LIVES BEHIND THE LAWS

# Lives behind the Laws

## THE WORLD OF THE *CODEX HERMOGENIANUS*

*Serena Connolly*

Indiana University Press

*Bloomington & Indianapolis*

*This book is a publication of*

Indiana University Press
601 North Morton Street
Bloomington, IN 47404-3797 USA

www.iupress.indiana.edu

*Telephone orders*   800-842-6796
*Fax orders*   812-855-7931
*Orders by e-mail*   iuporder@indiana.edu

♾The paper used in this publication
meets the minimum requirements
of American National Standard for
Information Sciences—Permanence
of Paper for Printed Library Materials,
ANSI Z39.48-192.

Manufactured in the United States of
America

Library of Congress Cataloging-in-
Publication Data

Connolly, Serena.
  Lives behind the laws : the world of
the Codex Hermogenianus / Serena
Connolly.
    p. cm.
  Includes bibliographical references and
index.
  ISBN 978-0-253-35401-3 (cloth : alk.
paper)—ISBN 978-0-253-22147-6 (pbk.
: alk. paper) 1. Codex Hermogenianus.
2. Roman law. I. Title.
  KJA437.C66 2010
  340.5'4—dc22

                                    2009021895

1 2 3 4 5 15 14 13 12 11 10

*parentibus optimis*

# CONTENTS

The law constantly writes itself on bodies. It engraves itself on parchments made from the skin of its subjects. It articulates them in juridical corpus. It makes book out of them.

MICHEL DE CERTEAU, *THE PRACTICE OF EVERYDAY LIFE*

To ordinary Romans, the emperor must have seemed an enigmatic figure. On the one hand, he was everywhere: his face was on coins, his statue watched over his subjects in basilicas, and his name appeared on laws posted across the empire. Yet their opportunities for contact with the emperor were scarce. They might glimpse him from a crowd during a carefully staged event, or catch sight of him as he shuttled between imperial residences, governors' palaces, Senate houses, basilicas, and army camps. Only a fortunate few ever approached the emperor for a hearing.

Given the emperor's elusiveness, it is remarkable that hundreds, possibly thousands, of individuals communicated with him each year. The system of petition and response enabled Romans to write to the emperor about their legal problems and to receive a response that could offer information or guidance, or direct them to a legal official who could offer assistance or a hearing. Though petitioners did not often meet the emperor face-to-face, theirs was a more personal sort of communication that offered tangible benefits. It could benefit the emperor too, by bolstering his reputation as an authoritative yet responsive ruler, and it also provided employment to the legal experts who facilitated the system.

The early spring of 293 was a busy time at Sirmium. Diocletian had decided to accompany his newly crowned junior colleague Galerius part of the way to his new court at Antioch. Diocletian would leave him at Byzantium to head back to Sirmium, where he would stay until the following summer, overseeing Roman efforts to repel barbarian invaders from the north. In August 294 he would journey along the Danube frontier to see for himself the aftermath of the summer campaigning, before heading south via Byzantium to Nicomedia. Among the hundreds of imperial staff preparing themselves for the journey were the members of the *scrinium libellorum*. They had been answering a steady stream of petitions at Sirmium since the beginning of 293 and now faced about five months on the road, where they would meet nine hundred–plus petitioners.

The encounters between those officials and petitioners are the focus of this book. It presents a user-centered analysis of why and how petitions were sent and answered, to reveal a wide array of petitioners who petitioned for a wide range of reasons, the working methods of the team that answered them, and the emperors' reasons for investing in a system that provided free legal advice to non-elites. Petition and response emerges as a mutually beneficial undertaking—a means for ordinary people to help solve their legal problems and for emperors to advertise their legal authority and responsiveness. I shall argue that the process of petition and response, which provided subjects their most common—and personally helpful—contact with the emperor, suggests that the Roman imperial administration was a more collaborative enterprise than we might have imagined.

This book is concerned with the people who used and administered the system of petition and response—their problems and their daily experiences. Since petition and response was used by many people to help resolve their legal problems, reconstructing the system offers insights into the role that law played in shaping the lives of these ordinary subjects. Examining the many hundreds of extant responses to petitions ("rescripts") reveals the types of legal issues that subjects in the provinces confronted and therefore the types of cases that came before the imperial chancery, and considering them en masse helps us understand in some detail how the members of the imperial chancery worked and therefore also, given the ubiquity and popularity of petition and response, how law was administered in the Roman Empire. This book is concerned also with the role petition and response played in the administration of justice and claims that all participants in the system—petitioners, officials and the emperor—were bound in a mutual dependence that should alert us to the little-acknowledged political power of ordinary people in Roman governance.

Petition and response is a wide subject, both in terms of the time periods in which it is found and in the range of approaches employed to understand it. Trying to synthesize these approaches to understand petition and response in all these periods is an impossible (or at least inordinately lengthy) task. I have therefore decided that a profitable approach to the topic is to look at a span of time in which the evidence is most numerous and detailed. More than nine hundred rescripts are extant from the years AD 293–294, the greatest concentration of responses extant for any two-year period from the reigns of Hadrian to Diocletian and his co-rulers. Written by the *magister a libellis* Hermogenianus and his team in the reign of Diocletian, they provide a useful collection of evidence for analyzing petition and response because they represent the responses of a team operating under an individual legal expert active at particular time.

The rescripts are interesting in themselves, as chapter 4 will demonstrate. Moreover, given the lack of change to the system (Diocletian introduced many administrative reforms in other areas during his reign, but apart, perhaps, from providing increased access to the system, the rescripts do not reveal any significant changes brought about by these reforms) and given that there is no obvious departure from the content or form of previous years' rescripts, we can make inferences from these rescripts about the system not only at the time of the Tetrarchy but also before and after. Further, since, as I contend, the entries of 293–294 were kept primarily because of their legal content, not the identities of the recipients, we can analyze, albeit tentatively, the makeup of the recipients. While the conclusions I draw apply first and foremost to those years, I venture that because Diocletian seemingly made no significant changes to the rescript system, they may be valid for at least the second and third centuries. Possibly my claims about the significance of the system for understanding the interrelationship of rulers and subjects can be applied to all periods and places in which petition and response can be found, from earliest Near Eastern history to at least the medieval period. (They may also help us understand ordinary people's reasons for and ways of navigating legal systems.)

The system of petition and response as it operated in these two years, then, will be the subject matter of this book, and the focus will be on the people who used and ran the system. I want to move away from imagining petition and response as a static and theorized system of procedures to recreating it as a locus around which the emperor, his officials, and the people interacted. By means of this approach we can reconfigure the roles of the emperor, his staff, and his subjects as mutually dependent—all relied on the system of petition and response (and probably other systems too) to confirm their own positions within Roman society. Further, as I shall show in the introduction, some of our oldest written documents are petitions and responses that express the mutualism between ruler and ruled (and the facilitator, i.e., official). From these we see that, for example, Hittite rulers realized the benefits of responding to needy litigants, who in turn found that their obedience supported a system of rule that safeguarded their daily security. In the Roman world, petition and response acted also as a buttress against the predations of the powerful and as a partial treatment for ills inflicted in court by disinterested, ignorant, or prejudiced judges. The rescript system was much more than "a scheme of free legal aid," as Tony Honoré has described it.[1]

Chapter 1, using the well-known inscription of the Skaptopareni as a starting point, reconstructs the system to put together a picture of the process from beginning to end that is careful to insert the petitioners, whose experiences of the system seem to have been missed in other examinations. This chapter also examines the interaction between petitioners and *tabelliones,* the people who helped them compose their petitions. Chapter 2 looks at the system in motion, as it was managed on a daily basis, both at the imperial court and also on the move through the lower Danube provinces. It traces the movements of Diocletian and, more importantly, his court during AD 293–294 and looks at the interaction between petitioners and the team of officials of the *scrinium libellorum,* who I believe composed most rescripts under the leadership of their *magister,* Hermogenian.

Chapter 3 focuses more closely on the petitioners in a quantitative approach to the system. Building on the work of Huchthausen, this chapter analyzes the makeup of the petitioners whose rescripts are preserved in the *CJ* from AD 293–294 and seeks to discover the makeup of the total group of petitioners to the imperial court during those years. It also explores how petitioning helped different types of petitioners and what benefits and barriers existed in their use of the system. Chapter 4 moves from the quantitative to the analytical with a detailed examination of a selection of rescripts to look more closely at how individuals used the rescript system to resolve their legal problems. Analysis of the rescripts' content suggests that the petitioners, who belonged to the "middling sort"—a term I define below—with the crucial exception of those claimed as slaves, were united not by wealth, social status, or occupation, but by a shared sense of vulnerability. Officials responded to their petitions often with sympathy, but primarily with concern for justice and the law. This chapter focuses on the interrelationship of petitioners, officials, and the body of Roman law.

Chapter 5 takes a broader view of the rescript system. Beginning with the claim that petitioners perceived themselves to be "poor" in the sense of feeling vulnerable before others rather than by any objective criteria, this chapter argues that the emperor used his perceived responsiveness to poor petitioners to advertise his regal diligence and legal authority, in the manner of previous rulers in the ancient world and as his successors in the east and west would do. The high degree of interdependence of the emperor, his officials, and his subjects of the middling sort illustrated by the rescript system suggests that the importance of the middling sort to imperial stability has been overlooked and that they should be inserted as a party into the Roman system of law and legal administration.

The petitioners whose problems and lives are examined in this study come from what John Crook has described as the "non-pauper non-elite." Though these people accounted for a significant proportion of the population, finding descriptions, let alone definitions, of them requires sifting through evidence of many kinds. They form a large and diverse group that includes the small-scale commercial farmer, the small-business owner, and the town councilor who was stretched too thin. Augustine knew the latter well. His father, whom he described as a *tenuis municeps* ("a burgess of slender means," in Peter Brown's elegant rendering),[2] was one of them. The family had a roof over their heads and food to eat, but the school fees could not always be paid.

John Crook's description of these people is useful: "A true middle class has political and economic 'clout': the people I mean had none of the former but some of the latter (i.e. purchasing power, witnessed, e.g., by the less grand sorts of wall-decoration)."[3]

Money purchases property, enables business transactions, and creates a need for people to draw up wills—all of which can lead to the sorts of legal problems we find tackled in the rescripts. People lacking money also suffer legal problems, such as marital breakup, assault, and unlawful eviction, but such individuals can do little except tolerate them as best they can or retaliate using extra-legal means. The non-pauper non-elite or middling sort, as I shall call them for the sake of brevity, while they may have lacked sufficient money to hire a lawyer (or were shy of doing so without establishing greater need), formed the bulk of those who sent petitions to emperors asking for legal information or advice. These were people who could normally support themselves financially (and if they now owed money, they had at some point been considered good for the debt) with enough spare cash or liquidity, opportunity, and wherewithal to consider petitioning and perhaps even use subsequent litigation to rectify a legal problem.

Putting a figure on the worth of the middling sort is a slippery task. The incomes of many are set out in Diocletian's Edict on Maximum Prices and thus supply us with a range that includes the muleteer, veterinarian, barber, teacher, and scribe, but most likely not the advocate. It is possible to define that range with help from John Crook, who has rallied evidence to suggest an upper limit for a middling sort income:

> I would note that *ampla pecunia* begins, for the jurist Gaius, at 100,000, and freedmen count as *locupletiores* from that figure up (Gai., *Inst.* IX.140 with Saller at *PCPhS* 209 (1983), 72–76); that 12,000 was the legionary retirement bonus; that Augustus could only find 215 *cives Romani* in Crete/Cyrene with a fortune above 10,000 (the richer element there were peregrine); and that at Irni the level for *iudices* began at 5,000 (cf. *Digest* L.2.12, Callistratus).[4]

At the other end, the lower limit is demarcated by those whose lives were occasionally blighted by *paupertas,* "a poverty that is not the complete indigence of the desperate outsider, but a precarious dependence among the less well-off members of the community," as Purcell explains.[5] We might expect to find the sewer cleaner and cloak attendant of Diocletian's Edict among their number.

While economically diverse, members of the middling sort were united by their lack of formal legal education. Most probably received a rudimentary general education until the age of eleven or twelve and were subsequently apprenticed and trained in an occupation.[6] A general education in law and the navigation of local or central bureaucracy would not have been part of their formative years (nor is it today). Their legal education was probably acquired through experience or social interaction—speaking with others and learning of their experiences—rather than through a program of learning. It was informal and ad hoc, focused on the most common issues that arose in petitioners' lives. Problems such as those faced by Zosimus and Anicetus, two petitioners facing property disputes whom we will meet in chapter 4, must have occurred frequently in a time when there seem to have been no zoning restrictions and planning permission was not required until after the fact. Yet the knowledge they did have was piecemeal enough that they needed to petition to fill in gaps.

Petition and response is a popular topic that is attracting increasing attention from ancient historians with a wide range of interests—in the Greek, Egyptian, and Roman worlds, in law, in politics, and in administrative and social history—and for good reason. From my experience of discussing the subject with individuals outside of Classics and outside of academe, the basic notion that ordinary people could petition ancient rulers, including Roman emperors, for legal advice and help is surprising and intriguing—surprising because they assume rulers were aloof and unresponsive; intriguing because they want to know what sort of people these were, what they petitioned about, and why rulers received and answered their queries. Answering their questions is an important part of this book. Professional and lay interest in petition and response derives, I think, from the fact that the topic is literally "popular": it deals with ordinary people's problems, be they mundane or outlandish, common or unusual. We feel an affinity with petitioners. We too encounter complications and obstructions in our legal dealings, and we have all experienced frustration and impatience as we have sought help or information from or complained to large organizations, governmental or corporate. We have all been petitioners.

The increase in scholarly interest has arisen from three developments. The first is the exponential growth in the discovery and study of documentary evidence, such as inscriptions, papyri, and law codes, which are the main repositories of petitions and responses. The second is the increase in the number of scholars engaged in interdisciplinary research. This increase has come about in part as a result of increased use of documentary evidence, as scholars have integrated inscriptions and papyri into their research. Ancient and medieval historians' growing use of legal evidence, especially law codes, has contributed greatly to our understanding of petition and response and has helped make evidence for it more accessible to the wider academic community. The third is a change in the way history is being written. Influenced by the work of historians of the African American civil rights movement, who have compellingly and effectively integrated testimonies into their analyses (and also the work of sociologists, whose work is based on case studies as well as data sets), historians of other periods and places have realized the power of real first-person or imagined third-person accounts in supporting arguments and coloring a narrative. This is especially the case with the history of non-elites, and petitions make for good stories.

Alongside these factors, there is also much concern at the time of writing with questions of governmental accountability, which has in turn piqued historians' interest in the question of what motivates loyalty to rulers and in the notion of government as a system of exchange between ruler and ruled. These issues have not so far exercised scholars working primarily on petition and response, but they are of central importance to many scholars concerned with the imperial office, many of whom have used petitions and the responses to them as supporting evidence and whose work is in turn influencing research on that evidence. And just as interest in petition and response has increased with developments in the field of ancient history (and beyond), so focus within the topic has changed over time, from concern with the mechanics of the system of petitioning, to analyses of the makeup of the petitioners, to exploring the rhetorical structure of petitions.

This book has its origins in a dissertation that was inspired by a remark from John Matthews. In a conversation several years ago he mused that, according to our evidence, up to one-quarter of the people who received answers to their petitions from emperors were women. I was surprised at the extent of women's participation in a legal process and at their contact with the imperial administration. Then I wondered why I was surprised. Many questions followed. Was I right to be surprised? Who were these women? What did they petition about? Who were the other petitioners and what were their concerns? How did the system of petition and response work?

Why did people petition? And why did the system exist? The resulting book is a product of my curiosity and a desire to answer these questions.

I have benefited greatly from the path-breaking work of Tony Honoré and Fergus Millar, and though they differ in their views of petition and response, both have influenced my thinking. Their work, together with that of Judith Evans Grubbs, has done much to make the system more widely known. Liselot Huchthausen and Simon Corcoran's examinations of the petitioners provided a solid basis for my own analysis. My discussion of the political importance of rescripts continues and elaborates Corcoran's observation that the rescripts served no obvious legislative function and were not legally innovative; Clifford Ando's work on imperial communication set me thinking about why petitioners and emperors alike continued to invest in petition and response. I have taken a cue from John Crook's practice of integrating narrative into theoretical discussion and have also been much influenced by Chris Kelly's compelling depiction of an administrative "system in motion," so much so that I have borrowed the phrase for the title of one of my chapter sections, in which I have attempted to breathe life into a system usually discussed in a rather abstract fashion. Finally, modern sociological work on ordinary people and their encounters with the law has stimulated me into new ways of thinking about familiar material and situations.

This book is an examination of ordinary Romans' interactions in the course of finding help and navigating processes. I too have been aided by interactions with friends and colleagues over the last few years. Several years ago, Carlos Noreña brought to my attention Graham Burton's recent work on the interpretation of evidence, and our discussions helped me think about my findings in the broader context of imperial history. More recently, I have benefited from the suggestions and insights of Simon Corcoran. Michael Peachin has pushed me to think harder about crucial issues, and the book has benefited greatly as a result. Dennis Kehoe has offered encouragement, and his clear vision for the book has revealed much to me. I am grateful to the Department of Classics at Yale University, where the book has its roots, and to my new colleagues at Rutgers, who have provided support in the closing stages. I am also very pleased to acknowledge the assistance of the Frederick W. Hilles Publication Fund of Yale University in publishing this book.

John Matthews suggested the project and has been throughout its realization the ideal adviser. I have benefited enormously from his knowledge and insights and from his enthusiasm for my work, and I have enjoyed his good humor. I could not have had a better guide.

Finally I owe thanks to my parents, Roger and Hazel, for their support and affection, and to Paul Walberg, for everything.

# ABBREVIATIONS

Abbreviations of papyri follow John F. Oates et al., *Checklist of Editions of Greek, Latin, Demotic, and Coptic Papyri, Ostraca, and Tablets*, 5th ed., *Bulletin of the American Society of Papyrologists*, suppl. no. 9 (Oakville, Conn.: American Society of Papyrologists, 2001).

Abbreviations of journals follow *L'Année Philologique*. Abbreviations of literary works follow Simon Hornblower and Antony Spawforth, *The Oxford Classical Dictionary*, 3rd ed. (Oxford: Oxford University Press, 2003).

| | |
|---|---|
| AHB | *Ancient History Bulletin* |
| AJAH | *American Journal of Ancient History* |
| AJPH | *American Journal of Philology* |
| ANTARD | *Antiquité tardive* |
| APULEIUS, MUN. | Apuleius, *De mundo* |
| AUGUSTINE, CONF. | Augustine, *Confessions* |
| BASP | *Bulletin of the American Society of Papyrologists* |
| BMCR | *Bryn Mawr Classical Review* |
| CG | *Codex Gregorianus* |
| CGL | *Corpus Glossariorum Latinorum* |
| CH | *Codex Hermogenianus* |

CHV    *Epitome Codicis Hermogeniani Visigothica* (*FIRA*²
ii, 665)

CIG    *Corpus Inscriptionum Graecarum*

CIL    *Corpus Inscriptionum Latinarum*

CJ    *Codex Justinianus*

CONS.    *Consultatio Veteris Cuiusdam Iurisconsulti* (*FIRA*²
ii, 594–613)

CPH    *Classical Philology*

CPR    *Corpus Papyrorum Raineri*

CSEL    *Corpus Scriptorum Ecclesiasticorum Latinorum*

CTH    *Codex Theodosianus*

D    *Digesta Justiniani*

E&L¹    Tony Honoré, *Emperors and Lawyers,* 1st ed.
(London: Duckworth, 1981).

E&L²    Tony Honoré, *Emperors and Lawyers,* 2nd ed.
(Oxford: Clarendon, 1994).

EDRL    Adolf Berger, "Encyclopedic Dictionary of Roman
Law," *Transactions of the American Philosophical
Society,* new ser., vol. 43, pt. 2 (1953).

EMP    *Edictum de Maximis Pretiis*

ERW¹    Fergus Millar, *The Emperor in the Roman World:
31 BC–AD 337,* 1st ed. (London: Duckworth, 1977).

ERW²    Fergus Millar, *The Emperor in the Roman World:
31 BC–AD 337,* 2nd ed. (Ithaca, N.Y.: Cornell
University Press, 1992).

FEST.    Festus, *De verborum significatu*

FIRA    Salvatore Riccobono, Giovanni Baviera,
and Contardo Ferrini, *Fontes iuris romani
antejustiniani* (Florentiae: apud S. A. G. Barbèra,
1908).

| | |
|---|---|
| *FIRA*² | Salvatore Riccobono, *Fontes iuris romani antejustiniani,* 2nd ed. (Florence: S. A. G. Barbèra, 1968). |
| *FV* | *Fragmenta Vaticana* |
| *G&R* | *Greece and Rome* |
| GAIUS *INST.* | Gaius, *Institutes* |
| *HA, ALEX. SEV.* | *Historia Augusta, Alexander Severus* |
| *HA, HADRIAN* | *Historia Augusta, Hadrian* |
| *IG* | *Inscriptiones Graecae* |
| *IGBULG* | *Inscriptiones Graecae in Bulgaria repertae* |
| *IGRR* | *Inscriptiones Graecae ad res Romanas pertinentes* |
| *IGSK* | *Inschriften griechischer Städte aus Kleinasien* |
| *ILS* | *Inscriptiones Latinae Selectae* |
| *JRA* | *Journal of Roman Archaeology* |
| *JRS* | *Journal of Roman Studies* |
| JULIAN *EP.* | Julian, *Epistulae* |
| JUST. *EPIT.* | Justinus, *Epitome* |
| JUVENAL, *SAT.* | Juvenal, *Satires* |
| *LSJ* | Henry George Liddell, Robert Scott, Henry Stuart Jones, and Roderick McKenzie, *A Greek-English Lexicon,* rev. and augm. (Oxford: Clarendon, 1996). |
| *MEFR (A)* | *Mélanges de l'École Française de Rome. Antiquité* |
| NOT. DIG. OCC./OR. | *Notitia dignitatum omnium tam civilium quam militarium in partibus occidentalis/orientis* |
| *NOV.* | *Novellae Iustiniani* |
| OLD | P. G. W. Glare, *Oxford Latin Dictionary* (Oxford: Clarendon, 1982). |

P.AMH. *The Amherst Papyri, Being an Account of the Greek Papyri in the Collection of the Right Hon. Lord Amherst of Hackney, F.S.A. at Didlington Hall, Norfolk.*

P.BABATHA *The Documents from the Bar Kochba Period in the Cave of Letters*

P.BERL. MÖLLER *Griechische Papyri aus dem Berliner Museum*

P.CAIRO MASP. *Papyrus grecs d'époque byzantine, Catalogue général des antiquités égyptiennes du Musée du Caire*

P.COL. *Columbia Papyri*

P.DURA *The Excavations at Dura-Europos conducted by Yale University and the French Academy of Inscriptions and Letters,* Final Report V, Part I, *The Parchments and Papyri.*

P.ENTEUX. *ENTEUXEIS: Requêtes et plaintes adressées au Roi d'Égypte au IIIe siècle avant J.-C.*

P.EUPHRATES "Documents d'archives romains inédits du Moyen Euphrates," ed. D Feissel and J. Gascou

P.HAMB. *Griechische Papyrusurkunden der Hamburger Staats- und Universitätsbibliothek*

P.LIPS. *Griechische Urkunden der Papyrussammlung zu Leipzig*

P.MICH. *Michigan Papyri*

P.OSLO *Papyri Osloenses*

P.OXY. *The Oxyrhynchus Papyri*

P. PANOP.BEATTY *Papyri from Panopolis in the Chester Beatty Library Dublin*

P.PRINC. *Papyri in the Princeton University Collections*

P.RYL. *Catalogue of the Greek and Latin Papyri in the John Rylands Library, Manchester*

| | |
|---|---|
| P.SAKAON | *The Archive of Aurelius Sakaon: Papers of an Egyptian Farmer in the last Century of Theadelphia* |
| P.STRAS. | *Griechische Papyrus der Kaiserlichen Universitäts- und Landes-bibliothek zu Strassburg* |
| P.TEBT. | *The Tebtunis Papyri* |
| P.THEAD. | *Papyrus de Théadelphie* |
| P.VINDOB. | *Papyri in the Possession of the Österreichische Nationalbibliothek* |
| P.WISC. | *The Wisconsin Papyri* |
| P.YALE | *Yale Papyri in the Beinecke Rare Book and Manuscript Library* |
| PAN. LAT. | Charles E. V. Nixon and B. S. Rodgers, *In Praise of Later Roman Emperors: The Panegyrici Latini: Introduction, Translation, and Historical Commentary, with the Latin Text of R.A.B. Mynors* (Berkeley: University of California Press, 1994). |
| PLUT. DEMETR. | Plutarch, *Demetrius* |
| PLUT. MOR. | Plutarch, *Moralia* |
| PLUT. ROM. | Plutarch, *Romulus* |
| PLUT. SERT. | Plutarch, *Sertorius* |
| PSI | *Papiri greci e latini* |
| RE | August Friedrich von Pauly, Georg Wissowa, Wilhelm Kroll, and Kurt Witte, *Paulys Real-Encyclopädie der classischen Altertumswissenschaft: Neue Bearbeitung* (Stuttgart: J.B. Metzler, 1894). |
| RIDA | *Revue internationale des droits de l'antiquité* |
| SB | *Sammelbuch griechischer Urkunden aus Aegypten* |
| SDHI | *Studia et Documenta Historiae et Iuris* |
| SIDONIUS APOLLINARIS, EP. | Sidonius Apollinaris, *Epistulae* |

| | |
|---|---|
| STOBAEUS, *FLOR.* | Stobaeus, *Florilegium* |
| SUET. *DIV. AUG.* | Suetonius, *Divus Augustus* |
| SUET. *DIV. IUL.* | Suetonius, *Divus Iulius* |
| SUET. *NER.* | Suetonius, *Nero* |
| SUET., *VESP.* | Suetonius, *Divus Vespasianus* |
| SYLL³ | *Sylloge inscriptionum graecarum*, 3rd ed. |
| T.VINDOL. II | Alan K. Bowman, J. David Thomas, and J. N. Adams, *The Vindolanda Writing-Tablets (Tabulae Vindolandenses II)* (London: British Museum, 1994). |
| TD/RHD | *Tijdschrift voor Rechtsgeschiedenis/Revue d'histoire du droit* |
| TIR L 34 | Soproni, Sándor. *Tabula Imperii Romani: Aquincum, Sarmizegetusa, Sirmium, L 34 Budapest* (Amsterdam: A. M. Hakkert, 1968). |
| TNA SC | The National Archives (UK), Special Collections: Ancient Petitions. |
| ZPE | *Zeitschrift für Papyrologie und Epigraphik* |
| ZRG RÖM. ABT. | *Zeitschrift der Savigny-Stiftung für Rechtsgeschichte. Römische Abteilung* |

LIVES BEHIND THE LAWS

# INTRODUCTION

Thou hast let thy hands fall . . .
Thou didst not judge the case of the widow
nor uphold the suit of the oppressed.
Descend from thy rule that I may reign.

KRT[1]

The right of petition, I have said, was not conferred on the People by the
Constitution, but was a pre-existing right, reserved by the People out of
the grants of power made to Congress.

CALEB CUSHING, *THE RIGHT OF PETITION*[2]

From the Code of Hammurabi, dating to around 1780 BC, which contains
a provision binding the ruler to provide protection and justice to the weak,
to the First Amendment of the U.S. Constitution of AD 1791, granting (or,
in Cushing's opinion, confirming to) Americans the right to petition their
government for redress of grievances, protecting the weak and responding
to their petitions have been a feature of various governments around the
Near (now Middle) East, Europe, and beyond.[3] Petitions appear among
our earliest surviving documents, and a brief survey of some of these texts
reveals themes and procedures that have persisted through 4,700 years.

In the ancient world, these systems, whose roots lay in ancient rulers' responsibility for their vulnerable subjects, offered an opportunity to gain favor with the masses and helped to portray the ruler as a godlike figure who overcame social iniquities and victimization and thereby safeguarded the justice that came from the gods. Indeed, many petitions to rulers have the structure of a prayer: they call on the mercy and justice of the ruler and promise loyalty in return for help. Rulers who demonstrated charity toward the most vulnerable in their kingdom, many of whom must have petitioned them, were in turn praised by their subjects.[4]

An early Mesopotamian cuneiform letter of the late third or early second millennium BC from a certain Ur-saga to a king expresses concern at the possible seizure of his father's household and reveals the reverence with which rulers were addressed: "You are fashioned like the son of An. As with the words of a god, what you say is irrevocable. Your words, like rain pouring from the skies, are uncountable."[5] Surviving Sumerian letters of petition addressed to gods and officials express similar reverence. Many of them are actually scribal school exercises, a finding that suggests scribes were frequently paid to write them.[6] The petitioners, who complain of sickness, intimidation, and deprivation of inheritance, seek to persuade the recipients of their deservedness with declarations of their piety and status and with promises of future piety and obedience if their petitions are answered favorably.[7]

The familiar petition structure emerges in the Mesad Hashavyahu ostracon, otherwise known as the Yavneh-Yam ostracon. Written in Hebrew and dating to 639–609 BC, it is the petition of a harvester who claims that an official took his garment and demands its return. The petitioner acknowledges that the official's action was not unlawful but claims that it was unfair, a theme found in other petitions seeking protection, rather than a correction of illegal activity.[8] The structure of the petition leaves much unknown. There is no address or greeting, nor is the petitioner's identity disclosed. Given the absence of these identifying elements, the petition was probably either presented in person or delivered with an accompanying text. The brief text follows a pattern that will emerge. It opens with a formulaic plea, asking for the recipient to listen, outlines the situation, and then makes a request: if I'm innocent, get me my garment back; if not, let the governor hear my case. These written petitions retained the basic structure found on the ostracon: an outline of the circumstances followed by a request.[9]

It has been suggested that the ostracon summarized the case and was used simply to receive an audience during which the petition could be presented orally in full.[10] The practice of oral presentation gave the ruler the opportunity to be seen holding audience and thereby caring for the vulnerable. It was followed by Jews as well as others, including Bedouin sheikhs.[11] Oral presentation must have been an intimidating experience for many petitioners. Perhaps as a result, by the fifth century BC petitions across much of the ancient Near East were written texts that were delivered either by the petitioner or a representative, or were left at the base of a cult statue in a temple.

Egyptian pharaohs shared the Near Eastern notion that rulers have a responsibility to the weak. The vizier Rekhmire (c. 1479–1425 BC) proudly records:

> I judged both [the insignificant] and the influential; I rescued the weak man from the strong man; I deflected the fury of the evil man and subdued the greedy man in his hour . . . I succoured the widow who has no husband; I established the son and heir on the seat of his father. I gave [bread to the hungry], water to the thirsty, and meat, oil and clothes to him who had nothing . . . I was not at all deaf to the indigent. Indeed I never took a bribe from anyone . . .[12]

Two viziers (officials with viceregal powers) controlled Egypt's administrative departments, but also found time to receive petitions. In the Old Kingdom (2700–2200 BC) they received petitions daily from would-be litigants and from the poor asking for aid.[13] Rekhmire's tombstone preserves an astute insight by the vizier into the mentality of petitioners: "a petitioner better likes to be allowed to pour out his grievances than that they should be put right."[14] The fact that petitioners wanted to have their problems validated as worthy of the time of the most important officials in the land—sometimes more than they wanted a solution—reveals the psychological importance of petitioning. As well as giving officials an opportunity to fulfill their obligations to justice, it gave the poor, the vulnerable, and the oppressed an opportunity to feel powerful, benefits that have also been noted by sociologists studying modern (would-be) litigants.[15]

The Ptolemaic kings adopted their pharaonic predecessors' willingness to answer petitions. For example, pre-Ptolemaic Egyptian rulers had responded to petitioners asking for manumission, a practice that continued into the Ptolemaic period, when the responses were called *enteuxeis*, "acts of relief."[16] Though the Ptolemaic kings did not necessarily respond to more petitions than did their predecessors, happily for us evidence of petition and their response increases during this period.

One of the earliest Ptolemaic examples is a petition dating to the mid-third century BC from a lentil cook at Philadelphia who complains that his business is being ruined by rivals purveying roasted pumpkins and asks for extra time to pay his tax to the king, a dispensation that, so he says, had been granted in Crocodilopolis.[17] The text appears as follows:

> To Philiscus greetings from Harentotes, lentil-cook of Philadelphia. I give the product of 35 artabae a month and I do my best to pay the tax every month in order that you may have no complaint against me. Now the folk in the town are roasting pumpkins. For that reason then nobody buys lentils from me at the present time. I beg and beseech you then, if you think fit, to be allowed more time, just as has been done in Crocodilopolis, for paying the tax to the king. For in the morning they straightway sit down beside the lentils selling their pumpkins and give me no chance to sell my lentils.[18]

The petitioner, a humble man who probably had few chances to gain access to an official, carefully records how much tax he has paid in the past and how diligently he has maintained his payments. He also mentions that there is a precedent for what he asks. What is striking about this text is that Harentotes knew the value of portraying himself as a loyal and dependable subject worthy of pity and understood the importance of mentioning a precedent, whose existence would prompt the official to extend equity to him on the same basis.

The lentil cook's petition is significant not only for the care with which he presents his situation, but also for the structure of the text, which remained almost unchanged throughout the Roman period in Egypt and then spread across the Roman Empire. The petition opens with a greeting from the petitioner to the addressee and is followed by the petitioner's name, then an outline of the problem and finally a request for help.[19]

White believes that responses preserved on the backs of some Ptolemaic petitions were probably produced by a *strategos*, though they were supposedly written by the king. One response, on the verso of P.Enteux. 26 of 220 BC, reads as follows:

ἔτους ι, Γορπιαίου 30, Τῦβι 13.
Κτησικλῆς πρὸς Διονύσιον καὶ
Νίκην τὴν θυγατέρα περὶ χειρογραφίας.

We have delegated . . .
Year 1, Gorpiaeus 30, Tubi 13.
Ctesicles against Dionysius and
Nice his daughter concerning a written oath.

This papyrus, which seems to be the original, may have been handed back to the petitioner, though there are also docketed petitions that are described as copies and were handed back to petitioners, while the originals were kept in official archives.

The petitions from Ptolemaic Egypt concern broken agreements, intimidation, official wrongdoing, and requests for remission of taxes or release from local office. The range of subjects was large, reflecting the widespread use of petitions. Indeed petitions were so much a part of everyday life in Egypt that they appeared even in folk tales. The Tale of the Eloquent Peasant, dating to 2000–1500 BC, tells of a poor man who seeks justice by petitioning the son of a high steward and the king nine times.[20] The tale, which relies presumably on verisimilitude for the effectiveness of its themes, contains the petitions, and these, like the Near Eastern examples I have shown, flatter the recipient and describe him as a source of justice to the vulnerable. The tale demonstrates that petitioning was a readily recognizable means of securing justice. The number of petitions may be excessive but reflects the fact that people could expect to take a long time and might need to complete many legal procedures before finally gaining justice.

The Egyptian system of petition and response seems to have continued without interruption into the Roman period, since the structure of petitions remained the same and the nature of the complaints did not change. While many Ptolemaic petitions were written to monarchs, most of our extant Romano-Egyptian petitions are addressed to officials rather than the emperor; the only other differences between them are minor and structural.

While in Egypt the petitioning practices of the Ptolemaic period continued into the Roman period, elsewhere in the Roman world they had probably grown from another tradition. Answering petitions was most likely originally a function of the praetors, from whom it was adopted first by Caesar and then by the emperors.[21] The role of the praetor as chief administrator of Roman justice, his concern with supplementing existing law with equitable remedies, and his function of overseeing litigation, in which petitions were used to serve notice of the various stages of litigation, naturally led him to be the most likely official to receive petitions asking for help or advice. Some petitions of the Principate asked for equitable remedies for problems otherwise neglected or unjustly dealt with in law. If such petitions were sent also during the republic, successive praetors may have incorporated the responses to them into their edicts.

Praetors under the republic were of two sorts: *praetores urbani* and *praetores peregrini*. The former dealt with matters between citizens, the latter with cases concerning non-citizens. This willingness to extend the jurisdiction of Roman law and its accompanying protections and procedures to non-citizens applied also to the system of petition and response. Before AD 212, even non-citizens could petition Roman officials (including the emperor), as P.Babatha 13, a draft petition of a non-citizen Jewish woman to the provincial governor in Judea in AD 124 illustrates.[22]

Roman petitions were called *libelli*, a term that could also be used to describe any text written on a small sheet of papyrus, from a notice of upcoming games to a declaration of an impending marriage.[23] Caesar, on his fateful entrance into the Senate house on the Ides of March, was handed a *libellus* that contained details of the assassination plot about to unfold, which, as Suetonius tells us, he held in his hands along with other *libelli*.[24] The first *libellus* was simply a memorandum; it is possible the others may have contained petitions.

Suetonius tells us that Caesar personally answered petitions even at the games, though he also appointed an official to have his ring, presumably so that some official business could be transacted without his direct involvement.[25] Augustus's decision not to work at the games, ostensibly because he did not want to displease the people by working instead of watching the entertainment, may reflect an increased bureaucratization of petition and response. Tiberius went one step further and employed an official either to receive petitions or write answers to them. Epigraphic evidence records an *acceptor a subscr(iptionibus)* working for the emperor.[26]

This official was the forerunner of the *a libellis*, who answered most *libelli* in the name of the emperor. In the first and second centuries AD, the post of *a libellis* seems to have been part of the *cursus honorum* and was attained upon completion of tenures in military and procuratorial positions. Our sources do not tell us exactly what the *a libellis,* or *magister libellorum,* as he was known from the end of the third century, did. Lacking training in the law, the early *a libellis* likely managed the flow of petitions to the emperor. But from the third century, holders of the post had significant legal experience.[27] An entry in the Digest suggests that one *a libellis,* Papinian, managed petitions in some unspecified way and that responses were given out by the emperor.[28] The *Notitia Dignitatum* gives the duties of the fourth-century *magister libellorum* as dealing with hearings and petitions, a description that is equally vague.[29] It might be supposed that the *a libellis* supervised the receipt of petitions and passed them on to the emperor to be answered, but two factors argue against the emperor having sole responsibility for producing responses: first, the high volume of petitions that required responses from the emperor; second, the possibility that stylistic changes in the wording of responses correlate with the tenure of a new *a libellis,* not a new emperor. This is not to exclude the emperor from the process, simply to point out that there was a mechanism in place to relieve him of much of the responsibility. The duties of the *magister* will be discussed in greater detail in chapter 3.

It is possible that in the first and early second centuries AD, emperors received some petitioners in person, perhaps simply greeting them but possibly also hearing some of the petitions. From the third century, some petitioners, possibly important groups, continued to be heard personally by the emperor and the exchanges are preserved as *interlocutiones de plano.*[30] All other petitioners from the reign of Hadrian or perhaps from the third century received their responses in writing. According to Cassius Dio, Caracalla's mother, Julia Domna, also answered petitions, but only those that were less important. If true, this was an exceptional situation; otherwise responses from the imperial court were given only in the name of the emperor(s).[31]

From the reign of Hadrian to the end of the Tetrarchy the system changed little. It has often been assumed that Hadrian and Septimius Severus brought the system to its most advanced stage, though this claim is based on the survival of a plethora of petitions and responses from their reigns that may be owed more to jurists' activity during that period than to deliberate advertisement of the system from the center.[32] There were, however, some changes in terminology over three hundred years: petitions were called not only *libelli*, but also *preces, supplicationes,* and *petitiones;* responses were called first *subscriptiones,* then *rescripta.* In Greek, petitions were known as ὑπομνήματα, but from the second century as βιβλίδια and from the fourth century as βιβλία and λιβέλλοι.[33]

The bulk of our evidence for the Roman system of petition and response comes from papyri, inscriptions, literary-documentary evidence, and legal collections. The earliest document on papyrus to reference the system is P.Tebt. II 286, which preserves a quotation from a Hadrianic rescript (ll. 4–9) and also refers to one or more Trajanic rescripts. Our papyrological evidence burgeons, however, around the start of the third century AD under Septimius Severus and Caracalla, especially during their visit to Egypt in AD 199–200.[34]

Epigraphic evidence is a little more helpful in providing early evidence of the Roman system. At Aphrodisias, two inscriptions dating to the reign of Augustus may record the emperor's response to petitions sent by the community. Although whether the Aphrodisians sent a letter or a petition remains controversial, later evidence, such as the inscription from Skaptopara discussed in the next chapter, suggests that communities could send private petitions.[35]

Our best known literary-documentary evidence for the system is a couple of letters, 10.47 and 48, sent by Pliny the Younger to the emperor Trajan. In letter 47, Pliny writes that he is forwarding to the emperor a petition by the inhabitants of Apamea; in 48 Trajan confirms receipt of the *libellus.* Pliny's cautious language betrays the strangeness of his request. As we will see in chapter 1, petitions could not normally be sent on by an official but were handed in by a petitioner or a representative. Other literary evidence comes from the numerous anecdotes attesting (supposedly) to various emperors' handling of the system, which I shall discuss in chapter 5.

Much of our evidence for petition and response is preserved in late Roman legal collections, the prime example being the *Codex Justinianus* (*CJ*), in which the *Codex Gregorianus* (*CG*) and *Codex Hermogenianus* (*CH*) are partially preserved. The earliest rescript dates to the reign of Hadrian, the latest to the early fourth century. The Digest, companion to the *CJ* in Justinian's sixth-century *Corpus Iuris Civilis,* also preserves a few rescripts. For example, part of a Hadrianic response is recorded in *D* 48.22.1, which also refers to an earlier response by Trajan.[36] This period furnishes us with the most detailed information about the system, its users, and the people who ran it, and it will be the focus of the remaining chapters of this book.

From AD 304, our evidence, familiar and abundant during the Tetrarchy, changes significantly. The entries in the *CJ* belonging to the post-Diocletianic period look less like rescripts and more like letters, edicts, or *leges generales*.[37] Most historians assume, given that the rescripts seem to have disappeared from the Theodosian and Justinianic compilations, that they were no longer written under Constantine, though this conclusion may derive from a misunderstanding of that evidence and from a conception of later Roman emperors as authoritative and distant from their subjects.[38] But as we have already seen, the *Notitia Dignitatum* tells us that late Roman emperors still employed a *magister libellorum,* who had some involvement with *cognitiones* and dealt with petitions (*preces tractat*).[39] It is improbable that these officials were employed to deal with private petitions yet did not do so because none could be handed in. On the contrary, from the reign of Constantine a few rescripts preserved in the *Fragmenta Vaticana* follow the regular form.[40]

Petition and response was still being used at the local level—to initiate litigation. Cases were conducted *per rescriptum:* they could only be initiated by *editio rescripti,* a rescript from a local official in response to a litigant's petition.[41] This was not the only change. A law of Zeno dating to AD 477 also tells us that responses to petitions could come in the form of *adnotationes* and *pragmaticae sanctiones,* though the latter were issued in response only to petitions from organizations or community groups.[42] The first group includes those given *in personam precantium*—directly to the petitioner. *Adnotationes* were previously used to sanction imperial decisions given *contra ius;* subsequently the term was used simply to describe a brief response addressed to a petitioner.[43] The second contains rescripts *ad quemlibet iudicem,* also known as *pragmaticae sanctiones,* which were longer than *adnotationes* and were sent to officials when their accompanying *adnotationes* were felt to have general importance. It also gave sanction to what was written in the *adnotatio.* Without it, the response was invalid.[44] The reorganization of the *scrinium libellorum,* which was responsible for rescripts, and the *scrinium epistularum,* which produced letters to officials under the *quaestor* perhaps as early as AD 314 aided the production of both types of response and led eventually to the inclusion of some *pragmaticae sanctiones* in the Codes of Theodosius and Justinian.[45]

Though there were some other procedural changes, petitioning in the later Roman Empire continued.[46] The evidence for it, however, is of a different nature and quantity than before. Denis Feissel's compilation of known petitions (as well as letters) and responses dating to the fourth through the sixth centuries and Kramer's list of fourth-century petitions reveal that while many of those petitioning the emperor were private individuals, the bulk were Church officials, especially bishops, who wrote to the emperors about Church matters.[47] The preponderance of ecclesiastical petitioners may be an accident of the evidence. Church records, from which much of the evidence comes, have proven to be a long-lasting and stable repository of petitions.[48] Nevertheless, a wide range of petitions exists in these collections. Aside from those asking for privileges or inquiring about Church business, others ask for legal advice or for permission to bring a legal case before an official.[49]

Administrative officials may have received a greater share of overall petitions from the fourth century than in the earlier imperial period, and we also find the owners of large estates responding to local citizens' queries and complaints. But most significantly, the Church assumed an increasingly important role in answering petitions.[50] At a time when an increasing number of petitions were also being sent by clergy, it is unsurprising that Church rather than secular officials should have undertaken to answer them.[51] Christian leaders had been answering petitions from their followers since at least the second century, a practice made official by Constantine, who gave bishops and even holy men authority to act as arbiters. Symeon Stylites was known to have acted in this capacity.[52]

These new rights (or responsibilities) eased the pressure on provincial officials, and bishops took on the function of notarizing transactions (e.g., manumissions) with such efficiency that secular officials seem to have abandoned their notarial responsibilities.[53] The *episcopalis audientia* also helped the Church. According to Richard Finn, almsgiving provided Christians a way to show that they had the power to be generous, and their activities enabled them "to find an advantageous place for themselves in the common discourse and power-politics of generosity."[54] Having the authority to give responses also endowed them with a reputation for generosity, which previously only emperors, and by extension provincial officials, had enjoyed. The growth of the *episcopalis audientia* must also have helped to ease the burden on the secular courts. While employees in the secular administration may have been grateful to have their responsibilities reduced, some Church officials complained about their increased burden.[55] The Church responded not only to the rich in their congregations but also the poor, adjudicating rent disputes and intervening in the sale of children by poor parents.[56]

As the Church assumed greater judicial responsibilities, rulings by its officials acquired legal force. Papal decretals, as bishops' responses to petitions were known, gave judgments mostly on religious issues. Usually written in response to appeals, they provided precedents for future similar cases.[57] As the Church gained increasing influence, however, decretals dealt also with secular issues such as marriage and property. As decretals increased in number and use of them as precedent increased correspondingly, they assumed greater prominence in the body of late antique and then medieval law. Successive compilations followed into the medieval period, most notably Gratian's *Decretum*.[58]

Late Roman petitions to ecclesiastical officials and their secular counterparts became increasingly elaborate, in line with developments in petitions to the emperors. Not only did their language become more ornate, but petitioners' self-presentation also underwent changes. Late Roman petitioners began to call themselves slaves, not in a juridical sense but to express the fact that, first, they were subordinate to the responding official and, second, they were deserving of pity.[59] The reason for this change may be twofold. First, as the Church responded to increasing numbers of lower-status petitioners and as elites began to constitute the majority of recipients of later imperial responses, humble petitioners may have perceived that a limit had been placed on their chances of attaining justice. Presenting oneself as humbly as possible may have been a tactic to gain the sympathy of a recipient in the Church, and petitioners to the emperor may also have used this tactic. Given that evidence of private trials and courts in Egypt disappears in the sixth century, petitioning may have been the only available source of justice in some areas.[60] The need to present oneself as desperate is easily understood.

The second reason for the new style of presentation may come from the Near East. It is possible that petitions in the eastern part of the empire came under the influence of Near Eastern systems of petition and response. In the earliest Sumerian petitions, petitioners described themselves as slaves. We encounter similar formulas in the medieval period in Arabic petitions, now expressed with phrases such as "the slave [i.e., the petitioner] kisses the ground."[61] Statements of poverty are also common. The lentil cook from Ptolemaic Egypt who petitioned in the fifth century BC asked for more time to pay his taxes (see above). The *Hilferufe* of the second and third centuries AD also include statements that petitioners are facing poverty as a result of predatory officials and soldiers.[62] In the medieval period Christian, Muslim, and Jewish petitioners all also sought financial help, often in the form of a request for a change in the assessment of their poll tax rates.[63]

The Genizah texts from Cairo, which date from the ninth to the twelfth centuries, are a good repository of petitions. The collection concerns people and events from as far afield as Spain, Kiev, Iraq, and Provence, as well as Egypt, and contains both petitions and responses from Muslim and Jewish petitioners who approached caliphs, sultans, and viziers, as well as other lower-ranking officials.[64] Of the petitioners who pleaded poverty, some asked for money while others sought reinstatement of their employment and its accompanying allowance or a change in the rate of the poll tax levied on them. Some sought judicial remedies by asking that the recipient send a rescript to the other party in order to force them to stop their action. Others complained about theft and business deals gone awry.

The system that produced these petitions and responses had been in use in the Near East and Egypt from at least the eighth century. Petitions preserved from the beginning of that century concern, among other topics, a dishonest trader and a tenant who failed to pay rent. Other petitioners asked for help against predatory creditors, for employment with an allowance, and even for assistance in pursuing a murder investigation.[65] A significant proportion of their authors are women, many of whom had scribes writing on their behalf. Illiterate and often widowed with children, these women were among the most vulnerable people in society. One petition was even sent by a widow who was blind.[66] Local officials received the bulk of petitions. Among Jewish petitioners, women petitioned officials only in the local community, while men petitioned more widely. It seems that women were unwilling to petition strangers or were dissuaded by society from doing so.[67]

Just as petitioning continued in the Near East (Saladin is said to have received petitions and worked assiduously to answer them),[68] a little farther west, the system in the Byzantine Empire retained many of the features of its Roman predecessor.[69] While we have no original responses—our only examples are copies—we do know that they contained a date and the seal of the emperor. Significantly, when an imperial department was involved in composing the response, it was named. This is certainly not the case in Roman system, where the question of authorship of responses remains contested. Byzantine petitions are highly formulaic. In addition to following a pattern with regard to structure, petitioners were careful also to use tried and tested forms of address and to stress their humility, as Ruth Macrides has shown.[70] Some wrote in verse to impress the emperor with their literary skills; others presented themselves (or their customers) as stock characters: "the hen-pecked husband, the poor father of a large family, the monk looking for a secure place, the starving intellectual."[71] Such poses may have been adopted on a regular basis presumably so that a poor father, for example, could demonstrate eloquently that he was deserving of charity because he was suffering in all the ways that other poor fathers suffered. By following a standard mode of presentation, a petitioner guaranteed that he or she mentioned only persuasive points that had already been effective for others (to second-guess what would persuade the emperor was risky) but could then personalize the text with literary embellishment.

Petition and response endured in the west too, despite the fragmentation of the Roman Empire. We know that the Goths were using it in the reign of Theoderic,[72] but our evidence then becomes sparse. It redoubles in the later medieval period. The UK National Archives contain approximately 17,000 ancient petitions dating from the 1260s to the 1480s.[73] Sent by a wide range of individuals—rich and poor, male and female—they include complaints about predatory local officials (a common theme in petitions through the ages), pleas for help against those threatening violence or those demanding unjust repayment of debt, requests for help in securing personal liberty and inheritances, and even requests by outlaws for pardon. The topics are familiar to anyone working on Roman petitions. So too is nature of the petitions: they are formulaic and full of the expected humility. Unsurprisingly, we have evidence that scribes assisted in their composition.[74]

Sixteenth-century letters of remission are a rich source of evidence for communication between French non-elites and their rulers and contain carefully wrought narratives of murder and pleas for leniency that were written with professional help; and now notaries were institutionalized at the royal court. Historians of this period enjoy a surfeit of evidence relative to that available to ancient scholars and can even read notaries' style books. They have discovered that following a long procedure akin to a Roman appeals process, the king could grant or deny the suppliant's request. The king alone had this right; the Parisian Parlement could only reduce sentences for homicide. The process of sending letters of remission shares important features with the system of petition and response: both required the careful molding of a series of events into a sympathetic narrative, drew on professional help, and were enabled by the clemency of the ruler. And the pleaders were mostly non-elites, individuals of the middling sort. Natalie Zemon Davis has brilliantly analyzed the construction of a selection of the letters, discovering that these texts were replete with literary devices and figures, designed to affect the reader and reassure his subconscious with their traditional elements. If we had as many complete Roman and other ancient petitions, we would surely discover much more about the talents of provincial notaries.[75]

Petition and response has continued in various forms into the present day. Yemen is one of a number of Middle Eastern countries that continue to use a system of petition and response for administrative procedures. A recent newspaper editorial on Yemeni petitioners' experiences contains complaints from a disgruntled commentator about intimidating bureaucracy, unexplained and labyrinthine procedures, delay and expense, inefficiency, and queue jumping.[76] One wonders whether Romans had similar complaints.

In the West, the right to petition is enshrined in the U.S. Constitution, and every citizen of the European Union can petition the European Parliament.[77] The United Nations also receives petitions.[78] The World Wide Web has facilitated, especially among Westerners, collective petitioning, which is employed to redress grievances shared by special interest groups even across national borders; collective petitions to governments may concern issues of national or even international importance.[79]

The standardized forms, such as requests for planning permission, tax exemptions, federal loans, visas, and commercial licenses that people fill out and send to government departments, are today's equivalents of the Roman petitions that asked for privileges, such as the right of a senator to marry far below his rank, or for exemptions, for example, from liturgies.[80] The opportunity to petition the government for pre-trial legal advice and judgment, however, seems to have had no post-Roman successors. Today, people with legal difficulties have recourse only to lawyers, whose advice is usually expensive. While their letters may persuade an opponent to settle, they lack the authority of documents composed by a legal expert and signed in the name of the country's leader.

# ONE

# Seeking Justice in the Roman World

In addition to costs, however, our respondents also acknowledged the significant consequences of players' different levels of skill and experience. In other words, legality comes with costs that are differently burdensome, and thus legality is differentially available.

"They called me and we went up, you know, to the table. And I don't even know what the judge said, I couldn't even understand what he was saying. And the lawyer told me, he said 'okay,' he said 'that's it, it's all over.' I was right there and I don't know . . . I didn't even know what he was talking about."

EWICK AND SILBEY, *COMMON PLACE OF LAW*

Petition and response has been a feature of systems of justice in the West and Near East for thousands of years, indicating that it has fulfilled the needs of non-elites in search of justice. The Romans used it for understandable reasons. Their legal system was a complex mass of laws, procedures, and offices, so an individual with a legal problem stood little chance of taking an opponent to court, defending himself in court, or even finding out what to do about the problem on his own. Petition and response was not the only source of help, but as I shall show, it had advantages over the others.

For the Roman with a legal problem, patrons were a good source of advice, especially for freedmen, not least because as former master the patron had experience of the legal process of manumission and therefore might know some of the legal issues arising from it, such as inheritance and the status (and relationship to a master) of children born to a slave. To the freed or freeborn client, the patron was someone who was perhaps more worldly, certainly more wealthy and more influential. Even if he lacked expert knowledge of the laws and legal system, he probably had some experience of using the law or knew others who had, he had the money to help his client's legal undertaking, and he enjoyed elevated status, which he could bring to bear on behalf of his client. As far back as the *leges regiae,* patrician patrons were obliged to explain to clients the laws of which they were ignorant, to bring a suit on their behalf when they were wronged over a contract, and to defend clients against those who brought charges. Indeed it has been suggested that the duty of a patron to his client was the basis for petition and response.[1] With the institution of the imperial office, emperors became the patrons of all the people, especially the plebs. Finding later evidence for the influence and advice of patrons, however, is extremely difficult (unless we assume that some of those who signed on behalf of an illiterate party in our extant legal documents were patrons).[2] And of course patrons could not be guaranteed to offer expert advice.

Without the help of a patron, a Roman could ask a legal professional for legal information or advice. There was a range of such people to whom one could turn: advocates, jurists, and *tabelliones,* or notaries. Surprisingly, advocates were not the repository of legal information we might expect; many of them had only a shaky grasp of Roman law.[3] Quintilian makes clear the unimportance of the law for their professional development. Toward the close of the *Institutes,* a training manual for orators, he recommends that the orator also (*quoque*) have knowledge of law; otherwise he will be embarrassed by his ignorance during debate with the opposing counsel.[4] Before the appearance of official late Roman legal compilations, advocates in training and in practice relied on handbooks and memory. As Jill Harries notes, "Many of the references to the past in late antique texts are in fact formulaic; lawyers knew, for example, the basics of the requirements of the *lex Cincia* on gift-giving, without having to go back to a text now some six hundred years old. . . . Nor could the texts themselves have remained immune from the ravages of the centuries, from emendation or copyists' errors."[5]

Though knowledgeable (or well equipped with handbooks), the advocates, with their elevated social status, may have been off-putting to many seeking advice and help, and their fees were prohibitive to most. The Edict on Maximum Prices places a cap of 250 *denarii* on an advocate's fee for opening a case (*postulatio*), 1,000 *denarii* for pleading a case (*cognitio*).[6] These sums are considerable; for example, a farm laborer working for a maximum daily wage of 25 *denarii* would have spent fifty days' earnings on legal representation in court.[7] Advocates' consultation fees were probably also too high for most.

Jurists were the best repository of legal information. Trained in law schools and deriving their income from their knowledge and interpretive expertise, they were ideally placed to answer any legal question. Such legal expertise, however, belonged to only a few, who were not readily accessible and had many demands on their time, responding to requests for information, writing books, and increasingly from the second century providing their services to the Roman government. They were thus able to charge high fees. Lucky was the Roman who received their help.

So *tabelliones* were a good and frequently used source of legal advice for the middling sort. First attested by papyri in Egypt in the second century and by Ulpian in the third, they were responsible for drafting documents for use both in and out of court—wills, gifts or donations, contracts and settlements of sale, exchange, pledge, gifts, lease, and adoption—that contained promises which were binding in law and liable by law to penalties if broken.[8] Importantly for us, jurists also composed petitions to various officials for relief, dispensations, honors, or advice and also documents that were used in court as *narrationes*.[9] *Tabelliones* probably were the legal figures to whom non-elites turned most often with their legal questions. They understood classifications and legal procedure and, given the variety of documents they were expected to draw up, a substantial amount of law.[10] Some *tabelliones* may be named in the papyri as writing for a petitioner, though any named individuals who appear may simply be literate men writing for illiterate friends.[11] The input of *tabelliones* in the wording of petitions must be more subtly discerned than this, as I show later in this chapter. They were accessible, operating from city and town *fora* or offices (*stationes*), and they charged little: a maximum of 10 *denarii* per hundred lines, according to the Edict on Maximum Prices.[12] Further, they were bound by codes of conduct, which ensured minimum standards of competence.[13]

Upon receiving advice from an advocate, an expert, or more likely a *tabellio* about a legal problem, an individual had a number of possible remedies: he could go to court, ask for an arbitrator, or use the system of petition and response. To appreciate the obstacles a litigant of the middling sort faced in court, I turn first to P.Sakaon 31 (= P.Thead. 15) of AD 280 or 281, an account of a court proceeding. An Egyptian widow, Aurelia Artemis, was plaintiff against a local tax collector, Syrion, who, she claimed, had seized the family's livestock upon the death of her husband.[14] The document comprises three elements: the case that her advocate presents on her behalf, which simply tells her story and makes no mention of any relevant law, the reply of a public official, who claims that Syrion is absent on official business and is therefore unable to attend, and the judgment of the *epistrategos*—the provincial prefect's deputy who presided over the court—that the case be thrown out and that Aurelia Artemis send a petition to him. Aurelia had already petitioned the governor complaining about the actions of Syrion,[15] and he directed her to the *epistrategos,* who summoned Syrion to court for a trial over which he presided. That aborted trial was set to follow the model of the so-called *cognitio extra ordinem,* which by the third century was the standard trial procedure in the provinces.

In this trial procedure, litigants approached the provincial governor, who would either hear the case or pass it to a subordinate. The governor or his junior was responsible as judge for issuing the summons to court and for condemning parties in their absence. A judge was then chosen, often the governor but perhaps a junior official or a member of the local elite. The choice of judge sometimes depended on the case. Taxation cases under Diocletian had to be held before a representative of the *fiscus,* presumably at or near his place of work. Sometimes it depended on the status of the litigants: the higher the litigants' social status, the higher the judge's office.

In theory there were safeguards to ensure that the less well off could use the courts. Lawyers could not charge exorbitant sums for their services,[16] and later Constantine abolished the levying of charges by chiefs of the office staffs, their assistants, *apparitores* (who assisted magistrates with the running of the court), and *exceptores* (who wrote up court records). In place of these individual charges, Constantine seems to have introduced flat rates. However, his good intentions failed.[17]

Aurelia Artemis and others similarly vulnerable to more powerful opponents faced various disadvantages. The most obvious were pecuniary.

Plaintiffs had to put up a "wager of law," which, if they lost, was forfeited. In criminal prosecutions unsuccessful plaintiffs even had to face whatever penalties defendants might otherwise suffer. And there were hidden costs too, for example, charges for a summons to be drafted, written, and issued.[18] Aside from lawyers' fees, litigants also had to bear the cost of travel to court and time spent away from earning an income.[19] For those with little spare cash, these costs could threaten their livelihood, even the roof over their head.

Social prejudice was another disadvantage in court. Women, wards, soldiers, "infamous" persons, and freedmen acting against their patrons were barred from putting forward charges.[20] There were a few dispensations for women. At first, the *ius trium liberorum* allowed some women to be *sui iuris*; later, increasing numbers of women acted independently regardless of the size of their family. But to the other groups, the courts remained closed. The original ban reflects the position of the judiciary: not everyone should or could participate in law, an attitude probably shared by most judges.[21] Local magistrates could be prejudiced by their knowledge of a party's background or reputation, especially if that party moved in the same social circle.[22] The middling sort were sometimes protected, however, by patrons and, according to Harries, "being made to appear the weaker party may even have been an advantage in some cases."[23]

A third disadvantage was linguistic. While legal documents such as wills could be written in any language, court documents were written in Latin or Greek, and court cases were also conducted in those languages.[24] So an individual who knew neither Latin nor Greek was unable to read his or her court documents and could not understand what was happening in court. There were always bilingual legal professionals and friends who could help, but for inhabitants of the Roman Empire of moderate means and status, whose first language was neither Latin nor Greek, going to court must have been a bewildering and alien experience.[25] Even in one's own language, trial procedure can sometimes be so arcane as to be unintelligible, as demonstrated at the start of this chapter by the words of a woman who appeared in court on a charge of driving without insurance.

It was because of the disadvantages—financial, social, and linguistic—inherent in standard trial procedure that people of the middling sort used alternative methods to solve legal problems. Probably the most popular alternative to litigation was force. In the absence of police, settlement by force usually went unchallenged and unpunished. A more social option was arbitration. Less costly and less divisive than going to court and less dangerous than the use of force, arbitration offered quicker and less complex resolution.[26] The process was begun with the parties agreeing to choose an arbiter and abide by his decision.[27] There is little information about the people who acted as arbiters. They are not mentioned in arbitration documents, which simply outline the agreement between the two parties. It is likely that they were respected members of the community, perhaps from the elite, and possibly, though not necessarily, officials in the local administration.[28] The arbiter formally summoned the parties to appear, who argued their cases themselves or with the help of more eloquent and knowledgeable friends. The arbiter made his decision and concluded proceedings with an agreement in the name of the parties, which recorded the judgment.[29] The agreement was binding on both moral and legal grounds; a party that reneged was usually fined. If the fine went unpaid, the local administration could begin proceedings against him or her.[30]

Negotiation was also a popular option, undertaken directly between the two parties or by means of a third party. Another method widely used but seldom discussed was the exchanging of oaths before a judge.[31] The first party would challenge another to swear the veracity of his or her suit. If the second party swore, he or she won; if the second party failed to swear, the first party won. Exchange of oaths was swift and inexpensive (no advocates were needed, just a *tabellio* to draw up the oath), but it relied on individuals' good conscience and on their concern for their reputation in the community.

The final source of legal redress or help was the system of petition and response, which provided the most effective and readily available means by which the middling sort could receive advice about their legal problems and find a solution to them. As we will see, a favorable response could support a case in court or could help persuade an opponent faced with the increased prospect of defeat to settle. Neither so rich that they did not need the system nor so poor that they lacked the wherewithal to use it, I think it reasonable to suggest that most petitioners belonged to the middling sort—"de condition moyenne ou humble."[32]

I shall argue in this book that petitioners, though most were from the middling sort, shared a sense that they were "poor," not because they were necessarily financially deprived but because they perceived themselves as lacking power in the face of an opponent and therefore as vulnerable. Since the system of petition and response did not limit the opportunity to petition to certain individuals, petitioners defined themselves as needing help, usually because they were unable to seek the private advice of an advocate or were too weak to ensure that existing laws protecting them were enforced. These are the individuals about whom we know little relative to their numbers. They are the mostly silent majority. But their use of petition and response is evidenced in abundance in law codes, papyri, and inscriptions, in texts that offer valuable information about the lives of these ordinary people.

## Petitioning in the Roman World

Putting it in writing or filing a complaint is seen as a necessary step in engaging or mobilizing the institutional machinery. In a world of anonymous bureaucracies, writing is a modern mythical practice that has the capacity to transform immediate, ephemeral, and idiosyncratic experiences into a stable and legible form. Even as writing abstracts events and experiences from one context—that of immediate social action—it endows them with the characteristics necessary to exist in a more formal, timeless, institutional context.

EWICK AND SILBEY, *COMMON PLACE*

In AD 238, the residents of Skaptopara, a village in Thrace, complained to the emperor Gordian III about their suffering as a result of the successive exactions of soldiers, visitors, and provincial officials. Previously an edict that guaranteed no exactions except those sanctioned by the provincial governor had protected them, but now it was being ignored. The desperate residents claimed that they had been reduced to poverty; finding no satisfaction from an approach to senior provincial officials, they had decided to appeal to the emperor. The text and a translation are supplied in appendix 1. Their complaint was in the form of a petition, and they used the system of petition and response to receive help. The answer, along with the petition, was preserved by them on stone.[33]

There were various types of petition, for example, "Local officials are harassing me in the following ways. Please make them stop." This type of petition could be answered with an assurance that because the harassment described was unacceptable, the matter would be raised with the provincial governor and the officials ordered to cease their activity. This type of petition is preserved in inscriptions such as that of the Skaptopareni, which I shall discuss as a paradigm in this chapter. Another type of petition was, "I am involved in the following legal dispute. What is your opinion of the matter and what do you suggest I do?" The response would be of the form "Given the facts of the situation, as presented by you, and given the following pertinent law, you are in the right." Responses of this type constitute the bulk of the entries in the *CJ* and are the focus of chapters 2–4.[34] Finally, petitions could also read like this: "I, a senator, wish to marry an actress. May I receive your permission to do so?" A response would grant or deny the special request.[35]

Petitions in each category were called *libelli;* responses were called *rescripta.* The text written in response beneath a *libellus* was at first called a *subscriptio,* literally a piece of writing underneath the petition. In the third century the more general term *rescriptum* was usually employed in its place (usually anglicized as rescript), though the answer may still have been written below the petition.

Petitions of the types listed above were sent by private groups and individuals such as the Skaptopareni and the petitioners whose names are recorded in the *Codex Justinianus (CJ).* Individuals acting in an official capacity could also petition the emperor with a request for advice or assistance with an administrative problem, and their petitions are generally known as *epistulae,* or letters; confusingly, responses to them are commonly known as *rescripta,* the same word used for responses to private petitions.[36] A small number of *rescripta* written to officials date to AD 293–294. These years will be the focus of subsequent chapters but the *rescripta* are recognizable as responses to letters from their format. The recipient's name can appear in the accusative case following *ad* or in the dative case accompanied by a title or in a more complex formulation such as *have Heraclida carissime nobis* or *Serapioni suo salutem.*[37] Responses to petitions simply give the recipient's name in the dative.

Private groups and individuals had a wide choice of recipients for their petitions. Most petitioned one of a number of local officials, their choice being based on the respective officials' authority to pass judgment or initiate legal procedure and their accessibility.[38] Provincial governors, the highest-ranking local officials, received many petitions while at their palaces and as they toured important cities on the regular *conventus*. P.Yale I 61 records that an Egyptian prefect received 1,804 petitions over three days. This high number suggests that, since 1,804 petitions were handed in at a single stage of that year's *conventus*, the system of petition and response was very popular; that petitioners waited for the arrival of the prefect because they knew that he received petitions when traveling; and that the task of answering petitions was too onerous for the governor alone, even with several weeks for the task. These considerations also apply to the system run out of the imperial court. Other provincial officials who answered petitions included *epistrategoi* and centurions. Centurions occasionally answered civilians' petitions, but were more often the first source of legal help or advice for petitioning soldiers. Far above the centurions were the *duces*, the military counterparts of provincial governors. According to the *Notitia Dignitatum*, the *duces* of Moesia Secunda, Moesia Prima, and Dacia Ripensis were served by *scrinia libellorum*, which presumably answered petitions from soldiers.[39]

While most petitioners sought out local officials, some approached the emperor, as evidenced by the *CJ*. Petitioners used almost the same system for anyone they approached,[40] and the similarity of the systems at the imperial court and in the provinces helped them. The regularity of the governors' *conventus*, at which petitions could be handed in and answers received, served to heighten public awareness of the power of petitions, and the practice of posting those answers in prominent public spaces increased awareness still further. The availability of junior officials as respondents in addition to the governors helped to make petition and response a procedure that a wide array of people, knowing of it and understanding it, were willing and able to use. Petition and response as a mode of communication was also popular among Romans because it was found elsewhere and earlier in time and because they saw that it was being used by petitioners as a deterrent against opponents and that others in the community abided by responses. Finally, petitioners accepted that an imperial response had authority. Potential petitioners' familiarity with the system in the provinces and emperors' willingness to answer them at home and abroad enabled and emboldened ordinary Romans to bring their complaints or queries to the empire's highest legal authority. The number of responses preserved from the *Codex Hermogenianus*—over 970 in two years—bears witness to the success of many of them. Conversely, a Roman who had petitioned the emperor and had been directed to approach the provincial governor with the emperor's response knew from this experience how to fulfill the next step in his search for help. The similarity of the provincial and imperial systems also offered petitioners a choice of recipient. If petitioning the emperor directly was unfeasible, petitioning the governor was an effective and simple alternative.

Both emperors and officials received petitions on a wide variety of subjects. As will be shown in chapter 4, individuals petitioned the emperor about bad business deals, property disputes, inheritance, theft, and family problems—subjects that appear in petitions to officials and emperors alike. While we have hundreds of rescripts from the imperial court, we have fewer from provincial officials. It is therefore impossible to make any claims about qualitative differences in the answers petitioners received. It has been suggested to me on several occasions that surely petitioners directed less important matters to provincial officials and more important matters to emperors. Yet, unsurprisingly, there is no evidence for this. Some topics seem to have been the preserve of officials. We find on papyrus, for example, a petition notifying an official about a family member's disappearance; another petitioner asks why his son has been left off the *ephebe* list; another complains about the level of tax levied on him; some ask for exemption from liturgies; others request guardians.[41] These topics are not, to my knowledge, found in petitions to or responses from emperors, and perhaps a local official was best placed to respond to them. There is no evidence, however, that they could not have been the subjects of petitions to emperors. On the whole, would-be petitioners who knew that the emperor was coming to town are unlikely to have kept their petitions for a visit to the provincial governor because they deemed them more suitable for his attention. The recipient of a petition was probably determined by financial and geographical factors, not by subject matter. Besides, as will be discussed in chapter 4, one successful petitioner to the emperor complained about his neighbor knocking a window into a shared wall. While many would consider the problem trivial, to the petitioner it was worthy of the emperor's attention.

Most petitions were cries for help couched in legal terms.[42] The individual or group sending a petition hoped for or expected a response that would be effective in one of three ways. First, it would guarantee that the emperor or local official would resolve the legal problem at issue. Second, it could be shown to a legal opponent to pressure him to settle out of court. Even letting an opponent know of the intention to petition might have persuaded an opponent to desist from whatever harmful action he was carrying out and save the petitioner the potential expense of a trial.[43] A supporting rescript was a bonus, though sending a petition could also provoke retaliation from an opponent. For example, a group of *coloni* from the *saltus Burunitanus* complained in a petition that news of their petition could incite their opponents (the *procurator* and *conductores* of the estate) to harsher treatment of them.[44] They could only hope for a swift and favorable answer.[45]

A petition could help a willing litigant bring about a trial. The Egyptian widow Aurelia Artemis, whom we met in the introduction, had petitioned the prefect about a local tax collector's (Syrion) seizure of the family's livestock upon the death of her husband. Her petition, preserved in P.Sakaon 36, received the response . . . κατὰ τὸ δικαιότατον δοκιμάσει ὁ κράτιστος [ἐπιστράτηγο]ς ("the most powerful governor will pass judgment according to what is most just"): she was to take her situation to the *epistrategos*, who would summon Syrion to court. From an account of the court proceedings, P.Sakaon 31, we know that Syrion failed to attend and Aurelia Artemis was forced to petition again. But the story shows how a petition could set in motion a trial that would otherwise never have been initiated.

Alternatively, a petition could influence court proceedings. For example, a petition could request that an official or the emperor respond with an attestation of the facts as presented in the petition. In P.Euphrates 5, a woman petitioned a centurion to certify a deposition in an affair regarding murder and the usurpation of goods. She states that two people, a soldier and a veteran, can attest to the murder and seizure, and asks the centurion to confirm that they can act as witnesses.[46] Finally, petitions could also be used to validate the existence and content of a document.[47]

A petitioner could also use his response in court, offsetting trial costs with the increased likelihood of a favorable outcome. A favorable response in court was valuable because if the presiding judge found the facts of the case to be as they were presented in the petition, he would use the response as the basis for his favorable judgment, especially if the response had come from the office of someone more powerful.[48] Even the most favorable response, however, could be countered with a petition by and response to the other party; if even one detail of the original petition was revealed in court as inaccurate, the response to it was rendered invalid.[49] On the pitfalls of inaccurate representation in writing, Ewick and Silbey note that "inscription creates a material impediment to reinterpretation and thus limits the influence we might exert over the interpretation others might make. Because inscription permits—indeed encourages—interpretation dissociated in time and space from one's own participation, the ability to actively intervene in future interpretations is reduced."[50]

Petitions were also effective in another way. Although they could not force adjournment in a trial already under way, they could ask that an investigation (*quaestio*) or legal process (*actio*) such as that taken against an adulterous wife be stopped. And they could be used in the appeals process following a declaration of intent to appeal. Receipt of a petition lodging an appeal obliged the recipient official to guarantee that the appellant would not be imprisoned, tortured, or subject to inquiry.[51]

The efficacy of petitions and responses in each of these situations—initiation of a trial, management of it, and appeal—derives from the fact that they were public documents. Their power came from the authorizing signature of an official, the authentication of them by the imperial or provincial archives, and the witness of members of the public.[52] It was therefore essential that petitioners compose or have composed for them documents that depicted their situation accurately and presented their plight persuasively (though even if there were errors or omissions in a petition, they did not permit prejudgment of a case). The benefits, however, of the petition and its response were everlasting. The opinion expressed in the response was always valid for the situation detailed in the petition, though there could be a time limit on undertaking an action based on it.[53]

The Skaptopareni suffered such serious privations and humiliation at the hands of local officials and soldiers that they chose to petition the emperor. The inscription they commissioned to commemorate their undertaking is useful for understanding the process of petition and response. It comprises their petition, the emperor's rescript, and an introduction describing the origin of both texts, and is the fullest single piece of evidence for petition and response. Taken together with other third-century inscriptions and papyri, it can give us a general outline of how petitions were sent and answered in the third century.

The content of the inscription, however, cannot tell us what the experience of petitioning was like for the Skaptopareni. That must be inferred from the content of the petition and the system as we can recreate it from this and other inscriptions. Nor can it tell us why the Skaptopareni chose to petition the emperor rather than, say, barrage the provincial governor with individual petitions or form a movement to resist their predators. Such things have to be imagined from the evidence we have and from common sense. We cannot know how the experience of the Skaptopareni would have differed if they had each petitioned as individuals. Indeed, all petitioners would have had a different experience, depending on what their problems were, who their opponents were, where they lived, how much money they had, what legal experience they had.

Moreover, the Skaptopareni petitioned as a group, and we should not overlook the differences in experience between petitioning collectively and petitioning individually. Though each member of the group had suffered individually, as the number of their complaints grew, the villagers decided to seek help collectively. They realized that acting as a group could solve their problems most efficiently, since they could share the expense of writing and sending a single petition. Others too realized the benefits of collective action. Petitions preserved on inscriptions, such as that of the Skaptopareni, were for the most part sent by groups, most often members of a geographical community. First, group petitioners may together have had more money and therefore more opportunity to use a representative to deliver their petition, as the Skaptopareni did, though individual petitioners may have had families and other interested parties who contributed toward any necessary costs. Second, given that they had a better chance of using a representative, group petitioners may have been more likely to petition the emperor though he was far away. Individual petitioners, if they had less money for a representative, were more likely to petition the emperor only if he was reasonably close, and they might petition the provincial governor if he was closer, especially if approaching the emperor was unfeasible. Diocletian's journey through the lower Danube provinces, therefore, in 293–294 offered a large number of individuals greater opportunity to petition than they might otherwise have enjoyed.

The petitions whose responses are collected in the *CJ* were sent mostly by single individuals; fewer than 10 of the 966 entries of AD 293–294 were without doubt addressed to more than one recipient. The experience of individual petitioners was somewhat different from that of groups. Individuals had on average less money to pay for help with composing a petition or delivering it (as well as paying court fees), and they had less knowledge on average about the process of petitioning and how to use it. On the other hand, they needed to worry only that their petitions accurately reflected their situation, and the same institutions and resources were theoretically available to them as to groups, such as professionals who could help compose petitions, representatives to bring them, and of course the *scrinium* to answer them. Groups had to make sure that their petition reflected the needs of all members. They needed to have the same involvement in legal terms in the situation for the rescript to apply to all of them.[54]

The inscription of the Skaptopareni, then, will be used to give a general impression of how petition and response worked. It is likely that the experience of the recipients of the rescripts extant from 293–294 was similar to that of the Skaptopareni except that, as I shall argue in chapter 3, the former for the most part handed in petitions and took copies of the rescripts themselves, rather than use representatives.

## PETITION

The stone on which the petition of the Skaptopareni is preserved was found in 1868 at Cumaja in Bulgaria (then in Turkey). The stone, seventy centimeters wide and one meter long, was broken into four pieces at that time or soon after and is now untraceable. Almost-complete texts have been constructed on the basis of records of squeezes and copies.[55] The inscription opens with a greeting, an authentication of the rescript, and confirmation of Pyrrus's delivery of the petition, all in Latin. The petition and a speech delivered by Pyrrus before the provincial governor, both in Greek, follow. The emperor's rescript and witnesses' seals, both in Latin, close the inscription.

The petition of the Skaptopareni followed a commonly used format: it outlined the legal situation at hand and then asked the emperor to solve the problem in a particular way. (Petitions asking for advice also outlined the situation and then requested suggestions for further action.) Yet the format of this and other petitions is not as simple as first appears. Analyses of the few extant Roman petitions have revealed the care with which they were written. Their structure follows principles of rhetoric, as I shall show;

their content is emotive and compelling.[56] The petition of the Skaptopareni was carefully written because its presentation was crucial to their success. It had to distill the experiences of the community—a series of distressing and probably confused incidents—into an accurate, reasonable, and persuasive account that would prompt a response that removed all causes of the petitioners' difficulties. Its accuracy was important because a petition made an individual's experience a matter of permanent public record, unalterable and incontestable until proven in court. If imprecisely formulated, a petition could misrepresent that experience, elicit an unhelpful or even damaging rescript (that could be seen by the public), and finally prejudice the judge in court, if the petitioner was still able to bring his or her case that far.

Writing a petition, then, was no easy matter and was the first obstacle facing would-be petitioners. The petition may have been written by one of the villagers—an accomplished writer or perhaps a reasonably good writer with access to petitions sent in previous years by his or another community or kept in family archives. Other petitions provided a structural template, and local inscriptions could be harvested for flattering phrases and modes of address. The wording of extant petitions suggests that care was taken to choose formulations that were effective by virtue of being not just familiar but also in current usage.

Yet even with the most generous estimates of basic literacy, the chances that one of the petitioners was a writer adept at composing legal documents were slim. A number of options were available to a petitioner or a group of petitioners who lacked skill in composition. The knowledge and experience of family members, friends, or acquaintances could be called upon. Alternatively, petitioners could employ the skills of a professional writer. The services of scribes were widely available in the Greco-Roman world. They may have been numbered among those who wrote for illiterate parties in Egyptian legal documents and would also have been qualified to aid petitioners. Petitioners may also have hired lawyers, though their fees were high. Some petitioners may have sought to minimize lawyers' costs by outlining the case themselves and then asking a professional to fill in the formulaic elements and supply supporting documents.[57]

Notaries, or *tabelliones,* whom we met above, were skilled in both writing and composing legal documents and could have assisted would-be petitioners. Their role in drafting legal documents is suggested by the *formula Baetica,* a notary's master template for a loan agreement, from which he could create standard documents, requiring only the addition of particular information; the fees for notaries' services are mentioned in Diocletian's Prices Edict.[58] Their input in petitions is suggested by the use of abbreviations, which a layman is unlikely to have used: λβ for λίβελλος and στρατ λεγ for στρατιώτην λεγεῶνος ("legionary soldier"), for example.[59] Their skills may be detected in petitions containing citations of supporting documents that are legally appropriate and compelling, although such inclusions could be the work of legal researchers hired by notaries.

The petition of the Skaptopareni is long—the longest of all extant petitions—and collects in one document elements found scattered through other existing examples. Opening with an *inscriptio,* it moves to an *exordium,* then the *narratio* of the problem, and closes with the request for help (*preces*). This format follows rhetorical guidelines that were laid out in handbooks and were used in many petitions, as Tor Hauken has shown.[60] Staying within these guidelines was important for petitioners. A standard format was what the recipient expected (responses to petitions also followed a format), and it provided a normalizing framework in which the issues at stake could be considered. To deviate from that format was to risk transferring the reader's attention from the details of the complaint to its unusual presentation. The Skaptopareni seemed to realize that a format that had worked for other petitioners offered them the best chance of success.

The careful composition of this extensive document is apparent from its opening. It begins with the *inscriptio* and the name of the emperor, Gordian III. The formulation of the name is significant. While emperors' full names and titles appeared on edicts and provincial documents and were proclaimed aloud at state events, a standard abbreviated form appeared on petitions and was used by the imperial court in its responses.[61] The Skaptopareni used this special form, either copying from available petitions and responses or relying on the expertise of a professional writer.

Further precision is shown in the next part of the document. Its purpose is stated with the technical word δεήσις, the Greek equivalent of *precatio.* In the original document, this word would probably have been set off from the preceding and subsequent text, as the texts of extant petitions on papyri demonstrate.[62] The name of the petitioner or petitioners comes in the genitive case following παρά. Some (but not all) petitioners included their office and occasionally their place of origin. There seems not to have been a standardized system of naming for petitioners as there was for emperors. Indeed petitioners did not even name themselves in the same way twice. In one petition a petitioner might include a title and patronymic to impress the recipient; in another he might omit such details to gain his sympathy.[63] As the *exordium* that follows makes clear, touching the emperor emotionally was important. The petitioners contrast the benefits that Gordian's rule bestows on the world with their suffering.

The body of the text follows, outlining their complaint (*narratio*) and making a plea for help (*preces*). At the end of the original petition came a copy of a speech made by Pyrrus on behalf of the Skaptopareni before the Thracian governor. Other petitioners included documents such as edicts, excerpts from trial proceedings, their own previous petitions and the responses to them, and other people's petitions and responses. So compelling were these documents that they could read like lawyers' court arguments or *narrationes*. Indeed petitions could be used like *narrationes* both in and out of court. The plaintiff's advocate could begin court proceedings by reading out a petition or could use a petition as a means of rebutting the facts of an opponent's petition before going to trial.[64]

Next, the petitioners had to get their petition to the emperor. Most of the recipients of rescripts from 293–294, as I argue later, delivered their petitions themselves. If that was not possible because of time or physical constraints, an alternative method needed to be found. The Skaptopareni used a representative, who is named in the inscription as Pyrrus. Representatives could be family members or friends, or a group could select one of its members. An individual who was traveling to Rome anyway would carry the petition for less money than the petitioners would have spent to deliver it themselves. But even if he (or, less likely, she) was making the trip solely to deliver the petition, he would have spent less money than a group of petitioners. Petitioners could also reduce their time and money costs by delivering their petitions with a representative carrying others from the same area.

Representatives were crucial to petitioners living far from the imperial capital, given the time and financial costs of a journey, as well as its dangers. Unreliable communications could make even short journeys hazardous, and whether a petitioner carried his or her precious text in person or sent it through a representative, there was no guarantee that it (or the deliverer) would arrive. Emperors were willing to receive petitions as they traveled, offering petitioners or their representatives the possibility of a shorter journey. They would have to find out where he would be and when; if he was on campaign, it seems unlikely that petitioners could have approached him. For some people, petitioning local officials or even going to court may have been safer options. Nevertheless, papyri from Oxyrhynchus preserve petitions answered at Alexandria by Severus and Caracalla, and the *CJ* contains responses produced in places all over the empire, including the lower Danube provinces, through which Diocletian traveled in AD 293–294.[65]

Many petitioners were deterred from delivering their petitions in person by the distance and expense, by their immobility or work commitments, or by poor security, and the state rarely offered assistance. Pliny the Younger once forwarded to the emperor Trajan a petition from a centurion seeking citizen status for his daughter. Trajan replied that he read the petition and would grant the request. Pliny sent on the petition by public post, but most likely received only the letter from Trajan. The emperor's response to the centurion was probably posted at Rome for the centurion to collect. Pliny's act of generosity is exceptional, and although a *patronus* might often have done this, no other examples of such a favor have been found.[66]

While it has been suggested that individuals could bring petitions for governors to send on to the imperial court, it seems unlikely that the state would have supported a practice so burdensome to the public post. Governors would have to know where to send the petitions—to the imperial capital or to wherever the emperor was traveling. Moreover, the practice would have been complicated and would have created extra work for the imperial court. It would have obliged the court, which kept the originals for the archives, to make copies to send back to petitioners. Further, if the court was on the move, those copies would have to be made en route and sent via public post, hopefully to the right recipients in the right places, all over the empire.[67] Given that responses were not returned to them, the onus was therefore on petitioners either to deliver their petitions in person or to choose the right representative.

Petitioners or their representatives had to know where and how to hand in a petition. There is evidence that approaching provincial governors during the *conventus* was sometimes difficult. They were busy men, pressed by the demands of hundreds, sometimes thousands of petitioners.[68] Approaching the imperial court was probably little different.[69] Furthermore, petitioners seem to have received little guidance about where to hand in petitions. Those petitioning the provincial governor were told simply ἔντυχέμοι πρὸ βήματος ("petition me at the tribunal"), wherever that was, while those petitioning the emperor needed to know that the *scrinium libellorum* received petitions.[70] Individuals who were alert to announcements of the emperor's itinerary and knew in advance where to hand in their petitions would find themselves toward the front of the queue when the emperor came to town. Those with cash to spare might persuade officials in the *scrinium* by means of a financial incentive to move them nearer the front, though money was not supposed to help petitioners move their way up the queue.[71]

## RESPONSE

The representative of the Skaptopareni, Pyrrus, secured a response to their petition, formulated and written by an official in the *scrinium libellorum*. It was originally written beneath the villagers' petition and was followed by the official's declaration *rescripsi*, included to ensure that no further text could be added by someone else. The response was then verified by the *magister a libellis*, who wrote *recognovi* ("I have examined").[72]

As will be argued more fully in the following chapter, members of the *scrinium libellorum* are more likely than the emperor to have composed and written responses to petitions. Emperors, lacking time and expertise, would not have employed a *magister a libellis* and his officials unless they played a role in the answering of petitions. Moreover, the fact that responses were written in the name of the emperors endowed them with the authority of the empire's most senior judge. That authority would not have increased if they were actually written by the emperors. It is possible that the petition of the Skaptopareni was answered not by Gordian III, but by an official in the *scrinium libellorum*. Many similar petitions had been brought to emperors over the years, and the complaints of the Skaptopareni, while critical to them, did not present any unique or constitutionally significant legal problems. Moreover the answer is not legally interesting. It simply directs the petitioners to the provincial governor, who can hear all sides of the story and then take appropriate action.[73] It is unlikely that the emperor would have been asked by his *magister a libellis* to authorize a simple direction to the provincial court.

The response was written either underneath the original petition or on another piece of parchment or papyrus and cross-referenced.[74] The authentication contains the emperor's name (*imperatore Caesare Marco Antonio Gordiano Pio Felice Augusto*), the standard format also employed by the Skaptopareni in their petition, who presumably took their Greek version from the introductions to other petitions, which were in turn translations of Latin titles on responses. It is addressed to the villagers represented by Pyrrus but uses the second person singular *debeas,* directed at Pyrrus. The response is an instruction to approach the provincial governor, who would check the veracity of their claims and then presumably castigate their harassers. It was more apt to the situation than a judgment from the emperor. The latter would have appeared more helpful to the petitioners but would probably have required enforcement by the provincial governor.

Though the emperor's answer only directed them back to the governor, the villagers felt that it was important enough to be inscribed. The inscription does not preserve the judgment of the *praeses,* an omission that may reflect the fact that the inscription "is not primarily a record of the efforts of the village and its results, but a private or semi-official record of the meritorious efforts of Aurelius Pyrrus on behalf of his village."[75] True, Pyrrus emerges as the central figure in the sequence of events and documents. But there may be other reasons for the omission. Perhaps the villagers felt that the imperial response was sufficient to intimidate their harassers, even if the governor did not find in their favor. Or perhaps the governor did find the facts as they had been presented in the petition and the Skaptopareni wanted to celebrate this fact.

A delivery note in which Pyrrus is named as the *conpossessor* also appears in the inscription and was presumably added to the original petition, perhaps between it and the imperial response. Both the delivery note and response are in Latin. The choice of language must have been frustrating for many petitioners, including the Skaptopareni, who had petitioned in their first language, Greek. Petitions from Greek-speaking areas were answered in Latin; our extant responses in the *CJ,* which come from all over the Roman Empire, are in Latin. This was yet another obstacle to petitioners, some of whom would have paid for the help of translators who spotted a good business opportunity. Though unhelpful to many, the choice of Latin is understandable. The official language of the imperial administration, it was used for official civilian and military documents even in the Near East, and was presumably the working language of the *scrinium libellorum.* It has been suggested that responses produced in Greek-speaking areas were written in Greek and then translated into Latin for archival copies to be held at Rome or the imperial capitals under the Tetrarchy.[76] But the enormity of the task of translating and transporting the responses argues against the suggestion. If Greek-speaking petitioners wanted their responses in Latin, they would have them translated when they had copies made. The answer to the Skaptopareni was in Latin. They were told what the response said and felt no need to have it translated; their harassers, who were soldiers and officials, would have understood it. Our few extant responses in Greek are most likely translations from the Latin originals.[77]

Pyrrus went to a somewhat unlikely location to receive the response: the portico of the baths of Trajan, as we are told in the protocol at the start of the inscription. Other locations used for advertising responses were at various times temples—the temple of Apollo on the Oppian Hill in Rome was used before Trajan's baths—and the *stoa* of gymnasia.[78] At the baths Pyrrus would have found pinned up long sheets of petitions that had been glued at the top and bottom.[79] Searching through the mass of petitions and responses, he would have found his original petition and the response to it written below. Noting its content, perhaps with the help of a translator standing by to offer his services, he then ordered a copy.

Pyrrus and the petitioners suffered a series of obstacles as they composed the petition, sent it, and received the response. Those who most likely offered help—*tabelliones,* representatives, translators—were private individuals who might charge for their services. It does not appear that the imperial court offered help at any stage in the process, save for answering the petitions it received. While the system of petition and response helped ordinary people with legal problems and queries, it did no more than answer them. Those using petition and response needed determination.

The final stage in the process was for Pyrrus to bring a copy of the response to his fellow petitioners. But petitioners collecting responses on their own behalf had to decide whether taking their own copy was necessary or even prudent—keeping a copy of an unfavorable response would seriously undermine one's attempts to resolve a legal problem. Pyrrus's copy was an official document, as would have been clear from its presentation and meticulous authentication. It would have been written in a highly competent hand that demarcated the separate sections of the document and began each with an ornate first letter, and it would have opened with a statement that the text was taken from the original posted at Rome in the portico of the baths of Trajan, a location precise enough to provide authenticating detail.[80] The authenticity of a copy was further guaranteed by witnesses. The Skaptoparean copy was signed (*signatum*) by possibly seven witnesses. The inscription shows VI, and six witnesses appear in other documents.[81] But as seven was the standard number of witnesses to a Roman legal document, it is universally accepted that the inscription should be amended to VI[I]. The witnesses were presumably individuals paid a small fee by petitioners or representatives to help them at the archives.

The Skaptoparean text had been copied (*descriptum*) and validated (*recognitum*) from one of the sheets of petitions and responses (*factum ex libro libellorum rescriptorum*). In some copies we find roll and sheet numbers, revealing that the long sheets were stored rolled up in the imperial archives.[82] A petitioner wishing to produce a response in court would have brought his or her copy, which could have been checked against the original held at Rome or the imperial capital. Copies of petitions and responses had to record the texts of the original documents in full to guard against fraud, and indeed Diocletian and Maximian declared that responses could only be presented with wording identical to the original, guaranteed as genuine, and without abbreviation.[83]

Responses were collected and edited into an abbreviated form by lawyers, who used them to create a private archive of statements of important principles for trials and cogent expressions for legal documents.[84] One example of such a collection is P.Oxy. XII 1407, a fragmentary papyrus containing an imperial letter and approximately three responses from several decades, addressed presumably to different recipients and taken from different locations, including Neapolis (which Neapolis is not specified) and Rome, as the author records. The names of the recipients seem to have been omitted (though too little text remains to be certain on this point), and the texts were probably abbreviated. Much of the remaining text contains the titles of the emperors. The only discernable topic seems to be an official appointment; the texts of the other documents are too meager to interpret. The content of this papyrus yields few clues as to its original content. Of the remaining extant collections, some collected rescripts on similar topics, while the others did not.[85] This and similar collections are testament to the importance of these imperial legal pronouncements not just to their recipients, but also to the wider legal community who provided services to potential litigants. They may have been the work of legal collectives that pooled their documentary resources.[86]

While copies of petitions and responses were used for a myriad of purposes by petitioners and others, the originals were simply stored in rolls in the archives. On at least two occasions those rolls were undone and read through; any rescripts thought to be worth maintaining (for reasons unknown to us) were copied, reorganized, and bound in codex form. The compilations known to have been made in this way are the *Codex Gregorianus* and the *Codex Hermogenianus*. The second of these is the focus of the succeeding chapters.

# TWO

# The Rescript System

## The *Codex Hermogenianus*

The predecessor to the *Codex Hermogenianus (CH)* was the *Codex Gregorianus (CG)*, the earliest known official collection of rescripts, which comprised texts illustrating various points of law from both halves of the empire that dated from AD 196 to 291 and was organized by title.[1] The *CH*, named after Hermogenian, *magister a libellis* to Diocletian, followed the model of the *CG*, comprising responses from AD 293–294 composed by the eastern imperial petitions department, headed by Hermogenian.[2] He probably compiled the code as he worked during those two years, putting the finishing touches to it in early AD 295. Later that year he moved west to head the western *scrinium libellorum*. Sometime between 296 and 305, when he became praetorian prefect at the court of Maximian in the west, he may have added the few western entries that appear in the code. Perhaps after this time, Hermogenian was given senatorial honors, his career culminating with the urban prefecture. Sometime before 324 a final version of the *CH* containing yet more western texts was produced at the court of Licinius or at the Beirut law school.[3]

Hermogenian used the model of the *CG* to sort through and rearrange the responses he and his team produced in AD 293–294. Work on the *CG* may have been prompted in AD 291–292 by the fact that the imperial archives contained at least one hundred years' worth of responses arranged by date, not topic, a mass of material that would have made searching for the most important or most recent statement on a legal point burdensome and time-consuming. The archives had grown too big to be efficient, so Gregorian seems to have intended to supplement the imperial archives with a library of responses. The archives could then preserve responses for officials and petitioners, while the library would constitute a permanent reference collection for legal officials, experts, and scholars.[4] In addition to bringing together the newest and most important responses, the reference collection would also gather responses held at the various imperial capitals. Before the Tetrarchy, the imperial archives were presumably based at Rome, the sole imperial capital. But when Diocletian instituted multiple imperial courts, the imperial archives were probably divided between Sirmium and Rome. The division hindered officials, jurists, lawyers, and students wishing to access imperial responses, but Gregorian's compilation gave easier access to the responses that would be most useful to the greatest number of people. Gregorian made his collection more useful still by rearranging the entries from chronological sequence into topics.

Hermogenian's code was a false start. Following the model of the *CG*, it was possibly meant to have initiated a custom, subsequently neglected, of preserving every few years the responses that best illustrated new and important legal principles, though this is not stated anywhere as a fundamental rule. (Although we cannot know for certain that Gregorian and Hermogenian collected only some responses and discarded the rest, it seems reasonable to suggest that Gregorian did just this, for otherwise his compilation seems to have served little purpose apart from transforming the archives from roll to codex format. Hermogenian probably followed Gregorian's model.) The *CH* may also have been meant to preserve not just the most important eastern responses, but those from the west also. In its first editions the code contained just those rescripts to which Hermogenian had access in the east. But when he moved west he added a number of rescripts produced by Maximian's court. Though later collections, such as the *Fragmenta Vaticana,* included some of the entries from the *CG* and *CH* as well as later texts, no subsequent *magister a libellis* seems to have made a collection of responses from their years of tenure. Hermogenian's compilation may also have helped to iron out any discrepancies in responses between the eastern and western courts. While a response that was contradicted or superseded by another could not be destroyed, it could be omitted from the compilation in favor of the second, thus reducing the chances that it would later be used in a legal argument. While Gregorian may have used the writing of his compilation as an opportunity to clear out some of the oldest entries in the archives, Hermogenian could not follow his predecessor's model here. The petitioners of AD 293–294 still needed the original documents to verify their copies. So he had to leave the archives intact.

Gregorian may have been inspired by Salvius Julianus's codification of the Praetor's Edict in the reign of Hadrian, which was seen by some as the precursor to imperial responses and perhaps helped remove contradictory entries and present material more systematically.[5] Codification of rescripts now made available important responses previously little known or overlooked in the archives, of which there may have been many. The numbers of responses in the archives would have been immense—far more than any individual could be expected to be familiar with—but codification made them accessible, searchable, and intelligible. Copied and bound into codex form, they were now also portable and easier to store than in the old roll format.[6] These collections, which included many of the most legally important and recent responses, were perhaps sent to legal officials at the courts and in the provinces and were also made available for study in law schools.[7]

Both the *CG* and the *CH* were commissioned by Diocletian. It has been claimed that the *CH* was a private enterprise, since in the first edition Hermogenian obviously did not have access to the western archives; the presence of western rescripts in subsequent editions, however, undermines this argument. Much has also been made of the fact that neither the *CG* nor the *CH* was named *Codex Diocletianus* (or *Maximianus*). Indeed, the collection now known as the *Codex Theodosianus,* though strictly speaking not its original name, was certainly commissioned by Theodosius. Support for identifying both codes as official comes from the fact that both Gregorian and Hermogenian used the imperial archives. Furthermore, it is unlikely that Gregorian and Hermogenian, as current or former *magistri a libellis,* would have been able to put together compilations of imperial constitutions taken from the imperial archives, edit them for brevity (they certainly left out the petitions), and send them to law schools without imperial permission.[8] The *CG* and *CH* were probably named for their compilers in recognition of the importance of their role in supporting the effective preservation and transmission of the law and thereby maintaining the emperors' legal authority.

The *CG* and *CH* are long lost. Excerpted repeatedly and subsumed into various subsequent codifications, they must be reconstructed from a variety of sources: the Justinianic *Digest* and *CJ,* later Visigothic codes, and post-classical jurists' work, such as the *Fragmenta Vaticana* (*FV*). We are left with around three thousand responses—and no petitions. The editors of the *FV* in the early fourth century certainly left out the petitions, and it seems reasonable to suggest that the petitions had already been omitted from the *CG* and *CH* for reasons of space. The main repository of entries from the *CG* and *CH* is the *Codex Justinianus,* though some of its entries may come from outside the two earlier codes. The *CJ* does not preserve all the entries from the *CG* and *CH*; a few omitted from the *CJ* were preserved in other sources, such as the *FV* and *Consultatio.* When the compilers of the *CJ* lifted entries from the fifteen-plus books of the *CG* and the nineteen-odd titles of the *CH,* they redistributed them within the *CJ*'s new titles and imposed a chronological order within each.[9]

Hermogenian, and Gregorian before him, may have edited the entries they preserved in their codes. Subsequent editors certainly left their mark on the rescripts, as we can see from the fact that different collections preserve different texts of the same rescript. For example, one entry originally from the *CH* contains 191 words as *FV* 293, but only 79 as *CJ* 4.38.4, suggesting that other entries were likewise edited and interpolated before inclusion into the *CJ*. Editing and interpolating are different processes. The former involves amending a text to render it intelligible for publication; through the latter a text is altered by deleting sections or adding foreign material so as to make it conform to a purpose or audience not its own. The *CH* was edited for inclusion into the *CJ* by keeping only those texts that best illustrated the new titles and by removing responses that contradicted one another or the law. Some entries were not removed but interpolated to make them agree with post-Tetrarchic legislation.

The responses that found their way into the *CJ* were accompanied by some contemporary letters and edicts. The rest of the *CJ* comprises letters and edicts that date from 295 to the reign of Justinian. Material in the *CJ* or other collections that postdates AD 294 does not come from the *CG* or the first editions of the *CH*. A few responses dating to the reign of Constantine have been attributed to the *CH,* though these were never part of the code as Hermogenian left it. One imagines a conscientious official of the fourth or fifth century, inspired by Gregorian and Hermogenian's achievements, adding to their codes.[10] Or an individual inserting Constantinian texts into his own copy because they were useful or interesting to him; as his copy was recopied, so the extra texts became part of the *CH*.

The entries in the *CJ* do not look like the response received by the Skaptopareni because they have been edited for the sake of brevity. They open with the name of the emperor only in abbreviated form—*Diocletianus et Maximianus AA*—rather than in full and with imperial titles. Where two successive entries date to the same year, the name of the emperor(s) in the second is replaced simply with *id(d)*. The identities of recipients are preserved usually with only one name, very occasionally with two or more. The texts of the responses themselves have probably been edited, as we can tell from the fact that some responses appear in fuller form in smaller collections than they do in the *CJ*. Days and months are abbreviated, as they are on the Skaptopara inscription, but the names of consuls, which appear in full in the inscription, are also abbreviated in the *CJ*. On the inscription, the date introduces the authentication of the copy, while in the *CJ* it follows the text of the response; its position on the original sheets is unknown. Nor do we know the position of the location on the originals. In the inscription it appears in the authentication of the copy and is detailed: at Rome in the portico of the baths of Trajan. In the *CJ* it is inserted between the month and the consular year and is limited to the name of the city. Finally, the closing formula in the Skaptoparean response—*Rescripsi. Recognovi.*—does not appear in the *CJ*.

The following example illustrates the format of entries in the stereotype edition of the *CJ*:[11]

> Impp. Diocletianus et Maximianus AA. et CC. Euelpisto. Res obligatas sibi creditorem vi rapientem non rem licitam facere, sed crimen committere convenit, eumque etiam vi bonorum raptorum infra annum utilem in quadruplum, post simpli actione conveniri posse non ambigitur. S. vii id. Ian. Sirmi AA. Conss. (*CJ* 9.33.3)

Some entries in the *CJ* do not contain even these abbreviated elements. Because of problems in transmission, dates are sometimes missing or partially missing, and records of locations have disappeared or have been miscopied. Occasionally missing locations can be supplied from complete dates, or approximate dates can be given based on a location. The opportunities for compensating for absent elements are discussed and explored in appendix 2, a catalog of entries in the *CH*. Such omissions may shed light on the compilation of the *CH* and the *CJ*; for example, the occasional lack of place names suggests that entries in Hermogenian's original code could have been organized chronologically and that only some entries, perhaps the first at each new place and the first on each new page, contained the name of the location.

An element that appears in most *CJ* entries but not on the Skaptopara inscription is a notation. It appears immediately following the text of the response and before the day—on the example above it is *S*. Other entries bear the notations *D* and *PP*. There are a few others, though these are variants and may sometimes be the result of scribal error.[12] *S* has usually been interpreted as *scripta* or *subscripta*; *D* has often been understood as *data*; *PP* is probably an abbreviation of *proposita*.

It has been suggested that the notation *D* could signify handing back a rescript to the petitioner by hand, but there is no obvious explanation as to why some responses would have been posted and others given by hand. Another proposal is that *S* and *D* both stand for the date on which the response was written and made available to the petitioner. However, it seems odd that the *scrinium* would use two different notations to signify a process that may not have necessarily taken one day.[13] While there is no current obvious explanation for the significance of *D*, there are patterns that eventually with closer examination may suggest one. *PP* predominates in all titles among entries dating up to and including AD 293–294. In 293–294; however, *S* is the most common notation, followed by *D*, while *PP* is far less common. In these two years, notations are often clustered within titles; for example, *D* appears overwhelmingly in *CJ* titles 3.32, 4.19, 5.12, 6.2, and 6.42. *S* is found overwhelmingly in *CJ* 4.2, 4.49, 8.13, 8.42, and 8.44. From AD 295, *D* predominates among entries, with *PP* second in frequency, as table 2.1 illustrates.

The system of petition and response was a boon to ordinary Romans needing advice on legal problems. Though some were deterred by time and distance, many others used the system, as inscriptions, papyri, and the *CJ* demonstrate. The system seems to have been set up for the ease of the *scrinium libellorum* rather than for petitioners, who could not use the public post for sending petitions or receiving responses and had to arrange for an official copy to be made if they wanted to use the texts in court (if this is how we should understand *CJ* 1.23.3).[14] The members of the *scrinium* simply received petitions, answered them (or handed them on to the emperor), and posted the responses wherever they happened to be. Eventually the simplicity of the system also benefited petitioners. It enabled

Table 2.1 Notations Found on Rescripts in the CJ

|  | S | D | PP |
|---|---|---|---|
| AD 197–283 | 8 | 169 | 1021 |
| AD 284–293 | 8 | 46 | 172 |
| AD 293–294 | 408 | 295 | 70 |
| AD 295–528 | 51 | 3498 | 1737 |
| Total | 475 | 4008 | 3000 |

the *scrinium* to continue its work as it accompanied emperors on the road and thereby answer petitioners over a wider geographical area than would otherwise have been possible. The responses that the *scrinium* produced in AD 293–294 under the leadership of Hermogenian were produced both at the imperial residence, Sirmium, and en route through the lower Danube provinces, using one streamlined system. It is these responses that constituted the *CH*, now partially preserved in the *CJ* and other sources.

The entries of the *CH* were edited and interpolated from the reign of Diocletian to Justinian over a period of nearly 250 years. Many were discarded; those that remained were rearranged and abbreviated to make them as useful as possible to legal officials and lawyers. Though the code of Hermogenian was probably compiled for the use of legal professionals, superfluous elements remained: the names of the rescripts' recipients, the locations at which the rescripts were written or posted publicly, and their dates. But these elements, together with what remains of the responses, allow us to recreate the system of response as it operated in AD 293–294 and to understand better the experiences and motivations of the people petitioning and responding in those years.

Many people in the Danube region took the opportunity to petition the empire's ultimate legal authority, and the *CH* as we have it preserves some, though certainly not all, of their rescripts. Only rescripts containing legal precepts have been preserved; administrative rescripts (of the type: "you may approach the provincial governor" to have a process completed or permission granted) were discarded.[15] Their loss reduces the general exemplariness of the surviving rescripts, since administrative rescripts may have formed the bulk of answers written each day. These rescripts were preserved by Justinian's compilers (and possibly Hermogenian too) because they contained legal precepts, not because of their recipients, and the *CJ* contains more rescripts—nearly a thousand—for these two years than for any others; therefore the entries for 293–294 offer the best evidence for the variety of petitioners.[16]

Though they contain varying numbers of entries for each year, it is hard to determine from the *CG* and *CH* whether more petitions were answered in some periods than in others, since some of their rescripts were preserved for the *CJ* because they contained legal principles, not for their numbers or any other criteria. Nevertheless, we can discern a marked reduction in the number of rescripts preserved in the *CJ* from the middle of the third century, which could reflect the administration's inability to answer petitions in troubled times. It is just as likely, however, to reflect the poor state of the imperial archives during the period. I do not believe that Diocletian answered more petitions than other emperors; rather, the high numbers of rescripts preserved is a function of good archives and Hermogenian's codification. Consequently the lower number of rescripts from 250–280 is probably also a function of the care of the archives. My supposition is supported by the fact that we still have a good amount of papyrological and epigraphic evidence for the system during this period. Our evidence redoubles under Diocletian, when administrative and archiving procedures returned to the normality of the early third century, and when the emperor decided to commission compilations of rescripts. Despite the occasional omissions, the *CG*, so far as it can be recovered, offers a large number of texts to analyze: approximately 1,400 rescripts from the time of Hadrian to the accession of Diocletian. However, they are unevenly spread over a long period and across the empire. The value of the *CH* is that it comprises hundreds of rescripts that come almost exclusively from two years and from a defined area.

## The Rescript System in Motion

Voyager c'est gouverner.

The *Codex Hermogenianus* is a collection of about 970 responses produced as the emperor Diocletian toured the lower Danube provinces in AD 293–294. By looking at how petition and response worked while he toured, we can draw several conclusions about the system: a diverse group of petitioners used the system to ask about a wide range of issues; a team working in the *scrinium a libellis* answered them; the system worked well for the officials administering it because of its simplicity, but it was less convenient for the petitioners. Just as the Skaptoparene inscription records the villagers' rescript as posted at Rome, so the rescripts extant from 293–294 probably once all recorded the places at which they were produced. Today only 433 still have recorded locations; the others were lost in the many centuries of editing.[17] But 433 is a number high enough to enable us to plot the journey.

The route has been traced before. Mommsen, Ensslin, and Barnes have all produced their own versions, always with the assumption that the rescripts reveal Diocletian's location. In fact, the rescripts chart precisely the progress of the *scrinium,* not necessarily that of the emperor. He may have left early from or arrived early at some of the locations while the *scrinium* followed on behind. He may also have undertaken brief visits unaccompanied by the *scrinium* to locations which therefore went unrecorded.

In tracing anew Diocletian's journey from the rescripts, amendments needed to be made to the editions produced by Krüger. Having arranged the rescripts that survive in the *CJ* from 293–294 into chronological order, he moved entries that did not correspond with the probable route or whose dates and/or locations were wrong based on a reasonable speed of travel. The partial revision of the entries extant from 293–294 is presented in appendix 2, accompanied by explanatory notes. A map showing the route of the *scrinium* is also included at the end of this volume.

Emperors traveled for many reasons. As head of the Roman army, the emperor was expected to lead his troops against serious attacks on the empire.

In his capacity as controller of the government of the empire, getting to know provincial officials and locals could aid him in the smooth running of administration in the provinces. (This was perhaps Hadrian's reason for inspecting his provinces.) An emperor could also secure continued support by being present in places that were under threat from barbarian incursions, were suffering from internal strife, or had been hit by a natural disaster.[18] Meeting and being seen to meet with different social groups and showing responsiveness to local problems, even to those caused by imperial policies or practices, would give the impression of concern and empathy, a useful tool in minimizing potential disloyalty. Travel also gave emperors an opportunity to advertise their power. In the *profectio*, or setting-off, the highest-ranking senators or the imperial family would accompany a departing emperor part of the way on his journey, and welcoming ceremonies could be expected along the route.[19] Finally, emperors traveled because they could: the center of the empire was where the emperor was. So while Severus visited Egypt in 199/200 AD ostensibly to show support for Alexandria's autonomy, his tour also indulged his interests in Egyptian religion, antiquities, and wildlife.[20]

Diocletian's reasons for traveling may have been a combination of the above. Following the investiture at Sirmium, he accompanied his new Caesar Galerius as far as Byzantium, while Galerius continued to Antioch and then Egypt. The journey by the two men helped advertise Galerius's new status in the region over which he would come to have control. Diocletian's slow return to Sirmium enabled him to meet with high-ranking officials and locals in some of the most important towns and cities in the Balkans at a time when he may have been considering the feasibility of further dividing existing provinces. Once at Sirmium, he spent the winter, spring, and summer of 294 repelling an invasion by the Sarmatians. His movements in and around the city are evidence of his responsibilities for overseeing the campaign. His tour along the Danube in the autumn has been explained as a trip, following that invasion, to inspect the forts and garrisons along the frontier. The journey to Nicomedia was undertaken for personal reasons: he had built a home for his wife in the city and was perhaps joining her for the winter.

Court administrators were tied to emperors and therefore traveled with them. The presence of the court on Diocletian's journey is proven by the mass of legislative output produced as they traveled with him. With their help, Diocletian gave out edicts, sent letters to provincial officials, and answered private individuals' petitions. Emperors maintained their judicial responsibilities when traveling, and from the evidence of Diocletian's journey, they also answered petitions.

Though Diocletian's legislative output on the move was high, solving his subjects' legal problems was not one of his motivations to travel. Rather, his route was dictated by military, political, and personal concerns. If he had been concerned primarily with addressing judicial issues, he might have followed the routes of the Danube governors' *conventus*. And indeed he did visit some of the sites probably on those routes (including Viminacium, Philippopolis, Heraclea, Byzantium, and Adrianople); others he left out (such as Nicopolis ad Istrum and Naissus). But he also stopped at some places that probably would not have been included, such as the small settlements of Transmarisca, Tzirallum, and Burtudizum. His legal output was high because the system of petition and response, as we saw in the previous chapter, was accessible to petitioners and offered them an easy way to solve their legal problems, not because the route was designed to benefit petitioners.

By convention, the itinerary of an imperial journey was made public before the emperor and his court set out. Plans were drawn up that included each day's route, the name of every *mansio* (stopping place), and a list of supply locations.[21] Once these arrangements were finalized, word was sent out two months in advance to allow provincial officials time to find suitable accommodation and prepare supplies of animals and food.[22] Advertising also gave petitioners time to make their way to a convenient stopping point on the emperor's journey.

Accommodation for the traveling emperor was of great political consequence in provincial communities. When Diocletian stayed in Nicomedia, he enjoyed his own private accommodation,[23] and at other locations where long or regular stays were anticipated he may have had a home specially built.[24] But in places he seldom visited, the emperor lodged with the provincial governor or a prominent family.[25] Despite the heavy, sometimes crippling costs incurred, a host could gain favor with the emperor and win local prestige. In major towns and cities, Diocletian probably enjoyed a high degree of luxury with his hosts, though in smaller towns he was probably less comfortable. Sometimes unconventional arrangements had to be made. On his stay in Egypt, Diocletian stayed in a small local temple that had been converted for the purpose.[26] In the fort towns along the Danube, he probably stayed with local commanders. If the court was trying to cover distance quickly, the emperor may have stayed at large lodging places or even small route stations and forts as he traveled. If we believe the stories of his early years, Diocletian was probably not unduly discomforted by such surroundings.[27]

While Diocletian was usually well looked after, his court (including the *scrinium libellorum*) was less fortunate. He probably brought his full court with him, consisting of hundreds of officials and slaves. According to Philo, when Caligula set out for Egypt, he planned to take the equivalent of a full military escort with him, which would have numbered in the thousands.[28] With the Sarmatian threat in the north, Diocletian was probably also joined by a military guard and his total retinue may have rivaled Caligula's. The court likely pitched camp at each stop on the journey; the logistics of billeting hundreds (if not thousands) of officials, servants, and soldiers with locals, even in cities, were impossible.[29]

Though the imperial train may have provided its own accommodations, it had to obtain supplies along the way. The procurator of each province was in charge of arrangements. Animals and food were provided by suppliers to the *cursus publicus*, while financial and logistical support for the necessary requisitioning seems to have come from the παραπομπή, a specially formed group of high-status locals in each city at which emperor stayed.[30] Local worthies relished the opportunity, albeit burdensome, to be seen aiding the emperor's stay, but ordinary people suffered as they struggled to provide the court with animals, food, and goods. It is ironic that many of our best-preserved petitions from the late third century concern the crippling demands of requisitioning.[31]

Diocletian's court probably produced two itineraries.[32] The first was for a journey beginning in March 293 from Sirmium to Byzantium and back. This journey took them south along a major route through the Danube region, via Heraclea. After a brief sojourn at the imperial villa at Melantias, they finally arrived at Byzantium, where they remained until mid-April. They began the return journey in late spring, retracing their route through Melantias, Heraclea, Tzirallum, Adrianople, Philippopolis, Serdica, and Viminacium, until they reached Sirmium in early September. The emperor remained at his residence from the autumn of 293 until the autumn of 294.

Occupied with the Sarmatians during these months, he made brief trips to Lucionum, Tricornium, and Aureus Mons, probably on military business, though officials accompanied him and answered petitions.

The second itinerary outlined a journey from Sirmium due east along the Danube. The court stopped at Singidunum, Viminacium, and a string of smaller towns and forts: Cuppae (also known as Scupi), Ratiaria, Crebrus, Varianae, and Transmarisca. At Durostorum they turned south, traveling down through unidentified Reginassi and Marcianopolis to Anchialos, then to Heraclea via Develtus, Adrianople, and Burtudizum. Stopping briefly at Melantias once more, they reached Byzantium, from where they crossed over the Bosphorus and continued through Pantichium, stopping finally in November 294 at Nicomedia. They remained here for the rest of 294 and the spring of 295. They had covered 2,500 miles in two years.

Diocletian's court probably stopped at locations in addition to those recorded in the extant rescripts of 293–294. Some of these may have been isolated stopping places, containing a coaching inn and little else; with no petitioners waiting for the court, no responses were recorded at these places. Other larger locations probably were sites for administrative activity, but mention of them has disappeared with the rescripts that were discarded by Justinian's codifiers. There are entries that lack place-names; these may once have revealed that the court stopped at Naissus, for example. Many more responses that never made it into the *CJ* may have recorded otherwise unknown stops.

The court's itinerary can be plotted by using the locations recorded in the extant rescripts from 293–294 and by assuming that it stopped at major locations and took routes that were most convenient to a large train. The *Itinerarium Antonini* of the early third century and the Peutinger Map of the fourth provide valuable evidence for contemporary routes. The former, supposedly prepared for Caracalla's travels, was still being used at the time of the Tetrarchy and reveals, for example, that a route from Develtus to Burtudizum does not pass through Adrianople but goes straight down to Burtudizum, and thus a rescript placed at Adrianople on that same route is probably erroneous.[33] The latter, though dated to the fourth century, was probably based on a second-century map and also preserves routes. It demonstrates clearly, for example, that a direct journey from Taliata to Egeta via Gerulatis and Una was a possible alternative to the longer route via Tabula Traiana and Caput Bovis that followed the Danube.

The precise course of some parts of the journey can be determined only by taking into account the time needed to travel from one named point to another. To choose between alternative routes, a reasonable speed for the court also needs to be calculated. Gaius assumed that litigants who were required to travel to another town or city's court could cover twenty miles per day.[34] Although Diocletian's train probably encountered fewer delays than did a lone private traveler and benefited from a planned itinerary and possibly a local escort that would prevent it getting lost, it would sometimes have faced difficult terrain and harsh weather. Moreover, it was a large, bulky caravan that could travel only as fast as its slowest member. Gaius's calculation seems therefore a reasonable average speed for Diocletian and his entourage.[35]

On the basis of this speed and the records of places and dates in the extant rescripts, Diocletian's route can be more precisely plotted. The following examples show how routes were chosen and how approximate departure and arrival dates were arrived at. First, the *Barrington Atlas* (map 21) shows two possible routes between Taliata to Egeta, one hugging the Danube, the other passing almost in a straight line between the two points. But the Peutinger Map (seg. VII) shows only the latter. The last dated and placed entry before the route split was *CJ* 8.44.28 at Cuppae on October 5, 294; an unplaced rescript, *CJ* 6.59.7, follows on October 6. The next rescript is *CJ* 4.33.5 on October 10 at Ratiaria, located after the alternative routes recombined. The total distance according to the shorter route on the Peutinger Map is approximately 150 Roman miles or approximately 138 modern miles,[36] which could be covered in about seven days (assuming a speed of 20 miles per day). The number of full traveling days allowed to the court was three days (October 7, 8, 9), giving them an additional four and a half days for the journey.[37] The longer route, however, which is 197 miles long, would have required nearly ten days. If the court was traveling quickly (about 30 miles each day), it could have followed the longer route, though it is more likely that they took the shortcut. Second, calculating accurately the distance between two locations and the time taken to travel from one to the other helps to assign locations to otherwise unplaced rescripts and thereby to recreate Diocletian's itinerary in greater detail. A straightforward example, presented in table 2.2, concerns three a set of three rescripts. The distance from Pantichium to Nicomedia was forty-one miles, which could be traveled in just over two days. Assuming that the court did not stop

Table 2.2 Rescripts from the Journey between Pantichium and Nicomedia

| CJ Entry | Date | Location |
|----------|------|----------|
| 4.29.18 | 11.11.294 | Pantichium |
| 7.16.34 | 11.13.294 | no location |
| 4.2.13 | 11.14.294 | Nicomedia |

anywhere for more than a night's sleep, a meal, or a change of animals, it is most likely that they left Pantichium during the day of October 11, traveled the rest of that day and the next, and arrived at Nicomedia sometime on October 13. The rescript dating to October 13 can therefore be located at Nicomedia.

A more complicated example in table 2.3 demonstrates how unlocated rescripts can sometimes be placed in general areas, if not specific locations. At first sight, the list looks unpromisingly sparse, but calculating the distance and time to travel between Adrianople and Philippopolis helps to fill in the gaps. Philippopolis (modern Plovdiv in Bulgaria) lies 119 miles from Adrianople (Turkish Edirne), a distance that the imperial train could have covered in six days, assuming a speed of twenty miles per day. The rescripts dating to October 14, 16t, 17, and 18 come either from Adrianople or from somewhere close by; Burdenis, Castris Rubris, and Arzus are possible places. Those on October 23 and 24 probably belong to Philippopolis or a neighboring town or village; likely stopping points include Parambole or Ramlus and Pizus. Though there are rescripts from small locations, any that are unplaced and cannot be securely located most likely come from a larger place rather than a smaller. The majority of the unplaced rescripts in the example above, therefore, probably come from either Adrianople or Philippopolis.

An allowance of twenty miles per day takes into account only time spent moving. More difficult to factor into calculations of speed is the time spent arriving at and departing from each location, though allowance should be made for it. For example, an emperor's *adventus* at a location was an important and time-consuming event. Locals thronged to the city walls and dignitaries stood on ceremony to receive their ruler as he entered through the gates in spectacular splendor. Ammianus Marcellinus's classic account of Constantius II's *adventus* (16.10) could mutatis mutandis describe Diocletian's arrival at cities and large garrison towns in AD 293–294.

**Table 2.3  Rescripts from the Journey between Adrianople and Philippopolis**

| CJ Entry | Date | Location |
|----------|----------|--------------|
| 8.13.16 | 05.12.293 | Adrianople |
| 8.50.10 | 05.13.293 | Adrianople |
| 8.42.12 | 05.13.293 | no location |
| 4.6.6 | 05.14.293 | no location |
| 8.53.12 | 05.16.293 | no location |
| 4.57.6 | 05.17.293 | no location |
| 8.13.17 | 05.18.293 | no location |
| 7.16.17 | 05.23.293 | no location |
| 6.3.12 | 05.24.293 | no location |
| 2.17.3 | 05.25.293 | Philippopolis |
| 2.52.4 | 05.25.293 | Philippopolis |

At smaller towns and villages there were probably fewer VIPs to greet and less pomp, but the ceremony was essentially the same. After the emperor had arrived and been welcomed, his retinue had to see to his luggage and their luggage and to setting up their accommodation.

Despite these burdens on the court's time, the legal output from the journey of AD 293–294 was substantial. The number and spread of constitutions is all the more impressive when one considers strings of rescripts from 293–294, such as those shown in table 2.4. Diocletian's court left Heraclea on November 8, covered fifty-five miles that day and the following, the emperor or the *scrinium*—more likely the latter—answered at least one petition on the day he reached Melantias.[38] Leaving on November 10, it traveled the final seventeen miles to Byzantium, finding time to answer a petition upon arrival.

The revelation of this tight schedule leads to two conclusions. First, the emperor did not answer most petitions personally, nor did the *magister a libellis* answer them alone; a team of officials that included the *magister* and traveled with the emperor was responsible for producing most of the rescripts of 293–294. Second, some petitions were probably answered en route.

**Table 2.4  Rescripts from the Journey between**
**Heraclea, Melantias, and Byzantium**

| CJ *Entry* | *Date* | *Location* |
|------------|--------|------------|
| 2.4.34 | 11.08.294 | [Heraclea] |
| 2.4.33 | 11.09.294 | [Melantias] |
| 7.16.33 | 11.10.294 | unplaced |
| 2.4.31 | 11.10.294 | Byzantium |

## The Work of the *scrinium libellorum*

The suggestion that members of the *scrinium libellorum* accompanied emperors on their travels is not without foundation. We know that important officials traveled with emperors. When the emperor Valerian was captured by Šapor, his praetorian prefect was held with him; Ammianus Marcellinus reports that Valens left his praetorian prefect and other important officials hidden in the city of Adrianople while his army fought the Goths.[39] *CJ* 1.18.2 also supports the claim. It was written in the name of a teenage Gordian III, who had just fought the Goths on his way to fight the Persians. Gordian was surely incapable of answering petitions and would in any case have had concerns more pressing than the inheritances of his subjects, so a member of his *scrinium libellorum* would have written it for him.

The evidence of the rescripts of 293–294 supports the idea that the *scrinium* not only accompanied Diocletian but also answered petitions for the emperor as a team under the direction of Hermogenian. They were produced on a tight schedule, and the burden of producing numerous responses each day was probably too heavy for the emperor alone to bear. For example, sixteen entries dating to December 1, 293, have been preserved, and the original number may have been higher. It is impossible to know what proportion of the responses produced in those two years was kept in the *CJ*; it is unlikely that the *CJ, FV* and other collections preserve all of the code's entries. (The fact that our sources for the rescripts of 293–294 do not contain all the same entries and that shared entries sometimes contain different wording suggests only partial preservation of Hermogenian's Code.) Furthermore, Hermogenian may not have kept for the original codex every response produced for Diocletian in AD 293–294. But sixteen is probably not an unusually large number of responses for one day. Indeed, sixteen could be an average or even a small number. Allowing just half an hour to read a petition and compose a response, processing sixteen petitions in one day would require eight hours' solid work—surely too much for the emperor or even the *magister a libellis* working alone. It may be objected that taking the burden of answering petitions from the emperor might suggest that the emperor did not answer officials' letters or draft legislation either, and that to remove all these responsibilities raises a bigger question for historians than it answers: if the emperor does not carry out these tasks, then what does he do? We might suggest that he filled his time receiving embassies and directing diplomatic, military, administrative, and legal and judicial policy, just like modern rulers (though I am not suggesting that my argument for the *scrinium* answering petitions is based on what modern governments do). Moreover, the length of some of the responses argues against imperial authorship. One petitioner, Aurelia Euodia, received an answer of 185 words in taut, legally precise prose.[40]

Another piece of evidence supports the notion that a team produced may of the rescripts. In P.Oxy. XLII 3017, dating to AD 218, an Egyptian prefect decreed that responses in the form ἔντυχέ μοι πρὸ βήματος (l. 5) ("petition me at the tribunal") handed in to him would be answered within ten days. If petitioners were accustomed to such rapid responses from provincial officials, they might expect similar service from the imperial court. Indeed, from the emperor's point of view, there was little point in using one or only a few officials to answer petitions slowly. A backlog would quickly form, and the masses might become disenchanted at an unresponsive emperor.

A team could prevent a backlog from forming. It could help the system operate more efficiently by answering more petitions and answering more of them swiftly because of their competence—the emperor was not a legal expert, but members of the *scrinia* were and may even have been chosen for their knowledge about particular fields in which they could answer petitions. It is, of course, possible that the emperor did all this work, but he would have done so with far less available time than a team had and with less expertise.

My claim that a team answered many of the petitions puts into question Fergus Millar's assertion that emperors alone composed the responses.[41] The punishing schedule of traveling, running the empire, directing military campaigns, and answering petitions was surely too much for one man. The existence of the *scrinium libellorum* and the expertise of Hermogenian, its *magister*, argue against lone imperial authorship; the tight schedule for answering petitions on the road and the numbers of responses further strengthen that argument. It also puts into question Tony Honoré's claim that *magistri a libellis* were their sole authors. He believes that the responses contain stylistic traits that distinguish individual *magistri* during their years in office.[42]

Had the emperor alone been responsible for answering petitions, it is perhaps the case that nothing like the number of entries that exists in the *CJ* and other collections would have been produced. And had the *magister a libellis* been sole author, it is doubtful that even sixteen entries could have been produced in one day. Petitioners were usually answered by a team, and the system of petition and response was designed to maximize the team's efficiency. Although the system inconvenienced a few petitioners, it enabled many more people to ask for imperial legal help than would otherwise have been possible. If, as seems probable, team members answered petitions in their field of expertise, they could answer more petitions in less time than if the petitions were shared out evenly among them. The system also allowed the team to receive and answer petitions wherever they happened to be and (perhaps with a few exceptions) did not require them to send back responses. And it placed the onus on petitioners to find their response and request that a copy be made.

A team that shared the burden of producing responses could answer more petitions each day than a lone emperor or official. But their daily schedule during AD 293–294 was still often demanding. Their days consisted of reading petitions and researching and writing answers, and as was shown above, they often worked and traveled considerable distances on the same day. Furthermore, strings of rescripts for as many as twelve days in a row show that at least some members of the team were working every day. There is no evidence for how the team divided up its work, but perhaps members answered petitions in their field of expertise, while the *magister* had final editorial control.

Though doubtless trained in the law, the team would have brought reference materials on the journey: some rescripts quote from or paraphrase constitutions of earlier emperors.[43] *CJ* 3.33.3, a response by Caracalla was copied in part for a response by Diocletian's team in AD 293 and provides evidence that the team was able and willing to draw on earlier material, which could save valuable time. The fact that the Antonine text is preserved in a rescript of 293–294 may suggest that the team was carrying a copy of the *Codex Gregorianus*: rescripts that predate AD 292 seem to have come entirely or mostly from that collection.[44] One imagines members of the team working together, dividing up petitions, poring over jurists' handbooks and official legal collections, crafting precise answers, conferring over particularly tricky problems, and from time to time wondering at the complexity or improbability of some petitioners' situations.

For a total of 15 months in AD 293–294, this work was carried out in Sirmium. But for the remaining months, the team worked away from home, in locations as diverse as the metropolis of Byzantium and the tiny fort town of Transmarisca. It is unlikely that their families accompanied them, and the separation probably encouraged members of the imperial retinue to form a close-knit community.[45] A possible limitation on the cohesion of the *scrinium* team, however, is that senior members of departments did not hold their positions for more than a limited period of time, sometimes for only a few years and sometimes not in successive years. Hermogenian himself served Diocletian as *magister libellorum* for only two years, replacing perhaps Arcadius Charisius, who held the post for one year, and Gregorian, whose tenure was for two years. Another limitation is that the *magister* may also have employed *supernumerarii*. These men, who drew no salary, only fees, were employed simply to mop-up extra work when the department was over-burdened. If the *scrinium* charged petitioners fees (and there is no evidence for this), it could attract individuals trained in law to take on its extra work, and one would expect to find high-caliber members (as indeed one does at the level of *magister*).[46] Still, the fact that the team may have included as many as 34 officials perhaps helped to compensate for the disruption caused by changes in personnel at higher levels.[47] The burden of work on the team was also somewhat lifted by working en route.

This way of working meant that some petitioners handed in a petition at place A, but received the answer to it at place B. The representative of the Skaptopareni, Pyrrus, received his response at Rome, where he had handed in the petition. Most petitioners in 293–294 would also have handed in their petitions and received responses at the same location, but not all were so lucky. A number of extant rescripts were posted on the day of arrival at a new location, as the set of rescripts in Table 2.5 illustrates. Table 2.5 is an expanded version of Table 2.4 above. *FV* 314 was posted up on the day the court arrived at Melantias, and *CJ* 2.4.31 when it reached Byzantium.

Table 2.5 Rescripts from the Journey between
Heraclea, Melantias, and Byzantium (expanded version)

| Entry Number | Date | Location | Notation |
|---|---|---|---|
| CJ 2.4.34 | 11.08.294 | [Heraclea] | pp |
| FV 314 | 11.09.294 | Melantias | pp |
| CJ 2.4.33 | 11.09.294 | [Melantias] | s |
| CJ 7.16.33 | 11.10.294 | Byzantium | s |
| CJ 2.4.31 | 11.10.294 | Byzantium | pp |

The recipient of *FV* 314 had presumably handed in his petition at Heraclea, while the recipient of *CJ* 2.4.31 may have handed in his at either Heraclea or Melantias. These two unlucky men were expected to make a journey of between fifty-five and seventy-two miles or (approximately) three and four days to receive their responses.[48]

Most petitioners who handed in their petitions at one location, but received responses at another had time to have a copy made at that second location, as responses were probably posted for several days.[49] The unlucky recipient of *FV* 314, however, may have handed in the petition at Heraclea and seen the response posted briefly at Melantias, but was not able to request a copy until reaching Byzantium.[50] Few petitioners would have been in this unfortunate situation compared with the numbers who could read their responses and have them copied in one location. Moreover, publicizing Diocletian's itinerary would have helped petitioners to avoid handing in petitions at locations where the court's stay was brief or in the few days before the court moved on to another location. The result was that the scheme described above was inconvenient for only a few petitioners and relieved pressure from the emperor and the members of the *scrinium*. It may, however, have doubly impacted petitioners from far away. Not only did they have to find where the emperor was and run the risk of traveling with him to receive a response, but it is possible that they were answered last, if the imperial court followed the model of the governor, who answered local petitioners first.[51]

Although Diocletian's court would have made public his itinerary in late AD 292 or early 293, nevertheless some petitioners may have arrived at Sirmium hoping to hand in petitions. Upon finding that the emperor (and the *scrinium libellorum*) was away, some may have waited for his return.

Others may have followed the imperial train, using the itinerary to catch up with it at a convenient location. Still others may have handed in their petitions at Sirmium, hoping that they would be sent on to a location where the court was scheduled to stay for some time. Once answered, the responses were posted where the court happened to be; whoever delivered the petition would have to get the answer back to the petitioner.[52] These petitioners would have relied on representatives perhaps bringing other important documents from the capital to the emperor and his officials.

Assigning dates to each rescript with as much confidence as is reasonable reveals an uneven spread of responses over each month in AD 293–294, the cause of which is simple: responses initially included in the CH were perhaps preserved in the CJ because they stated a legal principle. Assuming that a steady stream of petitions was handed in over the two years, since there was no correlation between the dates and legal interest or complexity of petitions, we should expect over each month a random spread of responses.

Nevertheless, over the two years, there are marked increases and decreases in the number of rescripts, which could reflect correlative surges and lulls in the total numbers of petitions being handed in. For example, during Diocletian's stay at Sirmium from September 293 to August 294, rescripts for the months of September, October, and November 293 numbered 13, 25, and 21 respectively.[53] The number increased significantly in December, however, to 90. Likewise at Nicomedia in 294, there are 67 extant rescripts in November and 123 in December. December may have been a constitutionally busy period, during which petitioners tried to attend to their legal business before the end of the year.[54]

Another fluctuation probably reflects political events. The month-to-month spread of entries over 294 is presented in Table 2.6. The numbers are fairly constant through the spring, but suddenly decline during the summer months. They rise again in the autumn, with a sharp increase at the end of the year. From January through mid September Diocletian was at Sirmium, so the summer decline cannot be connected to changes in the court's location. Rather, the cause of the fluctuations was probably the Sarmatian invasion, during which few petitioners were willing to travel to the city.[55]

**Table 2.6  Month-to-Month Spread of Entries over AD 294**

| | |
|---|---|
| January | 34 |
| February | 54 |
| March | 38 |
| April | 60 |
| May | 7 |
| June | 2 |
| July | 5 |
| August | 7 |
| September | 13 |
| October | 25 |
| November | 21 |
| December | 90 |

The experiences of petitioners of AD 293–294 varied. While some enjoyed close proximity to the imperial capital or lived in a location visited by the emperor on his journey, others faced long journeys to hand in petitions, and perhaps had to follow the traveling court to receive their responses. Many were doubtless prevented from petitioning by the military action along the Danube frontier in 294. But all benefited from the fact that petitions were answered by a team employing a system that was as simple as possible.

The emperor's presence allowed the system to function, though he did not himself operate it. Indeed, justice could be administered in all its forms with the emperor present because his presence necessitated also the presence of the full panoply of legal officials—some to answer letters from officials, some to help with ambassadorial presentations, others to assist with hearings, and others to respond to petitions. While petitioners may not have known how their petitions would be answered and by whom, they did know that the presence of the emperor signified that petitions were being answered. So while the rescripts extant from 293–294 allow us to trace the journey of the *scrinium*, the route was that of Diocletian and to reach him was the goal of the petitioners. Petitioners addressed their petitions to the emperor, traveled to him to deliver them, received answers in his name, and may even have believed that he wrote them. The *scrinium*, however, probably wrote the majority of them.

The system was clearly important for Diocletian: he used a team of experts to run it with efficiency and he brought them on his journeys. He used them to enable as many petitioners to be answered as possible and to allow every petition to be answered by an expert, who could take his time to conduct the necessary research to produce a legally sound response to which Diocletian and Maximian's names could be added with confidence. All this was done because the system of petition and response was one of the commonest ways ordinary people came into contact with the emperor or with his pronouncements, as I shall argue more fully in chapter 5.

The very fact that Hermogenian was authorized to collect and codify rescripts illustrates their importance to the emperor. The *Codex Hermogenianus* was so named by Diocletian in recognition of the important role his *magister a libellis* played in producing responses. The members of the *scrinium libellorum,* the authors of many hundreds of rescripts, also played an important role. In 293–294 their expertise provided legal advice to diverse petitioners on a wide array of issues across the Danube provinces, in bustling cities, sleepy towns, and frontier garrisons. But except for the title of the *CH,* their work went unacknowledged: petitions were addressed to the emperors and the responses were written in their name; only the identity of their boss survives. Their customers' names, however, survive in their hundreds.

# THREE

# The Rescript System in Context

The area that is the source of the rescripts comprised the provinces of Pannonia Inferior, Moesia Superior and Inferior, Thracia, and finally Bithynia and Pontus.[1] To the west was Greece, long part of the empire; to the north was a frequently breached frontier dotted with garrisons; to the south was the eastern Mediterranean; to the east was the Black Sea, an area attacked by Goths during Diocletian's reign. The population of the area was diverse. The empire's Greek-Latin linguistic divide ran through the middle, yet it was home to a local, native, pre-Roman culture, of which there were still some traces during this period.

The provinces along the lower Danube are characterized also by stark physical contrasts. Inland are mountain ranges and flood-prone rivers that thwart all but the hardiest travelers. The harsh conditions of the Black Sea coast are well-known, made famous by Ovid's relegation (though he exaggerated them), but weather along the southern Adriatic coast is considerably kinder. The plains in the northwest endure long, cold winters, broken by short summers; to the east, and south of the Danube, the climate is milder, but there is snow and regular flooding.[2] Though largely agricultural (as all of Rome's provinces were), the region was dotted with villages, towns, and major cities, linked by some of the most important military arterial routes in the empire.

The difficult terrain and seldom clement weather thwarted the attempts first of the Greeks and then of the Romans to colonize the area. In the south, along the Sea of Marmara, the local Thracian population was Hellenized, but inland the Greeks made less progress. The city population changed, but the country dwellers did not.[3] Later the Roman way of life came to dominate in the west and along the Danube frontier, and made significant inroads into the hinterland. The south, though nominally Roman, remained Greek. But the Thracians' language and remnants of their religion persisted throughout the provinces. Some families kept their traditional names, and inscriptions show that some native people of the region still identified themselves by their tribe, not their place of birth or residence.[4]

The area was split linguistically. Latin dominated west of the Pass of Succi and along the northern frontier, while Greek held fast in the rest of the region. Thracian was still spoken throughout. Gerov, who has analyzed the linguistic split, points out that inscriptions in Latin or Greek do not prove that the local people spoke either language, but that some wrote in them, while perhaps keeping Thracian as their spoken language. The choice between Latin and Greek as a written language tended to follow provincial boundaries, the division being maintained in the hills but not in flat areas, where there were pockets of one language in a place dominated by the other.[5]

Our knowledge of the Balkan population and its surroundings, particularly the available legal services, is spotty. Inscriptions from the region tell us about individual locals' provenance, names, gender, occupation, and legal status, but their numbers are too few to reliably reflect the composition of an area's population. For example, areas with a large immigrant population (especially soldiers and veterans) will probably have more inscriptions than those comprising mostly natives. Wealthy people, who could afford the stone and the inscribing, are more likely to be recorded than those who lacked the means, and they tended to be either from Roman families that had recently immigrated or Romanized locals, whose Roman names obscure their origins. Soldiers were also regularly represented on inscriptions; women and children were always under-represented.[6] The usefulness of inscriptions is tempered also by location. Cities and garrison towns are the source of most inscriptions, where the desire to advertise one's position was strong; people in smaller towns and the countryside were slower to adopt the epigraphic habit. But even cities outside Rome offer few inscriptions. It seems there were fewer of them in the third century, though private ones can rarely be dated.[7]

Archaeology can help redress the shortcomings of inscriptions in revealing evidence for local populations and the location of buildings that could be used for judicial purposes. Following the restrictions of communism and the disturbances from the wars of the 1990s, work in the Balkans is now gathering pace at a few sites, though the lack of detailed and comprehensive investigations into many sites presents problems for the lower Danube, and conclusions about one site in the west should not be held to apply to another.[8] Comparative material from urban studies can also help to reconstruct what buildings and related services may have been present in settlements of various sizes, though any conclusions are necessarily generalizations. The sizes of third-century populations of sites are often unclear, but even knowing the location of the town walls, the part of a settlement most often found, can help on this issue.[9] Ventzislav Dintchev has estimated that the city walls of Philippopolis encompassed approximately eighty hectares, and the city could therefore have been home to about 46,000 people.[10]

Certain buildings can be expected to have existed in Danubian cities and large towns. Some may have had legal and judicial functions and provided space for trials and offices for magistrates, registrars, lawyers, and notaries. These, as well as the legal services and resources that surrounded them, supplied residents of small cities and towns access to justice without requiring them to go to the provincial capital. Visiting these buildings or knowing people who had visited them in the past helped the petitioners of 293–294 to discover how petitioning could benefit them and how it could be done. Magistrates, on the model of the *epistrategoi, strategoi,* and *exegetes* in Egypt, probably received petitions, presumably posting the answers to them publicly. Advocates were on hand to provide legal advice to would-be petitioners or to defend them in court, should the need arise. Notaries could draw up petitioners' documents, drawing on the *acta publica* held in local registry offices to make their claims.

By Diocletian's time for reasons that are unclear, magistrates' courts had lost much of their power to the provincial courts, which makes finding evidence for spaces where courts could operate or the functioning of them difficult.[11] For court spaces at the provincial capitals, there are a few literary references to the noise at Alexandria's legal hearings, to the *conventus* and the people associated with it, and to the reading of an imperial edict at a *conventus*. And there are also hints in the later *acta consistorii* of the emperors Julian and Theodosius I that legal hearings were held sometimes in public, sometimes in private.[12] Archaeologists, whose interests at this stage of excavation in the Danube provinces necessarily lie in finding walls, temples, and grand houses, not in uncovering administrative spaces and speculating over their functions, have rarely uncovered court spaces and court offices. But one clue as to their probable location is the phrase *praescriptio fori,* which described the rules determining where a case was heard. Cases must once have been held in the forum, although *forum* came later to be used figuratively for places where trials were held and for towns on a governor's *conventus* route.[13] Close to the forum (or agora) at Rome, Cyrene, Madauros, and other sites, a rectangular structure with an open hall extending from end to end has been found: the basilica. This building served as a market, meeting hall, and judicial space, and at its ends were *chalcidica,* rooms that served as judges' chambers. The fact that the basilica at Rome measured 169 meters in length but the one at Madauros only 14.6 meters suggests that settlements large and small had basilicas in which public business was conducted. Around them were presumably clustered advocates' and notaries' offices or *stationes.*[14]

Notaries and lawyers may have had offices even in small towns, but as magistrates' offices were not so common, many petitioners and would-be litigants had to travel to their nearest magistrate.[15] With the decline of magistrates' courts, in many places only governors' courts could offer hearings. Some governors were helped in their judicial duties by officials, such as the *iudices pedanei,* yet they remained overworked.[16] The prospect of a long journey to the capital, together with a long wait to gain the attention of an official once there, must have deterred many litigants.

The development of the Tetrarchy in the early 290s gave petitioners the opportunity to petition the imperial court nearest to them and therefore gives us grounds to believe that the majority of recipients of rescripts in 293–294 came from the lower Danube provinces. Petitioners from farther afield were more likely to approach the courts of Maximian, Licinius, and Galerius. Morever, as I shall explain later in this chapter, it may be possible that a significant number of the individual recipients had not traveled far to petition and were simply taking advantage of the nearby presence of the emperor to send petitions that were intended for the provincial court, or that had been stored up in anticipation of traveling to the imperial or provincial court, or that had been written because of the emperor's imminent arrival by individuals who had nevertheless explored other avenues of advice and resolution. Analyzing both the legal services available at the locations where they received their rescripts and their local populations may therefore give us additional information about some of the recipients in 293–294. But even if petitioners were not local to the places I discuss in detail in this chapter, they were most likely local to the lower Danube provinces.

Whether the majority of petitioners were Danubians or not, and whether they lived close to the places where they received their rescripts or not, the issues about which they petitioned were rarely regionally specific. So while we might be able to claim that a rescript received at Sirmium concerning hire of a boat referred to commercial activity on the nearby Danube River, even if we cannot, we still have discussion of over nine hundred issues that could have arisen anywhere in the empire and therefore represent the types of problems the imperial government faced. Problems that would have held good only in certain areas are less likely to have been preserved by Justinian's compilers. The value of the rescripts, therefore, lies in the insights they can provide about many shared aspects of ordinary people's lives across the empire.

## Petitioners

From the years AD 293 and 294, the *CJ* and other collections preserve 917 rescripts produced by Diocletian's court. These were addressed to 942 people (some of the entries were addressed to two individuals), as well as one group addressed as the heirs of Maximus. These numbers exclude rescripts from the east that cannot be fixed to sometime during those years and rescripts that were produced by Maximian's court in the west. Of the rescripts to groups, some were addressed to a named individual plus unnamed others (*et alii,* or similar); others, although they were addressed to one named recipient, refer to *vos* or use a form of *vester* in the text. Rescripts that lack either of these group identifiers may still have been addressed to groups. Given that this group is of unknown size, for the purposes of this chapter, rescripts addressed to a named individual "and others" have been counted as being received by only one person.

On the basis of the names preserved in many of the rescripts, the designations *miles* or *veteranus* that were included when appropriate, and the content of the entries, the recipients can be divided into five groups: women, slaves (male and female), soldiers, and male civilians, groupings that are easily detected in the entries, as Liselot Huchthausen and Simon Corcoran have already shown.[17] I shall use these categories in the rest of the chapter.

I begin with the issue of the extent to which the makeup of the recipients of rescripts in the *CJ* reflects that of all those intending to petition Diocletian in 293–294. I shall map the relationship between the two groups by considering how the former developed into the latter.

GROUP A:

PETITIONERS WHO APPROACHED DIOCLETIAN IN 293–294

This group comprises all people who decided to petition the emperor Diocletian for advice about their legal problems. It comprised adult (minors would have been represented by an adult guardian) men and women (on the assumption that there were women at this time acting without guardians).[18] Possible petitioners could include all adults living in the empire who contemplated legal action, be it in court or arbitrated outside of court, at every financial level in society, and of every legal category too. People kept as slaves could petition about disputed status (see below for further discussion).

Most individuals likely to petition belonged to the "middling sort" (as defined earlier), who had enough money and property that they could and would undertake legal transactions, but not enough money that they could easily consult a lawyer and subsequently retain him for a court case. They probably included more men than women. Some women might be dissuaded by the dangers or inconvenience of traveling; others might not petition for themselves but have a male representative or guardian petition on their behalf. Those using representatives would still be named as petitioners; those using guardians would not. Petitioners were more likely free than servile. Petitioners kept as slaves could petition only on one topic and could face severe limitations on their opportunities to petition. Soldiers, on the other hand, enjoyed a steady income, some social prestige, and probably easier access to judicial administration than did civilians. But their opportunities to petition may have been hampered by the time and geographical demands of their duties. Individuals living in densely populated areas were more likely to petition than country dwellers. They had a greater chance of learning from peers about the benefits and process of petitioning and they enjoyed easier access to magistrates, provincial governors, or the emperor.

Group A therefore probably comprises mostly men, soldiers in proportion to their numbers in the general population, a significant number of women (though certainly less than 50 percent of the total), and a small number of people claimed as slaves. It also included those living in the eastern half of the empire, who were closer to Diocletian's court than to Galerius's or were traveling in the area. Those in the west most likely approached the courts of Maximian or Constantius.

GROUP B:

PETITIONERS WHO WERE ANSWERED BY DIOCLETIAN'S
COURT IN 293–294

Out of Group A comes Group B, comprising those whose petitions were answered. It can be divided into three subgroups. The first comprises petitioners whose petitions were answered because they addressed a justiciable situation and so were suitable to be answered. The second includes those whose petitions were answered in the time available. Given that answering petitions was not the primary purpose of Diocletian's journey in 293–294, it is possible that some petitioners, unable to hand in petitions at one location before the court moved on, were unable to follow to the next stop. Others may have handed in their petitions so late that the court could not answer them in the time available to them, either where they were or even at their next stop. It seems unlikely that petitioners in any particular one of the five categories would have been especially disadvantaged in this way.

The third subgroup comprises petitioners to whom officials may have been favorably or unfavorably disposed. While there is no evidence that officials favored some petitioners over others, it is possible that they may have been more willing to answer the petition of anyone—male or female, free or slave—who gave a monetary incentive. Groups may therefore have enjoyed an advantage. Some officials may have been biased toward answering male civilians, others toward soldiers, perhaps under direction from the emperor, though there is no proof for this. Unfavored petitioners may have included individuals from outside whichever province Diocletian happened to be in or from the west, depending on whether and how the recommendation that governors first answer locals on the *conventus* was applied to the imperial situation. Positive or negative discrimination may have been especially marked if officials were pressed for time; discrimination may have also have derived from the attitudes expressed by legal experts that women were inherently weak and that slaves were to be trusted only under torture.[19] It may be argued that women and people claimed as slaves were favored by the *scrinium* precisely because they were otherwise disadvantaged, and rulers professed to care for the disadvantaged. But they did not mention either women or slaves as inherently deserving; rather, it is their circumstances that would be deserving. So to claim that there could be more women and people claimed as slaves in this group is, I think, to project our modern aspirations for government's role in justice onto the Roman period. Group B, then, would probably have included proportionally more male civilians, soldiers, and local petitioners than did Group A. There may also have been slightly more petitioners with money, or at least enough cash to hand over as a sweetener.

## GROUP C:
### PETITIONERS WHOSE RESCRIPTS WERE PRESERVED IN THE *CODEX HERMOGENIANUS*

It is likely that the *CH* contained only some of the rescripts to petitioners in Group B. Given the existence of archives into which all rescripts were placed, the code would have been unnecessary if it simply duplicated the contents of those archives. But we know that it did not, since its entries were arranged by topic: the first thirteen books followed the Praetor's Edict, the fourteenth concerned criminal law and the final two were given over to public law. It is very probable that groups of entries in the archives contained duplicated information, of which only one would entry be kept for the *CH*.

Legally interesting and precisely formulated responses were therefore more likely to be preserved. The status of the petitioner probably played a less important role at this stage (though see below under Group D). Group C was picked primarily because rescripts to its members were the most legally interesting and well-written examples from Group B. Therefore we should expect to see in Group C a cross-section of Group A.

## GROUP D:
## PETITIONERS WHOSE RESCRIPTS ARE PRESERVED IN THE
## *CODEX JUSTINIANUS* AND OTHER COLLECTIONS

Petitioners whose rescripts are securely datable to 293 or 294 and are extant in the *CJ, FV,* and *Coll.* constitute the final group. It is very likely that all the petitioners in Group D were also in Group C, and it is also likely that the compilers of the *CJ* and other collections chose their entries on the basis of their legal principles, rather than the status—be it legal, financial, or gendered—of the petitioners. We can assess the probability of this proposition by testing two opposing hypotheses against what we know of Group D. The first hypothesis is that the post-Tetrarchic compilers selected entries solely on the basis of the status. If this were true, we would expect to see a strong divergence between groups A and D; in particular there would be few women and virtually no slaves—entries concerning *quaestio status* would be selected that answered only free people concerning those they claimed as slaves (of which there are many). Soldiers might be strongly represented; the overwhelming majority of entries would be to male civilians.

The second hypothesis is that the compilers selected entries solely on the basis of legal principle. If this were true, we would expect to see virtually no divergence between Groups A and D. So, while women would number fewer than 50 percent of the petitioners, they would still be present in significant numbers. The proportion of soldier-petitioners would reflect the number of soldiers in the general population: if the army under Diocletian was about 500,000 strong and the overall adult population numbered about 36 million, we should expect soldiers to constitute about 1.4 percent of Group D (13 out of a total of 942).[20] Estimates of the number of slaves in the empire range from 2 million (3.7 percent of the total population) to 3.6 million (10 percent), so slaves should number from 35 to 94 of the total of 942 petitioners.[21] We would also expect to see groups that tended to petition about legally complex issues advantaged, as more of the rescripts to them would be preserved. Women, male civilians, and soldiers were probably equally likely to petition about legally complex issues; only slaves would be advantaged. A key title in the *CJ* concerning status, 7.16 *de liberali causa,* contains forty rescripts, a number far higher than the norm.

**Table 3.1 Recipients of Rescripts Preserved in the *CJ* and Other Collections**

| | Greek Name(s) | Latin Name(s) | Greek or Latin | Other Name(s) | Unnamed | Total |
|---|---|---|---|---|---|---|
| Male civilians | 316 | 273 | 24 | 10 | — | 623 (66%) |
| Women | 104 | 134 | 5 | 3 | 1 | 247 (26%) |
| Male slaves | 22 | 18 | — | 1 | — | 41 (4%) |
| Female slaves | 11 | 10 | — | — | — | 21 (2%) |
| Soldiers | 2 | 6 | — | 1 | — | 9 (1%) |
| Not specified | — | — | — | — | 1 | 1 (<1%) |
| Total | 455 | 441 | 29 | 15 | 2 | 942 |
| Unspecified groups | — | — | — | — | — | 1 |

*Note:* All percentages in this table are rounded to the nearest whole number.

The numbers of petitioners in Group D belonging to the various status groups are presented in table 3.1.

Women account for slightly more than 25 percent of recipients. This number is significantly lower than 50 percent, though 50 percent would be unexpected, as some women would have used guardians whose names would have appeared in place of theirs. Slaves number sixty-two, or 6 percent, and so account for a smaller proportion of Group D than in the general population. The low number reflects the restricted issues about which slaves could petition, but is higher than we might expect if compilers were actively avoiding slave recipients, in which case there would be almost none, and may reflect the legal complexity of status issues. Soldiers number only nine, or 1 percent. If rescripts to them were chosen because of their status, they should number substantially more than thirteen; if their entries were preserved because they contained legal principles clearly stated, we should expect around thirteen, making the second hypothesis more likely. Male civilians number approximately two-thirds of all recipients of extant rescripts, a substantial but not overwhelming majority.

From these numbers, it seems that legal principle played a more important role in determining petitioners' inclusion in the *CJ* and other collections than did status. The members of Group D, petitioners named in these collections, cannot be claimed to be representative of the adult population in the lower Danube provinces in AD 293–294. But they are roughly representative of the members of Group A, those who intended to hand in petitions and were able to do so. What follows is a brief analysis of the members of Group D, based on table 3.1 above, the rescripts to them, and the locations in which they were answered, the conclusions from which can be held to apply broadly to Group A also. We are thus rewarded with a series of insights into the characteristics of those who chose to use the system of petition and response in the time of Diocletian.

## MALE CIVILIANS

That male civilians constitute the great majority of Group D is no surprise. We can be confident that they are drawn mostly from the middling sort, since none of the extant rescripts to them contain vocabulary suggesting that the recipient was of senatorial or equestrian status, though nine rescripts entries were certainly written to decurions, whose curial status is explicitly referred to, and three possibly.[22] It is very probable that there were other decurions among the male civilians of Group D, though the subject matter of their entries does not reveal their status.

The small number of obviously elite recipients confirms what comes out clearly in the epigraphic evidence for the system of petition and response, and in Egyptian evidence too: that it is a system for people with no other recourse to legal help.[23] Deborah Hobson has concluded, based on her examination of the evidence, that "one did not go to law on the principle of the matter, but only because it was necessary to do so in order to assert one's rights or claim one's rightful property or even to re-establish one's dignity; in other words, if you could do this for yourself, you didn't make a petition." One entry shows, however, that sometimes elites used the system and that they needed help navigating it. Leontius, the recipient of *CJ* 10.32.6, had petitioned the emperor asking whether decurions, or town councilors, were exempt from their curial *munera* if they were illiterate. The answer was no. If we are to believe Leontius, he must have asked a professional (or a skilled friend) to write for him, as surely many others did also.[24] It is unlikely that officials in the *scrinium libellorum* were prejudiced against elite petitioners, such as Leontius. The recipient of *CJ* 2.53.3 (AD 285) is recorded as *Proculo decurioni* (his title perhaps the sole relic of a regular practice of including curial signifiers) and is unlikely to have drawn attention to his status, which in this case is irrelevant to his legal situation, if it was likely to harm him.

## SOLDIERS

Soldiers are as easy to identify as decurions may once have been, since their names are accompanied by the designation *miles* or *veteranus*.[25] It has been argued that this distinction reflects their legal privileges, and the fact that 8.5 percent of rescripts dating to AD 211–244 and preserved in the *CJ* were received by soldiers has led Brian Campbell to argue that soldiers were favored petitioners of the emperor.[26] But soldiers number only 1 percent of recipients in 293–294. If soldiers could expect the emperor to be more responsive to them than to civilians, especially since the current emperor was a man of the army, it is striking that so few rescripts were addressed to them in these two years. It is likely that Campbell happened to find thirty-three years in which an unusually high number of rescripts to soldiers are preserved.[27]

Soldiers had as many opportunities to petition as had civilians. They could petition centurions and, far above them, *duces,* the military counterparts of provincial governors. According to the *Notitia Dignitatum,* the *duces* of Moesia Secunda, Moesia Prima, and Dacia Ripensis were served by their own *scrinia libellorum,* which presumably answered petitions from soldiers.[28] Army reforms had moved many professional soldiers from the frontier to urban centers to form a "mobile elite" ready for campaigns, rather than everyday defensive skirmishes,[29] and this change could explain why rescripts to soldiers come mostly from urban locations. Diocletian's route, which took in a number of important cities in the region, therefore provided to soldiers in particular good opportunities to petition. One limitation on their access, however, was that a soldier could not leave the province in which he was serving unless authorized to do so as a courier.[30] For soldier-petitioners, representatives were therefore very important; the imperial administration's willingness to receive petitions from them was a boon to those in military service.

Soldiers do not seem to have been marginalized by the compilers of the *CJ* and other collections on account of the subject matter of the rescripts to them. The extant rescripts concern, among other topics, a dispute between two soldier brothers, one appropriating the other's military pay; the wrongful sale of part of an estate; an invalid agreement; the division of *donationes* between *socii*; a conflict with a deceased father's fellow guild members; the difference between *donatio* and *venditio*; age at inheritance.[31] Given the subject matter of the entries in AD 293–294 and given that soldiers received a reasonably steady income, we can assume that the soldier petitioners were, like their civilian counterparts, from the middling sort. Soldiers were certainly not economic paupers. They had property to disburse, they were involved in transactions of great enough value to be the subject of serious dispute, and they were receiving *donationes* substantial enough to cause arguments over distribution.[32] These men were not hastily drafted local militia, nor were they officers of the highest ranks; they were middling career soldiers.

The topics of the extant rescripts are as likely to have been of concern to soldiers as to civilians; the sole title in the *CJ* that contains rescripts concerning only soldiers is *CJ* 6.21, *de testamento militis*, which has one entry dating to AD 293–294, *CJ* 6.21.14, addressed to the heirs of a soldier's sister. Given that all of the extant rescripts to soldiers in AD 293–294 concern non-military matters, the number of them is probably a more accurate reflection of the numbers of military petitioners than is the total of the rescripts to soldiers in preceding years, which concern military (as well as some civilian) issues and have therefore been preserved because of their subject matter, not because more soldiers petitioned and more often than did the civilian population.

## WOMEN

Women comprised 247 of the recipients, or 26 percent. The consistency of this number with earlier figures is striking. Women constituted 30 percent of recipients of rescripts extant from the time of Hadrian to AD 292 (and contained in the *CG*) and 29 percent of the authors of petitions to officials extant in Egypt.[33] The similarity among the three groups suggests first that the proportion of women in Group D (see above) most likely reflects the proportion of women in Group A. Otherwise one must argue that preserving rescripts to women was always favored or disfavored on the basis of their gender to the same degree, from the time of Hadrian through to Diocletian, and then under Justinian, and second that Hermogenian was neither unusually favorable or unfavorable to keeping rescripts to women. Furthermore, the fact that the proportion of women petitioners in Egypt is comparable with the proportion of women recipients of rescripts strongly suggests that Justinian's compilers did not discriminate in favor of or against female petitioners.

Not all female recipients of rescripts extant from 293–294 are explicitly identifiable. While some women sent their own petitions, others may have had petitions written by guardians on their behalf. That is to say, women may have been interested parties in many more of the petitions but let men represent them. Of the four rescripts to groups of petitioners, all have a male civilian as the one named recipient, even though women may have numbered among the unnamed recipients. However, the existence of a couple of entries that are directed to individual named women but address plural recipients (by using *vos,* etc.) who are fellow heirs raises the possibility that women were named as recipients even if some members of the recipient group were male and that women may even have acted as representatives of a group.[34]

Female recipients who can be identified by their names were from the middling sort. They received rescripts concerning, for example, property, their slaves, and their businesses.[35] Slightly less than half of the women were recipients of rescripts concerning the *familia.* There are two surprising aspects to this finding. First, one might have expected a *pater familias,* or another male relative, to undertake inquiries about family matters. The fact that women were petitioning on their own behalf supports evidence from Egypt and the East that from the third century women were less commonly using guardians to represent them in law.[36] Second, if fewer than half of rescripts to women concerned the *familia,* correspondingly more than half concerned matters outside the home. Some of these will be discussed in the following chapter. The preponderance of rescripts unrelated to the family reflects nicely the fact that, although women have tended to appear in literary sources as wealthy, leisured, and ensconced in the house, many women, especially those of the middling sort, were earning a living or were actively engaged in managing money and property, as papyrologists have long been aware.[37]

Low numbers of rescripts at smaller locations prevent us from gauging whether women were disadvantaged among smaller populations, as seems to be the case in Egypt.[38] If they were, an explanation may lie in the importance of sociability. The greater numbers of women living in large towns and cities may have shared legal advice and information, and the numbers of women appearing in court were higher. Women in cities also had better access to legal advice and more opportunities for legal experience. Though relative proportions of female recipients in urban and rural locations are hard to detect, there may be clues in the patterns in the frequency of rescripts to women, which may reveal female cooperation in towns and cities. For example, during Diocletian's visit to Heraclea in April 293, there is a sudden and substantial increase in the number of rescripts to women over the three-day visit, which could suggest that word had spread among women that the emperor was arriving and would accept petitions. Unfortunately, it is equally likely that the glut, created by the selection of Justinian's compilers, was unintended. Another explanation for the high numbers of urban petitioners is that women from towns and villages may have been deterred by the prospect of travel to provincial and imperial capitals.

### SLAVES

Not all female recipients were free; twenty-one were slaves or claimed as slaves (2 percent of all recipients). They include freedwomen threatened with a return to slavery, free women considered by others as slaves, and free women held as slaves.[39] Forty-one males (4 percent of the total) found themselves in similar situations. Slaves, of course, should not have been eligible to receive rescripts, but a rescript from Diocletian allowed the rule to be waived in exceptional circumstances—and it seems that all those claimed as slaves who received rescripts were considered as being in exceptional circumstances.[40] Diocletian's dispensation may have been encouraged by the Roman legal concept of *favor libertatis*.[41] Though most citations of this phrase quoted by jurists concern issues of testamentary manumission, the concept was probably influential also in allowing slaves to petition. They claimed themselves free or freed on the basis of birth, a *fideicommissum*, or another type of manumission. One might at first imagine that such claims were easily proven—our literary sources divide individuals clearly into the categories of free, freed, and servile. But as we'll see in the next chapter, the rescripts reveal that such distinctions were less fixed than we might assume.

Among the entries of AD 293–294 there are more rescripts to slaves, the least favored petitioners, than there are to soldiers, thought by some to be privileged petitioners. Yet relative to their numbers in the general population, slaves were still under-represented among petitioners, an unsurprising finding. More surprising is that the ratio of men to women among slave recipients reflects that of free men to free women, despite the fact that women claimed as slaves were probably among the most marginalized, vulnerable inhabitants of the empire.[42]

There are nearly as many Latin names as Greek among the slaves, an unexpected discovery, given the tradition of taking slaves from the East. But by the late third century many slaves in Latin-speaking areas may have acquired Latin names; moreover, we should remember that these individuals were disputing their status and may have had names that were comparable with names belonging to the incontestably free. The explanation may be geographical. Most slaves' rescripts came from Sirmium, where Latin and Greek names were roughly equal in number; the remainder of slave rescripts were found primarily at other cities.

The predominance of slave rescripts at urban locations has three explanations: either accidents of preservation and selection retained urban rather than rural rescripts, or the majority of all rescripts were placed at cities, or cities were home to the majority of slaves. The first cannot be proven or disproven and should simply be accepted as a possibility. The second explanation probably carries the most weight, but given the population density in cities and the court's route in 293–294, the importance of the third should not be underestimated. Analysis of epigraphic evidence from Pannonia suggests that the majority of slaves worked in cities. But because epigraphy is an urban phenomenon, a false impression of the concentration of slaves in urban contexts may be created. Inscriptions can tell us what urban slaves did. They were in domestic service and served in low-level administrative positions, mostly for governors and procurators; they are also found working in military camps, where soldiers often owned them.[43] In an urban environment slaves could easily have discovered that they could petition, especially if they worked in the provincial administration, or if they came into contact with many free and freed people and fellow slaves. An urban social network among slaves may explain how individuals claimed and/or kept as slaves had some degree of legal awareness, evidenced by the fact that they understood their position in law, that their status was a function of birth or manumission, and that a faulty will or familial misunderstanding could impact that status. It has been claimed that the few slaves working in the countryside tended to be overseers for landowners, individuals who were perhaps more capable of petitioning than many free civilians. Yet rural slave petitioners in a small community may have found it more difficult than their free or urban counterparts to petition about such delicate issues as status.[44]

The slave rescripts provide a useful insight into why the rescript system was used. Free petitioners used petition and response because it could help force settlements and avoid costly court cases. If the system did not suit their purposes, however, there were alternatives, as I explained in the introduction. Slaves (or people claimed as slaves), on the other hand, used it because they had no other choice: "There is no way for slaves to go to law against their masters, since they are absolutely not recognized by the *ius civile,* by the *ius praetorium,* or *extra ordinem.*"[45] Their only hope was the decision of the emperor.

## GROUPS

Four rescripts are addressed to groups. Three are directed to a named recipient, followed by *et aliis* or *et ceteris;* one is given to *heredibus Maximae.*[46] The named recipients are all males, perhaps chosen as the most senior or socially elevated members of the groups. Three of the rescripts concern inheritance, of which two are to an individual's children, the third to Maxima's heirs; the fourth rescript deals with the unlawful sale of "your" (plural) slave. While these groups' rescripts confirm what we already know from inscriptions—that people could send petitions as a group—they also call into question the typicality of the inscribed rescripts. Most of the epigraphic evidence records petitions by and rescripts to communities about intimidation and harassment by provincial officials, but extant rescripts to groups record families' questions about inheritance. It is unclear whether harassment or inheritance is the more usual subject of group rescripts and whether communities or families are the more usual constituents of groups. But the topics of rescripts to groups extant from 293–294 and the nature of those groups prompt us to question the typicality of the inscriptions, on which so much of our knowledge of the rescript system has been based.

The small numbers of rescripts to groups should also give us pause. Groups should have been advantaged. They collectively had more money than did individual petitioners and so could use representatives to deliver their petitions. It is therefore possible that the individuals in Group D had more money and made more use of representatives than did groups.

The question of whether many individual petitioners used representatives is important for helping us to consider several issues; first, whether petitioners tended to be groups or individuals; second, whether our rescripts extant from 293–294 were written to people living near the location of Diocletian's court at the time; and third, whether we can therefore analyze the makeup of recipients of those years within a specific geographical context.

### NAMES

It is a curious feature of the rescripts preserved in the *CJ* and other collections that the names of the petitioners dating to Diocletian's reign and earlier have been preserved, though they served no identifiable purpose for officials or lawyers in the time of Justinian, save as an aide-mémoire. For us, however, they enable further investigation of the individuals whose rescripts have been preserved from AD 293–294. While most of the recipients are recorded with a single name, over one hundred have been recorded with two, three, or even four elements—Aurelia Asteria, Pullius Iulianus Eucharistus, and Antiochus Atticus Calpurnianus Democrates, for example.[47] All but two of these multiple names come either from a source outside the *CJ,* such as the *Fragmenta Vaticana* or the *Collatio,* or from the second half of the fourth book of the *CJ.*[48] Given that the compilers of the Theodosian Code generally used single names for the recipients of edicts and letters, a practice found also in the *CJ,* it is possible that the compilers of the *CJ* were drawing their entries from a compilation of the *CG* and *CH* that postdated the Tetrarchy and the fourth-century *FV* and *Collatio.* Because it was edited in a similar fashion to the *CTh,* the missing compilation probably dated to the fifth century and was also arranged into the titles we find in the *CJ.*[49] By the time Justinian's compilers used it, however, the end of book 4 seems to have been lost. So they took entries from an earlier compilation of the *CG* and *CH,* which contained the unedited names of the recipients, and kept them in full.[50]

The single names that appear in the *CJ* are *cognomina,* as we can tell from series of rescripts. For example, *Cons* 6.18, *CJ* 6.59.04, and *CJ* 7.16.27 were addressed to Aurelius Asterius, but in *CJ* 3.31.08 he is called simply by his *cognomen,* Asterius. From the first century AD (or perhaps earlier), the *praenomen* gave way to the *cognomen* as the major signifier of an individual's identity, and some people dispensed with the *praenomen* altogether; others, however, kept three or more names, as we can see from book 4 of the *CJ.* Another major shift in the composition of Roman names came at the end of the third century, around the time of the Tetrarchy. Increasing numbers of people no longer identified themselves with *gentilicia* but used the *cognomen* only. This practice is mirrored in the *CTh* and *CJ,* in which officials are addressed only with their *cognomina* and titles. The editing of recipients' names originally in the *CH* from multiple to single names, which happened perhaps in the fifth century, may have reflected this trend, which had begun much earlier, and hence we find multiple names in the *FV* and *Collatio.* Alternatively, a fifth-century editor or scribe may simply have found it more time-efficient to record only *cognomina.* The compilers of the *FV* and *Collatio* felt differently—and so retained the multiple names.

Although most recipients in the *CJ* can be identified by only one name, when we analyze these single names in large enough numbers at various locations in the lower Danube provinces to discover whether the names are mostly Greek or Latin or neither, we can gain an impression of the cultural ancestry of petitioner populations.[51] While this is a fairly simple process for most of the 942 names, some are hard to categorize and are unattested in the standard onomastic *repertoria,* which draw mainly on epigraphic and literary sources. Consequently reasonable guesses have had to be made about these.[52] Moreover, some names are unidentifiable in their current form because scribes have sometimes tried to make an unfamiliar name Latin or Greek; other times they have misspelled Latin or Greek names, making them appear foreign.[53]

Any conclusions drawn about the relationship between names and cultural ancestry are necessarily impressionistic. The ethnicity of a person's name does not always correlate with his or her ethnic background. For example, a slave with a Greek name was not necessarily Greek. Roman masters often gave slaves Greek names regardless of their background.[54] Greek former slaves with Greek names often gave their freeborn children Latin names, though ethnically they were Greek. And then, as Solin warns, "we have to distinguish between Romans or Italics settled in the East and their Hellenized descendants; provincial Greeks with Roman citizenship; and any Orientals who bore a Latin name in lieu of a Greek or local one."[55] Nevertheless, since the Danube provinces were an area of linguistic, and therefore onomastic, diversity, the numbers of petitioners who are western in ethnicity but eastern by name, and vice versa, probably cancel each other out. Moreover, the numbers of such people are most likely small enough as to be negligible.

More difficult is the fact that the elements we are missing may reveal individuals with two names: one Latin or Greek and the other Thracian, for example. Since there is little way to assess how many individuals were named in this way, we simply note that the phenomenon exists and that some of those with Latin or Greek names also had other names.[56] Some names are neither Greek nor Latin, but they account for just over 1 percent of our total. The names are Thracian, eastern (probably Persian), Semitic, and African, with Thracian being the most common.[57] A petitioner might have a name that was not Greco-Roman for a number of reasons; for example, he or she began living in Roman territory only recently or belonged to a recently settled family. Alternatively, such a name might reflect a late Roman "rediscovery" of an earlier local culture that was neither Greek nor Roman,[58] a suggestion supported by the fact that the locations of recipients with non-Latin, non-Greek names correspond broadly to the probable location of the petitioners. For example, one finds Thracian names in Thracia and eastern names in the easternmost locations Diocletian visited.

The frequency of non-Greco-Roman names among the petitioners is probably not a good reflection of the number of such people in the general population. For example, there may have been many more recent immigrants who did not petition the emperor, who had settled among the immigrant populations in isolated areas or along the borders.[59] They were culturally, and probably linguistically, isolated and therefore unlikely to avail themselves of Roman institutional procedures, such as the rescript system. Other immigrants moved into the cities or joined the army; they probably became Romanized quickly and gave Latin or Greek names to their children, who cannot be detected among the petitioners.

What we can infer from names is that because the recipients had Greek and Roman names in roughly equal proportions, they most likely came from both the Latin-speaking western half of the empire and the

Greek-speaking eastern half. Given the location of Diocletian's court in the linguistically divided center of the empire and given the existence of other courts farther west and east, the majority of recipients probably also came from this central area; the rest came from farther west and east in roughly equal numbers.

Conclusions based on names that survive among the extant rescripts of 293–294 are necessarily impressionistic and can be applied only in the most general way to existing ideas about the history of locations and the linguistic divide in the region. But they will aid the discussion of petitioners and places that follows. Further work on Latin names in the Greek east would probably allow us to draw more sophisticated conclusions.[60]

## Places

The populations local to Sirmium and Heraclea are the focus of this examination, and the locations will act as case studies. Examining the entries at these two locations will allow us a more accurate estimate of the extent to which the makeup of recipients of rescripts extant from 293–294 were reflective of local populations of petitioners and, if they were not, to suggest what factors might have caused the discrepancy. It will be helpful also to see the degree to which status and ethnic diversity among recipients in the populations local to Sirmium and Heraclea reflect overall diversity among recipients and thus whether individual discrepancies have conspired to produce the overall figures pertaining to Group D and presented in table 3.1. Finally, it will allow us to look at some of the topics of petitions that were handed in at these two locations, not for the purpose of discerning locally specific topics but to gain a sense of the kinds of issues petitioners were concerned with and to see how knowing the location at which a petition was answered can help us understand better the issue at hand. Finally, it will serve as an introduction to the following chapter, in which petitioners and their problems will be examined more closely.

Not all recipients of rescripts at Heraclea and Sirmium were locals, but I suggest that the majority were. Given that Diocletian and his court stopped at many locations, large and small, some only a day's journey apart, it is likely that most of the individuals petitioning at Heraclea were local to the city, that is, lived within a day or two's journey.[61] It is less likely that as many petitioners at Sirmium were locals, but a comparison with evidence that gives insight into the makeup of the local population may reveal whether this is true. The possibility that the governor on his *conventus* answered locals first may have increased the likelihood that the petitioning population was local.[62] Petitioners were local also because of necessity and opportunity.

Sirmium was an imperial residence where Diocletian stayed for considerable periods during the two years, and it offers us an opportunity to see who used the rescript system when the court was stationary. From Sirmium, Diocletian traveled down to Byzantium in 293, accompanying Galerius on his journey to Nicomedia. On the way back, he stopped at Heraclea on the southern coast of Thrace for several weeks in April, perhaps in order to open a mint there.[63] He stopped again briefly in November 294 on his way down to Nicomedia. While Sirmium was one of Diocletian's residences, Heraclea was simply a stopping point. It will therefore serve as a good example of what happened in a city when the emperor stayed for only a short time. These two locations, each of which supplied more than thirty rescripts preserved in the *CJ*, allow me a reasonable size data set for use in a statistical analysis.

## SIRMIUM

### *Legal Services*

Anicetus's next door neighbor, Julianus, had made some home improvements perhaps in 292, adding to the height of his property and putting a window into a wall that belonged to Anicetus. So at the start of 293, Anicetus petitioned the emperor about the problem. He was told that, while Julianus was allowed to build as high as he liked so long as there was no servitude on the property, if he had indeed put in the window without Anicetus's agreement, he had to remove it and restore the wall at his own cost.[64] Such were the problems of urban living.

Sirmium, on the site of modern Sremska Mitrovica in Serbia, is where Diocletian's journey began in 293, and also where he spent the winter of 293 through to the late summer of 294. The city gained stature with the rise of the Danubian soldier-emperors in the third century, and under Diocletian it became an imperial residence. But it was never the capital of

Pannonia Inferior: that distinction had been bestowed on Aquincum.[65] So, like Rome, Sirmium lacked a provincial governor but enjoyed the services offered by the imperial court. When the court was away, however, residents of Sirmium had to travel to Aquincum for their cases to be heard or to present petitions to the governor, or they could wait for him on the *conventus*.[66] Local magistrates and decurions likely presided over smaller courts, which surely were needed for a population of approximately 57,000 people.[67]

Given the nature of his problem, Anicetus probably lived in the densely populated city. *Insulae* excavated at Sirmium reveal residential spaces comprised of small rooms. Shops, artisan workshops, and warehouses have also been found, as well as some luxurious buildings with mosaics, suggesting that the city was home to an economically diverse population.[68] Around the forum, the remains of very large public buildings have been found. The building on the southwest corner may have been a basilica, given its rectangular shape measuring about forty-five meters in length and its inner portico.[69] Here magistrates and decurions would have heard local cases, including perhaps that of Anicetus (although the provincial governor's court is also a possible setting). Also nearby would have been a registry office, where Anicetus (or Julianus) could have found documents indicating whether there was a servitude on Julianus's property. Anicetus would have presented his petition probably at the imperial palace, which lay in the south of the city, although it is unclear whether the court offices were located here. Anicetus's answer could have been put up at the imperial palace, in the forum, or at one of a number of bath complexes found in the city.[70]

## Local Petitioners

As he walked through the streets to the forum or the palace to deliver his petition, Anicetus would have been surrounded by a great variety of people, including locals and people from neighboring towns and villages, coming to the city's markets and shops. Archaeological evidence points to a wide variety of trades in the city. Some may have been artisans, employed by the arms factory, the weaving industry, or the *horrea*.[71] Anicetus may also have seen visitors from far-off places, including Africa, according to one rescript.[72] Given the fact that Sirmium was an imperial residence, we will in all likelihood find a higher proportion of non-locals among the petitioning population at Sirmium than at smaller stopping points on

Diocletian's journey. However, with Diocletian's later institution of multiple imperial capitals, the numbers of petitioners from outside the local area would not be so large as to distort seriously this analysis of the recipients of rescripts at Sirmium.

In table 3.2 I have tabulated the numbers of petitioners at Sirmium according to the five status groups discussed earlier in this chapter, further dividing by name, whether Greek, Latin, or neither. There are slightly more women than in Group D (table 3.1), slightly fewer slaves, slightly fewer male civilians, and the same percentage of soldiers. Archaeological evidence points to a military presence in the city, though there are only four rescripts to soldiers. Barracks have been discovered opposite the hippodrome, a finding which supports the description in the *Notitia Dignitatum* of the city as a host to infantry and cavalry, as well as a naval fleet.[73] Inscriptions from the city provide more detail about soldiers at Sirmium. Of five named soldiers, two have Latin names and three are Syrian-named brothers.[74] The soldiers presumably petitioned and received their rescripts just as Anicetus did. Considerable social cohesion among soldiers may have helped would-be petitioners receive advice, and the central location of the barracks meant that they suffered no geographical disadvantages in petitioning. Soldiers, like their civilian counterparts, would have used the administrative and legal institutions of the place they were living in. The number of soldiers is very low, but as they petitioned about non-military matters, their rescripts were as likely to be preserved as anyone else's, and chance may have denied their rescripts preservation. Equally, their titles may have been lost during transmission. The low number of soldiers may also be attributed to the fact that there was never a permanent garrison at Sirmium; instead, legions moved in and out of the city area. Moreover, archaeological evidence suggests that the legions were based not in the city (where there is no evidence for a military area) but on the outskirts. A temporary camp has been found three miles from city, which may have been located near a more permanent site.[75]

It is surprising that while only four soldiers' rescripts were preserved, we have in this group eighteen rescripts to slaves. Archaeology and inscriptions preserve no information about the numbers or backgrounds of slaves at Sirmium. Common sense suggests that in a population of 57,000 there were slaves present, but only the rescripts provide firm evidence of their existence. Women were also well represented, accounting for approximately

**Table 3.2  Recipients of Rescripts at Sirmium**

|                | Greek | Latin | Greek or Latin | Other Name(s) | Unnamed | Total |
|----------------|-------|-------|----------------|---------------|---------|-------|
| Male civilians | 106   | 133   | 7              | 2             | —       | 248 (63%) |
| Women          | 53    | 63    | 2              | 2             | 1       | 121 (31%) |
| Male slaves    | 5     | 4     | —              | —             | —       | 9 (2%) |
| Female slaves  | 4     | 5     | —              | —             | —       | 9 (2%) |
| Soldiers       | —     | 3     | —              | 1             | —       | 4 (1%) |
| Total          | 168   | 208   | 9              | 5             | 1       | 391   |

*Note:* All percentages in this table are rounded to the nearest whole number.

one-third of the recipients, whereas only 5 of the 104 inscriptions from the city mention women.[76] It is unlikely that the discrepancy can be explained by the arrival at the city of large numbers of non-local female petitioners.

An analysis of petitioners' names reveals that there were more petitioners at Sirmium with Latin names than with Greek names—208 to 168 (including Anicetus). Another nine had names that could be either Latin or Greek, and a further five had names that were neither Greek nor Latin (two Thracian, two eastern, and one Semitic). The predominance of Latin names is unsurprising: Sirmium lay west of the Pass of Succi and had not been subject to Hellenization. It is striking, however, that the other source of evidence for names in the city, the inscriptions, are almost all in Latin and that nearly all the names mentioned in them are Latin (including many soldiers); only a few are Greek, Thracian, and Illyrian names. There are only eight Greek inscriptions, of which one contains names and they are all Greek.[77] From the evidence of the inscriptions, the inhabitants were almost exclusively Latin-named writers of Latin. Yet the names of the rescripts' recipients suggest a more mixed population. If, as is claimed, inscriptions tend to be commissioned by wealthy elite males, they probably do not feature as good a cross-section of the population as do the rescripts. It is also possible that many of the petitioners at Sirmium traveled to the city from east of the Pass of Succi.

At Byzantium and Nicomedia, two other locations at which high numbers of rescripts are recorded, the relative proportions of Greek and Latin names correspond with their distance from the Latin-Greek divide. At Byzantium, there are roughly equal numbers of Greek and Latin names;

Table 3.3  Recipients of Rescripts at Nicomedia

| | Greek | Latin | Greek or Latin | Other Name(s) | Unnamed | Total |
|---|---|---|---|---|---|---|
| Male civilians | 14 | 13 | 1 | — | — | 28 (74%) |
| Women | 2 | 5 | — | — | — | 7 (18%) |
| Male slaves | 1 | 1 | — | — | — | 2 (5%) |
| Female slaves | 1 | — | — | — | — | 1 (3%) |
| Soldiers | — | — | — | — | — | — |
| Total | 18 | 19 | 1 | — | — | 38 |

Note: All percentages in this table are rounded to the nearest whole number.

farther east at Nicomedia, Greek names predominate—an unsurprising finding—as table 3.3 demonstrates. It is striking that at Nicomedia, the distribution of the recipients between our initial groups—male civilians, women, slaves, and soldiers—is comparable with that at Sirmium, as table 3.3 shows. At Byzantium too, though there are far fewer entries, the makeup is not dissimilar, as table 3.4 shows. The fact that the relative proportions of groups of petitioners found at these large and well represented locations are fairly consistent suggests that groups of petitioners would have been represented in similar proportions at other major locations in AD 293–294, though the fact that there are fewer entries at the other locations means that this possibility cannot be verified.

Would-be petitioners normally had to travel to Aquincum to petition the provincial governor or to Nicomedia, Diocletian's other residence, or to Rome, Maximian's main residence. So the presence of Diocletian in AD 293–294 for extended periods was a boon, especially to local women and slaves, who might otherwise have found it hard to travel. Petitioners outside of the Sirmium area would likewise have needed to travel to Aquincum, so Diocletian's presence at Sirmium offered many of them too a closer and more powerful alternative. Still, some people surely faced obstacles such as inclement weather, bad local roads, and intimidation. Yet the numbers and identities of the recipients at Sirmium do not suggest that any group suffered particular discrimination, and the appearance of recipients from the city and its environs, as I shall show, suggests that geographical obstacles could be overcome.

Table 3.4 Recipients of Rescripts at Byzantium

| | Greek | Latin | Greek or Latin | Other Name(s) | Unnamed | Total |
|---|---|---|---|---|---|---|
| Male civilians | 75 | 39 | 4 | — | — | 118 (71%) |
| Women | 20 | 14 | — | 1 | — | 35 (21%) |
| Male slaves | 7 | 2 | — | — | — | 9 (5%) |
| Female slaves | 2 | 1 | — | — | — | 3 (2%) |
| Soldiers | 1 | — | — | — | — | 1 (>1%) |
| Total | 105 | 56 | 4 | 1 | — | 166 |

Note: All percentages in this table are rounded to the nearest whole number.

There was most likely greater diversity among petitioners in Sirmium than at the other locations Diocletian visited, which could be explained by the presence of foreign traders or settlers. As we saw of the recipients of rescripts at Sirmium, five had names that are neither Greek nor Latin: two Thracian, two eastern, and one Semitic. These people probably lived or were working in or around Sirmium; petitioners in the east more likely approached Galerius. Foreigners at Sirmium may have been engaged in manufacturing, having arrived in the waves of immigration from Syria in the second and third centuries.[78] Others, as the inscriptions reveal, enlisted in the army. Aside from soldiers, few foreigners appear in the epigraphic record, probably because they were not necessarily long-standing members of the resident community.[79] One rescript concerns a traveling trader, Alexander, who had purchased a *pondus* of gold in Gaul with a partner, Syntrophus. He asked his partner to sell the gold at Rome but never received his share of the proceeds. With his partner now dead, Alexander presumably returned to the Sirmium area to take action for himself and Syntrophus's heirs.[80] Another rescript at Sirmium refers to a relative being captured by a Palmyrene faction. The entry probably refers to events during Aurelian's overthrow of Palmyra, or shortly thereafter.[81] The rescript does not mention that the relative was a soldier, leaving open the possibility that he was a civilian, perhaps a trader.

Given that Sirmium was an imperial capital and that people may have traveled some distance to present a petition there when the court was present, the city's surroundings are worth considering. Within a twenty-mile radius, there were some large settlements (Bassiana, Malata, Cuccium, Budalia), over twenty smaller sites (only two of which are certainly ancient), six *castella* and *oppidula,* and four *mansiones.*[82] Beyond these settlements "some sort of small village was located every 7–12 Roman miles along the roads."[83] The many settlements—which the Bordeaux and Antonine itineraries further confirm—and the lack of any serious topographical hindrances to travel in the area, combined with the fact that December 293, in the very depths of winter, was a very busy month for the *scrinium,* suggest that there were no significant geographical hindrances to travel. Farther out into the Danube plains, however, there may have been more serious obstacles.

## Local Problems

The activities of people living outside Sirmium are revealed in the rescripts. Fifteen entries are addressed to people concerning farms,[84] including a *praedium rusticum.*[85] A local pattern of small-scale landholding is suggested by rescripts to the tenant of an *ager* and to a woman who has a contract with a group of *coloni.*[86] We know that some of the local landholdings supported herds; rescripts that mention livestock concern debt, harm to the animals, and sale of the meat.[87] We also know of local viticulture, as two rescripts concern wine contracts.[88] The first deals with a faulty stipulation, the second with trading standards. It seems that Egus Crispinus (perhaps the owner of a *taverna*) had been sold an expensive wine but received a cheaper substitute. Another rescript discusses sale of vines.[89]

Moving back into the city, most of the rescripts concern inheritance, tutelage, slavery, possession, and debt. But there are some more notable entries. Apart from Anicetus's rescript, there are two others concerning building regulations.[90] Further rescripts tell us about trade. One woman received a rescript concerning her purchase of a year's harvest of olive oil, which must, given the location of Sirmium, have been transported from the southern coast.[91] Another entry to a woman concerns her hire of a *magister navis,* presumably to transport goods along the Danube.[92] Both of these rescripts offer us insights into the rarely seen business activities of women and into the complex legal issues with which they had to deal. I am not claiming that these topics could only have been found in petitions at Sirmium—they could have been found in many other locations too;

rather, I am demonstrating that sometimes knowing the location at which a petition was produced can elucidate the background to the text.

A few rescripts dealing with miscellaneous matters should be mentioned. One concerns the rights of people involved in legal trials to change their names (the answer is that they can, provided they are not intending to defraud); the entry is noteworthy for its evidence that the *tria nomina* was still used at the end of the third century.[93] Another entry declares that learning and practicing geometry is in the public interest, but the damnable art of mathematics is forbidden.[94] Finally, one rescript confirms the existence of prostitution at Sirmium and testifies to some individuals' stunning naïveté. It also provides a good example of the moral indignation also found in some other rescripts of the period.[95]

Some of the rescripts refer to laws: *senatus consulta,* the Carbonian edict, the *lex Falcidia,* the *lex Cornelia,* an opinion of Papinian, and a constitution of Antoninus Pius.[96] These references would not have been meaningful to most recipients, many of whom were chastised for their legal ignorance.[97] They are instead evidence that rescripts were often used in court. At a time when so much law was inaccessible, obscure, or confused, a clear statement of law from a legal expert in the form of a rescript was an enormous help to potential litigants and their advocates. The frequency of recipients' appearances in court also emerges from the rescripts. Many recipients were directed to, or had already appeared before, the *praeses,*[98] who was stationed at Aquincum, several hundred miles from Sirmium, but traveled around the province on his annual *conventus.* Some recipients were also directed to *procuratores,*[99] who were stationed at Sirmium.

HERACLEA

## Legal Services

The city, formerly known as Perinthus, received its change of name under Diocletian sometime before AD 293.[100] No systematic excavation work has been carried out at the site in the modern Turkish city of Marmara Ereglisi, so we lack detailed knowledge about the ancient city's layout and buildings, although ancient references and surveys have led to the identification of some monuments. Perinthus had been an important Greek city with a long history. Septimius Severus, who received support from the city despite Byzantium's support for Pescennius Niger, rewarded it by building over the former city and up onto the promontory and extending it down onto flat land to the north. The new Roman city was an impressive home to approximately 27,000 people, containing a theater and a 240 meter stadium.[101] As the provincial capital of Thracia and then, following Diocletian's provincial reorganization, the capital of Europa, it always had a provincial governor and the associated officials and services. Indeed, the legal resources and services at Heraclea may have been more extensive than those at Sirmium. An *exedra* dating from the early Principate and located at the central square of the modern city, near the ancient forum and the main ancient and modern road into the city, has been identified as part of either a palace complex or a large church. But given the shape and location of the excavated structure, it is most likely the basilica, a location for judicial hearings, though the governor may also have conducted hearings at his palace.[102]

One of the people taking advantage of the emperor's arrival at Heraclea in April 293 was Capitolina. Her late husband had taken items belonging to her and bequeathed them to his relatives. Now she wanted them back. The answer to her petition was measured: it was now up to Capitolina to prove, presumably in court, whether she had gifted the items to him, in which case she was entitled only to the amount he had been enriched by enjoyment of them.[103] Like Anicetus at Sirmium, Capitolina probably used local legal professionals to have her petition composed. In the forum there would also have been notaries to assist her. A rescript from Heraclea offers yet more evidence that notaries composed petitions. It was here that Leontius, the decurion, petitioned the emperor asking whether his illiteracy exempted him from curial duties.[104]

If Capitolina and Leontius had petitioned the governor, they would have handed in their petitions at the provincial palace. The emperor's *scrinium libellorum* probably set up its office here or perhaps at the basilica, two locations that were familiar to people who had petitioned before or had been involved in a legal dispute. The *scrinium* would have posted the answers either in the forum, at the palace, or at another public place, such as the baths or gymnasium.

## Local Petitioners

Though Heraclea was originally a Greek city, it is striking that of the two recipients mentioned so far, Capitolina has a Latin name and Leontius can be either Greek or Latin. In fact, in this Greek city there are nearly as many Latin names among the recipients as there are Greek, as table 3.5 shows.

Unsurprisingly male civilians form the largest group of recipients. Their rescripts concern common issues: family matters, property, contracts, and transactions, among others. Although the rescripts do not make it clear, we can surmise from inscriptions some of the businesses in which these men were involved: wine and grain production, for example, and oil imports, which were important local businesses.[105] Judging from local inscriptions, other men could have been textile manufacturers, butchers, stone masons, barbers, and goldsmiths.[106] Only one rescript (to Leontius) refers to curial duties; no other rescripts belong to people obviously from the local elite.

While the numbers, names, and concerns of the male civilians offer few surprises, the recipients at Heraclea are notable for the numbers of women among them: twenty-two, or 36 percent of the total. The clustering of entries to women around April 20, 24, and 27–29, 293, and November 8–9, 294, was probably the result of chance. An alternative explanation is that groups of women were delivering petitions together. Women in urban locations probably enjoyed greater interaction than their small-town and rural counterparts, more of them were probably involved in business and had concerns outside the home, and more of them had already gone to court or sought legal advice. Most of the women at Heraclea petitioned on matters concerning the *familia,* but others had questions about contracts or business, and yet others received rescripts concerning trials, which are testimony to women's need or willingness to go to court over legal matters.

Entries to soldiers are conspicuous by their absence. The city has been called a "Sammelplatz der Heere,"[107] a description supported by the large numbers of soldiers' gravestones. Its military center was the harbor, where the *Classis Perinthia* was stationed as the first line of defense of the Propontis. The harbor was also a strategically important point for moving troops from Thrace to Asia Minor.[108] The surprising lack of entries to soldiers could be explained by chance or by the suggestion that even though there were considerable numbers of soldiers at Heraclea performing an

**Table 3.5 Recipients of Rescripts at Heraclea**

|  | Greek | Latin | Greek or Latin | Other Name(s) | Unnamed | Total |
|---|---|---|---|---|---|---|
| Male civilians | 22 | 9 | 3 | — | — | 34 (56%) |
| Women | 5 | 15 | 2 | — | — | 22 (36%) |
| Male slaves | 2 | 1 | — | — | — | 3 (5%) |
| Female slaves | 1 | 1 | — | — | — | 2 (3%) |
| Soldiers | — | — | — | — | — | — |
| Total | 30 | 26 | 5 | — | — | 61 |

Note: All percentages in this table are rounded to the nearest whole number.

important role, nevertheless they were not unduly favored petitioners. Or (as explained above) they had other ways of solving their problems.

There were five entries to slaves, or 8 percent of the total, a proportion mirroring that at Sirmium, Nicomedia, and Byzantium. At those locations, at least one-third of the overall number of slave recipients were female, a proportion that is comparable to their representation in Group D. At Sirmium, male and female slaves are represented in equal numbers; in Heraclea the proportion is 3 to 2. The general pattern that emerges is that female slaves were represented in significant numbers, though not as strongly as male slaves; the pattern among their free counterparts is the same.

As was the case at Sirmium, inscriptions extant from the city provide useful evidence for comparison with the Heraclean rescripts. Excluding inscriptions that name high-ranking officials and members of local elite families, who probably had little need for the system of petition and response, we find among the remaining individuals seventy-nine Greek names (69 percent) and thirty Latin (26 percent), plus a few others.[109] Likewise among male civilians named in the rescripts, there are more than twice as many Greek names (65 percent) as Latin (26 percent). Among women recipients, however, we find a surprising result: fifteen have Latin names, but only five have Greek. The preponderance of Latin names among female recipients could be variously explained. They could, by chance, have come from Latin-speaking or Romanized families; they could be the wives of local troops, most of whom had Latin names; they could have traveled from Latin-speaking areas (but as these are outside the province, this last explanation is the least likely). Alternatively, many more entries to recipients with Greek names than with Latin names were by chance omitted by Hermogenian and then Justinian's compilers.

Extant from the city are sixteen funerary monuments to soldiers, of whom six have Latin names, two Greek, one Germanic, and one unknown, probably Thracian or Celtic. One inscription refers to a Latin-named soldier who seems to have come from Pannonia and was serving in Heraclea when he died, as *tropaiophoro fratre* (a nice example of linguistic borrowing).[110] It is possible, though of course unverifiable, that the original group of soldier recipients of rescripts would have been similarly composed.

Despite the maritime location of this major settlement, there are no entries from Heraclea to recipients with names that were neither Greek nor Latin. There is indirect evidence of foreigners in the city: references to a Gothic population in the third century. On the model of other cities it is likely that eastern craftsmen and skilled workers moved in. Some Thracian names appeared among Romanized families during that time, and Thracians could even become emperors, like Maximinus "Thrax."[111] The dominance of Greco-Roman names could be explained as the product of chance, though there is another possibility, illustrated by a name preserved in *CIG* 2.2019. Though admittedly unclear (I have not seen the stone), it could be read *Apollonius [ ]arkos kai Dizas*. The second name looks to be Roman with a Greek inflection, which would probably have been the name preserved if this man had been recorded in a rescript subsequently preserved in the *CJ*. Dizas, his Thracian alias, however, would have been omitted, and his Thracian heritage would have been obscured.

Though Heraclea was a *Straßenknotenpunkt* surrounded by a few towns (Tzirallum, Daunioteichos, and Heraionteichos), eight smaller settlements, a *mutatio* (a halting place that offered services for the maintenance of carriages and animals), and a *mansio* (a rest stop with a coaching inn), its environs appear to have been less densely populated than those of Sirmium.[112] The population along the coast was denser than inland and enjoyed a good road network. But with Byzantium only a short distance away, few petitioners needed to travel long distances to hand in petitions to Diocletian at Heraclea. Those isolated in the middle of the province of Thracia, who would customarily have come to Heraclea to petition the governor, would have found the journey more difficult. Indeed, apart from one reference to a *praedium rusticum*,[113] no other entry can be tied with certainty to an out-of-town petitioner. There was, however, some respite for inland residents. In AD 293–294, those lucky enough to be living near the main roads did not have to travel to Heraclea. Diocletian's officials answered petitions at Beroea, Burtudizum, and Tzirallum, as well as Adrianople.[114] The emperor's arrival was for them an unusual and enormous boon.[115] Those who did travel to the city in April 293 would have enjoyed seasonably fine weather and good roads and therefore easy access to the city.

### Local Problems

There is little that is surprising or notable in the content of rescripts at Heraclea. People here petitioned mostly about family matters, especially tutelage, inheritance, and dowries, just as Capitolina did. A few rescripts refer to trials that are taking place or have just finished; one woman is in a contest with someone of senatorial status, presumably a local. There are other references to local elites, such as Leontius the decurion. As we saw at Sirmium, there are references to specific laws (the *lex Fabia* and the *lex Julia de vi*) to aid recipients' advocates in court, and one rescript mentions the role of *consuetudo regionis* in rental agreements, which is accorded the same status as that of *lex contractus*.[116]

The usual home of Hermogenian's department and the rest of the court was Sirmium. So when Diocletian arrived there in September 293, Hermogenian and the other officials simply returned to their permanent offices and homes. But when they arrived at Heraclea, new accommodations, food, and supplies needed to be found for them. The knock-on effects of the court's arrival were dramatic for locals. Resident merchants increased prices in anticipation of the court's needs and were joined by other eager traders hoping to supply the enlarged population. The court was followed by an unofficial train of petitioners, ambassadors, and hangers-on.[117] Lawyers and notaries from out of town would also be drawn by a large customer base. If the emperor needed to billet members of his retinue in Heraclea's surrounding towns and villages, they too may have seen increased trade and new arrivals. Cities at which emperors would stay often or for longer periods of time might also benefit indirectly from the court's arrival. The erection of new buildings, such as baths, theaters, even palaces, would require local labor, skills, and materials.[118]

Diocletian's arrival in towns and cities through the lower Danube provinces offered opportunities to a wide array of people in the local population, especially providers of local services and petitioners. But not everyone could take advantage of Diocletian's visits equally. Slaves and women were probably the most disadvantaged of the petitioners. At smaller locations they probably lacked the social interactions within their group that would have given them legal advice. Soldiers are perhaps the least represented group, though their status is unlikely to have disadvantaged them. Male civilians seem to have enjoyed the most opportunities to petition and receive responses. In the course of two years, petitioners approached Diocletian across the mountains and valleys of the Danube provinces, in bad weather and on poor roads. Though these difficult conditions are not perceptible in the rescripts, slaves and women at isolated locations probably had less opportunity or courage to travel to where Diocletian was staying.

If the majority of recipients of rescripts in 293–294 were from the lower Danube provinces as I think likely, and if a significant number of them were local to the places at which they received their rescripts, we have a group of petitioners who were taking advantage of the emperor's travels and who would otherwise have probably approached a provincial official. The experience of this group was in one sense unusual: far more people petitioned local officials than petitioned emperors. But it was typical of people who petitioned emperors: some lived where the emperor visited frequently; others had to travel. Given the largely local nature of the recipient group, one could argue that petitioning the emperor had only a marginal effect in redressing widespread imbalances of justice on a local level. Yet with the multiplication of courts by Diocletian and the travels of the emperors, local injustices were righted on a wider scale, at a range of places that could not always be anticipated by the bullies, cheats, and thieves who plagued many of the middling sort. The fact that petition and response was now accessible in more places at any given time than had previously been the case also created more opportunities for individuals to seek the protection of Roman courts than if they had to rely simply on local institutions.

In the stories of Anicetus's home improvement woes and Capitolina's greedy husband, and in all the other petitioners' legal problems, we understand more about ordinary people outside Egypt in the third century than we can from any other source, as we will see in the next chapter.

FOUR

# Using the System

As Diocletian arrived at Philippopolis, one of the petitioners waiting to hand in a petition was Sisola. She had lent a man a single cow, which met its end as a result of a hostile incursion. This was the answer she received from Hermogenian and his fellow officials:

> *CJ* 4.23.1 (Sisolae d. 27 May 293 Philippopolis). Ea quidem, quae vi maiore auferuntur, detrimento eorum quibus res commodantur imputari non solent. sed cum is, qui a te commodari sibi bovem postulabat, hostilis incursionis contemplatione periculum amissionis ac fortunam futuri damni in se suscepisse proponatur, praeses provinciae, si probaveris eum indemnitatem tibi promisisse, placitum conventionis implere eum compellet.[1]

> Those things indeed, which are taken away by force majeure, tend not be reckoned as a cost to those to whom the items of property were rented. But since the man who asked that the cow be leased to him by you, is shown to have taken upon himself the risk of loss and the chance of a future penalty with regard to a hostile incursion, the provincial governor, if you prove that he promised you security from loss, will force him to fulfill the terms of the agreement.

This little text illustrates what rescripts can tell us about the administration of justice. This chapter will closely examine case studies that illustrate how responses once helped petitioners in practical terms and now help historians seeking to understand the interactions of ordinary people with the machinery of the Roman state as they solved their problems. They also reveal more about people's lives under the Tetrarchy.[2] The texts of the entries reveal abundant detail about the people who used the system of petition and response and the legal problems they suffered. Much of the original detail of the problems has been lost, but enough remains to produce a snapshot of people's problems and the ways in which rescripts could help to solve them.

The entries of 293–294 were kept for the *CJ* solely for the legal principles they illustrated, and I do not claim that they reflect all the rescripts that were ever produced or indeed that the stories behind them reflect the stories in all the petitions that were ever sent. The nine hundred–plus rescripts are typical only of themselves, but they shed light on over nine hundred situations in which people sought justice—a considerable number by the standards of ancient historians, especially those focusing outside Egypt. They result from problems that were unusual enough for there perhaps not already to be a clear statement of law in an earlier rescript, yet not so unusual that the *scrinium* could not apply Roman law to them and later compilers did not deem an authoritative rescript worth keeping in several successive editions. The case studies in this chapter are even less reflective of the universality of the these documents, but as I shall show, they do illustrate the place of the rescript system within the Roman system of legal administration and the ways in which they helped people to seek justice.[3] They have been chosen from among the longest rescripts for the simplicity and human interest of their subject matter.

Key themes and aspects of rescripts that will be addressed in this chapter are the clarity of their structure despite the complexity of some of them; their role in legal processes and their importance in disseminating legal information; their value in protecting vulnerable petitioners as well as the risks of receiving an unfavorable rescript; the importance of legal knowledge in using a rescript (and the extent of some petitioners' ignorance); the commitment of the *scrinium* to answering petitions that arose from issues affecting the middling sort; the importance for the *scrinium* of upholding justice and the laws in rescripts; and social and political influences on the content of rescripts.

I shall be examining responses to petitions that were useful for the compilers of several legal compilations and codifications. Of course, not all rescripts made it into the *CH* and indeed not all petitions were necessarily answered. The criteria for answering a petition are unknown (see above), but it seems reasonable to suggest that it had to contain a query about the law or procedure concerning a justiciable situation. Petitions probably went unanswered that concerned situations without a legal aspect or problem cases, which Merry defines as having "the characteristics of mutual fault, history, emotional intensity, and ongoing relationships."[4] Problem cases are those better solved through mediation than a court trial.

A recent sociological study by Patricia Ewick and Susan Silbey of American attitudes toward the law identified a number of strategies employed by individuals suffering legal problems: aligning themselves with the law, putting themselves before the law, and acting against the law.[5] Taking each in turn, I shall demonstrate that my case studies used them too.

According to the study, the first strategy among Americans is to approach law as a game, as a terrain for tactical encounters in which people are bound by a set of rules they might try to change, and to regard legality as simply one element of commonplace events and activities. They are solving their problems *with the law,* regarding the law as an "arena of contest."[6] Similarly, the wealthier decurions, equestrians, and senators, who encountered law frequently and had little to lose in defending in their actions and solving their problems, had this attitude. Some of the more confident members of the middling sort may have shared this attitude and used the rescript system as one element in a tactical schema to win a legal dispute. For them, the law was to be upheld when it was in their favor, but contested or manipulated when it could go against them, for example, by using status-based intimidation. Some may have misrepresented their situation so as gain an unduly favorable rescript, which they could then show to their opponents, hoping to bamboozle them into submission with legal complexity and the emperor's imprimatur.

Some Americans place themselves *before the law,* believing it to be an immovable and disinterested independent entity, distant from the lives of ordinary people. They respect it and follow it, but avoid using it to their benefit unless absolutely necessary. Among those ancient Romans with legal problems, we can imagine that most of them would have taken a similar stance: intimidated by the law and its institutions, they would have taken legal action as a last resort, even if they could afford it or knew how to do it.[7] Given that the middling sort, of all groups in society, most often took advantage of legal aid or inexpensive advice, some of them may also have had this attitude, petitioning simply to see where they stood in relation to the law.[8] Petitioners standing before the law gained an opportunity to hear another voice, one that seemed to lack bias and whose words were incontrovertible. This was particularly important for petitioners who felt they were being forced into an unfair situation but could not argue because they lacked legal knowledge and know-how.

The third attitude found among Americans is that law is a product of power and is arbitrary and capricious, not to be stood before but to be acted against. Americans with this attitude found themselves in situations *they* felt to be unfair (or inconvenient) but had been forced on them by the law, and felt themselves driven to act *against the law*.[9] Some Romans, eschewing any contact with the administration, may have used extra-legal means, such as intimidation or even violence, against those putting legal pressure on them. But others, especially the middling sort, petitioned to find out how successful they could be in opposing laws they felt were inhibiting their (often questionable) activities.

The Skaptopareni may have fallen into this category, though not exclusively. There is some overlap between these attitudes. Ewick and Silbey have seen in their case studies that an individual may display all three at different times during a legal dispute. So, when the Skaptopareni first encountered trouble, they probably stood *before the law*—in awe of it. Then as their problems worsened, they realized that approaching the provincial governor for assistance in reforming requisitioning practices might help them. So they petitioned. But as their problems resumed, they probably found themselves wondering what they could do. They decided to act *with the law,* using a petition and rescript to bring the legal authorities at the imperial level on their side and thereby overcome the superior status of their opponents. They may have taken to direct action against the soldiers and local officials, but were careful not to allude to this in their petition. Their last action, possibly tampering with the rescript's wording for the inscription, is an example of acting *against the law.*

The Skaptopareni were acting as a group and probably had the support of everyone, or nearly everyone, in their community—except local officials. But for individuals, acting with the law could be risky. If they were in legal disputes with relatives, neighbors, or community members, they might attract the opprobrium of the community by being seen to go outside the community for help.

Just as repeated encounters with the legal administration seem to increase Americans' confidence in dealing with legal issues, some Romans might be expected to gain confidence with the protection afforded by the emperor's rescript. It is therefore likely that those petitioners whose problems had not been solved by appealing to their neighbors or the community or by approaching the provincial authorities were well placed to petition the imperial court, and some clearly felt that petitioning was easier or more worthwhile than putting up with an ongoing problem. Likewise, the Skaptopareni, following their initial encounter with the provincial court, may have become more confident about their case. The response they received directed them back to that court but this time with a rescript and greater experience. The petition of the Skaptopareni may present them as vulnerable and helpless, but their repeated requests for help would have emboldened them, and they may have combined their increasing skill in navigating administrative systems such as the rescript and court systems with an understanding of the importance of presenting themselves in their petition and in court as humble and helpless.[10]

### "With the Law"

The rescript to Sisola informed her that force majeure, which would not normally have granted her any compensation, did not apply in this situation because her lessee had agreed to be responsible in any situation (at least according to Sisola). He had presumably learned following the hostile incursion that his full agreement had been unnecessary and now refused to reimburse Sisola for her loss, since it was the result of force majeure.[11] We no longer have Sisola's petition, but elements of it can plausibly be reconstructed on the basis of the rescript. We can assume, for example, that she outlined the contract by which the lease had been undertaken, described the circumstances in which the cow perished, and recounted her disagreement with the lessee. The basis of the disagreement was whether the lessee was bound by his original agreement to do something from which he was exempt by law.[12]

We do not know whether Sisola knew the details of *vis maior*—or knew anything about it when her lessee agreed to the original contract (and thus she was acting with the law) or found out when the lessee first objected to covering her loss. But she probably had some understanding of it to feel the need to petition. (It is also possible that Sisola had no idea about force majeure and petitioned knowing simply that she lost her cow and wanted compensation.) Behind every rescript was a petition based on general awareness or precise knowledge of legal concepts gained through social interaction or legal experience. While the petitioner group was small compared to the rest of society, its members differed in the extent of their legal knowledge, and these differences mattered greatly in legal disputes.[13] Petitioners such as Sisola may have acquired knowledge of contract law and the concept of *vis maior* gradually through experience. Perhaps she spoke about the situation with legally informed friends or even sought legal advice.[14]

Others would have been spurred to action by a sense of injustice gained from social interaction and shared values. These are often reflected in common expressions in everyday discourse: we might imagine such expressions as "live somewhere long enough and it becomes yours" and "you can't make a free man a slave."[15] If their sense that an injustice had been committed was borne out in law, the rescript would confirm this. In the process of petition and response, state and subject interacted as the state re-expressed in legal terminology the complaint of the subject. With so few examples of petitions extant, it is impossible to gauge the extent to which they were explicitly formulated in terms of Roman law (though it is more likely that they simply described a problem that seemed to the petitioner justiciable according to common concepts of fairness) and responded to it in such a way that it was now justiciable within the framework of Roman legal administration (i.e., the courts). So Sisola complained that her lessee, though having agreed to compensate her for loss in any situation, was now reneging. Complaints that did not have an existing expression and solution in Roman law could also be addressed. Members of the *scrinium* could create equitable remedies, which would become law and help others.[16]

Whether Sisola and the many other recipients of 293–294 knew much about Roman law probably mattered little to their situation. Their legal affairs were most likely ordered according to Roman law, though they didn't realize it. The contracts and documents that Romans used to order and make official their relationships and undertakings—marriage documents, wills, lease agreements, employment contracts—need not be expressly made in accordance with Roman law, but they could not contradict it.[17] Any problems that resulted from them were therefore also problems that were justiciable in terms of Roman law, even if not dealt with explicitly by Roman law in existing Roman legislation.

Sisola's complaint elicited a response that was entered into the *CH* and later the *CJ* because it treated a problem that either had not been encountered before or had not been addressed with a clear and precise solution. Of course, other entries may have been equally worthy of inclusion, but the rescript to Sisola survived sufficient accidents of fate to be included. The rescript was preserved through successive compilations, even though in economic terms, the scale of her loss was small. It seems to have comprised only one cow, suggesting that this was the only item of property leased. The rescripts reveal the trifling subjects that came before emperors, and it is perhaps surprising that the imperial court, let alone the emperor, should have been concerned with Sisola's cow. Yet the subjects were not trifling to petitioners. For a smallholder, the loss of a cow could have serious financial repercussions, and he or she, being in a precarious position, was surely justified in taking advantage of the opportunity to petition the emperor. And the emperor, in the role of patron, was expected to do this. The fact that problems as small in scale as Sisola's were addressed by the court must have emboldened others to petition. And even if they (perhaps mistakenly) believed that they had no real chance of being answered, they could at the very least tell their opponents that they had petitioned and were awaiting an answer from the emperor himself.

Petitioners such as Sisola had reason to be confident. Though the scale of their problems may have been small, their legal import was not. For example, there were vast numbers of individuals throughout the empire leasing or hiring livestock, who might benefit from a clarification on the scope of force majeure. The rescript she received is important not only because there were many livestock owners or lessees, but also because there were significant numbers of attacks on Romans. The nature of the incursion in which Sisola's cow was killed is unclear and the people responsible unknown, perhaps a gang of brigands operating within the empire or barbarians raiding Roman territory for plunder. (Or even some lawless neighbor.) It is possible, though this is speculative, that the rescript to Sisola was kept for the *CH* because it was the first expression of (or perhaps even the catalyst for) a new policy that no longer classed a hostile attack as an act of force majeure. It may therefore also reflect the frequency and severity of contemporary attacks on Roman property. Successive governments, under pressure from successive invasions, could have continued that policy; hence Justinian's compilers preserved the rescript to Sisola. Collections of rescripts, including that to Sisola, also served to show the emperor at work helping his subjects. The preamble to the Edict on Maximum Prices likewise advertises Diocletian's concern for his subjects, in that case his soldiers.

Viewed in this light, the rescript is an important one with wide-ranging consequences. The issue that prompted it was important enough for Sisola to petition and to consider pursuing through the courts (the assumption that she would bring the case to court is based on *probaveris* in the rescript). And it was important for the court, which wrote rescripts essentially for two reasons: concern for justice and concern for law. Rulers' concern for justice and for answering subjects' petitions so as to maintain the legitimacy of their position, as we have seen, has long been a feature of conscientious rule. Sisola's lessee was refusing to cover the loss he had formerly agreed to cover. Rulers' concern for law had several motivations. The first was political: concern for the law gave an impression of stable and responsible government. The second was academic: members of the *scrinium*, who were legal experts, may have considered responding to petitioners' legal problems a duty to their discipline, in the mold of jurists' activities in composing works that compiled or explained aspects of Roman law.[18]

However, the rescripts were most immediately important and useful for their recipients in following legal processes. They contained legally accurate wording that Sisola could reproduce in any subsequent document. She could show her rescript to the lessee and demand repayment for the loss of the cow; she could adduce the rescript in a court case, having proven that in the original contract the lessee agreed to cover loss suffered even under force majeure; she could ask the governor for an action against the lessee on the basis of a mistake of law if she had already covered the loss herself. The wording of many other rescripts suggests that the petitioners were engaged in disputes that either threatened to come to court or had already reached the trial stage. The rescripts they received could persuade an opponent to settle or could sway a judge in court. Thus rescripts fitted neatly into Roman judicial procedure, not (at least until later in the fourth or fifth century) as procedural devices themselves but as instruments that could avert or influence a procedure.

The structure of rescripts also helped petitioners. Sisola's rescript provides a good example. It has a tripartite structure, like many rescripts. An introduction expresses briefly a legal principle: *ea quidem, quae vi maiore auferuntur, detrimento eorum quibus res commodantur imputari non solent.* This is followed by a clause that outlines the core legal issue in the recipient's problem: *sed cum is, qui a te commodari sibi bovem postulabat, hostilis incursionis contemplatione periculum amissionis ac fortunam futuri damni in se suscepisse proponatur.* The rescript closes with a clause that applies the initial legal principle to the recipient's problem and gives a judgment: *praeses provinciae, si probaveris eum indemnitatem tibi promisisse, placitum conventionis implere eum compellet.* The opening statement of law reveals the basis for the disagreement and confirms to the petitioner the justiciable nature of the problem and the area of law in which it lies, a detail that could be passed to counsel as the basis for a case. The outline of the problem normalizes it into a justiciable framework to which the law can be applied. This outline could be repeated in court, with supplementary detail to prove that the facts of the case were as they had been presented in the petition. The application clause is most important. It provides a judgment on whether the law (or some equitable variation on it) could be in favor of the petitioner (depending on the true facts of the case), and it sometimes explains to the recipients how they should solve the problem. The former could help the petitioner already in court; the latter is useful for the petitioner at the pre-trial stage.

Another woman taking advantage of the rescript system was Antigone, who was engaged in moving goods presumably along the Danube.

> *CJ* 4.25.4 (Antigonae d. 17 Oct 293 Sirmium) Et si a muliere magister navis (n. *firmant Gr.*) praepositus fuerit, ex contractibus eius ea exercitoria actione ad similitudinem institoriae tenetur.

> Even if the master of a ship had been appointed with command by a woman, given the contract, she is held by an action on controlling the ship, which is considered similar to an action on managing it.

Antigone was probably the owner or lessee of a boat, which she was using to transport either her own goods or someone else's, and she had hired a *magister navis* to oversee the job. (It is also possible that she was an interested third party, such as the owner of another boat that had been damaged.) The following scenario may have prompted her petition: while transporting the goods, the *magister navis* damaged a second party's vessel on the river. That party, wishing to claim damages, approached Antigone, who remonstrated that the *magister* was liable as the author of the accident. The second party, however, disagreed, and Antigone decided to seek a second opinion by means of a petition. The answer she received was perhaps not to her liking: as *exercitor* (i.e., owner or lessee) of the boat, she was liable. The author of the rescript adds that an action against her as *exercitor* was similar to an action against the manager of a commercial business (*actio institoria*), information that may have been added as clarification not just for Antigone but also for a judge in a future trial or future readers of the rescript. Alternatively, it may be a later interpolation meant to help Justinianic readers. Like Sisola, Antigone was keen to avoid being penalized for a loss and was using the rescript system as one part of her strategy for dealing "with the law."

The importance of the rescript for the administration of law in the empire is that it helps us understand the importance of posting up responses. The rescript was given at Sirmium, an important center for Danube shipping. The act of putting up the rescript with its petition advertised its judgment to local people, many of whom were involved in trading on the Danube. Also among that community would have been lawyers or notaries, some of whom would have offered their services in drawing up contracts for or giving legal advice to maritime traders. The compiler of the *Apokrimata* may have been a lawyer who kept rescripts for his personal reference library; his later Danubian counterparts may have found the rescript to Antigone especially useful for their local clientele.[19]

Finally, the rescript is interesting for its equity. Antigone was told that the owner or lessee of the boat is liable for any damage inflicted by it (even if she was not steering). If this were legal advice from a lawyer, we might expect some explanation of how she could evade liability. But the imperial court, at least in the rescript as it survives, states only that she is liable. While disappointing for Antigone, this rescript advertised to the local community and later readers of the *CH* and *CJ* how justice should operate in this situation.

While publishing the rescript to Antigone may have informed people in the local trading community and reduced the number of petitions on the same subject, most petitioners did not live near enough for publication of rescripts to spread much legal awareness. For example, Alexander received the following rescript:

*CJ* 4.2.9 (Alexandro s. 18 Dec 293) Cum te in Gallia cum Syntropho certum auri pondus itemque numeratam pecuniam mutuo dedisse, ut Romae solveretur, precibus adseveras, aditus competens iudex, si duos reos stipulandi vel re pro solido tibi quaesitam actionem sive ab heredibus Syntrophi procuratorem te factum animadverterit, totum debitum, alioquin quod dedisti solum restitui tibi iubebit.

Since you assert in your petition that when you were in Gaul with Syntrophus you had lent a fixed weight of gold and likewise a certain amount of money that was to be paid back at Rome, an eligible judge once approached, if he perceives that there are two debtors on what has been stipulated or that you have sought an action on the whole amount or that you were made agent by the heirs of Syntrophus, he will order that the entire debt, or only what you gave, be restored to you.

Two locations are mentioned in this rescript: Gaul and Rome. We can imagine that Alexander and Syntrophus were businessmen moving around the empire. Alexander had made a short-term loan to Syntrophus, which was to be paid back in Rome. Unfortunately for Alexander, this did not happen. Syntrophus subsequently died, leaving Alexander to seek compensation either by initiating an action against the two debtors or by claiming the money through Syntrophus's estate, having been made procurator of it. From local problems with cargo on the Danube and livestock, we have moved into the sphere of long-distance traders. Alexander, we can imagine, would have applied his business savvy to his legal problem and viewed petitioning as a powerful tool in his dealings with the law.

This text shows that most rescripts were not geographically focused. Even if not universally known, the legal principles of a rescript from the emperor were, on the whole, valid anywhere in the empire. Of course, rescripts were not always unique to a local situation: one could not necessarily look simply at their content and know where they were from or what particular local problems they were dealing with. Therefore publishing them did not necessarily reduce the number of future petitions on the same subject. Nevertheless, despite only local publication and infrequent compilation, the court presumably continued to respond to all petitions, many on similar subjects. In this light, Honoré's description of the rescript system as "a scheme of free legal aid" rings true.[20]

While the rescript system brought benefits to successful petitioners, the legal system remained burdensome for many of them.

*CJ* 1.18.6 (Tauro et Pollioni d. 27 Apr 294) Si non transactionis causa, sed indebitam errore facti olei materiam vos Archantico stipulanti dare spopondisse rector animadverterit provinciae, reddito quod debetis residui liberationem condicentes audiet.

If the rector of the province should notice that you in a stipulation agreed to give to Archanticus a certain amount of the oil, not because of a transaction, but by an error of fact, he will listen to both of you, having paid off what you owe, pleading together for the liberation of the remainder.

The structure of this rescript differs slightly from the paradigm we saw above. The opening statement of law, often discrete from the rest of the text, is missing (though it may have been lost through successive copying), and the statement of the petitioners' situation is combined with the section that usually closes a rescript advising the recipients on their next course of action.

Taurus and Pollio are advised that since they handed over too much oil because they misunderstood how much they owed, not because they expected payment for the extra quantity, they should approach the *rector provinciae* (another name for the governor). Assuming that Taurus and Pollio resided in Upper Moesia (their rescript had something done to it at Sirmium), they were obliged to travel to Aquincum, the provincial capital, if they wished to obtain justice. Moreover, they were advised that they should present their case speaking together (*condicentes*), and therefore needed to make the journey together. Given that governors presumably faced a heavy load of cases, our two litigants were now subject not only to the expense of the journey, but also the loss in business caused by their need to wait for a trial. The possibility that once in court their rescript would help them offered solace to would-be litigants faced with considerable costs of money, time, and business opportunity. And while would-be litigants faced short-term costs in acquiring a rescript and going to court, they might benefit in the long-term from overcoming potentially expensive and long-running legal problems.

Finally, it is interesting that Archanticus's name is preserved. Other rescripts (such as *CJ* 7.45.8) also contain the names of other parties. Just as the *CJ* preserves the names of recipients of the rescripts probably to aid memorization, so retaining names probably aided memory and comprehension better than if the names were replaced by pronouns.[21]

Thus far, we have looked at contracts concerning goods and services. But transactions could be of human capital also. While Hadrian allowed all slaves to bring actions against their masters for excessive cruelty, only slaves contesting their status could petition the imperial court and receive a response. Therefore, those I am (for the sake of brevity) calling slaves in this section were not necessarily of slave status. These individuals' ability to petition is probably based on the fact that, while to some they were slaves, nevertheless in the eyes of the law there was the possibility that they were free. On this subject the court's concern for justice is very apparent. Status was an important issue for legal officials in the imperial court, given the Roman discomfort with slavery.[22]

That discomfort comes out clearly in the following rescript.

*CJ* 7.16.19 (Paulo before 27 Aug 293) Principaliter causam eius de quo supplicas esse quam tuam perspicimus. nam cum te eum ad libertatem produxisse profitearis, illius interest magis sollemniter suum tueri statum et consequenter tua etiam agetur causa: nam si ab eo, contra quem fundis preces, servus dicatur eique libertas ex manumissione tua vindicetur, probatio servitutis originis et beneficium manumissionis libertatem illi adsignans tuum etiam ius patronatus tuetur. si vero consentiat servituti, tunc iure concesso adito praeside provinciae eum invitum etiam defendere poteris.

We see that the man, about whom you are supplicating, is the principal affected party in this case, not you. For since you profess that you promoted him to freedom, it is in the interest of him to guard his own status in the proper way and in consequence his will also be a case that has interest for you: for if he is called a slave by the man, against whom you are pouring forth your petition and his liberty is being claimed on the basis of the manumission you bestowed, with proof of his servile origin and your benefaction of manumission giving liberty to him, these things also preserve your right of patronage. If he truly agrees to servitude, then with that right given up, having approached the provincial governor, you can defend him even though he is unwilling.

Paulus had been the master of slave X (who is unnamed in the rescript), whom he manumitted; X then became Paulus's freedman. But a third party was now claiming X as his slave. X seems to have agreed to resume his servile status, though Paulus suspected that he was being coerced. Paulus wished to undertake a case against the third party, presumably because he had been deprived of his freedman and the services he was obliged to offer.

If this was the case, we can view Paulus as a man who was willing to work with legal services and processes to resolve his legal problems. Viewed more charitably, he may have wished to protect his former slave. Roman law stated that a family member could undertake a case on behalf of an individual who had willingly submitted to servitude despite being freeborn.[23] This rescript is a clear example of the strong concern behind that law: the *scrinium* assumes that the freedman would not have willingly given up his freedom and allows Paulus to mount a defense on his behalf. Once again, we see the court showing care for upholding justice and the laws.

The rescript is striking because Paulus's freedman was claimed by someone else as a slave and seems to have returned to his servile state willingly. It seems fitting to end this section, which looks at petitioners who were more willing than most to *use* the law to their advantage, with an analysis of a rescript that shows a petitioner clawing his way up in status from slave to decurion's son, from the bottom of the group of petitioners to the top.

> *CJ* 6.55.6 (Posidonio sp./d. 8/10 Feb 294) Ex libera conceptus et servo velut spurius habetur nec ut decurionis filius, quamvis pater eius naturalis manumissus et natalibus suis restitutus hunc fuit adeptus honorem, defendi potest.

> Someone born of a free woman and a slave is considered as if fatherless and cannot be claimed to be the son of a decurion, even though his natural father, manumitted and having received the privileges of the free-born, had acquired this honor.

Posidonius was presumably the spurious child referred to in the rescript, his father the slave who was manumitted and rose to the position of decurion. Possibly Posidonius was in trouble and wanted the protection afforded the sons of decurions. But because his father was a former slave, he was denied those privileges.[24] This rescript demonstrates that while the imperial court was concerned with people being held as slaves in contradiction of their true status, it did not recognize the achievement of social mobility. Posidonius's father had raised himself from slavery to a position of local honor, but his son could not enjoy the benefits that would have accrued to him had his father been born with the privileges of the curial class, though he did not shy away from putting his case to the imperial court. The *scrinium* had to respect existing *mores*.

## "Before the Law"

The individuals we have just looked at worked *with the law* to gain the best outcome from their situations and used the rescript system as one element in their legal strategy. In the second category, we find people who placed themselves *before the law*. Less confident of their situation, they used the rescript system simply for help and advice. It is unsurprising that the majority of recipients of rescripts I am discussing in this chapter either were victims or suffered as a result of their ignorance and now were humbled before the law. One such victim was Egus Crispinus, whose rescript concerned substitution of goods.

> *CJ* 4.2.10 (Egi Crispino s. 4 Feb 294 Sirmium) Eo, quod a multis proprii debiti singulorum obligationis uno tantum instrumento probatio continetur, exactio non interpelletur. nam si pro pecunia quam mutuo dedisti tibi vinum stipulanti qui debuerant spoponderunt, negotii gesti paenitentia contractum habitum recte non constituit irritum. *CJ* 4.49.12 (ibid.) Sicut periculum vini mutati, quod certum fuerat comparatum, ad emptorem, ita commodum aucti pretii pertinet. utque hoc verum est, sic certae qualitatis ac mensurae distracto vino fidem placitis servandam convenit: quo non restituto non pretii quantitatis, sed quanti interest empti competit actio.

> For the reason that proof of debt belonging each individual is held in only one instrument of obligation [but] by many persons, the process of recovery of the debt is not forbidden to you. For if in place of the money which you had loaned, you had both agreed that they could owe you wine, a change of mind over the business which was undertaken does not make void a contract which was considered legally valid. Just as the danger of substituted wine, which had been acquired for a fixed price, pertains to the purchaser, so does the profit from an increase in price. And since this is true, if wine is sold of a certain quality and amount, it is right that the good faith of the terms of the agreement be preserved: but if the [correct] wine is not handed over, an action pertains not on the amount of the price, but of its value once handed over.

This rescript is split between two titles. To the person undertaking to recreate a recipient's legal problem, the splitting of a rescript into several parts indicates a text's complexity (which is not to say that texts preserved seemingly whole are not complex; many of these too have their difficulties). The first section confirms that a person who had entered into a contract as part of a group could take action on a debt as an individual and that a loan in one form could be repaid in another, providing the value was maintained. The second, concerning the quantity of the debt that could be recovered, states that if Egus were to take action, he would receive the sum for which he could sell the contracted wine, rather than the price he had agreed to pay.[25]

According to the rescript, the law states *sicut periculum vini mutati, quod certum fuerat comparatum, ad emptorem, ita commodum aucti pretii pertinet.* Egus Crispinus's situation is that wine had been substituted and the application of the law to it resulted in the following statement: *sic certae qualitatis ac mensurae distracto vino fidem placitis servandam convenit: quo non restituto non pretii quantitatis, sed quanti interest empti competit actio.*

Separating Egus Crispinus's situation into two parts reveals that it may have required the skills and knowledge of experts who could respond with authority on both issues, and the resulting rescript was the product of considerable time and care. Probably some text is missing between the two parts, sacrificed as confusing or superfluous to the intelligibility of the separate sections. The intervening text may have disappeared accidentally with successive copying; more likely the compilers took the text, kept only parts of it, and divided them across several titles. Alternatively (though less likely), Egus Crispinus inquired about the two issues in discrete questions, which explains the abrupt transition from the first part of the text to the second.

Some rescripts furnished the recipient with valuable information and could provide considerable guidance to a judge. In fact, so thorough are some rescripts in setting out the law on a particular issue that they may actually be addressed to magistrates, not petitioners.[26] This should come as no surprise. The *CJ* contains a variety of types of text, including rescripts to private individuals, letters clearly addressed to magistrates, and recordings of imperial audiences and judgments.[27] The vagaries of transmission may have rendered letters to officials, usually signified by the address to the official in the accusative case following *ad*, identical in form to rescripts to individuals, who were named in the dative case. Alternatively, sometimes magistrates may have been addressed in the dative case, as had happened before the Roman period.[28] If some rescripts were in fact addressed to magistrates, the makeup of petitioners may change slightly—the officials would all be male, slightly increasing the preponderance of female recipients

among the private recipients. We would also see that the guidance to magistrates is barely distinguishable from that to private individuals and that
members of the imperial *scrinia* took as much care in explaining the law to
a wine trader as to a provincial official. Legal experts' care for justice and
the law may have overridden their concerns about rank. The rescript to
Egus Crispinus may be one such text. Written entirely in the third person,
it never addresses him as a private individual who has suffered as a result
of the broken contract.

Before tamper-proof seals, substitution of goods must have been a
common occurrence. Egus, if he was indeed a private individual and not
an official, was either operating on a small scale or was new to the business,
had been duped by someone with more experience, more money, or simply
more gall, and in his ignorance simply wanted answers to his questions
about the legality of the situation. Alternatively, he may have known what
the answer would be but wanted a rescript that he could use to show to
his opponent before or in court. If this is the case, and if many others did
the same, it is all the more remarkable that their petitions were answered.
But the rescript system was an established part of the imperial administrative system, its symbolism so important, and filtering out petitions
whose topics had previously been addressed so cumbersome that petitions
such as Egus's continued to be answered.[29] Moreover, codification did not
guarantee that petitions on these questions would no longer be answered.
The workload for the *scrinium* was surely enormous, but the benefit for
petitioners greater. The rescript system decreased the likelihood that an
individual could be bullied by an opponent into court or into covering a
loss unduly, and it increased the numbers of cases that were being decided
in accordance with the law.

Egus Crispinus's rescript was split by Justinian's compilers because
various elements of it illustrated different legal points. Another split
rescript is that to Aurelia Euodia.

*CJ* 2.19.9 (Aureliae Euodiae d. 1 Dec 293). Imperatores Diocletianus, Maximianus. Metum non iactationibus tantum vel contestationibus, sed atroc-
itate facti probari convenit. *CJ*.2.20.6 (ibid.) Dolum ex insidiis perspicuis
probari convenit. *CJ* 2.31.2 (ibid.) Si ex persona minorum in integrum
restitutio adversus transactum propter aetatis auxilium imploretur, tibi
quoque agenti ex integro vel replicatione contra exceptionem pacti vel,

si peremptam constet pristinam obligationem, ex instauratione negotii
tributa actione consulendum est. *CJ* 4.44.8 (ibid.) Si voluntate tua fundum
tuum filius tuus venumdedit, dolus ex calliditate atque insidiis emptoris
argui debet vel metus mortis vel cruciatus corporis imminens detegi, ne
habeatur rata venditio. hoc enim solum, quod paulo minori pretio fundum
venumdatum significas, ad rescindendam emptionem invalidum est. quod
videlicet si contractus emptionis atque venditionis cogitasses substantiam
et quod emptor viliori comparandi, venditor cariori distrahendi votum ge-
rentes ad hunc contractum accedant vixque post multas contentiones, pau-
latim venditore de eo quod petierat detrahente, emptore autem huic quod
obtulerat addente, ad certum consentiant pretium, profecto perspiceres
neque bonam fidem, quae emptionis atque venditionis conventionem tuetur, pati neque ullam rationem concedere rescindi propter hoc consensu
finitum contractum vel statim vel post pretii quantitatis disceptationem:
nisi minus dimidia iusti pretii, quod fuerat tempore venditionis, datum est,
electione iam emptori praestita servanda.

It is agreed that intimidation be proven not only by claims and public declarations, but by the awfulness of the deed. It is right that deceit be proven
by obvious plotting. If on behalf of someone underage, reinstatement into
a former legal position is asked for on account of the person's age to counteract an act of protection undertaken, your interests will be considered,
whether you bring an action *ex integro* or an exception in response to the
exception on the agreement or, if it is agreed that the former obligation was
null and void, by the granting of an action of resumption of the business.
If your son sold your farm with your wishes, deceit ought to be proven by
the shrewdness and plotting of the purchaser or fear of death or imminent
torturing of the body ought to be uncovered, lest the sale is considered to
have been legally valid. For, this alone, the fact that you report that the farm
was sold for a little less than its value, is not valid for annulling the sale.
Because clearly if you had considered the nature of the contract of sale and
purchase and because the purchaser wishing to buy for less and the seller to
sell for more have come to this agreement and after many deliberations, the
seller gradually drawing back from what he had sought, and also with the
purchaser adding to what he offered, they agree to a fixed price, assuredly
you would see clearly that neither good faith, which guards the agreement
of sale and purchase, allows nor any reason grants that a contract that has
been closed with agreement be rescinded on this account, either immediately or after the amount of the price has been subject to dispute, unless less
than half of the lawful price, as it stood at the time of sale, had been given,
the purchaser reserved the right to keep what he was offered.

What remains of this entry has been divided into four parts (some of the original text may be missing). The opening two sections of the text concern intimidation and the third concerns restoration of a minor (though a guardian is nowhere mentioned) to an inheritance despite a transaction or division of the property, while the bulk of the text concerns the rescission of a sale.[30] The situation seems to be that Aurelia Euodia's underage son was threatened into selling his estate (*fundus*) for a price lower than initially agreed or perhaps less than a previous valuation. What makes this text complicated is that there are three aspects to the problem. The first is intimidation. Aurelia Euodia wishes to claim that her son has been the victim of deliberate intimidation, a claim she presumably used to explain the other two aspects. Her son has sold property, but Aurelia Euodia wishes it to be returned to him. For that, she must claim that the intimidation so affected him, being a minor, that he was an unwilling party to a contract to sell that property—his unwillingness is the second aspect. Finally, she wishes to claim that the sale was not valid because the money her son received for the property was less than the sum he wished for at the beginning of negotiations. As the author of the rescript points out, she needs to prove that intimidation, not the natural process of bargaining, was the cause of the difference.

So complex is this text, with each part depending on the previous one, that the tripartite structure is not used. Legal principles are still stated, as is the case with the opening sections concerning intimidation. The final, long section of the text concerning sale of the farm starts with a premise—that if a purchaser pays a price lower than that he had hoped for, the sale remains valid—and leads into a justification for that premise.

The role of the mother concerning her son is curious. As Roman mothers could not act as guardians for their children, Aurelia Euodia was not a party to the sale, simply an interested party. She may still have been living at the farm, and she may have petitioned the emperor so as use his answer to persuade her son's guardian of how to remedy the situation. Yet the legal nature of her role is puzzling, especially given the use of the second person in the advice concerning *restitutio* of a minor. Certainly women could send a petition and receive a response on behalf of their children.[31] Later on in the litigation process, however, they needed the input of a man, presumably a father, relative, or tutor. I am hesitant to suggest that Aurelia Euodia was indeed acting as guardian on the model of Egyptian and

Arabian examples, such as that most famously provided by Babatha, but the wording of the rescript may imply it.[32] Aurelia Euodia does not appear in a good light in this reconstruction of her situation. She was perhaps a victim, but she was also ignorant of the law, an unfortunate state to be in given that she was in a legally complex situation. This rescript illustrates that though Roman jurists were (and still are) famed for their exhaustive and precise analysis of legally complex situations, the parties in them rarely shared their understanding.

The rescript to Aurelia Euodia was not wholly favorable, and its author seems inclined to disbelieve her claim of an unfair sale. The following rescript to Bithus shows that the imperial court could criticize those who came before the law, ignorant of it.

> *CJ* 4.7.5 (Bitho s. 10 May 294/293) Promercalem te habuisse uxorem proponis: unde intellegis et confessionem lenocinii preces tuas continere et cautae quantitatis ob turpem causam exactioni locum non esse. quamvis enim utriusque turpitudo versatur ac soluta quantitate cessat repetitio, tamen ex huiusmodi stipulatione contra bonos mores interposita denegandas esse actiones iuris auctoritate demonstratur.

> You say that you considered your wife for sale on the open market: wherefore you understand that your petition contains a confession of pimping and there is no (room for) action on the secured amount on account of the shameful reason for taking the payment. For although the shame was practiced by both sides and with payment of the amount the claim would cease, nevertheless since they arise from a stipulation made against good morals, by the authority of the law, it is shown that the actions are to be denied.

Bithus had arranged for a man to sleep with his wife but had not been paid as agreed. He presumably wanted to know how he could pursue a claim against the man, but in the response was told that there was no claim; he should not have prostituted his wife in the first place. Though publishing this rescript did not advertise a ruling on a particularly local issue—and of course most rescripts do not do this—it did make clear to Bithus and those crowding round the rescripts posted at Heraclea that the imperial court would chastise those it felt worthy of censure. In the rescripts we have seen above, the greatest risk to petitioners is confirmation that they would lose their case if it came to court. But for others like Bithus, to receive an unfavorable response was to risk having one's legal transgression made public.

In Bithus's case, he may not have suffered any repercussions of his exposure, save an inability to claim against the other man. While the imperial court naturally did not bring proceedings against such people (petitions are, after all, presentations of hypothetical situations, whose facts must be proven in court), others might have done so. Bithus, on the other hand, did not have to do anything with the response. No petitioner was obliged to follow what was set out in a rescript and could simply hope that it was forgotten soon after publication.

The author(s) of the rescript to Bithus condemned him in strong terms.[33] Members of the *scrinium* seem to have felt a duty to see justice done, so they imply that Bithus would have had a claim, but for the fact that he admitted pimping. This is an important legal point; the *scrinium* strove to maintain standards of decency through adherence to the law. Bithus was exposed by the conscientiousness of the *scrinium;* others too may have felt that their rescripts were a bane rather than a boon.

Some of the examples we have seen above, including the rescript to Bithus, concerned contract law. They have illustrated that rescripts could be used to avoid a trial or improve the chances of winning it, that they contained sufficient legal information to educate the recipient and were usually structured in three parts, and that they were concerned with upholding justice and the laws, even if that meant pointing out that a petitioner was to blame, castigating him or her for it, and omitting to advise on how to avoid causing imperial displeasure.

Aurelia Euodia complained about intimidation concerning property. Other rescripts relating to property also concerned neighbors who probably intimidated petitioners, either directly with threats or indirectly by virtue of having more money or higher social status. In the area of property, the concern of government to protect the weak from the strong is clear. We have already met Anicetus from Sirmium. His next door neighbor, Julianus, had been making some home improvements perhaps during the course of 292. Not only had he been adding to the height of his property, he had also put a window in a wall that belonged to Anicetus. So at the start of 293, Anicetus petitioned the emperor about the problem.

*CJ* 3.34.8: (Aniceto d. 1 Jan 293 Sirmium) Altius quidem aedificia tollere, si domus servitutem non debeat, dominus eius minime prohibetur. in pariete vero tuo si fenestram Iulianus vi vel clam fecisse convincatur, sumptibus suis opus tollere et integrum parietem restituere compellitur.

The owner of a house is not at all prohibited from raising buildings higher in fact, if the house has no servitude on it. But if Julianus is shown to have made a window in your wall either by force or in stealth, he is compelled to re-do the work at his own expense and to make good again the wall.

Zosimus had a similar problem.

> *CJ* 3.34.9 (Zosimo pp. 28 Dec/27 June 293 Sirmium) Si in aedibus vicini tibi debita servitute parietem altius aedificavit Heraclius, novum opus suis sumptibus per praesidem provinciae tollere compellitur. sed si te servitutem habuisse non probetur, tollendi altius aedificium vicino non est interdictum.

> If Heraclius built a wall higher than the servitude owed to you allows against the building of a neighbor, through the provincial governor he will be compelled to re-do the work at his own expense. But if it is not proven that you had a servitude, your neighbor is not prohibited from putting up a taller building.

The rescripts to Anicetus and Zosimus are strikingly similar. Both concern neighbors adding to the height of their properties. What distinguishes them is that in the first, Anicetus asked about his neighbor both raising the height of his building and knocking a window into an adjoining wall (presumably in a garden, rather than a house, though the latter is not impossible), while in the second, Zosimus inquired only about the first issue. Given the overlap between the two entries, the inclusion of the rescript to Zosimus proves that the *scrinium* was not averse to responding to petitions that could be addressed wholly or in part with answers that had been given to other petitions, and they may have done so frequently. The rescripts to Anicetus and Zosimus are dated about six months apart, and there were surely many other urban dwellers whose neighbors were undertaking building work. It also shows that the compilers first of the *CH* and then the *CJ* were not so concerned with economy that they could not tolerate repetition in their codes. The entry to Zosimus may have been included to instruct the reader that applications to have a neighbor remove unauthorized work should be made through the provincial governor and to advise him (or her) that a servitude could specify either that no increase to the height of a building was permitted or that the increase was limited to a specific measurement.

The rescript also demonstrates that rescripts were one element in the process of legal self-education that litigants needed to undertake. Anicetus and Zosimus may have had some vague familiarity with the concept of servitudes before they petitioned. Based on the recognition that some property owners could add to their properties while others could not, they petitioned the emperor. Upon receipt of their rescripts, they needed to discover whether there were servitudes on their neighbors' property and what effect those had. They needed to find out where they could view documents of purchase for those properties and then how to incorporate what they found into a case. Finally they needed advice on how to present their cases to their neighbors and, if necessary, how to initiate trial proceedings. Sending a petition and receiving a response were two stages in the process of navigating through social institutions, administrative procedures, and the judicial system. At each stage, the petitioner and potential litigant needed to learn how to move to the next stage. Anyone purchasing property or borrowing money for the first time can attest that the learning curve is very steep, and timely acquisition of the right knowledge is essential for moving forward to a successful conclusion. Though time-consuming, petitioners' self-education in law and legal procedure in an area important to them was a lifelong investment.

Individuals also petitioned to encourage opponents to desist, an important goal given that intimidation may have been common in property disputes. In Pompeii, at least, we believe neighborhoods contained a mix of commercial and residential space for a range of incomes.[34] Anicetus and Zosimus may have been inferior in status to Julianus and Heraclius and therefore used the rescript system to find out what action they needed to take in order to have their neighbors' work stopped or removed. They may also have used the responses to humiliate publicly their neighbors. We see here once again the importance on a local scale of publishing rescripts. Those from the imperial court protected petitioners not only against soldiers and over-exacting officials but against private individuals who were not necessarily powerful in the eyes of the court, but were enough of a threat in the eyes of petitioners that they were driven to seek justice through petitioning. Julianus and Heraclius may not have been of senatorial or even equestrian rank, but their rank relative to that of Anicetus and Zosimus in a hierarchy of prestige may have been higher. Intimidation needs only a small difference in rank, along with an intention to bully, to be effective, and a society that functions in this way adds to it.

Status depends on local conditions, on how others around you compare you to themselves. If you live in a small town, tens of miles from the nearest city, you may live in a fairly homogeneous population. The criteria according to which others grant you high or low status may be different from those by which inhabitants of the cosmopolitan city would judge you. The small town "big man," a moderately wealthy equestrian from a family enfranchised in 212, would have seemed inferior to a city bigwig, a senator or equestrian from a long enfranchised family with plenty of old money, but could still intimidate those around him. Petitioners, especially those who were before the law, regarded themselves as needing to use the rescript system simply because they were vulnerable to the depredations of another or ignorant of how best to look after their interests. They did not define themselves by their income or profession, and the imperial court did not limit their access to the system according to either criterion. Even the lowliest of imperial subjects could petition.

What is remarkable about the rescripts concerning status is the extent to which a person's servile status was unknown or could be hidden. The following entry provides an example of ignorance of background that reflects the degree to which slaves' parentage within a household could be uncertain.[35]

> CJ 7.16.22 (Pardaleae d. 27 Nov 293) Parentes natales, non confessio adsignat. quapropter si ex ancilla nata post ad libertatem manumissa pervenisti, te velut ex altera natam ancilla servam professa quaesitam manumissione libertatem huiusmodi simulatione vel errore amittere minime potuisti, cum servi nascantur ratione certa, non confessione constituantur.

> Birth parents, not a public statement, provide the designation. Wherefore, if born of a slave girl afterwards you were manumitted and obtained freedom, having acknowledged that you were born of another slave girl, the liberty you sought by manumission you cannot at all lose by a false claim of this sort or by error, since people are born slaves by certain rules, they are not constituted as such by a public statement.

Pardalea had been born a slave in a household; this much she knew. Her manumission seems to have been contested, and in the course of her successful defense, she had named a particular member of her former household as her mother. But she subsequently realized that the person she had named had not borne her and so declared publicly the identity of her real mother. (Possibly Pardalea had falsely claimed birth from the wrong woman so as to claim her freedom illegally.) Afraid that her freedom was now in jeopardy, she petitioned the emperor. The rescript she received reassured her that because her former slave status and subsequent manumission were based on certain legal rules and concepts, not on the identity of her mother, she remained free.

Pardalea's uncertainty about her parentage could have arisen from a deliberate policy of separating family groups within her household, probably not a rare occurrence.[36] Keeping children from parents reduced the likelihood that children would know their family history or indeed how they had come into the household—whether through birth or purchase. It would also destroy ties to a birth family and increase loyalty to the larger household. Given a lack of information about their background, many others working in households, either in a private house or a business owned by the master, possibly did not know their true status, since they had been separated from their birth parents and, in urban settings, slaves and the poor free often worked alongside each other, performing similar duties. For example, in a rescript to Diogenia, we find that she was kept as a slave but then discovered that she was free.[37] While status was clearly delineated in Roman law and literature, the reality was less clear-cut on the ground.

Members of the *scrinium* were aware of the problem and were willing to answer petitions from people who were, at least in the eyes of some, slaves. Their willingness was based on the premise that the petitioner might in fact be free, and it illustrates once again their concern for justice, by giving petitioners the opportunity to have their cases heard, and for law, by making sure that the *rationes* by which people were free or slaves were also seen to be upheld in court. Their responses, in helping to ensure that the free remained free and slaves remained slaves, preserved equity in society. Each person got what he or she deserved according to the law, no more, no less. Their willingness also reflects the concern of the free population that they not be mistaken for slaves.

That concern is reflected in rescripts whose wording seems to reflect a desperate tone—unsurprising among those who placed themselves before the law—in the petitions they answered. For example, Reginus had petitioned about his brothers who, like him, had been born free (so he claimed). This was the response he received.

*CJ* 7.16.17 (Regino s. 23 May 293) Multis rationibus natalibus ingenuis fratribus natis, post delictis vel casibus intervenientibus singulorum causae status separantur. Nihil itaque prohibet eundem et tibi non movere quaestionem et eos, quos fratres tuos adseveras, in servitutem vindicare sive retinere. Igitur ad demonstrandam fratrum tuorum libertatem aliae sunt probationes necessariae: nam quod tibi non movetur quaestio libertatis, eorum non idoneam constat habere probationem.

For many reasons associated with their birth, though your brothers were born free, after private wrongdoings or accidents may have threatened their free birth, so the defense of each one's status is conducted separately. Therefore, nothing prevents the same investigation being brought as to whether those you assert are your brothers should be released from or kept in servitude. Thus different proofs are required to demonstrate the free status of your brothers: for just because an investigation of liberty is not moved against you, so it is agreed that they cannot show proof on that basis.

Though presumably born to the same parents and under the same circumstances, his brothers had subsequently faced threats to their status because of *delictis vel casibus*. This phrase is probably a summary of incidents that Reginus had described in his petition and therefore does not allow us to understand what exactly could have happened to undermine something as important and fundamental as the brothers' status. Nevertheless, the things that happened to them were the result either of willful wrongdoing (perhaps they were held against their will or were kidnapped) or accidents (the brothers may have been the victims of mistaken identity). The different situations of Reginus and his brothers may have come about because of early separation of the family; alternatively, Reginus's brothers may have left home as adults for work and then suffered from accidents or others' wrongdoing.

Several phrases in this rescript suggest that the imperial court was trying hard to help Reginus and his family. The first I have already discussed: *delictis vel casibus*. The use of the disjunctive conjunction *vel* indicates that Reginus had not been entirely clear in his petition. Therefore, the author(s) of the rescript seem to be confirming that whatever had happened to the brothers, whether intentionally or by accident, needed to be brought before a court in the *quaestio status*. But by suggesting the two alternatives, they were perhaps also proposing that the brothers' case would be strengthened by defining the nature of what had happened to them. Inclusion of the opening phrase *multis rationibus natalibus ingenuis fratribus natis* suggests that even if Reginus had already explained their birth status, nevertheless the court was urging him and his brothers to provide full evidence for their freeborn status.

Behind each of these phrases is an assumption of legal knowledge. Reginus's brothers needed to show why they were free (though it seems that they may have done so already) and why the incidents or accidents that had happened to them could not affect their status. They probably also needed to show that they had not entered willingly into a state of servitude. Each area of their case needed to be argued on the basis of careful presentation of the facts, as well as an understanding of the legal concepts behind them and the arguments that could be made on the basis of them. The court pointed Reginus and his brothers in the right direction; it was now up to them either to show the rescript to the brothers' opponents or to hire legal help to put together a defense. The provider of that help might also need the rescript. The less money a petitioner had to spend on legal counsel, the more that counsel might benefit from the legal direction of a rescript.[38]

The following rescript illustrates the problems of extricating oneself from wrongful servitude.

> *CJ* 7.14.5 (Crescenti d. 4 Apr 293) Defamari statum ingenuorum seu errore seu malignitate quorundam periniquum est, praesertim cum adfirmes diu praesidem unum atque alterum interpellatum a te vocitasse diversam partem, ut contradictionem faceret, si defensionibus suis confideret. unde constat merito rectorem provinciae commotum adlegationibus tuis sententiam dedisse, ne de cetero inquietudinem sustineres. si igitur adhuc diversa pars perseverat in eadem obstinatione, aditus praeses provinciae ab iniuria temperari praecipiet.

> It is very unjust for the status of certain free persons to be defamed either through error or from malice, especially since you claim that a long while ago the governor had called the other party summoned once and again by you, so that he might make an opposing claim, if he trusted in what he gave as a defense. Wherefore it is held that the rector of the province, moved by your allegations, had rightly given his judgment that you should not suffer aggravation concerning anything else. Therefore if the other party still perseveres in his stubbornness, approach the provincial governor who will order that you be shielded from harm.

The governor had confirmed Crescens's liberty after his status had been investigated, but his liberty was again being called into question. Several things are of interest in this entry. The use of the technical terms *defamari, inquietudinem,* and *iniuria* remind us of the need for legal knowledge and the role of rescripts in providing knowledge to recipients, their legal advisers, and the courts. The inclusion of the word *diu* is striking: with it, the *scrinium* acknowledges that Crescens's troubles have lasted a long time and with the words *periniquum* and *commotum* and the phrases *unum atque alterum* and *perseverat in eadem obstinatione* places itself in sympathy with his suffering and in opposition to his persecutor. The sympathetic coloring of these words reminds us of the humanity of the *scrinium,* of the recognition that petitioners' problems were real and often grave, and of the importance to the *scrinium* (and presumably to the emperor also) of justice as well as the law.

While the court offered information, guidance, and even sympathy to Reginus and Crescens, it could not help all petitioners. The following rescript is an example of the tragedy of lack of resolution for the deceased in matters of status.

> *CJ* 7.16.13 (Antistiae d. 27 Apr 293) Principaliter de statu defuncti agi non potest. si vero ex peculio quondam eius, quem tibi bona reliquisse commemoras, res vindicentur vel eius filiis moveatur status quaestio, haec omnia sollemniter praesidali notione decidi debent.

> It is not possible for there to be a trial concerning chiefly the status of someone deceased. If truly property is being claimed from the *peculium* of the deceased, whom you mention had left the items to you, or if an investigation into status is being brought against his sons, all these things should be decided in the proper manner by means of an examination by the provincial governor.

Antistia claimed that she had been made a beneficiary of a slave's *peculium.* But her claim was met with opposition. To make matters worse, the slave's offspring were now the subject of an investigation into status. The opening statement of the rescript seems to suggest that an investigation could not be held, a statement that is explained by the title of *CJ.*7.21: *Ne de statu defunctorum post quinquennium quaeratur.* The slave must have been dead for more than five years for the rescript to make sense. The word *principaliter* announces that this is the crux of the matter. We now realize that Antistia had either found out about her inheritance very late or that she had been struggling to claim her inheritance for so long that she was now unable to do so.

It is possible that the slave, tragically, had been free all along. He had never enjoyed freedom, nor would his sons be able to give him in death the free status he should have had while alive. Perhaps wise to this, the author of the rescript told Antistia that the issue of her inheritance and the slave's status (as well as the possibility of an investigation) should be decided *sollemniter*. The author of the rescript, in view of the situation Antistia faced, was careful to point out that the matter should be resolved in the right way before the provincial governor.

One wonders how the deceased man, if he really had been free, could have been taken for a slave. There are several examples among the rescripts of inquiries about the circumstances under which someone could become a slave, such as the following to Stratius.

> CJ 7.16.10 (Stratio d. 293) Liberos privatis pactis vel actus quacumque administrati ratione non posse mutata condicione servos fieri certi iuris est.

> It is certainly the case in law that free persons by private agreements or by some administrative undertaking cannot become slaves, their condition changed.

This rescript is a response to a petition that asked about the circumstances under which a free person (not a freedman, as was the situation in the rescript to Paulus) could become a slave. The answer was that there were none. (Given the brevity of this and the following rescript, it is likely that these texts have been edited from more complex responses.) Despite this blanket ban, which we might imagine would be well-known, Dionysia received this response:

> CJ 2.4.26 (Dionysiadae s. 13 Apr 294) Transactione matris filios eius non posse servos fieri notissimi iuris est.

> It is absolutely well-known in law that sons cannot become slaves by the transaction of their mother.

If Dionysia is the mother referred to in the rescript, then she seems to have inquired whether she could sell her son to someone as a slave.[39] This rescript may reveal a sad situation: Dionysia may have been so poor that she felt compelled to sell him. If this is the case, then we may have evidence that the rescript system was indeed open to a wide range of people, even those poor enough to be in such a desperate situation, and that it was a system that required little or no money to use. Dionysia stood to gain from the transition—and perhaps she justified her decision by believing that her son would also. Those in penury suffered lack of shelter and food, perhaps to the point of starvation; slaves, however, could expect shelter and food, even if meager, because they were too expensive to let starve. Alternatively, Dionysia simply wanted to make money by selling her offspring. In this case, we may have an instance of the parental detachment that is thought by some to have been more widespread in the ancient world than today.[40] (It is also possible that Dionysia was the purchaser of the son, who, doubting that the transaction was legal, was concerned that she could be cheated out of the purchase.)

Since the abolition of *nexum* (debt bondage) by the *lex Poetilia Papiria* in 326 BC, free men had not been allowed to become slaves, even voluntarily. But there was one situation in which a free person could be held in something akin to slavery. Romans held captive by barbarians in *barbaricum* were often ransomed by brokers, who brought them back to Roman territory. Until a prisoner paid back the amount of the ransom, he or she was bound to the broker in a form of servitude—rescripts on the subject are careful to point out that it is not servitude, but rather a state like it. The imperial court was therefore concerned that former prisoners held by brokers not be mistreated. For example, they could not be prostituted.

The law surrounding ransoming is complex, but the following example will demonstrate some of the myriad problems that arose from captivity.[41] A rescript to Julianus concerns the property he left behind when he was taken prisoner.

> *CJ* 3.32.24 (Iuliano d. 16 Nov 294) Nullo iusto titulo praecedente possidentes ratio iuris quaerere prohibet dominium. idcirco cum etiam usucapio cesset, intentio dominii non absumitur: unde hoc casu postliminio reverso citra beneficium actionis rescissoriae directa permanet integra vindicatio.

> With no just title coming first, the rule of law prohibits those in possession from seeking ownership. For this reason, although ownership by long-term possession may cease, the intention of ownership is not taken

away: wherefore with this situation having been reversed through *postliminium,* your direct claim remains whole, without the need for an action of rescindment.

Julianus had returned from captivity, presumably by rescue, escape, or ransom. If it was the latter (and this seems to have been the most common method of return), he had paid back the ransom only to discover that his property had been taken from him. According to Roman law, a prisoner's status was in suspension while he was held captive by enemies. Upon his return, his rights remained. If he had been free upon captivity, he stayed free, and his property was still in his possession. Other relationships, however, had to be restated or reproven, such as marriage and possession.

Julianus found that someone else had taken possession of his property and was trying to claim ownership on the basis of *usucapio.* Despite his absence, Julianus had never intended to relinquish his ownership. Indeed, given that his absence was accidental and his status and relationships upon return were governed by the laws of *postliminium,* his claim for ownership remained valid. An *actio rescissoria,* which annulled the *usucapio* that had arisen as a result of the original owner's captivity, was not necessary. Julianus was lucky, though one might also have sympathy for the individual who thought Julianus might never return and so had claimed his property on the basis of *usucapio;* his claim would have been valid had it not been for Julianus's captivity. (It is more likely that the individual was simply an opportunist who grabbed the property in Julianus's forced absence.) In an age when ownership was poorly documented, possession and subsequent *usucapio* may have been common. Those who lacked a secure title to their property or were squatting faced everyday the danger of eviction.

Invasions and uprisings, which were responsible for Julianus's troubles, created insecurity in people's daily lives, as the following example illustrates:

*CJ* 7.14.4 (Agrippae s. 10 Jan/29 Dec 293) Cum cognatum tuum ingenuum, factum Palmyrene factionis dominatione velut captivum, distractum esse dicas, praeses provinciae ingenuitatis suae reddi eum efficiet.

Since you say that your free born kinsman was torn away, made akin to a captive by the tyranny of a Palmyrene faction, the provincial governor will see to it that he is returned to his free birth.

The uprising in Palmyra, an attempt by Zenobia and her son Vaballathus at self-rule, met with defeat at the hands of Aurelian and his army at Emesa in 272; a second uprising precipitated the destruction of the city of Palmyra. Diocletian's subsequent concern with local defenses may have been the result of further unrest, during which Agrippa's relative was probably captured.[42]

This rescript illustrates a major danger of captivity: others might assume the returning captive had lost his freedom not only physically through captivity but also in law, and therefore try to claim him as a slave. This was the danger faced by the kinsman of Agrippa, who petitioned the court on his behalf. The response from the *scrinium* was that the laws on *postliminium* were applicable, and therefore the kinsman retained his status. This finding is somewhat surprising when one considers that *postliminium* was operable only when someone had been taken by a foreign enemy, *hostis*, not a domestic bandit. The Palmryene uprising took place within the empire and was fomented by Roman citizens, who should not therefore have been considered *hostes*; consequently *postliminium* should not have applied. But it seems that the uprising was considered more as a barbarian incursion than an internal dispute, and therefore the kinsman was *velut captivus*. Inclusion of *velut* makes it clear that the court knew the decision was not strictly in accordance with the laws, but it was a decision borne of a sense of justice—and probably political pressure too.

### "Against the Law"

In the third category are individuals for whom law was an unwelcome intrusion and who petitioned the emperor to find out their best course of action in their struggle *against the law.*

A rescript to participant in the olive oil trade, Antonia, demonstrates that the oil trade was cutthroat and that rescripts were valuable to more vulnerable traders.

> *CJ* 4.65.21 (Antoniae d. 8 Oct 293 Sirmium) Si olei certa ponderatione fructus anni locasti, de contractu bonae fidei habito propter hoc solum, quod alter maiorem obtulit ponderationem, recedi non oportet.

> If you rented out a year's harvest for a certain weight of oil, there should not be a withdrawal from the contract held in good faith, on account of this fact alone, that another person offered a greater weight (of oil).

Having entered into a contract, Antonia now wished to break it so as to receive a greater quantity of oil from someone else, who presumably had been carefully monitoring the potential harvest. At first sight, we might be surprised at Antonia's ignorance and gall. Surely she should have realized that a contract once undertaken could not be broken in this way.[43] But there were circumstances under which a contract could be broken: if both parties were willing, one could leave the agreement, providing no other legal situation was affected.[44] Antonia might not have been certain that she had terminated her contract contrary to law, but she was willing to take her chance with a petition. She had nothing to lose, whereas bringing a case to court and losing it would have cost her in penalties.

The rescript was important to the Roman government. It would be surprising if this was the first time someone had tried such a trick, but for Justinian's compilers at least, Antonia's rescript may have been the clearest statement of the principle that declared predatory contract offers illegal grounds for withdrawal. The court's ruling was important for maintaining order in trade, which would otherwise be seriously disrupted in fruitful years by attempts to double-sell—undertake to sell to one buyer and then, as the values of goods rise, sell to a second buyer instead—and perhaps also in barren years by threats to withdraw from unprofitable contracts.

Two more unscrupulous Romans appear in the next rescript.

*CJ* 1.18.9 (Gaio et Anthemio d. 8 Dec 294) Non idcirco minus, quod a vobis velut a liberis debitam accepisse pecuniam Samus dicitur, cum nullus sit errantis consensus, movere status quaestionem prohibentur eius heredes.

Even though Samus is said to have received the money borrowed by you as if from free people, since one who is in error is not in a position to agree, his heirs are no less prohibited from initiating an investigation into your status.

Gaius and Anthemius had borrowed money from an unnamed party in order to settle a debt with Samus incurred through either a loan or purchase. They presumably claimed that Samus did not realize that they were not free people—slaves were not allowed to borrow money from someone who was not their master as if free. Samus's heirs, suspecting that the pair were not free, had decided to begin a trial to investigate their status. The reasons for the heirs' decision, aside perhaps from public spiritedness, were surely financial, though this is not stated. Perhaps Gaius and Anthemius had not paid back the full amount with the correct interest.

The complexity of their financial arrangements suggests that Gaius and Anthemius were engaged in business, perhaps as traders. Though they had managed to fool both Samus and the other unnamed lender into believing that they were free, Samus's heirs were sufficiently suspicious to initiate proceedings against them. Local knowledge is the most likely source for their suspicions. They may have been informed by someone in the area similarly cheated by the pair, or they may have investigated the men's origins. The fact that Gaius and Anthemius were operating as partners was probably their undoing. Perhaps they were related or had belonged to the same household and escaped together, and were therefore more noticeable as a pair than if they had left the area and separated.

Surprisingly, this entry implies that Gaius and Anthemius had admitted to being slaves. The burden of proof in an investigation of status would fall on Samus's heirs. Gaius and Anthemius may have been confident that since Samus had not realized they were slaves and perhaps therefore had seen or heard nothing to suggest otherwise, his heirs would be unable to adduce any firm evidence. Therefore, they were confident that even with their admission, the heirs' legal action would be unsuccessful. They placed themselves firmly against the law, seeing it as something that thwarted their plans. What is remarkable about Gaius and Anthemius's situation is that they petitioned (perhaps they were hoping to intimidate their opponent by the simple act of petitioning), but their plan backfired. The heirs remained suspicious and might have been able to bring witnesses from the slaves' household or some other evidence as to their servile status. Moreover, publication of the rescript may have attracted attention to the slaves' case and encouraged others to furnish the heirs with the evidence they needed.

Despite their admission and their resulting inadvertent confession to a wrongdoing, Gaius and Anthemius, like Bithus, still received a response. And therefore, aside from the human interest in the story it tells, this rescript is important as an illustration of the court's concern for proper procedure in answering the slaves' legal inquiry and concern for the law in putting together an answer for two men who had unwittingly revealed themselves to be slaves. It is also interesting for considering how petitioning worked within a community. If the players in this story lived in the same area, one must imagine that Gaius and Anthemius petitioned and waited for their response amid increasing public awareness of their status.[45]

Another petitioner whose rescript suggests that he may have admitted his servile status (and was therefore by default acting against the law) was Philoserapis.

> *CJ* 7.16.38 (Philoserapi d. 17 Dec 294 Nicomedia) Non idcirco minus, quod te limenarcha creato nemo contradixit, rei publicae nomine moveri tibi status quaestio potest.

> Although when you were made harbor-master no one objected, an investigation into your status in the name of the state is no less able to be undertaken against you.[46]

Philoserapis may have been free and hoped to use the lack of opposition at the time of his appointment in his defense. Alternatively, he was a slave who hoped that the absence of opposition indicated that there was no evidence against him and he could therefore continue to hide. Perhaps he was hoping that his appointment to public office with the approval of the community rendered him free.[47] If this were true, this rescript would be a good example of the degree of some petitioners' ignorance.

The burden of proof was on the state, as Philoserapis may have acknowledged in his petition or as the rescript may have explained in a section that has not been preserved. It is possible, however, that it was not mentioned, leaving Philoserapis unaware that the burden of proof was not on him. Petitioners needed to ensure that they asked all the questions to which they did not know the answers.

If Philoserapis were a slave, he had perhaps escaped from his master to an area where he could pass himself off as free and become harbor master. Individuals who lived as free persons but whose status was challenged were considered as free during the course of proceedings.[48] But those being held as slaves and challenging their servility probably did not enjoy such protection in practice. A master (or mistress), upon hearing of a slave's intention to petition, could restrict the slave's movements, intimidate witnesses who might appear for the slave, and even destroy evidence.

What comes out in both of these rescripts is a determination on the part of the petitioner(s) to act out of pure self-interest, even to the detriment of others. The following rescript provides a sobering example of the harmful selfishness of some acting against the law.

> *CJ* 7.16.37 (Olympio before 17 Dec 294) Si filium tuum liberum genero ven-
> didisti, qui tam proxima necessitudine coniunctus condicionis ignorantiam
> simulare non potest, utrisque sociis criminis accusator deest.

> If you sold your free son to your son-in-law, who being bound in very much
> the closest relationship is unable to feign ignorance of the son's condition,
> the plaintiff of the charge is missing for you both.

Olympius seems to have been trying to sell his freeborn son to his son-in-law. The son could not have been borne by an *ancilla,* as he would have been a slave. This was a freeborn son and, as the rescript tells us, the son-in-law was not able to pretend to be unaware of his condition. It seems that the son-in-law, unable to continue the charade any longer, may have returned the son because, once he had done so, as the final phrase of the rescript indicates, no one could act as a plaintiff against either man. Olympius was concerned that he could be taken to court by someone who had known of his intentions, but it seems that any wrongdoing was negated by the fact that the son had been restored.

Rescripts such as this reveal terrible situations. We cannot help but wonder what Olympius's son made of his circumstances. It is possible that Olympius needed money, while his son-in-law needed help on his land or in his house, and therefore selling a son made practical sense. But legally it deprived the son (who was presumably underage given the absence of any mention of his opposition) of self-determination until he either initiated a *quaestio status,* was manumitted by his brother-in-law, or died. The son-in-law's change of heart ended the wrongdoing and therefore deprived the *accusator* of a case, though publication of the rescript would have advertised what had happened to the local community. The *accusator* must have been a concerned member of that community, perhaps even the family, who had indicated his intention to bring the matter to court. It is heartening to find, amid examples of sad situations, that the members of the *scrinium* were not alone in wanting to uphold justice. There were many others in society (perhaps like Paulus) with concern for what was right.

The cases discussed in this chapter have gone some way toward demonstrating the range of topics represented among the extant rescripts. Every one of these cases is real—Sisola really did lose her cow, Bithus prostituted his wife, and Egus Crispinus was cheated with inferior wine. These cases are not the stuff of grand history, but they are brief snapshots into the real lives of ordinary Romans. I could have included many more cases; indeed, no two cases are exactly the same, since rescripts, though perhaps kept by Hermogenian for a myriad of reasons, illustrated different legal principles. What is common to all of the rescripts, however, is that their recipients suffered legal problems. And while it is true that few Romans suffered *exactly* the problem encountered by Sisola, for example, it is not the case that the recipients of rescripts extant from 293–294 were unusual individuals who suffered from bizarrely unusual problems. Certainly for the *CJ,* perhaps the *CH* also, clearly expressed rescripts that would be useful to provincial officials and lawyers were preserved, and therefore the hundreds of recipients who received these extant rescripts were suffering the *sorts* of problems that were known to have been suffered by very many others in the empire. Moreover, the recipients I have discussed in this chapter are not unusual in suffering legal problems, since law is at the heart of all relationships in society. It enables and restricts the behavior of one person marrying or divorcing another, bequeathing to or inheriting from another, buying from or selling property to another, leasing to or hiring from another goods and services. In short, Romans belonged to families, lived in property, and earned income, and all of these activities were carried out according to and on the basis of law.[49]

For all petitioners, writing and receiving a response made their problems real in the eyes of the state and therefore necessary to take seriously.[50] Petitioners wanted their problems to be written into a document and to receive a response that disciplined their situation into law, because in a legal form their problems would have more weight in the eyes of their opponents, communities, and most importantly the courts.[51] A legal form would also give petitioners and their problems a sense of identity and importance (which would have been increased if they had known that their problems would become part of a legal code and their names would remain). Rescripts normalized petitioners' problems and thus suggested a solution or means of progress within legal institutions and processes. Sally Engle Merry, who has analyzed legal consciousness among working-class Americans, has observed that this normalization was largely achieved by turning petitioners' situations from "hot" problems to "cold" cases, by removing much of the emotion, hearsay, rumor, and back story (in some situations the long periods of simmering tension punctuated by moments of intensity), and reducing it to a frame comprised simply of action, shorn of legally irrelevant detail, to which law could be applied.[52]

A favorable rescript could increase a petitioner's status in the eyes of an opponent and perhaps the local community, and might counteract the daunting nature of the experience of handing in a petition to the *scrinium*.[53] Though the court and its emperor and indeed the law itself may have been intimidating to petitioners, yet the rescript system may also be seen as falling into a system of village law comprising small local courts, arbitration, and mediation, a system that was popular and accessible to many (as is the case in some non-Western communities today).[54] This is especially true considering that petitioning at the imperial level was probably similar to petitioning at the provincial level, a practice more familiar to Romans.[55] Dieter Nörr notes that petitioning a local official was far more common than petitioning the emperor; the latter was something extraordinary and complicated. While the petitioners in this chapter did not suffer strikingly unusual problems, they themselves were unusual by virtue of the fact that they petitioned the emperor. Most individuals lacked the opportunity, know-how, or courage to do so.

I have emphasized in this chapter the aid that rescripts could give to petitioners. But the help given by the imperial court to those suffering legal problems should not be overstated. Unlike provincial governors' annual assizes, the administration of justice and the production of rescripts was not the purpose of Diocletian's journey through the lower Danube provinces in AD 293–294. Indeed, looking at the stages in petition and response, we have seen that each was set up in such a way that inconvenienced the petitioner more than the *scrinium*. Moreover, the answers that petitioners received, while containing information and vocabulary that aided and informed, did not have the clarity of a textbook and could respond only to the petition as it was set out, not to the problem as it could be expressed from the mouth of the petitioner.[56] (This is an unfortunate consequence of the normalization and objectification of people's problems into petitions.)

Then again rescripts did not, from the point of view of the *scrinium*, need to have accompanying detail. Every rule in a legal system has a message of substance and a message of jurisdiction.[57] Rescripts state a legal principle and sometimes brief explanatory material. Likewise, a legal system needs no more than a statement of rules; it does not need to explain a rule's rationale (e.g., for murder) or its consequences for society, or for the accused in particular.[58] Indeed some rescripts, as we now have them in inscriptions and papyri, give only bald directions: "approach the provincial governor."

On a superficial level, petitioners petitioned because they could and members of the *scrinium* answered them because they were paid to do so. But there are less prosaic reasons for the writing of rescripts: they followed tradition, upheld the laws, and supported the sense of justice shared by the emperor, *scrinium,* and people. Petitioners asked the emperor (really the *scrinium*) to rule on a situation because they hoped to gain an advantage over their current situation and perhaps because they believed that law is a reflection of the ideal ordering of society, one in which their interests were looked after as much as anyone else's, and a rescript would bring their situation into that ideal state. It makes little sense for people to use a system which they know is corrupt and will work against them, if they do not have the means to make it work for them. Roman law did, on the whole, reflect society in its ideal state and society in turn accepted it; there was little opposition to Roman laws.[59] Though law could not rule on every situation imaginable, it did contain precepts that could be equitably applied to new situations, and thus situations that seemed unfair and contradicted the social order could be stopped within the law by means of equitable rescripts.

Rescripts based on an equitable interpretation of the law balanced the need to uphold reasonable standards of justice acceptable to society with the ideal of a rule of law.[60] Rescripts were produced to respond to specific individuals' situations, though they had some weight in others' situations too. They were preserved because they did not contradict Justinianic law, they adhered to standard legal precepts, and as equitable remedies they were acceptable, were not outlandish, and conformed to existing legal precepts, or proposed acceptable equitable remedies.

The petitions were a vibrant source of material with which the court could refine the law, and the resulting rescripts have provided a rich seam of material for historians to mine. In the next chapter, I shall show how the production of rescripts provided opportunities for connection and interaction between the ordinary person and the state.

# FIVE

# The Emperor and His Petitioners

In chapter 2, I claimed that Diocletian did not answer his subjects' petitions himself; in this chapter I want to suggest that he employed highly skilled officials to carry out the task, not simply to save him time and trouble but also to bolster his self-presentation. Literary and art-historical evidence, as well as the surviving rescripts of AD 293–294, suggest that the system of petition and response benefited emperors as well as their subjects. The needs of their subjects, the expertise of their officials, and their own imprimatur produced a system that presented emperors as authoritative but also accessible and responsive to individuals in need, no matter how humble they were, and as the supreme source of justice. The nexus of relationships between emperors, officials, and subjects produced by petition and response shows that the administration of the Roman Empire was a more collaborative enterprise than historians have previously proposed, and that the political importance of the co-dependent relationship between emperors and the middling sort has been underestimated or neglected.

Close examination of just a few of the rescripts extant from AD 293–294 has demonstrated that rescripts can offer a wealth of information about the lives of ordinary Romans in the Balkans under the Tetrarchy. It is possible that some of this information could be valid for other times and places in the empire. Of course, it is also possible that the Tetrarchic period may have been exceptional. It was a time of multiple emperors who traveled extensively around their provinces. Yet the general framework of petition and response and, as I shall show, the reasons for maintaining it were the same as they had been in earlier times. Moreover, the problems it dealt with and the makeup of the people who used it are unlikely to have been significantly different from those of earlier times.

In this final chapter, I shall argue that the system of petition and response offered political benefits to Diocletian, as well as to other Roman emperors and to rulers before and after the Roman period. I also claim that the system gave members of the middling sort influence in the creation and administration of Roman law, though this was never an imperial policy. This final chapter explores the nature of that influence and its manifestation in the relationships between non-elites, officials, and emperors.

## Petitioners in Need: The New Understanding of Poverty

At the beginning of this study, we saw that the Roman system of petition and response may have had its roots in Near Eastern conceptions of rulers' duties as including a commitment to protect the legal interests of their most vulnerable subjects. Hammurabi was concerned especially to look after the weak, widows, and orphans. Rekhmire, the Egyptian vizier, claimed to help the insignificant, the weak, widows, orphans, and those without food or clothing. What is striking about the categories of needy people is that only some of them—those lacking food or clothing—suffered poverty. The term weak does not necessarily denote someone in dire financial straits, and widows and orphans could be rich or poor (though usually poor). So Hammurabi and Rekhmire were claiming to help those who suffered from some sort of vulnerability, not necessarily financial, that prevented them from receiving the justice they deserved from the normal functioning of the judicial system. To understand poverty as vulnerability is, I think, the key to understanding who the petitioners were and why they were helped.

When I began work on the subject of petitioning, I wanted to construct profiles of typical petitioners who needed help in the Roman justice system. To do so, I considered analyzing petitioners on the basis of wealth from income or property, occupation, education, standing in the local community, gender, and marital status, but realized that this was an unproductive approach. As far as wealth was concerned, I decided that the very poorest people in society were unlikely to use it. They probably lacked the knowledge, means, and opportunity to use legal processes to solve their problems. The very wealthiest people—the top of the curial class in large and affluent places, equestrians, and senators—did not on the whole need to use it, though of course they may have availed themselves of it.[1] This leaves the middling sort, encompassing everyone from people just above peasant status (i.e., not tied to the land they worked) to the lower reaches of the curial class.

The middling sort included such a wide range of people that none of the other factors—property, local standing, gender, marital status—predominates. We find among the petitioners the man employed in a small workshop alongside slaves, the widow subsisting on whatever was left of her husband's smallholding, a trader who cheated on a deal, a wife whose dowry was squandered by her husband, and a decurion householder literally overshadowed by his neighbor's building work. Their only shared characteristic is that they were overcome or cheated by an opponent they felt unable to persuade to settle or to defeat in court. Given the diversity of the petitioners who received the responses in 293–294—men and women, slaves and decurions, soldiers and traders—there seems little bias against any particular type of petitioner whose cause can be discerned. Petitioners were united simply by their vulnerability and once they had petitioned, their chances of receiving an answer seem to have been based largely on whether the petition contained a legal question or problem that could be addressed.[2] (The possibility of discrimination on the basis of legal status cannot be discounted.)

Scholars have recently become interested in members of society who perceive themselves as vulnerable and in need of help.[3] Peter Brown describes them as "poor" because "in the Near Eastern model of society, the 'poor' were a judicial, not an economic, category. They were plaintiffs, not beggars."[4] A "poor" person might beg for money because he had less than nearly everyone else and was unable to look after himself in his current situation through no fault of his own. Likewise, a "poor" person might beg (or petition) for legal help because he had less purchase on the judicial system than did his opponent and was unable to gain justice for himself given his inferiority to his opponent in terms of wealth, local standing (lack of property), gender, and marital status, again through no fault of his own. He had no one to protect him against his opponent or against the biases inherent in the system of legal administration except its ultimate authority, the emperor. "The pauper was a person with a claim upon the great,"[5] and the great were expected to respond.

If poverty is in the eye of the beholder, and the beholder is someone who receives many petitions each day from "poor" people, the petitioner must determine which aspect of his or her situation is the most deserving of pity. So the Skaptopareni dwelled on the privations they suffered to their land and claimed that they had suffered so grievously for so long that they might have to move, unless the emperor could help them.[6] Another "poor" petitioner was Lollianus, a salaried grammarian living in Egypt in the AD 250s. Though he could not complain of total poverty, he had the eloquence to present himself well in his struggle with the local authorities to increase his salary. He elicited the emperor's pity by describing himself lacking τὰ πρὸς τὸν βίον χρ[ε]ιώδη, things necessary for life, and thus being unable to teach the local children. In an accompanying letter to a friend who has access to the court, he mentions that his salary is paid ἐν ὄξεσιν ἀγτὶ οἴνων καὶ σίτοις σητ[ο]κόποις, "in sour wine and worm-eaten grain,"[7] details which he probably hoped would be passed on to the *scrinium* that received his petition. Despite his claims, Lollianus was not destitute and was unlikely to be economically the poorest person in Oxyrhynchus. Poverty is a subjective concept with many possible determinants.

Vulnerability was the determinant of poverty among petitioners rather than lack of money or social rank because these criteria may have been hard to enforce. Nor may they have been important to the imperial court, which strove to help those who had identified themselves as needing it (rather than simply legally curious and wealthy), so that the emperor could display his concern, magnanimity, accessibility, responsiveness, and authority.

## The Roles of the Emperor

Even if Diocletian's travels in AD 293–294 were not motivated by a desire to answer as many petitions as possible for a specific purpose, the fact that he had the *magister a libellis* traveling with him, who answered over 864 of them in two years at locations large and small, indicates at least that he was willing to answer his people's petitions as he traveled. We know from the *CG* that Diocletian was answering petitions on his other journeys before 293,[8] and the existence of rescripts from during and after 293–294 from locations in the West suggests that Maximian also answered petitions, and that he did so as he traveled.[9]

It appears that the rescript system was not unimportant to the Tetrarchy, though nowhere in our evidence is there any explanation from the Roman government as to why emperors answered petitions. But reasonable explanations can be given on the basis of the function of other types of imperial communication and on the advantages to the emperor's effective government and his self-presentation of answering petitions.

Rescripts were not the only communication concerning law to emanate from the imperial court.[10] There were also *edicta, decreta,* and *epistulae,* categorized as *constitutiones principis* by Gaius in his *Institutes* (1.5), which were sent to high-ranking provincial officials and contained legal initiatives to be implemented either in specified parts of the empire or empire-wide. Letters could also be written to lower-level officials offering guidance or a ruling on a legal inquiry. The compilation of rescripts, first in the tenure of Gregorian and then under Hermogenian, and codification of them in the reign of Justinian put them in the mold of the other types of constitution and confirmed their equal status with them. The purpose of compilation (as I claimed earlier) was to create a usable store of rescripts for officials, lawyers, and legal students. There was some precedent for legal compilations in the codification of the Praetor's Edict and in the *Sententiae et epistulae Hadriani,* a collection of Hadrianic legislation.[11] The first compilation of rescripts, produced by Papirius Justus in the third century, was unofficial; rescripts were also included in the later-named *Fragmenta Vaticana* of the fourth or fifth century and the fifth-century *Consultatio veteris cuiusdam iurisconsulti.* But the first officially ordained collection was the *Codex Gregorianus,* followed by the *Codex Hermogenianus.*

As we saw in the previous chapter, the *scrinium libellorum,* staffed by legal experts, demonstrated concern for justice and law in their responses to petitioners. Whether addressed to prefects, provincial governors, low-level magistrates, or even the man in the street, every constitution that made its way into a legal compilation contained a statement of law (with the recipient being of less long-term importance to the maintenance of justice and a coherent legal system than the principle stated in it). Compilation was undertaken not only to make life easier for lawyers defending lowly clients, magistrates acting as judges in the provinces, and imperial court officials who had to ensure the consistency of law in the Roman Empire (though rescripts did not have to prescribe to judges)[12], it was also done because constitutions, including rescripts, contained a lot of law that, it seems, must have been important for the Roman government. This law, much of which was actually composed by the experts of the *scrinium,* was written in the name of the emperor. Putting the emperor's name to rescripts meant that they were important enough to have his authorizing signature or stamp, and codifying them gave them a status equal to that of the other constitutions.

### THE POLITICIAN

Rescripts may have been used to implement emperors' political and judicial programs.[13] In the law codes we find clusters of constitutions belonging to one emperor that dealt with one subject. For example, Theodosius issued a series of edicts in the 410s and 420s allowing estate owners to erect fortifications and compelling absentee owners to cultivate their landholdings. And among the rescripts, we often find a string of entries on a legal issue that date to a single year or reign. For example, in *CJ* 7.16 concerning slavery, we find sixteen entries dating from AD 293, fifteen from 294; before those years, there are only seven in total. Similarly, *CJ* 2.4, *de transactionibus,* contains fifteen entries dating prior to AD 293, seven entries from 293, and fully seventeen entries from 294 alone. Other years seem to be represented by no more than about four entries in any one title. But it is important to remember that these clusters of entries may be an accident of the evidence following the compilation work of Gregorian and Hermogenian, rather than a reflection of a policy to enact legal reform on that issue, as there are proportionally many more entries for AD 293–294 than for other years.

Moreover, legal reform through rescripts would have been piecemeal and not reliably successful.[14] For example, so far as we are aware, a rescript was published only for a limited time in one location, and its content would have responded directly to only one petition. Therefore, individuals wishing to know Diocletian's policy on *quaestiones status,* for example, would have had to consult all rescripts published on that topic, though the places of publication would have ranged across the lower Danube provinces. Alternatively, they could have consulted the imperial archives, which in the case of Diocletian were most likely located at Sirmium. Concerned or interested magistrates were notified of new and relevant edicts, letters, and *mandata,* and in turn circulated copies of the texts among their ju-niors.[15] In the case of rescripts, however, magistrates would have had to join the general public at the archives, since rescripts were addressed only to their recipients and seem not to have been circulated among magistrates, creating an inefficient process for disseminating policy.[16]

Producing rescripts did not publicize legal reform as efficiently as did other forms of imperial correspondence, and the fact that multiple peti-tions and responses exist on the same topic indicates the problem. For example, the petition of the Skaptopareni, who complain about officials' excessive demands for quartering and provisions without payment, is only one of a number of petitions on the subject of intimidation by government officials and soldiers who requisitioned goods and supplies. The very fact that these petitions were written suggests that some code of behavior was regularly being violated. Indeed legislation dating to the reign of Tiberi-us had already once addressed these very issues: "Shelter and hospitality should be provided without payment for all members of my own staff, for persons on military service from other provinces and for freedmen and slaves of the best of princes and for the animals of these persons in such a way that these do not exact other services without payment from people who are unwilling."[17] This text is an edict from the Pisidian *legatus pro praetore,* who writes that the regulations are based in turn on the *mandata* he received from the emperor. It is possible that the Skaptopareni and others knew of this or even of earlier legislation, such as the *lex Iulia de repetundis* dating to 59 BC, which seems to have formed the basis for the Tiberian edict, or one of the later statements of the rules.[18] But none of this legislation was referred to. More importantly, the Skaptopareni did not quote from earlier successful *Hilferufe.* Over several centuries, the Roman government received multiple petitions on similar subjects, suggesting that magistrates and soldiers did not cease their intimidation.

There is, however, some support for the notion that rescripts adver-tised legal policy. There are papyrus documents belonging to litigants who supported their cases with quotations from others' rescripts, though some of these rescripts are from different locations and years.[19] We can also infer (rather than prove) from some rescripts extant from 293–294 that the petitions prompting them were inspired by earlier petitions and their responses. For example, Diocletian's rescript of 292 allowing individuals claimed as slaves to petition about their status probably prompted some of the entries in title *CJ* 7.16. While geography lessened the influence of rescripts, the fact that they were written in response to petitions sent by ordinary people with problems with which others could identify did make them more intellectually accessible.

Moreover, some petitions not only prompted rescripts that supplemented or amended law but may also have prompted legislation expressed in a different form. If the imperial court received a number of petitions on a similar problem and it appeared that the problem could be suffered by a significant number of other people, the *scrinium* might report those petitions and the problem to another department or perhaps to the *magister memoriae,* who would then draft an edict to be promulgated where necessary or a letter to be sent to the relevant magistrate or magistrates. Honoré believes that the rescript system "was meant to ensure a degree of Romanization in the administration of law" by putting pressure on judges to adhere to the contents of rescripts.[20] This was, however, a rather hit-and-miss technique of ensuring empire-wide legal uniformity (as the petitions of the Skaptopareni and other *Hilferufe* demonstrate). With the advent of multiple courts under the Tetrarchy, rescripts could be important locally, regionally, or across the empire. The content of rescripts of import to a small region might be passed on from the court to surrounding provinces; rescripts of wider importance might be sent by the court to all governors or prefects in that part of the empire. Finally, rescripts of universal importance would be shared with all provinces, East and West. On an issue such as requisitioning, it is easy to see how petitions might have been an important element in a nexus of communications to and from the imperial court that contributed to the development of legislation.[21]

The rescript system may also have helped disseminate Roman law, which was not followed universally in the Empire. For example, from evidence in the Babatha archive, we know that some adherents of Mosaic law followed polygamy, a practice outlawed by Roman law. While we have no direct evidence of how the imperial court would have responded to a petition that inquired about a practice that was contrary to Roman law, we know from the response to Bithus discussed in the previous chapter that the court could condemn a petitioner's behavior. Perhaps such a response would advertise (at least to some extent) the court's (and therefore Roman law's) attitude toward the practice and might subsequently prompt a provincial edict on the subject. Even when not expressing disapproval of non-Roman legal practices, rescripts enhanced the authority of Roman law in the provinces by addressing widespread legal problems within the framework of Roman law. They also played a role in the development of Roman law across the empire. Coriat, examining the Severan period, has seen in the directions of the emperor to his officials in the rescripts a challenge to the formulary system, which he thinks may have strongly contributed to the development of the *cognitio extra ordinem*.[22]

Clusters of petitions on similar topics sometimes prompted new legislation, and indeed any petition could inspire legal reform. Some rescripts from 293–294 demonstrate that petitions may have prompted a political response also. As we have seen, the *scrinium* classed those responsible for an uprising in Palmyra—part of the Roman Empire—as *hostes,* a term generally used for foreign enemies. Though the Palmyrene rebels were not *hostes* in a legal sense, giving them that appellation served a worthwhile political purpose.[23] The rescript could have stood as a precedent for—and warning to—future resistance or separatist movements. Also politically advantageous was the ruling that former prisoners of war who had yet to pay back their ransomers were held as quasi-slaves. This ruling, reflected in the rescripts from the third century on, created an awkward legal situation—citizens could hold other citizens in a state of servitude (or one that resembled it)[24]—and was clearly the result of political pressure from the imperial court to increase the incentives for ransomers to return Roman captives.[25]

Answering petitions was also a consultation exercise that could help inform future policies in administration, law, or religion.[26] Through the activities of the *scrinium,* the emperor and his senior officials could find out what was going on in the empire—how citizens were suffering from barbarian invasions, how those improperly claimed as slaves were being protected, whether current planning regulations were maintaining social harmony in towns, what sorts of activities were being undertaken by unscrupulous traders. The *magister a libellis,* who sat on the *consilium principis,* was ideally placed to report to the emperor and his senior officials the legal problems facing his subjects.[27]

Diocletian's travels gave the *magister* the opportunity to find out what problems his people were facing. Imperial travel during these years may have coincided with his far-reaching administrative reforms that included reorganization of the provinces and of imperial rule itself. Diocletian and

Maximian were joined as emperors by Galerius and Licinius, who were elevated early in 293, and the number of the provinces was increased from about fifty to approximately one hundred. The number of provincial governors was correspondingly increased.[28] With more emperors and governors, petitioners had more opportunities to enquire about their legal problems (though I admit it is hard to imagine how the four courts and many provinces could have shared information about petitioners' concerns, if indeed they did). And in AD 293–294, uniquely or not, many of Diocletian's subjects seized that opportunity.

Instituting rule by four emperors and increasing the number of provincial governors may at first sight seem to be acts of decentralization. Yet they were perceived, most notoriously by Lactantius, as government interference,[29] or (otherwise expressed) as the concentration of imperial power, an activity consistent with Diocletian's increased concern for answering petitions. Rescripts' directions to praetors and governors also served as a means of control. Emperors could now direct the judicial activity of officials on particular points of law more efficiently through a rescript than a letter—the rescript would only come to the attention of the official if it was presented in court to him.[30] (Rescripts also enabled the authorization to judges to do—by equity—what they could otherwise not do.)[31] Rescripts could also spread Roman law throughout the empire, even to places that did not always use it, though they could also be a means for taking local law into consideration. They therefore served the important function of advertising that emperors could respond to problems on the ground.[32] Rescripts also allowed individuals' problems to be dealt with specifically, without the enormous subsequent correspondence that an empire-wide edict might have prompted.[33] Rescripts, in short, offered many advantages to the emperor and his people:

> Application ou rejet du droit local, recours au "Reichsrecht" de Rome ou seulement référence à celui-ci comme échelle de valeurs pour écarter un doute ou pallier une carence du droit local, les solutions adoptées selon les espèces expriment les mobiles du pouvoir central: souci de sauvegarder les intérêts de l'Empire, respect des traditions autochtones, esprit de tolérance et sentiment de justice proprement romain.[34]

Rescripts were "*la respiration*" of the Roman world.[35] The argument for regarding petition and response as part of a consultation exercise presupposes that emperors wanted to help people solve their problems. And there is no reason to think that this is not the case. For example, Diocletian's desire to act beneficently could explain his decision in a rescript of AD 290 to restate slaves' entitlement to petition in certain situations.[36] Emperors might want to help their subjects because it made for a more stable society. Giving people access to the law which governed their lives—to information and advice about it—helped them live in harmony with others and with society at large, and a harmonious people is a more easily governed people.[37] But the answering of petitions was not just legally and politically important. As far back as the New Kingdom of Egypt, responding to vulnerable individuals' requests for help had been an important element in rulers' self-presentation, and Roman emperors continued the tradition of responsiveness with the rescript system.

## THE PATRON OF THE POOR

So far we have looked at the rescript system as an administrative process evidenced through law codes, inscriptions, and papyri. But there is also evidence for the rescript system in literature and the visual arts that expresses the importance of the system in the emperor's presentation of himself, especially of his responsiveness.

Cassius Dio tells the following story about Hadrian and a petitioner: "When the emperor was on a journey, so the story runs, a woman approached him and asked for his attention. Hadrian replied that he had no time, at which the woman shouted, 'Then do not be a king!' So he turned round and gave her leave to speak."[38] The number of petitions, according to Suetonius, drove Julius Caesar to make time at the Circus for *epistulis libellisque legendis aut rescribendis*—the letters and petitions he had to read and respond to.[39] Suetonius tells us that his heir Augustus added to his *epistulae* the hour of the day (or night) at which they were composed and, like his predecessor, also replied personally to petitions, not only composing the responses but also applying his seal to guarantee his authorship.[40] Applying the seal to all *rescripta* was a demanding task, but Augustus undertook it to underline his legal authority. Subsequent emperors were more secure in their authority, yet they continued the practice of adding the imperial seal. For example, *signavi*, attested in the answer to the Skaptopareni, may refer to the signature or application of the imperial seal,[41] which could be carried out by the emperor or delegated to the *magister a libellis* (as I think was the case).

Augustus set a daunting precedent for assiduity (at least according to our sources). Caracalla complained of the burdens of the system of petition and response in the opening to the *Constitutio Antoniniana*. But some emperors followed it, including Marcus Aurelius, ever the diligent emperor, who judged late into the night, even when on campaign.[42] Emperors are also depicted in visual as well as literary sources as attending to the legal needs of their people. Coins were minted for emperors that either depicted a personification of justice, *Iustitia*, or simply included the Latin word as an inscription.[43] Structural reliefs also depict emperors dispensing justice, and late Roman manuscripts contain images of officials giving judgment. For example, the sixth-century Rossano Gospels contain a depiction of Christ coming before Pontius Pilate. Christ approaches the *dux consularis*, who is seated on a throne behind a table. Scroll in hand and flanked by provincial officials, Pilate is represented "radiating authority" as he passes judgment on Christ with the support of the Roman provincial administration around him.[44]

Some descriptions and images depict the emperor as the beneficent but harassed patron. Likening the emperor handing out rescripts to the patron distributing benefits to his clients may have some historical basis, but depicting the emperor as harassed when doing so is striking. While some of the emperors may have taken an interest in legal matters, I find it hard to believe that they allowed themselves to be overwhelmed by them. We should remember that emperors were burdened by the rescript system only in literary depictions and in carefully managed public appearances, which presented the emperor as working hard for his people. The reality was most likely different.

If the system created burdens for the most powerful man in the empire, it seems odd that he would agree to submit to it. As I stated in chapter 2, I think that the emperor often delegated that burden to the members of the *scrinium*. His major contribution to the system was to collect petitions on certain public occasions and thereby to bestow on the procedure a sense of ceremony. His presence created a moment of exchange: of his authority with their adulation, both of which were mutual creations. At these times, the emperor was close, literally and figuratively, to his people.

Likewise, the people were close to their emperor and took his accessibility as an opportunity not only to seek his help but also to complain about injustices they were suffering. There are records of popular protests during imperial visits,[45] and though they seem to have been fairly spontaneous and were concerned with problems of the moment, nevertheless they must sometimes have been irksome, even dangerous. On Caracalla's visit to Egypt, large gatherings had to be banned. Receiving petitions could on occasion be no less awkward, as Hadrian knew to his cost. From these stories of protest we realize that the people had some sort of power. They could make their displeasure about a particular issue known to the emperor and, as the anecdote concerning Hadrian indicates, sometimes that displeasure extended to the emperor's perceived inattentiveness. Protests seem to have happened most often in places where the emperor resided frequently or for long periods of time, where the people became accustomed to the emperor's presence and were emboldened to voice their opinions.[46] It was in those locations, in particular, that the rescript system, which had provided the people an opportunity for contact with magistrates, was probably most frequently used and its presence and availability most expected.

Despite the risks of public protest, the emperor's presence was important. Late Roman panegyrics often mention the emperor's *praesentia* as a cause for rejoicing; it was a source of comfort and gave reassurance that the emperor cared for his subjects.[47] Emperors, therefore, needed to be present at locations across the empire and they had to be accessible—to appear responsive to complaints, protests, and pleas for help. Moreover, they needed to publicize that accessibility, so they accepted petitions when in public places. The advent of the Tetrarchy increased the number of places that could enjoy the imperial presence. But they could not run the risk of facing public protests too frequently, and therefore needed to regulate people's access to their persons, both for the sake of security and to maintain their power and authority.

So emperors surrounded themselves with pomp and ceremony in public. For example, when an emperor arrived in a city, people flocked to the walls bearing altars to witness his *praesentia*. He responded to their reverence with a godlike appearance and presumably maintained his quasi-divine countenance throughout his visit.[48] As Coriat remarks, "Voyager c'est gouverner." Traveling was a political and ceremonial act for the emperor.[49]

The imperial *salutatio* can be viewed in the same way. The emperor's receipt of petitions was also a ceremonial, not simply an administrative, process, and like any ceremony, it was controlled. Emperors would receive only some petitions and only at certain points during a visit. Otherwise petitioners had to approach the court, wherever that happened to be. Individuals handing in petitions directly to the emperor were presumably carefully controlled, much like audience members seeking a handshake or conversation at a modern political rally. Suetonius records that Augustus allowed the *plebes* to attend *salutationes,* at which they could hand in *libelli,* an arrangement that may have been instituted to manage petitioners' access to the emperor.[50] And emperors themselves were probably also managed. They did not give extempore responses, thus avoiding the risk of giving an answer contrary to the laws or justice. Even when an emperor's response to an oral petition or case presentation is preserved, it was probably the work of legal advisers voiced by the emperor.[51]

The efficacy of an imperial rescript derived from the fact that the emperor was the most senior patron in the empire and the source of the law under which his clients lived. He was also a stranger to the local community and to the immediate situation that was the focus of any petition, rather like Peter Brown's holy man, who could settle matters within communities because he was an outsider untainted by suspicions who was not available to become a permanent focal point for resentment after giving judgment. In places the emperor visited infrequently, he was the seldom seen benefactor who came, gave pronouncements, and departed, leaving the town a better place. But in places he visited frequently, he cultivated his divine aspect.

## THE SUPREME JUDGE

Petitions to the emperor, a semi-divine figure, were akin to prayers and were often referred to by petitioners and the court as *preces.* Moshe Greenberg, who has analyzed the significance and development of biblical prayer, traces the evolution of the prayer from being a statement of information about a worshiper's problems accompanied by flattery to "a vehicle of humility, an expression of un-selfsufficiency, which in biblical thought, is the proper stance of humans before God."[52] As prayers became more like petitions and acknowledged humans' dependency on one or more gods,[53] conversely Near Eastern and Greek petitions often exhibited characteristics of prayers, as we saw in the introduction. Roman petitions also contain precatory postures. Petitioners emphasized their dependence on the emperor, aware that this was their best route to success, and downplayed any power they did have.[54] The publication of prayer-like petitions was also advantageous to the emperor; they advertised his concern for his people's problems, his accessibility, his ability to answer them, and his authority.

"To give 'justice' to the 'poor' was a sign of royal energy—whether this was the energy of a king or of a god. It was an attribute of royalty that was displayed most fully on the accession of the ruler. For in giving such justice, the new king showed the reach of his power."[55] For Roman emperors, that "energy" was derived not only from his status as king-like emperor but also from his role as *pontifex maximus,* who according to Festus was considered judge and arbiter of matters pertaining to the divine and the human (*iudex atque arbiter habetur rerum divinarum humanarumque*).[56] He was also a divine figure whose shrines and statues afforded protection to suppliants.[57] Like all other laws of the empire, rescripts were made in his name and thus advertised. They asserted his semi-divine authority, which enabled him to give definitive answers that could not be contradicted by anyone else.[58]

According to Michael Peachin, the emperor's legal authority derived from the fact that the legal system was without rigidity and consistency. In fact, Peachin argues, successive emperors maintained the *Formlosigkeit* of the Roman legal system so as to bolster their legal authority.[59] With ignorant judges and advocates, litigants suffered a high degree of legal insecurity, which could be assuaged only by the emperor's authority, expressed often in the rescripts with statements that advertise the generosity of the emperor: people should not be subject to repeated investigations as to their status; a testamentary manumission should be honored even if the will is technically faulty. The emperor's generosity derived from his authority, which was further strengthened by displays of *clementia*, φιλανθρωπία ("kindliness"), δικαιοσύνη ("righteousness") and ἐπιείκεια ("reasonableness"), qualities respected in Hellenistic rulers and later in Roman emperors.[60] Showing indulgence to petitioners, while keeping to the spirit of the law, supported the emperor's popularity and authority.[61]

Yet at several points in the rescripts of 293–294, we find statements that the emperor must keep to the law. This is something of an obfuscating claim. Politically it was unwise for the emperor to go against existing law, but legally he could and did, hence the rhetoric-laden *apologiae* that accompanied edicts changing the law.[62] It was a risky tactic; a wise emperor adhered to existing legislation as much as possible to support the inviolability of Roman law, which in turn ensured social security.[63]

Though the emperor did not write most rescripts, they were produced by or under the aegis of the most talented legal experts in the empire, who could ensure their legal correctness. Petitioners who received a rescript would associate the excellence of the response with the emperor's name, which also acted as a seal, attesting to the rescript's genuineness and persuading others of its definitiveness. The emperor also benefited from putting his name to these expert responses. They underlined the authority with which he was invested, which he could not, however, have maintained without the work of the *scrinium*. It not only saved the emperor time but also produced expert work.[64]

The emperor also benefited from the efficiency of the rescript system in advertising his responsiveness and concern for his subjects. Just as a provincial official might find that responding to a widow who asked for a little money produced cheaper and easier kudos than passing judgment on a messy legal problem, the emperor could improve the public's perception of his concern for his subjects more easily and cheaply by answering petitions (which, of course, he did not do personally) than by, for example, increasing the corn dole or public building works.[65] Moreover, many petitions, as we have seen in the case of the Skaptopareni, were answered with a direction to a local official. With such a response, the emperor was seen to be responsive, while actually offloading the petitioner's problem.

This was a system whose efficiency and symbolic importance helped to maintain peace and security among the people of the Roman Empire. Near Eastern rulers answered petitions asking for charity as well as legal help; likewise, the Roman emperor gave charity to the poor, using his bureaucracy to distribute doles of corn, pork, and wine so that his subjects were fed and contented and therefore unlikely to cause public disturbances (though we should distinguish Roman imperial charity, which targeted the better-off and especially the freeborn, from modern charity, which tends to be concerned for the poor).[66] The Roman rescript system also functioned as a means of maintaining public order. If the poor (i.e., those who felt themselves to be vulnerable in some way) did not have their legal queries responded to, they might try to use extra-legal means to solve their problems.[67]

## THE TRADITIONALIST

Diocletian was not the only emperor concerned with self-presentation and perceptions of his authority, as well as the pressures on his time. Emperors before him, beginning indeed with Augustus, shared them, as had chief magistrates under the republic and other ancient rulers. So the final explanation for why Diocletian (nominally) answered his subjects' petitions is that, as numerous anecdotes and the *CJ* suggest, (good) rulers had always done it. This may seem to be a facile statement, but it can, I think, explain why many bureaucratic procedures remain virtually unchanged despite changes in government or leader.[68]

Diocletian probably did not alter the system significantly, though given that there are far fewer extant rescripts dating to AD 292 or earlier than to the years 293–294, we have insufficient evidence to conduct a full analysis of the system in the two periods. There is, however, no compelling evidence to suggest that Diocletian's officials answered more or fewer petitions than any other emperor. I think Hermogenian and his staff answered as many petitions as they reasonably could, just as their predecessors had probably also done.[69] And there is no need to explain the rescripts of AD 293–294 as solely the by-products of a consultation exercise or of Diocletian's travels. His officials answered petitions because his predecessors' officials had done so, and it required little effort on his part to continue the tradition. Granted, the system depended on successive emperors to continue it and on their subjects' acceptance of emperors' legal authority as supreme. But the system had continued for centuries not because of the assiduity of some emperors, nor despite the lack of concern of others. It continued because none had stopped it and because it had continued to show the benefits described here. The range of recipients of rescripts extant from 293–294, then, does not reflect people's access to individual emperors but their access to the imperial bureaucracy.

## Limits on the Emperor

Diocletian continued the practice of answering petitions seemingly without change, despite his reforming zeal in most other areas of government. Remarkably, the rescript system had continued to function during the crisis-ridden years of the third century, despite a series of emperors and the dangers traveling petitioners faced from barbarian invasions and the plague. In 293–294 the empire was not free of its earlier troubles. Petitioners suffered inflated charges for scribes' services and, once en route to the court, faced neglected roads and the threat of bandits operating along them. But despite these problems and with increased governmental stability, local law courts may have been operating with greater effectiveness and local authorities may have been better able to enforce laws. The increasing number of litigants would have been grateful. The numbers of legal problems would have grown as trade and financial activity increased, masters bought more slaves, and property owners undertook new building work. The numbers of petitioners increased correspondingly, spurred on further by population growth.

The demand for rescripts may have grown again at the end of the third century. More emperors could have meant more petitions coming in overall, since petitions that would otherwise have gone to provincial governors and other officials would have come instead to the imperial court. Diocletian's administration would have needed to keep pace.[70] Earlier emperors' complaints about the burdens of the rescript system may not have been genuine; they may have been designed to advertise imperial diligence. But when Constantine complained of the burden, wanting to reduce the number of petitions and the cost of processing them, he may have been expressing his true feelings.[71] Changes to the system that happened around the time of his reign may have been prompted by his concerns at the increasing numbers of petitioners. Diocletian probably wished the same.

Any bureaucracy unable to cope with the numbers of applications for administrative procedures has two ways to deal with the situation. It can either make applying hard enough to create a manageable workload,[72] or it can increase the resources available to meet the demands on it. The latter seems to have happened in Diocletian's reign, though it was probably not the result of a deliberate policy but a side effect of other administrative reforms. Diocletian increased the number of provincial governors (and associated officials), thus increasing the opportunities for petitioners to petition at a lower level, and he also increased the number of emperors, helping those who wished to petition the emperor to do so. More emperors and officials meant more opportunities to petition, and the number of petitioners probably increased considerably. And as the numbers of extant rescripts from 293–294 demonstrate, the daily workload for the *scrinium* may have been considerable. It was the diligence and expertise of its officials that ensured the system continued regardless of the supposed diligence or disinterest of the emperors.

### The Nexus of Power: Emperor, Officials, Petitioners

The following story is told about a former U.S. president, Ronald Reagan. Finding one afternoon that he had no important presidential business to attend to, Reagan asked his Oval Office secretary to give him some letters from members of the public, so that he could fill the rest of his day answering them. The story shows Reagan in a good light: he chose to spend his spare time attending to his people (though presumably, like any president, he was given only those letters that required grateful acknowledgment rather than a statement of policy). The surprise is that Reagan should find himself at loose ends. How could the president of the world's most powerful nation have nothing better to do than answer people's letters?[73] Of course, the exception proves the rule: the president so rarely has the time to answer letters that he employs others to do it for him. Likewise, most emperors seldom answered petitions and surely did not do so without help.

Fergus Millar would interpret the story differently: it shows an American president getting round to answering his correspondence personally, as he always did. In his *Emperor in the Roman World*, he claimed that emperors answered all petitions personally. If authorship of imperial constitutions did not belong to the emperor, it was possible that many other functions associated with the emperor were actually not carried out by him, and the notion of the responsive ruler was thus undermined. What was left for the emperor to do? A proverbial can of worms had been opened.[74]

According to Millar's view, the function of the emperor was to respond to pressures coming to him from the empire, including petitions.[75] Government of the empire comprised the emperor's day-to-day reactions to demands placed on him by officials, citizens, and outside forces. His imperial correspondence was a never-ending stream of uncoordinated responses to immediate pressures. In this formulation, the emperor answered petitions because the people expected it. One could hypothesize an opposing view, that imperial rule was characterized as the imposition of the emperor's will without prompting by or response from the people, in which correspondence from the emperor takes on the form of diktats. According to this extreme view, the production of rescripts would have served little purpose, except as an expression of the emperor's power to make or amend law in the empire. I suggest that the nature of Roman imperial governance lies somewhere between these models. Since it is impossible to know for certain each year what proportions of petitions were answered solely by the *scrinium,* solely by the emperor, and as a joint effort, it is therefore possible that *some* emperors, *some* of the time, did behave like Millar's emperor.

Imperial governance can be regarded as a system of exchange that provided a fair and stable system of control to the people in return for their loyalty and financial support. According to this model, rescripts were produced because petitioners approached the emperor.[76] Petitioners knew that their petitions would be answered because they knew that other people's petitions were answered commonly enough to make the undertaking worthwhile.[77] And emperors accepted that petitions were a form of communication worthy (or perhaps necessary) to be answered. In this way, the rescript system was driven by the demands of the people. But the system would not have continued without the support (or cooperation) of successive emperors, who saw the political benefits of a system that helped to portray them as rulers who cared for their vulnerable subjects and that advertised their authority. And the basis of exchange in the relationship must surely be patronage, a system at the heart of Roman society. Such was the force of patronage in conditioning Roman relationships that participants in petition and response embraced the system since it offered similar benefits—guidance and protection, prestige and authority—to those derived from patronage. It was natural for Romans to believe that the emperor could provide them legal guidance and protection, and natural that he should do so. Ruler and ruled acted symbiotically, benefiting themselves and each other in a system of exchange that provided judicial assistance to the people in return for their appreciation and support of the emperor's legal authority.

The emperor and his subjects were not the only participants in the exchange; the officials of the *scrinium libellorum* were the enabling element. The emperor employed them to create for him an image of responsiveness, which their expertise imbued with legal capability, and to save him an immense burden in time. According to Michael Peachin, "The real indication of absolute monarchic power, is not a prince's capacity to subsume more of the work of governing. Rather, when an emperor can turn over the functions he is expected personally to perform to an officially labelled stand-in, then we are in the presence of a significant development in the nature of rule. For no longer would the person of the emperor seem to matter so much as would the position, the institution itself. What our judges make clear is that *the* emperor had become no longer so important to the daily routine as *an* emperor." While Peachin is referring to emperors' employment of *iudices vice sacra,* I think his comments can equally be applied to the *a libellis.*[78] Petitioners, probably unwittingly, also gained from the officials' skills, which helped to produce legally sound responses, and the officials themselves gained employment, much of it stimulating. Although some of the petitions they received probably required little skill to answer (perhaps these were reserved for less experienced members), others were more legally complex and probably tested the learning of senior officials, including Hermogenian. Corcoran claims that Diocletianic jurists answered rescripts rather than wrote their own juristic works and that their legal approaches found expression in this official work.[79] If I am right that the *scrinium* worked as a team to produce most responses and if, as Honoré believes, it is possible to discern the legal attitudes of individual *magistri* in the rescripts, the *magister* must have wielded considerable editorial authority over his juniors.

It is remarkable that a significant portion of our extant imperial constitutions were written in response to people of the middling sort about their legal problems. Considering the importance of rescripts as constitutions, we should not view members of the middling sort in the governance of the empire simply as victims or passive recipients, or indeed claimants on the emperor's time, but as participants in a nexus of constitutions and amendments that created Roman law and in a nexus of relationships with the emperor and his officials, many of whom also belonged to the middling sort.[80] The middling sort were both users and enablers.[81] The system of petition and response gave the emperor and the middling sort an opportunity to communicate not only their mutual recognition of their roles in Roman governance, but also their attitudes toward how life should be lived in the Roman Empire. The Skaptopareni objected to the behavior of the officials from the local elite; the emperor's response expressed his agreement with their stance and validated their objections.

Diocletian most famously expressed support for his subjects in his Edict on Maximum Prices. A dominant theme in scholarship on this text has been its inefficacy, but more important for my purposes is the fact that it advertises the emperor's attempt to regulate all things for his people.[82] Diocletian had this particular piece of legislation enacted in response to soldiers' complaints. These were not necessarily transmitted to him via the system of petition and response, but the fact that they were heard demonstrates that complaints (perhaps through various channels) were heard and sometimes acted upon, not just with a response but perhaps even with legislation.

Significantly, Diocletian chose to advertise his responsiveness in the edict, since responsiveness was a means of self-representation. Emperors could choose which petitions they answered—though they might do so with care—and which moments of responsiveness to advertise, for example, at the beginning of a reign. A large amount of scholarship has pointed out the importance of imperial self-representation, and responsiveness has been identified as a means by which emperors could mold an image of themselves.[83] But the middling sort has largely been missing from this work, not so much as a group that sometimes called on the emperor but as a group that the emperor felt it worthwhile to answer—and perhaps felt obliged to do so.[84]

# Conclusion

Ancient systems of petition and response existed around the Mediterranean with little variation for several thousand years, and that of the Roman Empire even survived its political demise. There were, I believe, several reasons for the Roman system's longevity. First, the system was not created ex nihilo, but rather was based on traditional practices, and there were incentives for the middling sort to use it. Limited opportunities existed for people of the middling sort to find advice about their legal problems as lawyers' advice and representation were too expensive for many, and they faced significant linguistic, social, and financial barriers to success in court. The alternative of petitioning the emperor for advice or help perhaps arose from or was analogous to the long-standing custom of calling on a patron's legal knowledge and thus may have been more accessible in the minds of the middling sort. So, the middling sort could now not only consult a lawyer or patron but also petition the emperor and (though few may have known it) the expert members of his *scrinium*. A favorable rescript could help persuade opponents to settle or judges to decide in a petitioner's favor and thus it offered significant advantages to the middling sort, especially given the availability of scribes, *tabelliones,* to assist them with composing a petition. Second, successive emperors, perhaps on the model of their earlier Near Eastern and Greek counterparts and certainly in emulation of Julius Caesar and Augustus, continued it, and their reputations were enhanced as a result (which stimulated them further to administer the system).

I have constructed a schema of the system from close analysis of the inscribed petition and response from Skaptopara and analyzed it primarily from the petitioner's point of view rather than that of the court. The result-ing system appears complex, and many scholars have noted its complexity in their attempts to fix its details. But few have recognized that the com-plexity was suffered primarily by the petitioners and most likely existed to maximize the convenience of the imperial court. When the system is stud-ied in motion, further details about how it operated emerge, in particular the fact that members of the *scrinium,* who answered most of the petitions, worked to a grueling schedule, despite the system's being designed for the court's convenience.

This system in motion, which can be recreated from examining the entries in the *Codex Hermogenianus* now extant in the *Codex Justinianus,* also reveals that the emperor did not answer all the petitions he received, but that the *scrinium* answered most of them, most of the time. The num-ber of petitions handed in daily to the court throughout the year, many of which required a legally complex answer, was simply too high for the em-peror to be the sole respondent. Petitioning continued while the imperial court traveled, though administration of the system was not the reason for traveling. (The court's attention to the system, however, would have helped the image of the emperor across a wide area.)

The very fact that petitioners were answered by the court on the move enables us to consider together the answers they received, their names as they were recorded, and the locations at which their rescripts were pro-cessed in order to understand better the lower Danube provinces, in par-ticular their cultural diversity, range of commercial activities, and familial and social interactions. While I do not claim that a regional history can be written from the rescripts alone, they are a fruitful addition (and some-times a useful corrective) to the existing archaeological and epigraphic evidence that reveals more complex and diverse communities.

The makeup of the petitioners themselves is also revealed and can be quantified, as others have shown. But it may be possible to push the evi-dence further than quantification, and I have suggested that where num-bers of petitioners from specific groups (e.g., women, slaves, and soldiers) are lower than their numbers in the general population, this is probably the result of social and practical restrictions rather than prejudice from the imperial court against answering them and compiling or codifying their answers. We may therefore use the existing rescripts to get a good sense of the kinds of problems that beset the middling sort and various subsets of them.

I hope that I have shown the case study approach, which I adopted in chapter 4, to be productive not only for understanding better the construction of the rescripts, but also for taking these terse legal texts and putting them in their social, human context. In that chapter I discussed a small number of texts that provide us with examples of rescripts' structure and content as well as demonstrate that sometimes we have sufficient information from them to recreate at least in part the back stories to the situations presented in petitions. We can sometimes also sketch out something of the next installments to these stories by analogy with what we know from texts such as the Skaptopara inscription. Considering the before, during, and after helps us to perceive the roles played by petition and response in the lives of the middling sort and how these roles varied with individuals' relationship with law—whether they were with the law, before it, or against it, according to Ewick and Silbey's scheme. I think that awareness of modern sociological work on individuals' interactions with law will deepen our mining of these texts, and there is much more to be done with them.[1]

One can also occasionally see that the court's social and political concerns were added to those for law (per se) and justice.

Examination of petition and response helps us understand more about the legal problems of the middling sort. Indeed the system provided probably the most common opportunity for contact (albeit in writing, not in person) between the emperor and his subjects. The participation of these people in the system and successive emperors' investment in it reveal the middling sort to be a significant constituency whose importance has been overlooked. Yet their problems and the court's perceived need to respond to them are behind the rescripts of the CJ, which constitute the bulk of this collection, a crowning achievement of Roman law and basis for Continental law.

The resulting picture is astonishing to behold: a system was set up because emperors felt obliged to answer those who perceived themselves as vulnerable, and a large body of literature was incorporated into law as a result. This picture reminds us of the power of expectation on both emperors and the middling sort. What the emperor can bestow is an important part of what defines imperial rule in the Roman period, as well as before and after it.

The middling sort may have been important legal participants throughout the ancient world. The participants in the ancient systems of petition and response we met in the introduction were from the middling sort—the Egyptian tomb worker, the Hellenistic lentil cook, the Skaptopareni, and the blind widow of the Cairo Genizah. The legal experts who contributed their skills and labor to producing responses in these systems likely were also of the middling sort. The relationship between these petitioners and officials has been hidden by many of our sources, yet it highlights the importance of the middling sort to the functioning of the Roman administration.

For all the expertise and hard work of the legal experts, stories about the rescript system mention only petitioners and rulers, who received petitions and seemingly responded to them personally. For example, in the Roman system, it was Julius Caesar who spent his time at the Circus in *epistulis libellisque legendis aut rescribendis;* Augustus after him carefully applied his seal to guarantee his authorship of the responses.[2] Severus Alexander "always gave up the afternoon hours to subscribing and reading letters, with the *ab epistulis,* ‹*a*› *libellis* and *a memoria* always in attendance."[3] And another example: "When the king goes out, he usually gets one of his suite to follow him with a leather bag, into which petitioners throw a statement of their case; on arrival at the palace, the king examines the merits of each case."[4] While this third-century Chinese account of the Roman Near East does not identify the king (it may also be a governor of Syria), it does reveal the formulaic nature of anecdotes about rulers dispensing justice. Whenever he is in a public place, the ruler should be available to his subjects so that they can hand in their problems to him. Each of these problems is then attended to and answered, presumably by the ruler.

Further examples of good, responsive rulers can be found in the later Roman period. Each week Leo I, ruling in the eastern half of the empire in the mid-fifth century, visited the *Pittákia,* a column at which petitioners from in and around the city deposited their petitions (*pittákia*). These petitions were guarded by local officials until the emperor arrived. Once they were handed to him, decisions (λύσεις) would then be produced (by whom is not specified, though Leo is probably assumed).[5] A little earlier in the West, we find Theoderic, king of the Visigoths, also receiving petitions, this time at his court: "At around the ninth hour begins again the toil of ruling. Back they come knocking at the doors; back they come to drive them away; everywhere busy litigants buzz to and fro, but the throng is weakened towards evening, held back by the arrival of the royal supper."[6] As at Leo's court, the receipt of petitions was regular and as many petitions were answered as there was time for, with petitioners jostling for attention and chattering as they waited. But it was the king (or more likely the court) who decided when to stop receiving. Justinian was praised as a ruler who maintained his authority and yet was accessible to his people, for he listened to them and was as welcoming to them in their plight as a windless harbor is to sailors.[7] In the age of Justinian, described as *l'apogée de la pétition*, Procopius claims that absolutely no one was prevented from having access to the emperor; more than that, he never offended those who were in his presence or even those who spoke to him without observing etiquette.[8]

From the Byzantine period and beyond, we find further descriptions of rulers receiving petitions in stories whose details are repeated—petitions are usually received outside, frequently under trees—so often that they seem representative, giving the overall descriptions symbolic, rather than historical importance.[9] In Central Asia in the early tenth century, "Isma'il b. Ahmad, the second of the princes of the house of Saman, used to make a regular practice of sitting on horseback in the open, before the hour of morning prayer, to listen to personal representations from any of his subjects who might wish to have an audience with him. In these sessions the Samanid ruler presented himself in the full panoply of war, as a visible indication that he had the power as well as the will to do justice . . . The Samanid ruler braved even the frost and snow of a Central Asian winter in order to be perpetually available to his subjects. He voluntarily endured this severe physical ordeal because, in his and his subjects' eyes alike, accessibility was of the essence of a ruler's duty."[10] A little later, the twelfth-century ruler Saladin "every day, either during the daytime or in the night . . . spent an hour with his secretary and minuted on each petition, in the terms that God suggested to him."[11] Later still in the West, the anecdotes continue. The sainted Louis IX is said to have received petitions in the Bois de Vincennes, a scene that reminds us of Byzantine emperors sitting under trees as petitioners approached them.[12] And in an evocative description, Arnold Toynbee tells of how a Georgian king of the eighteenth century would ride slowly on horseback through the streets of Tbilisi "dispensing justice impromptu *en route.*"[13]

Descriptions of publicly responsive modern rulers are harder to find. Rulers are too busy and inexperienced to answer petitions that pertain to complex modern legal systems, and access to them is limited because of security concerns. There are exceptions. Toynbee, once again, is the source of the following story. In the 1940s he recalled seeing a Turkish governor "giving audience" to his people. "Some of the petitioners were people in the humblest walks of life and were inarticulate, but all of them received a courteous and careful hearing and a prompt—and, of course, therefore unavoidably impromptu—decision on their case . . . This admirable direct method of administration is feasible only when the population is small and when public business is simple."[14] In Jordan, petitioners still enjoy access to their ruler. A newspaper journalist described a recent visit to a hospital by Abdullah II, who "frequently holds up the official procession so that patients and their families can hand him their petitions scribbled on bits of paper."[15] The Jordanian system is, however, an anomaly in the modern world.

Some ancient rulers were willfully unresponsive. Cyrus of Persia deliberately reduced his accessibility to the people by refusing to accept petitions passed on through officers.[16] The Hellenistic ruler Demetrius Poliorcetes was described by Plutarch as being so contemptuous of his administrative responsibilities that he emptied a lapful of petitions into a river.[17] Tiberius even went so far as to forbid petitioners approaching him at Capri.[18]

Both the positive and negative accounts of rulers' handling of petition and response are so stylized that they probably tell us more about the self-presentation or perception of a ruler than about his daily activities in judicial administration.[19] The positive accounts, for example, depict rulers as unrealistically diligent. It is hard to imagine that a ruler could answer petitions every night, even collect them every week, in the midst of war or during a domestic crisis.[20] It is more likely that rulers collected petitions in public and made a great show of the process, but probably worked on them when they had the time or inclination—at the start of their reign or at other politically important moments in order to advertise that they would be diligent and responsive emperors. It is possible (though improbable) that they may never have done these things, but were recorded as doing them by historians who used rulers' attitudes toward petition and response as a means of framing judgments about them and thus presented the rulers who were most conscientious about their subjects—Augustus, Justinian, Saladin—as doing them most regularly and carefully. The stories about Cyrus and Demetrius Poliorcetes were constructed in contrast to those of the good rulers. Because presentation of good and bad rulers is so stylized, we gain few insights into how most petitions were answered or how the emperor contributed to the process. Instead we learn generally about royal behavior and that systems of petition and response were a standard element in administrations and that rulers were expected to preserve them.

I have been arguing in this book that most emperors probably did not answer most petitions. The longevity of the rescript system under the empire with perhaps little input from the emperors and its persistence beyond the empire in multiple forms but under very different governments suggest that access to law is not necessarily tied to the accessibility of a ruler. It is more closely tied to the long-standing accessibility of administrative procedures.[21] These procedures had been open to those of the middling sort since the early Mesopotamian and Egyptian kingdoms, and remained open long after the demise of the Roman Empire.

As we saw in the introduction, systems of petition and response seem to have been designed for the purpose of fulfilling rulers' commitment to protect their vulnerable subjects. I have suggested that, as a result, the Roman system of petition and response reveals the significant contribution of the middling sort, especially those who regarded themselves as "poor," to the creation of law and administration of justice. The same may be true for other periods and places: in the ancient and medieval Near East, in the ancient and medieval West. It is from Western and Near (later Middle) Eastern rulers' shared and inherited sense of duty to the poor—a sense of duty that safeguarded their rule and reputation, even posthumously—that systems of petition and response grew, along with the development of charitable giving. And those systems gave the poor a voice.

Peter Brown believes that the Christian concept of the poor as deserving of aid came from Near Eastern attitudes toward petitioners asking for help of various sorts, such as food, shelter, and protection, as well as legal assistance.[22] It is possible, however, that the concept also developed from a Roman attitude toward the poor that gave rise to the system of petition and response that protected the interests mostly of the middling sort. We should not overstate the depth of concern the Roman imperial court may have had for the poor—there was no welfare state, no progressive taxation, and no legal aid.[23] But nor should we underestimate the contribution of the middling sort, and their demands, to Roman governance.

# The Skaptopara Inscription

*Bona fortuna**
‹F›ulvio Pio et ‹P›o‹n›tio Proculo cons(ulibus) XVII kal(endis) Iạn(uariis)
descriptum ‹e›t
⌐recognitum factum ‹e›x ‹l›ibro āliōbellorum rescript‹o›rum a do-⌐
⌐mino n(ostro) Imp(eratore) Cạ‹e›s(are) M(arco) Ạntonio Gordiano pio felice
Aug(usto) ‹e›t propo-⌐
5  ⌐‹s›it‹o›rum ‹R›oma‹e› in portico ‹th›ermarum Tr‹a›ianar‹u›m in ve‹r›ba ‹q(uae)›
i(nfra) s(cripta) s(unt).⌐
*Dat(um) p‹e›r Ạur(elium) Purrum mil(item) coh(ortis) X ‹pr(aetoriae)› ‹p›(iae)
‹f›(idelis) ‹G›ordianạ‹e› ‹c›(enturiae) Proculi
con‹vi›canu‹m› et conp{p}ossess‹o›rem.*

col. I  ⌐Αὐτοκράτορι Καίσαρι Μ(άρκῳ) Ἀντωνίῳ⌐
⌐Γορδιανῷ Εὐσεβεῖ Εὐτυχεῖ Σεβ(αστῷ) ‹δ›έησις⌐
10  ⌐παρὰ κωμητῶν Σκαπτοπαρηνων τῶν καὶ⌐
⌐ρησειτων· Ἐν τοῖς εὐτυχεστάτοις καὶ⌐
⌐αἰωνίοις σοῦ καιροῖς κατοικεῖσθαι καὶ⌐
⌐βελτιοῦσθαι τὰς κώμας ἤπερ ἀναστά1-
⌐τους γίγνεσθαι τοὺς ἐνοικοῦντας πολ1-
15  ⌐λάκ(ις) ἀντέγραψας· ἔστιν γ‹ὰρ› καὶ ἐπὶ τῇ τῶν⌐
⌐ἀνθρώπων σωτηρίᾳ τὸ τοιοῦτο καὶ ἐπὶ⌐
⌐τοῦ ἱερωτάτου σοῦ ταμείου ὠφελείᾳ·⌐
⌐ὅπερ καὶ αὐτοὶ ἔννομον ἱκεσίαν⌐
⌐τῇ θειότητί σου προσκομί‹ζ›ομεν εὐ1-
20  ⌐χόμενοι ἵλεως ἐπινεῦσαι ἡμεῖν⌐
⌐δεομένοις τὸν τρόπον τοῦτον. οἰκοῦ1-
⌐μεν καὶ κεκτήμεθα ἐν τῇ προγεγραμ1-

*Reprinted with permission from Klaus Hallof, "Die Inschrift von Skaptopara: Neue Dokumente und neue Lesungen," *Chiron* 24 (1994): 405–41.

⌜μένη κώμη οὔσῃ εὐεπεράστῳ διὰ τὸ⌝
⌜ἔχειν ὑδάτων θερμῶν χρῆσιν καὶ κεῖ⌝-
25 ⌜σθαι μέσον δύο στρατοπέδων τῶν ὄν⌝-
⌜των ἐν τῇ σῇ Θρᾴκῃ, καὶ ἐφ' οὗ μὲν τὸ⌝
⌜πάλλαι οἱ κατοικοῦντες ἀόχλητοι⌝
⌜καὶ ἀδειάσειστοι ἔμενον, ἀνενδεῶς
⌜τούς τε φόρους καὶ τὰ λοιπὰ ἐπιτάγ⌝ματα
30 ⌜συνετέλουν· ἐπεὶ δὲ κατὰ καιροὺς εἰς⌝
⌜‹ὕ›β‹ρ›‹ν› προχωρεῖν τινες κ⌝αὶ β⌜ιΆζε⌝σθαι
⌜ἤρξαντο, τηνικαῦτ⌝α ἐλαττοῦσθαι
⌜καὶ ἡ κώμη ἤρξατο· ἀ⌝πὸ γὰρ μειλίων δύ
⌜ο τῆς κώμης ἡ⌝μῶν πανηγύρεως]
35 ⌜ἐπιτελουμέν⌝ης διαβοήτου οἱ ἐκεῖσε
⌜τῆς πανηγύρ⌝εως εἵνεκεν ἐπιδημοῦν-
⌜τες ἡμέρ⌝αις πεντεκαίδεκα ἐν τῷ
⌜τόπῳ τ⌝ῆς πανηγύρεως οὐ κα⌜τ⌝αμ⌜έ⌝-
⌜νουσι⌝ν, ἀλ⌜λὰ⌝ ἀπολιμπάνοντ⌜ες ἐπέρ⌝-
40 ⌜χον⌝ται εἰς τὴν ἡμετέραν κώμ⌜η⌝ν
⌜καὶ ἀ⌝ναγκάζουσιν ἡμᾶ⌜ς⌝ ξενίας αὐ-
⌜τοῖς⌝ παρέχειν καὶ ἕτερα πλεῖστα ε⌜ἰ⌝ς ἀ-
νάλημψιν αὐτῶν ἄνευ ἀργ υρίου χο-
ρηγεῖν· πρὸς δὲ τούτοις καὶ στρατιῶται
45 ἀλλαχοῦ πεμπόμενοι καταλιμπά-
νοντες τὰς ἰδίας ὁδοὺς πρὸς ἡμᾶς πα-
ραγείν⌜ο⌝ι⌜νται καὶ ὁμοίω⌜ς⌝ κα⌜τ⌝ε⌜πεί⌝γουσιν
παρέχειν αὐτοῖς τὰς ξενίας καὶ τὰ ⌜ἐπι⌝-
τήδια μηδεμίαν τειμὴν κατ⌜αβ⌝ι⌜α⌝λόν⌜τ⌝ες·
50 ἐπιδημοῦ⌜σι⌝ν δὲ ὡς ἐπὶ τὸ πλεῖστον
διὰ ⌜τὴν⌝ τῶν ὑ⌜δ⌝άτων χρῆ⌜σι⌝ν οἵ τε ἡγού-
μενοι τῆς ἐπαρχίας, ἀλ⌜λ⌝ὰ καὶ οἱ ἐπί-
τροποί σου· ⌜κ⌝αὶ τὰς μὲν ἐξο⌜υ⌝σίας ⌜‹ἑὺ‹ξ›⌝ε-
νώτατα δεχ⌜όμ⌝ε⌜θα⌝ κατ⌜ὰ⌝ τὸ ⌜ἀ⌝ναγκαῖο⌜ν,⌝
55 τοὺς λ⌜οι⌝ποὺς ⌜ὑ⌝ποφέρε⌜ι⌝ν μὴ δυνάμε-
νοι ἐνετύχομεν πλειστά⌜κι⌝ς τοῖς ἡγε-
μόσι τῆς Θρᾴκης, οἵτινες ἀκολούθως
ταῖς θείαις ἐντολαῖς ἐκέλευσαν ἀοχλή-
τους ἡμᾶς εἶναι· ἐδηλώσαμεν γὰρ μη-
60 κέτ⌜ι⌝ ἡμ⌜ᾶ⌝ς δύνασθαι ὑπομένειν, ἀλλὰ καὶ ⌜νοῦ⌝ν ⌜ἔχ⌝ειν συνλείπειν καὶ τοὺς
πατ⌜ρ⌝ῴους θ⌜ίς⌝εμελίους διὰ τὴν τῶν
ἐπερχομένων ἡμεῖν βίαν· καὶ γὰρ
ὡς ἀληθῶς ἀπὸ πολλῶν οἰκοδεσπο-
65 τῶν εἰς ἐλαχίστους κατεληλύθα-
μεν· καὶ χρόνῳ μέν τινι ἴσχυσεν
67 τὰ προστάγματα τῶν ἡγ⌜ο⌝υμένων

col. II ⌜καὶ οὐδεὶς ἡμεῖν ἐνόχλησεν οὔτε⌝
⌜ξενίας ‹αἰτή›ματι οὔτε παροχῆς ἐπι⌝-
70 ⌜τηδείων, προϊόντων δὲ τῶν χρόνων⌝
⌜πάλιν ἐτόλμησαν ἐπιφύεσθαι ἡ⌝-
⌜μεῖν πλεῖστοι ὅσοι ‹τ›ῆς ἰδιωτίας⌝
⌜ἡμῶν καταφρονοῦντες· ἐπεὶ οὖν οὐ⌝-
⌜κέτι δυνάμεθα φέρειν τὰ βάρη⌝
75 ⌜καὶ ὡς ἀληθῶς κινδυνεύομεν ὅπερ⌝
⌜οἱ λοιποὶ τόδε καὶ ἡμεῖς προλιπεῖν⌝
⌜τοὺς προγονικοὺς θεμελίους, τού⌝-
⌜του χάριν δεόμεθά σου, ἀνίκητε⌝
⌜Σεβαστέ, ‹ὅ›πως διὰ θείας σου ἀντιγρα⌝-
80 ⌜φῆς κελεύσῃ‹ς› ἕκαστον τὴν ἰδίαν πο⌝-
⌜ρεύεσθαι ὁ⌜δὸ⌝ν ⌜καὶ μὴ ἀπολιμπάνοντας⌝
⌜αὐτοὺς τ⌝ὰς ἄλλας κ⌜ώ⌝μα⌜ς⌝ ἐφ᾽ ἡμᾶ⌝ς⌝
⌜ἔρχε⌝σθαι μήτε κατ⌜α⌝να⌜γκάζει⌝ν
ἡμᾶς χορηγ⌜εῖ⌝ν α⌜ὐ⌝το‹ὺ›ς προ⌜ῖ⌝κ⌜α τὰ⌝
85 ἐπιτήδια· ἀλλὰ μηδ⌜ὲ⌝ ξενία⌜ν⌝ αὐ⌜τοῖ⌝ς
παρέχειν, οἷ⌜ς⌝ μή ἐστιν ἀνά]γκη, — ὅ⌜τ⌝ι
γὰρ οἱ ἡγού⌜μεν⌝οι πλεο̣νάκις ἐκέλευσαν μὴ ἄλλῳ παρέχεσθαι ξε-
νίαν εἰ μὴ τοῖς ὑπὸ τῶν ἡγουμέ-
90 νων καὶ ἐπιτρόπων ἐκπεμ-
πομένοις εἰς ὑπηρεσίαν· ἐάν δε
βαρο̣ύμεθα, φευξόμεθα ἀπὸ τῶν
οἰ̣κε⌜ί⌝ων καὶ με⌜γίσ⌝τη̣ν ⌜ζ⌝ημία⌝ν⌝ τὸ
τ⌜α⌝μεῖον περιβληθήσε⌜τ⌝αι — ἵνα
95 ἐλεηθέντες διὰ τὴν θείαν σου
πρόνοιαν καὶ μείνα⌝ν⌝τ⌝ες ἐν
τοῖς ἰδίοις τούς ⌜τε⌝ ἱεροὺς φόρους
καὶ τὰ λοιπὰ τελέσματα παρασχεῖ⌝ν⌝
δυνησόμεθα· συμβήσεται δὲ
100 τοῦτο ἡμ⌜εῖν⌝ ἐν τοῖς εὐτυχεστάτοις σοῦ καιροῖς, ⌜ἐὰν κελεύσῃ⌜ς⌝
τὰ θεῖά σου ⌜γ⌝ρ⌜ά⌝μματα ἐν στή-
λῃ ⌜ἀ⌝ναγραφέντα δημοσίᾳ προ-
φ[α]ν⌜εῖ⌝σθα, ἵνα τούτου τυχόντες
105 τῇ Τύχῃ σοῦ χάριν ὁμολογεῖν
δυνησόμεθα, ὡς καὶ νῦν καθο̣[σ]-
107 [ι]ωμένοι σου ποιοῦμεν.
vacat 0,04
108 Adlegent ᵛᵃᶜ· Πύρρος ὁ πρα̣[ι]τωρι-
ανὸς ἀπὸ θείας φιλανθρωπί-
110 ας ἐπὶ τὴν ἔντευξιν ταύ-
την ἐλήλυθε̣ν· [κ]α̣ὶ δοκεῖ δέ̣
μοι θεῶν τ⌜ι⌝ς προνοήσασθαι

τῆς παρούσης ἀξιώσεως·
τὸ γὰρ ⌈τ⌉ὸν θειότατον ⌈αὐ⌉τ̣ο-
115  κράτορ⌈α π⌉ερὶ τούτων πέ⌈μ⌉-
ψαι τὴν δίανγνωσιν ἐπὶ
σέ ἔτι δε ἤδη φθάσαντα
118  περὶ τού⌈τ⌉‹ω›ν κα⌈ὶ⌉ προγράμ-

col. III  ⌈μασιν καὶ διατάγμασιν⌉
120  ⌈† δεδωκέναι †, τοῦτο ἐμοὶ δο⌉-
⌈κεῖ τῆς ἀγαθῆς τύχης ἔργον⌉
⌈εἶναι· ἣ‹ν› δὲ ἡ ἀξίωσις· Ἡ κώ⌉-
⌈μη ἡ τοῦ βοηθουμένου στρα⌉-
⌈τιώτου ἐστ‹ὶν› ἐν τῷ καλλί⌉-
125  ⌈στῳ τῆς πολιτείας τῆς ἡμε⌉-
⌈τέρας τῶν Πανταλιωτῶν πόλεως⌉
⌈κειμένη, καλῶς μὲν τῶν ὁρῶν⌉
⌈καὶ τῶν πεδίων ἔχουσα,⌉
⌈πρὸς δὲ τούτοις καὶ θερ⌉-
130  ⌈μῶν ὑδάτων λουτρὰ οὐ μό⌉-
⌈νον πρὸς τρυφήν, ἀλλὰ καὶ⌉
⌈ὑγείαν καὶ θεραπείαν σω⌉-
μάτων ⌈ἐπιτηδειότατα,⌉
πλησί⌈ον δὲ καὶ πανήγυρις⌉
135  π⌈ο⌉λλ⌈ά⌉κ⌈ι⌉ς μὲ⌈ν ἐν τῷ ἔτει⌉
συν⌈α⌉γ⌈ο⌉μένη πε⌈ρὶ δὲ ‹κ›α‹λ›(άνδας)⌉
Ὀκτωμ[βρίας καὶ εἰς πε⌈ντε⌉-
καίδεκα ἡμερῶν ἀτε̣λ̣⌈ής·⌉
συμβέβηκεν τοίνυν τὰ δ̣ο̣κο̣ῦ̣⌈ν⌉-
140  τα ⌈τ⌉ῆ̣ς κώμης ταύτης πλεον-
εκτήματα τῷ χρόνῳ περι-
εληλυθέναι αὐτῆς εἰς ἐ-
λαττώματα· — διὰ γὰρ τὰς
προειρημένας ταύτας
145  προφάσεις πολλοὶ πολλάκις στρατιῶται ἐνεπιδη-
μοῦντες ταῖς τε ἐπιξενώ-
⌈σεσι⌉ν καὶ ταῖς βαρήσεσιν
⌈ἐνο⌉χλοῦσιν τὴν κώμην·
150  κ[αὶ] διὰ τ̣α̣ύτ̣α̣ς αἰτίας πρό-
τερον αὐτὴν κ̣α̣ὶ πλουσιο-
τ⌈έ⌉ρ̣α̣ν κ̣α̣ὶ πολυάνθρωπον
μᾶ̣λ̣[λο]ν οὖσαν νῦν εἰς ἐσχά-
την ἀπορίαν ἐληλυθέναι·
155  περὶ τούτων ἐδ⌈ε⌉⌈ή⌉θη-
σαν πολλάκις καὶ τῶν ἡγε-
μόνων, ἀλλὰ κ̣α̣ὶ μέχρις τι-

νῶν ἴσχυσεν αὐτῶν τὰ
προστάγματ̣[α,] μετὰ δὲ
160    ταῦτα κατωλιγωρήθη
διὰ τὴν συγή̣[θ]ειαν τῆς
[τ]οιαύτης ἐνο̣[χ]λήσεως·
διὰ τοῦτο ἀναγκαίως κατ-
έφυγον ἐπὶ τὸν Σεβαστόν.
165   *Imp(erator) Caesar M(arcus) Antonius Gordianus pius felix Aug (ustus) vikanis*
*per Pyrrum mil(item) conposses-*
*sore[m·] id genus qu[a]erellae precibus intentum an VE .. ^ ....AT iustitia praesidis*
*‹p›otiʃus] super his quae adlegabuntur instructa discingere quam rescripto*
*pr[i]ncipali certam formam reportare deˇbeas. Rescripˇsi. Recognovi. Signavi.*

## I. Authentication (ll. 1–5)*

(ll. 1–5) Good Fortune. In the consulate of Fulvius Pius and Pontius Proculus
[238], on December 16 copied and examined from the collection of petitions
answered by our master, the emperor Caesar Marcus Antonius Gordianus Pius
Felix Augustus, and posted in Rome in the portico of the Baths of Trajan in the
words which are written below.

## II. Note of delivery (ll. 6–7)

(ll. 6–7) Presented by Aurelius Pyrrus soldier in the tenth praetorian cohort *pia
fidelis Gordiana*, of Proculus' century, fellow villager and owner.

## III. Petition to Gordian III (ll. 8–107)

*Inscriptio* (ll. 8–11)

(ll. 8–11) To the emperor Caesar Marcus Antonius Gordianus Pius Felix
Augustus. Petition from the villagers of Skaptopara, also called the Greseitai.

*Exordium* (ll. 11–21)

(ll. 11–15) That in your most happy and everlasting times the villages should be
inhabited and prosper, rather than the inhabitants should be driven off, you
have on many occasions stated in your rescripts. (ll. 15–17) This policy is both
salvation to the people and to the profit of your most sacred fisc. (ll. 18–21)
Therefore we too bring a legal supplication to your divinity, praying that you will
look graciously upon us when we entreat you in this way.

*Narratio* (ll. 21–77)

(ll. 21–26) We dwell and have our property in the village mentioned above; it is
most attractive because it has thermal springs and lies between the two military
camps which are in your [province of] Thracia. (ll. 26–30) In the past—as long
as the inhabitants were left alone and not subject to extortion—they contributed
faultlessly in full both taxes and the other impositions. (ll. 30–33) But when
some persons now and then started to get rough and use force, then the village

*Reprinted with permission from Tor Hauken, Petition and Response: An Epigraphic Study of Petitions to
Roman Emperors, 181–249, Monographs from the Norwegian Institute at Athens, Vol. 2. Bergen; Jonsered,
Sweden: Norwegian Institute at Athens; Distributor, P. Åstrøms förlag, 1998.*

too started to decline. (ll. 33–44) A famous market takes place two miles from our village. Those who stay there to attend the market, do not [however] remain at the marketplace for all the fifteen days—they leave it and turn up in our village and compel us to provide them with quartering and most of the other things for their entertainment without offering payment. (ll. 44–49) In addition to these soldiers that are despatched elsewhere leave their proper routes and appear among us and likewise press us hard to furnish them quartering and provisions without paying anything. (ll. 50–53) For the most part because of the thermal springs the provincial governors but also your procurators come here to stay. (ll. 53–59) We greet the authorities in a most hospitable way by necessity, but as we could not put up with the others, we have on many occasions appealed to the governors of Thracia, and they have—in accordance with the imperial instructions (*mandata*)—ordered that we shall be undisturbed (ll. 59–63). We explained that we can no longer remain, but that all of us have in mind to leave our ancestral homes because of the violence of those who assault us. (ll. 63–66) For in very truth from (being) landowners we have been reduced to very few. (ll. 66–73) For some time the orders of the governors held force and no one troubled us by demanding either quartering or provisions. But as time went on, numerous persons who despise our private status have again ventured to stick close.

*Preces* (ll. 73–107)
(ll. 73–77) So, since we can no longer sustain these burdens and, as the others, we too really face the risk of abandoning the settlements of our ancestors, (ll. 77–86) for this reason we beg you, invincible Augustus, to order by your sacred *rescriptum* that everyone shall keep to his proper route, that they shall not leave the other villages and come to us and compel us to offer them provisions at our expense, and that we shall not quarter those who are not entitled to [such service]. (ll. 86–94) For the governors have on many occasions ordered that quarters should not be provided for men other than those sent on service by governors and procurators. If we are oppressed, we shall flee our homes, and the fisc will be embroiled in the greatest loss. (ll. 94–99) If we are shown mercy by your divine foresights and remain in our homes, we will be able to provide both the sacred taxes and the other impositions. (ll. 99–107) This will happen to us in your most happy times if you order that your divine letter shall be written on a stele and set up in public so that we, when we have obtained this, can acknowledge our gratitude to your Genius, just as we do now because we [regard] you [with reverence].

IV. Speech delivered before the governor of Thracia (ll. 108–164)
*Exordium* (ll. 108–22)
(ll. 108–111) *Let them state.* Pyrrus the praetorian has come to this meeting by divine benevolence. (ll. 111–122) "It seems to me that some god has provided for the present petition: That the most divine emperor has referred the investigation of this case to you—whom he already knew had given [sentence] about this by edicts and instructions—this I think must be credited to good fortune."

*Narratio* (ll. 122–165)

(ll. 122–138) The petition. The village of the soldier who is being helped lies in the best [part] of our community, the town of the Pautalians. It is well endowed with mountains and plains; in addition [it has] thermal springs which are not only most suitable for pleasure, but also for health and healing of the body. Nearby there is also a market which is arranged many times a year, and around the first day of October it has tax immunity for fifteen days. (ll. 139–143) Now it has happened that what seemed to be an advantage to the village in time has turned to its disadvantage. (ll. 143–149) For the reasons we have mentioned above many soldiers on frequent occasions come to stay and they trouble the village by both the extra quartering and oppressive [requisitions]. (ll. 150–154) For these reasons the village, although it was formerly both quite prosperous and populous, has come to utter destruction. (ll 155–162) Even if they have on many occasions entreated the governors about this and their orders have for a while prevailed, the orders were later despised because of this habit of harassing it. (ll. 163–165) Because of this they perforce sought refuge in the [Augustus]

V. The subscriptio of Gordian III to Pyrrus, the representative of the village, Skaptopara. (ll. 165–168)

(ll. 166–69) The Emperor Marcus Antonius Gordianus Pius Felix Augustus to the villagers through Pyrrus, soldier and fellow owner. This kind of complaint submitted in a petition—if [correctly described]—you shall solve by notifying the court of the governor about what will be stated, rather than taking home some specific decision embodied in an imperial rescript.* I have answered. I have examined. [7] seals.

*Hauken, *Petition and Response*, 126, presents the following alternative translation based on Hallof's text of the *subscriptio*: "This kind of complaint submitted in a petition whether [it is true] the governor's sense of justice [ought] to decide—since it will be informed about the matters that will be alleged—rather than that you should take home a specific decision embodied in an imperial decision."

# Catalog of Extant Entries from the *Codex Hermogenianus*

The following catalog of extant entries from the *CH* is based on Paul Krüger's 1877 edition of the *CJ*.[1] Also included are entries dating to AD 293–294 which are found not in the *CJ*, but in other smaller collections. The new palingenesia was prompted by an attempt to recreate Diocletian's itinerary in AD 293–294, and so I have made emendations only to dates, locations, and names; I have not analyzed the texts themselves. I reconstituted the itinerary from entries whose locations coincided with a route confirmed by contemporary evidence and whose dates were consistent with a traveling speed of approximately twenty miles per day. A number of entries in Krüger's edition required emendation because their dates or locations did not fit this itinerary. I have taken into account Krüger and Mommsen's notes in the 1877 edition, many of which I have incorporated. I have also considered the changes suggested by Barnes and Honoré.[2]

Of an entry's date, location, and recipient, the first is the element most likely to be incorrect. Dates comprise the following parts: a day, for example, *iv non.*; a month, *Ian.*; a year, *AA* for AD 293, *CC* for AD 294. Of these parts, the day is the most prone to error. For example, *x*, *v*, and most frequently *i* may be left out; *v* may be written for *ii* and *v* for *x* (and vice versa). *k.*, *id.*, and *non.* are less frequently confused. Several pairs of months are prone to confusion: *Iun.* and *Ian.*, *Iun.* and *Iul.*, and *Mart.* and *Mai.* Other months are less likely to be miswritten, unless a month has been erroneously copied from a previous entry. Finally, some entries from AD 293 (*AA*) have been dated to 294 (*CC*) and vice versa. As far as is possible, I have made emendations that preserve the chronological sequence within the titles. But it seems that sometimes an error in dating could have occurred before the entries were arranged into their *CJ* titles and the corrected entries will therefore fall out of sequence. On a few occasions Honoré has provided in his palingenesia *termini ante quem* for undated rescripts by looking at the dates of subsequent entries. But he has omitted *termini post quem*, which are sometimes available and can narrow down potential dates and therefore locations. Where possible, both *termini* have been used to give such entries approximate dates and locations.[3]

Dates are more likely to be incorrect than are locations. Occasionally a scribe has mistakenly applied the place name of one entry to its successor also, but there seems to be no instance of two place names being confused. A few recipients' names have also been incorrectly copied, for example, *Rheso* for *Rhesae*. The extent of Krüger's efforts to determine petitioners' correct names is highlighted by just a cursory glance at a 1475 edition of the *CJ*: it has *Maxio militia* for Krüger's *Maximo mil.* (1.18.1), *Iuliano* for *Iulianae* (1.18.4), *Marcello* for *Martiali* (1.18.5) and *Tauro et Pallioni* for *Tauro et Pollioni* (1.18.6). It even names the recipients of *CJ* 2.28.2 as *Severae et Dementianae* instead of *Severae et Clementianae* (presumably copying an earlier error).[4]

What follows is a series of suggestions for how incorrect entries can be emended. Some entries contain dates or locations that are incorrect, but cannot be reconciled with other pieces of information. These have been kept as they appeared in Krüger's edition, but their problems are noted below. For others, only alterations that seem most reasonable have been included, but there may be others that turn out to be more suitable. I am aware that proposing changes to entries on the basis that their dates are incorrect raises the possibility that many other entries may also have the wrong date. Therefore, the catalog that follows is an attempt only to suggest changes to entries that obviously contradict a reasonable itinerary.

Locations given to unplaced entries on the basis of placed entries from the same day are marked in bold type. Locations given to unplaced entries on the basis of placed entries close in time are marked in italics. Entries with Western locations have been excluded from this catalog because they were not produced by Diocletian's court.[5]

Entries described as undateable belong to the years 293–304 but cannot be dated more precisely. It is therefore uncertain whether they were in the *Codex Hermogenianus*.

## Key

Sirmium = location recorded in entry
**Sirmium** = location supplemented on the basis of other entries placed at the location on the same day
*Sirmium* = location supplemented on the basis of other entries placed at the location shortly before or after

| CJ entry no. | Date | Location | Recipient |
|---|---|---|---|
| 5.74.2 | 1.1.293 | Sirmium | Alexander |
| 3.34.8 | 1.1.293 | Sirmium | Anicetus |
| 6.26.7 | 1.1.293 | Sirmium | Felicianus |
| 9.33.3 | 1.7.293 | Sirmium | Euelpistus |
| Cons 6.15 | 1.7.293 | **Sirmium** | Flaviana |
| 4.7.4 | 1.7.293 | Sirmium | Rufinus |
| 7.14.4 | 1.10.293 | *Sirmium* | Agrippa |
| 2.55.3 | 1.11.293 | *Sirmium* | Petronia |
| 8.17.7 | 1.16.293 | *Sirmium* | Iulianus |
| 7.29.2 | 1.28.293 | *Sirmium* | Marina |
| 6.42.23 | 1.28.293 | *Sirmium* | Stratonicus |
| 7.35.5 | 2.1.293 | *Sirmium* | Ianuarius |
| 4.44.3 | 2.6.293 | *Sirmium* | Titia & Marciana |

| *CJ* entry no. | Date | Location | Recipient |
|---|---|---|---|
| 6.2.9 | 2.7.293 | Sirmium | Aedesius |
| 3.38.5 | 2.8.293 | Sirmium | Fronto & Glafirio |
| 6.42.21 | 2.8.293 | **Sirmium** | Tiberius |
| 8.39.3 | 2.9.293 | Sirmium | Andronicus |
| FV 42 | 2.11.293 | Sirmium | Loreus, Aurelius et qui Enucentrius |
| 9.35.7 | 2.13.293 | Sirmium | Paenentianus |
| FV 312 | 2.21.293 | | Aurelius Onesimus |
| 2.5.1 | 2.24.293 | *Sirmium* | Aurelius Quartus |
| 4.34.6 | before 2.26.293 | *Sirmium* | Antonius Alexander & Ulpianus Antipater |
| 4.34.7 | before 2.26.293 | *Sirmium* | Antiochus Atticus Calpurnianus Democrates |
| 4.34.8 | 2.26.293 | Sirmium | Aurelius Alexander |
| 3.32.11 | 2.26.293 | Sirmium | Gaianus |
| 8.13.11 | 2.27.293 | *Sirmium* | Euphrosynus |
| 5.39.4 | 3.5.293 | | Maximiana |
| 2.4.16 | 3.11.293 | | Caecilius |
| 3.32.13 | 3.13.293 | | Eutychius |
| 5.51.7 | 3.14.293 | | Alexander |
| 8.13.12 | 3.28.293 | | Eusebius |
| 8.55.4 | 4.1.293 | Heraclea | Procula |
| 8.47.6 | 4.2.293 | Byzantium | Meliton |
| 5.30.2 | 4.3.293 | **Byzantium** | Asclepiodotus |
| 5.31.9 | " | Byzantium | " |
| 2.12.15 | 4.3.293 | **Byzantium** | Cornificius |
| 4.5.3 | 4.3.293 | Byzantium | Pamphilus |
| 4.9.2 | 4.3.293 | **Byzantium** | Scylacius |
| 7.14.5 | 4.4.293 | *Byzantium* | Crescens |
| 4.44.2 | 4.5.293 | Byzantium | Aurelius Felix |
| 4.10.5 | 4.5.293 | Byzantium | Camerinus & Marcianus |
| 4.26.7 | 4.5.293 | Byzantium | Crescens |
| 2.12.16 | 4.5.293 | Byzantium | Paconia |
| 5.10.4 | 4.5.293 | **Byzantium** | Rufus |
| 4.44.4 | 4.5.293 | Byzantium | Sempronius Eudoxius |
| 4.29.14M | 4.6.293 | Byzantium | Basilissa |
| 4.19.18M | 4.7.293 | Byzantium | Violentilla |
| 3.32.12 | 4.8.293 | **Byzantium** | Alexander |
| 4.26.8 | 4.8.293 | Byzantium | Isidorus |
| 4.49.6 | 4.8.293 | Byzantium | Neratius |
| 8.42.10 | 4.9.293 | Byzantium | Ambrosius |

| *CJ* entry no. | Date | Location | Recipient |
|---|---|---|---|
| 7.27.2 | 4.9.293 | **Byzantium** | Capiton |
| 8.8.2 | 4.9.293 | Byzantium | Cyrilla |
| 7.60.1M | 4.9.293 | Byzantium | Epagathus |
| 8.50.9 | 4.9.293 | **Byzantium** | Gregorius |
| 4.5.4 | 4.9.293 | Byzantium | Heraclius |
| 6.26.8 | 4.9.293 | **Byzantium** | Petronia |
| 7.33.4 | 4.10.293 | *Byzantium* | Hermus |
| 4.14.6 | 4.12.293 | Byzantium | Felicianus |
| 3.22.3 | 4.12.293 | Byzantium | Zenones |
| 5.70.4 | 4.13.293 | Byzantium | Asclepiodotus |
| 8.39.2 | 4.13.293 | Byzantium | Fabricius |
| 4.19.9 | 4.13.293 | **Byzantium** | Marciana |
| 3.19.1 | 4.13.293 | **Byzantium** | Pancratius |
| 6.42.22 | 4.13.293 | Byzantium | Plancianus |
| 7.60.2 | 4.13.293 | Byzantium | Severa |
| 7.32.6 | 4.13.293 | **Byzantium** | Valerius |
| 6.2.10M | " | " | " |
| 5.1.1 | 4.14.293 | | Bianor |
| 9.12.3M | " | | " |
| 5.51.8 | 4.14.293 | | Dalmatius |
| 4.19.10 | 4.14.293 | | Isidorus |
| 7.16.12 | 4.14.293 | | Secundus |
| 4.49.7 | 4.15.293 | Melantias | Diodorus |
| 8.53.9 | 4.16.293 | | Augustina |
| 3.35.4 | 4.17.293 | Heraclea | Zoilus |
| 4.5.5 | 4.18.293 | **Heraclea** | Attalus |
| 2.21.3 | 4.18.293 | Heraclea | Attianus |
| 6.9.4M | 4.18.293 | Heraclea | Marcellus |
| 4.16.3 | 4.18.293 | **Heraclea** | Maxima |
| 2.28.2 | 4.19.293 | *Heraclea* | Severa & Clementiana |
| 5.34.5 | 4.20.293 | *Heraclea* | Aeliana |
| 4.15.4 | 4.20.293 | *Heraclea* | Zosimus |
| 7.33.5M | 4.21.293 | *Heraclea* | Soterichus |
| 7.75.4 | 4.22.293 | **Heraclea** | Epagathus |
| 5.37.16 | 4.22.293 | Heraclea | Proculus |
| 5.12.11 | 4.22.293 | Heraclea | Severa |
| 5.16.17 | 4.24.293 | Heraclea | Capitolina |
| 8.42.11 | " | " | " |
| 2.45.1 | 4.24.293 | **Heraclea** | Eutychianus |
| 10.32.6 | 4.24.293 | **Heraclea** | Leontius |
| 5.12.12 | 4.24.293 | Heraclea | Rufina |

| *CJ* entry no. | Date | Location | Recipient |
|---|---|---|---|
| 7.14.6 | 4.25.293 | *Heraclea* | Dionysius |
| 6.20.9 | 4.26.293 | Heraclea | Onesimus |
| 7.16.13 | 4.27.293 | **Heraclea** | Antistia |
| 4.19.11 | 4.27.293 | Heraclea | Antonia |
| 4.49.8 | 4.27.293 | **Heraclea** | Aurelius Eusebius |
| 4.52.3M | " | " | " |
| 9.1.12 | 4.27.293 | **Heraclea** | Corinthia |
| 8.55.5 | 4.27.293 | Heraclea | Epagathus |
| 8.53.10 | 4.27.293 | **Heraclea** | Hermione |
| 2.21.4 | 4.27.293 | Heraclea | Isidorus |
| 2.24.4 | " | " | " |
| 4.65.19 | 4.27.293 | Heraclea | Iulius Valentinus |
| 3.42.8 | 4.27.293 | Heraclea | Photinus |
| 8.27.11 | 4.27.293 | Heraclea | Rufina |
| 2.21.5 | 4.27.293 | Heraclea | Rufus |
| 6.50.13 | 4.27.293 | Heraclea | Zethus |
| 7.16.14 | 4.28.293 | Heraclea | Quintiana |
| 4.65.20M | 4.29.293 | Heraclea | Aurelius Carpophorus |
| 4.26.9M | 4.29.293 | **Heraclea** | Diogenius |
| 8.38.4 | 4.29.293 | **Heraclea** | Domna |
| 8.13.13 | 4.29.293 | Heraclea | Matrona |
| 2.20.4M | 4.29.293 | Heraclea | Menandra |
| 9.41.13 | 4.29.293 | Heraclea | Philippa |
| 2.19.6M | 4.29.293 | Heraclea | Polla |
| 7.19.5M | 4.30.293 | Heraclea | Alephus |
| 9.33.4 | 4.30.293 | Heraclea | Attalus |
| 5.12.13 | 4.30.293 | Heraclea | Catula |
| 8.17.8 | 4.30.293 | Heraclea | Fabricius |
| 5.34.6 | 4.30.293 | **Heraclea** | Leontius |
| 5.71.12 | " | Heraclea | " |
| 8.53.11 | 4.30.293 | Heraclea | Septimius Sabinianus |
| 8.40.19 | " | " | " |
| 7.1.2 | 4.30.293 | **Heraclea** | Sallustius |
| 8.44.19 | 4.30.293 | **Heraclea** | Theodorus |
| 8.27.12 | 4.30.293 | Heraclea | Zoticus |
| 8.13.14 | 5.1.293 | Heraclea | Appianus |
| 9.20.9M | 5.1.293 | Heraclea | Eugenius |
| 8.16.6 | 5.1.293 | Heraclea | Rufus |
| 8.35.5 | 5.1.293 | Tzirallum | Basilius |
| 5.3.8 | 5.1.293 | Tzirallum | Euphrosynus |
| 6.30.7 | 5.1.293 | Tzirallum | Eusebius |

| *CJ* entry no. | Date | Location | Recipient |
|---|---|---|---|
| 2.3.21 | " | " | " |
| 6.53.6 | " | " | " |
| 4.2.5 | 5.3.293 | | Aristodemus & Proculus |
| 8.13.15 | 5.3.293 | *Adrianople* | Basilis |
| 5.14.6 | 5.3.293 | | Rufus |
| 4.37.1 | 5.5.293 | | Aurelius |
| 4.24.10 | 5.7.293 | | Apollodora |
| 6.14.2 | 5.9.293 | | Zosimus |
| 4.7.5 | 5.10.293 | **Adrianople** | Bithus |
| 7.16.16 | 5.10.293 | Adrianople | Diogenia |
| 8.13.16 | 5.12.293 | Adrianople | Herais |
| 8.50.10M | 5.13.293 | Adrianople | Apollodora |
| 8.42.12 | 5.13.293 | **Adrianople** | Eutychus |
| 4.6.6 | 5.14.293 | | Curio & Plotio |
| 8.53.12 | 5.16.293 | | Aurelius |
| 4.57.6 | 5.17.293 | | Helvidia Rufina |
| 8.13.17 | 5.18.293 | | Pontia |
| 7.16.17 | 5.23.293 | | Reginus |
| 6.3.12 | 5.24.293 | | Veneria |
| 2.17.3M | 5.25.293 | Philippopolis | Amphio |
| 2.52.4M | 5.25.293 | Philippopolis | Dionysius |
| 8.42.13 | 5.26.293 | *Philippopolis* | Philotimus |
| 4.23.1 | 5.27.293 | *Philippopolis* | Sisola |
| 4.38.4 | 5.29.293 | *Philippopolis* | Aurelius Lucianus |
| 5.12.14 | 6.2.293 | Philippopolis | Basilissa |
| 2.19.7M | 6.4.293 | *Philippopolis* | Cotys |
| 2.12.17 | 6.5.293 | Philippopolis | Mardonius |
| 2.4.17 | 6.9.293 | | Marcellus |
| 2.20.5 | 6.13.293 | | Aphrodisia |
| 5.24.1 | 6.14.293 | Beroea | Caelestina |
| 6.59.2M | 6.15.293 | Beroea | Apollinarius |
| 4.49.9 | 6.17.293 | Philippopolis | Aurelia Zania Antipatra |
| 7.67.1 | 6.17.293 | Philippopolis | Diophanes |
| 6.55.3 | 6.17.293 | **Philippopolis** | Fronto |
| 7.14.7 | 6.17.293 | **Philippopolis** | Matrona |
| 4.21.9 | 6.26.293 | *Philippopolis* | Aristaenetus |
| 3.33.8 | 6.26.293 | *Philippopolis* | Hiero |
| 8.44.20 | 6.27.293 | *Philippopolis* | Solidus et alii |
| 3.32.14 | 6.29.293 | *Philippopolis* | Septima |
| 9.33.5 | 7.2.293 | Philippopolis | Domina |
| 6.23.12 | 7.6.293 | Philippopolis | Matronia |

| *CJ* entry no. | Date | Location | Recipient |
|---|---|---|---|
| 5.34.7 | 7.6.293 | Philippopolis | Rufus |
| 6.23.11 | 7.6.293 | **Philippopolis** | Zethus |
| 6.26.6M | 7.10.293 | **Philippopolis** | Quintianus |
| 6.49.4 | " | Philippopolis | " |
| 8.42.14 | 7.11.293 | **Philippopolis** | Cuta |
| 8.15.6 | 7.11.293 | Philippopolis | Zosimus |
| 5.16.19M | 7.15.293 | Philippopolis | Dionysia |
| 7.16.18 | 7.15.293 | Philippopolis | Zoticus |
| 8.44.21 | 7.22.293 | Serdica | Heliodorus |
| 3.31.7 | 7.22.293 | **Serdica** | Restituta |
| 5.16.18 | 7.29.293 | Serdica | Materna |
| 4.5.6 | 8.8.293 | **Viminacium** | Mnaseas |
| 9.22.12 | 8.8.293 | Viminacium | Primus |
| 5.16.20M | 8.9.293 | Viminacium | Claudia |
| 5.16.21M | 8.11.293 | Viminacium | Cacalia |
| 9.46.6 | 8.17.293 | *Viminacium* | Domitius |
| 4.50.6 | 8.19.293 | Viminacium | Aurelius Dionysius |
| 4.50.7 | 8.19.293 | **Viminacium** | Aurelius Gerontius |
| 3.21.1 | " | " | " |
| 7.72.9 | " | " | " |
| 2.19.8 | 8.22.293 | Viminacium | Trophimus |
| 7.22.1 | 8.23.293 | *Viminacium* | Mucianus |
| 3.36.16 | 8.25.293 | *Viminacium* | Heraclianus |
| 6.2.11 | 8.26.293 | Viminacium | Demosthenes |
| 4.6.7 | 8.26.293 | **Viminacium** | Gerontius |
| 8.44.22 | 8.26.293 | Viminacium | Iulius |
| 7.16.20 | 8.27.293 | **Viminacium** | Aeternalis |
| 3.13.2 | 8.27.293 | **Viminacium** | Alexander |
| 2.9.3M | 8.27.293 | Viminacium | Ulpia |
| 2.4.20 | 8.28.293 | **Viminacium** | Antistia |
| 8.50.16 | 8.28.293 | Viminacium | Basilina |
| 9.9.25 | 8.28.293 | **Viminacium** | Crispinus |
| 8.42.15 | 8.28.293 | **Viminacium** | Quartio |
| 2.11.21 | 8.28.293 | **Viminacium** | Statius |
| 2.4.18 | 8.30.293 | *Viminacium* | Valentinianus |
| 8.35.6 | 9.1.293 | Viminacium | Helena |
| 5.71.13 | 9.6.293 | Sirmium | Zenonilla |
| 4.5.7 | 9.9.293 | *Sirmium* | Dionysia |
| 4.12.3 | 9.11.293 | Sirmium | Carpophorus |
| 3.32.15 | 9.17.293 | **Sirmium** | Aurelius Proculinus |
| 8.48.3 | 9.17.293 | Sirmium | Heliodorus |

| *CJ* entry no. | Date | Location | Recipient |
|---|---|---|---|
| 8.53.14 | 9.17.293 | **Sirmium** | Idaea |
| 2.4.19 | 9.18.293 | Sirmium | Irenaeus |
| 8.38.5 | 9.19.293 | **Sirmium** | Aquilina |
| 2.42.3 | 9.19.293 | Sirmium | Theodota |
| 4.35.18 | 9.25.293 | Sirmium | Tuscianus |
| 4.36.1 | 10.1.293 | Sirmium | Aurelia Dionysia |
| 4.26.10M | 10.3.293 | Sirmium | Aphrodisius |
| 4.19.12 | 10.3.293 | **Sirmium** | Chronia |
| 3.41.3 | 10.3.293 | Sirmium | Eutychius |
| 2.4.21 | 10.3.293 | **Sirmium** | Geminianus |
| 4.2.7 | 10.3.293 | **Sirmium** | Pactumeia |
| 6.38.2 | 10.7.293 | Sirmium | Rufinus |
| 7.16.21 | 10.7.293 | Sirmium | Thallusa |
| 4.65.21 | 10.8.293 | Sirmium | Antonia |
| 4.65.22 | 10.8.293–12.25.293 | *Sirmium* | Aurelius Priscus |
| 4.65.23 | 10.8.293–12.25.293 | *Sirmium* | Papinianus |
| 8.30.3 | 10.10.293 | *Sirmium* | Florus |
| 5.21.2 | 10.11.293 | *Sirmium* | Serenus |
| 6.15.3 | 10.15.293 | Sirmium | Felix |
| 6.2.12 | 10.15.293 | Sirmium | Quintilla |
| 4.25.4 | 10.17.293 | Sirmium | Antigone |
| 4.51.3 | 10.17.293 | Sirmium | Aurelius Valerianus |
| 6.5.1M | 10.17.293 | Sirmium | Claudius |
| 6.24.9 | 10.17.293 | Sirmium | Iulia |
| 5.37.17 | 10.17.293 | Sirmium | Martial |
| 2.39.2M | 10.17.293 | Sirmium | Sarapias |
| 8.42.16 | 10.18.293 | **Sirmium** | Charidemus |
| 3.35.5 | 10.18.293 | **Sirmium** | Claudius |
| 4.44.5 | 10.18.293 | Sirmium | Claudius Rufus |
| 9.35.8 | 10.18.293 | **Sirmium** | Marcianus |
| 4.44.7 | 10.18.293–11.30.293 | *Sirmium* | Mucatraulus |
| 4.44.6 | 10.18.293–11.30.293 | *Sirmium* | Novisius Gaius |
| 4.35.19 | 10.19.293 | Sirmium | Aurelius Eugenius |
| 6.17.1 | 10.21.293 | Sirmium | Flora |
| 6.57.3 | 10.21.293 | **Sirmium** | Iuliana |
| 8.40.21 | 10.22.293 | *Sirmium* | Iulianus |
| Cons 6.13 | 10.22.293 | *Sirmium* | Quintianus |
| 7.75.5 | 10.23.293 | *Sirmium* | Crescentinus |
| 3.34.11M | 10.27.293 | Sirmium | Aurelius |
| 4.23.2 | 11.4.293 | | Auluzanus |
| 9.20.11 | 11.5.293 | Lucione | Ampliata |

| *CJ* entry no. | Date | Location | Recipient |
|---|---|---|---|
| 9.20.10 | 11.5.293 | Lucione | Diza |
| 4.34.9 | 11.7.93 | Sirmium | Aurelius Menophilus et alii |
| 3.44.13M | 11.11.293 | Sirmium | Dionysius |
| 4.1.7 | 11.13.293 | **Sirmium** | Eutychiana |
| 3.32.16 | 11.13.293 | Sirmium | Ianuarius |
| 2.3.22 | 11.14.293 | Sirmium | Archelaus |
| 5.71.14 | 11.14.293 | **Sirmium** | Fronto |
| 4.2.6 | 11.17.293 | *Sirmium* | Nicander |
| 8.53.15 | 11.17.293 | *Sirmium* | Severa |
| 3.32.17 | 11.20.293 | Sirmium | Sabinus |
| 4.16.4 | 11.22.293 | Sirmium | Crispus |
| 5.51.12 | 11.22.293 | Sirmium | Quintilla |
| 5.10.5 | 11.24.293 | *Sirmium* | Dasumiana |
| 2.51.2 | 11.24.293 | *Sirmium* | Quintilianus |
| 5.71.15 | 11.24.293 | *Sirmium* | Sabina |
| 4.38.5 | 11.24.293 | *Sirmium* | Umbiga Gratia |
| 4.38.6 | 11.24.293–3.7.294 | *Sirmium* | Aurelius Lucretius |
| 3.36.17 | 11.25.293 | Sirmium | Commodianus |
| 6.20.10 | 11.26.293 | Sirmium | Irenea |
| 8.37.5 | 11.27.293 | *Sirmium* | Isidora |
| 7.16.22 | 11.27.293 | *Sirmium* | Pardalis |
| 7.16.23 | 11.27.293–12.28.293 | *Sirmium* | Muscia |
| 8.53.16 | 11.27.293 | *Sirmium* | Theodorus |
| 4.26.11M | 11.30.293 | Sirmium | Attalus |
| 2.4.22 | 12.1.293 | **Sirmium** | Alexander |
| 4.44.8 | 12.1.293 | **Sirmium** | Aurelia Euodia |
| 3.33.9 | 12.1.293 | **Sirmium** | Auxanusa |
| 8.42.17 | 12.1.293 | Sirmium | Cassius |
| 8.34.2 | 12.1.293 | Sirmium | Dionysius |
| 6.2.13 | 12.1.293 | Sirmium | Domnus |
| 8.13.18 | 12.1.293 | Sirmium | Euodius |
| 8.9.2 | 12.1.293 | Sirmium | Fabricius |
| 5.46.3 | 12.1.293 | **Sirmium** | Gaianus |
| 2.19.9 | 12.1.293 | **Sirmium** | Hymnoda |
| 2.20.6 | " | " | " |
| 4.19.13 | 12.1.293 | **Sirmium** | Iustinus |
| 6.42.24 | 12.1.293 | Sirmium | Menestratus |
| 4.19.14 | 12.1.293 | **Sirmium** | Mucianus |
| 8.25.10 | 12.1.293 | **Sirmium** | Quintilla |
| 7.2.12 | 12.1.293 | Sirmium | Rhizus |
| 1.22.2M | 12.1.293 | Sirmium | Statia |

| *CJ* entry no. | Date | Location | Recipient |
|---|---|---|---|
| 5.22.1M | 12.4.293 | *Sirmium* | Apollonaria |
| 5.21.3M | 12.4.293 | *Sirmium* | Quartio |
| 2.42.4 | 12.8.293 | *Sirmium* | Livius |
| 6.55.4 | 12.8.293 | *Sirmium* | Marcella |
| 7.32.7 | 12.9.293 | *Sirmium* | Asyncritus |
| 4.30.9 | 12.11.293 | *Sirmium* | Zoilus |
| 2.3.24 | 12.14.293 | Sirmium | Domna |
| 3.36.18 | " | " | " |
| 2.3.23 | 12.14.293 | Sirmium | Honoratus |
| 4.35.11 | 12.14.293–12.16.293 | *Sirmium* | Aurelius Gaius |
| Cons 4.11 | 12.15.293 | **Sirmium** | Zeuxianus Antoninus |
| 3.36.19 | 12.15.293 | **Sirmium** | Lysicratia |
| 3.41.4 | 12.15.293 | Sirmium | Sosius |
| 7.72.5 | 12.16.293 | **Sirmium** | Abydonius |
| 6.30.8 | 12.16.293 | Sirmium | Claudius |
| 4.35.12M | 12.16.293 | Sirmium | Firmus |
| 9.12.4 | 12.16.293 | Sirmium | Liberatius |
| 8.13.19 | 12.16.293 | **Sirmium** | Maximus |
| 8.27.14 | 12.16.293 | Sirmium | Modestus |
| 4.2.8 | 12.16.293 | **Sirmium** | Proculus |
| 4.49.10 | 12.16.293 | **Sirmium** | Titius Attalus |
| 2.17.4M | 12.17.293 | Sirmium | Achilles |
| 6.58.5M | 12.17.293 | Sirmium | Cyrilla |
| 8.19.2 | 12.17.293 | **Sirmium** | Endemia |
| 8.37.6 | 12.17.293 | Sirmium | Erotius |
| 6.27.3 | 12.17.293 | Sirmium | Felix |
| 8.3.1 | 12.17.293 | **Sirmium** | Latina |
| 6.30.9 | 12.17.293 | Sirmium | Plato |
| 6.30.10M | 12.17.293 | Sirmium | Sabina |
| 4.2.9 | 12.18.293 | **Sirmium** | Alexander |
| 6.39.3 | 12.18.293 | Sirmium | Aper & Pia |
| 3.28.19M | 12.18.293 | Sirmium | Apollinaris |
| 4.44.9 | 12.18.293 | Sirmium | Domitius Civalensis |
| 4.44.10 | 12.18.293–12.28.294 | | Aemilius Severus |
| 4.44.11 | 12.18.293–12.28.294 | | Aurelia Magna |
| 4.44.12 | 12.18.293–12.28.294 | | Antiochus |
| 4.44.13 | 12.18.293–12.28.294 | | Aurelius Nica Decaria |
| 8.50.11 | 12.18.293 | **Sirmium** | Eutychius |
| 9.25.1 | 12.18.293 | **Sirmium** | Iulianus |
| 8.53.13 | 12.18.293 | Sirmium | Urania |
| 9.2.12M | 12.19.293 | Sirmium | Aurelius |

| *CJ* entry no. | Date | Location | Recipient |
|---|---|---|---|
| 3.33.10 | 12.20.293 | Sirmium | Pomponius |
| 6.15.4 | 12.22.293 | Sirmium | Syrisca |
| 4.49.11 | 12.23.293 | *Sirmium* | Flavia Eucarpia |
| 3.32.18 | 12.24.293 | **Sirmium** | Clarus |
| 8.43.2 | " | " | " |
| 8.13.26 | 12.24.293 | Sirmium | Mauricius |
| 4.10.6M | " | " | " |
| 4.65.24 | 12.25.293 | Sirmium | Aurelius Antoninus |
| 3.32.19 | 12.25.293 | Sirmium | Callistratus |
| 5.3.10 | 12.25.293–2.7.294 | *Sirmium* | Dionysius |
| 5.3.11 | 12.25.293–2.7.294 | *Sirmium* | Nea |
| 6.2.14 | 12.25.293 | " | " |
| 6.5.2M | 12.25.293 | Sirmium | Iulia |
| 5.3.9 | 12.25.293 | **Sirmium** | Iulianus |
| 4.19.15 | 12.27.293 | **Sirmium** | Antoninus |
| 6.55.5 | 12.27.293 | Sirmium | Appianus |
| 8.15.7 | 12.27.293 | **Sirmium** | Cornelia |
| 8.53.17 | 12.27.293 | **Sirmium** | Hermias |
| 3.13.3 | 12.27.293 | **Sirmium** | Iuda |
| 9.22.13 | 12.27.293 | Sirmium | Marcus |
| 5.12.27 | 12.27.293 | Sirmium | Pompeianus |
| 4.24.11M | 12.28.293 | Sirmium | Ammianus |
| 6.20.11 | 12.28.293 | **Sirmium** | Artemia |
| 8.53.18 | 12.28.293 | **Sirmium** | Audianus |
| 2.4.39 | 12.28.293 | Sirmium | Marciana |
| 6.31.4 | 12.28.293 | Sirmium | Modestinus |
| 8.24.2 | 12.28.293 | **Sirmium** | Nonnosus & Antoninus |
| 8.1.3 | 12.28.293 | Sirmium | Pompeianus |
| 8.50.12 | 12.28.293 | **Sirmium** | Quintiana |
| 3.34.9M | 12.28.293 | **Sirmium** | Zosimus |
| 7.14.8 | 12.29.293 | *Sirmium* | Callimorphus |
| 7.14.9 | 12.29.293–3.6.294 | *Sirmium* | Potamon |
| 7.14.10 | 12.29.293–3.6.294 | *Sirmium* | Athenodora |
| 7.16.24 | 12.29.293 | *Sirmium* | Sebastianus |
| *Cons.* 4.9 | " | " | " |
| 7.19.6 | 12.30.293 | Sirmium | Alexandria |
| 4.65.25 | 12.30.293 | Sirmium | Aurelius Epagathus |
| 4.10.7 | 12.30.293 | Sirmium | Euelpistus |
| 9.22.14 | 12.30.293 | Sirmium | Gentiana |
| 8.56.3 | 12.30.293 | Sirmium | Heres |
| 5.17.4M | 12.30.293 | Sirmium | Piso |

| *CJ* entry no. | Date | Location | Recipient |
|---|---|---|---|
| 6.2.15 | 12.30.293 | Sirmium | Socratia |
| 7.33.7 | 12.31.293 | **Sirmium** | Anthea |
| 6.31.5 | 12.31.293 | Sirmium | Claudiana |
| 6.58.6 | " | " | " |
| 8.44.23 | 12.31.293 | Sirmium | Eustochia |
| 5.51.9 | 12.31.293 | **Sirmium** | Iulianus |
| 1.18.5 | 12.31.293 | **Sirmium** | Martial |
| 2.3.20M | " | " | " |
| 5.37.18 | 12.31.293 | Sirmium | Soterichus |
| 4.15.5 | 1.1.294 | *Sirmium* | Nanidia |
| 5.12.16M | 1.5.294 | Sirmium | Aemilianus |
| 5.61.2 | 1.5.294 | Sirmium | Alphocratio |
| 3.28.20 | 1.5.294 | Sirmium | Sabinianus |
| 5.12.17M | " | " | " |
| 5.18.7 | 1.9.294 | Sirmium | Erotius |
| 3.6.2 | 1.14.294 | *Sirmium* | Aurelia Agemacha |
| 8.13.20 | 1.15.294 | **Sirmium** | Alexander |
| 6.37.16 | 1.15.294 | Sirmium | Scylla |
| 8.37.7 | 1.16.294 | **Sirmium** | Antoninus |
| 4.29.16 | 1.16.294 | Sirmium | Rufinus |
| 8.53.19 | 1.17.294 | Sirmium | Alexandria |
| 6.50.16 | 1.17.294 | Sirmium | Diomedes |
| 6.50.15 | 1.17.294 | Sirmium | Pomponius |
| 5.12.18M | 1.19.294 | Sirmium | Menestratus |
| 5.12.19 | 1.20.294 | Sirmium | Achilles |
| 4.10.8 | 1.20.294 | Sirmium | Crescentio |
| 5.60.2 | 1.20.294 | **Sirmium** | Menippus |
| 9.22.15 | 1.20.294 | **Sirmium** | Rufus |
| 4.26.12 | 1.20.294 | Sirmium | Victor |
| 8.14.5 | 1.21.294 | **Sirmium** | Corinthia |
| 2.12.18 | 1.21.294 | Sirmium | Dionysia |
| 8.47.7 | 1.22.294 | Sirmium | Atticus |
| 6.20.12 | 1.22.294 | Sirmium | Nilanthia |
| 3.34.10 | 1.22.294 | Sirmium | Nymphidius |
| 5.51.10 | 1.22.294 | Sirmium | Pomponius |
| 4.19.16 | 1.23.294 | *Sirmium* | Philippus & Sebastiana |
| 8.53.20 | 1.26.294 | *Sirmium* | Helvius |
| 8.44.24 | 1.27.294 | Sirmium | Eutychius |
| 2.19.10 | 1.27.294 | **Sirmium** | Faustina |
| 6.46.5 | 1.27.294 | Sirmium | Faustinus |
| 5.62.23 | 1.27.294 | Sirmium | Neophytus |

| *CJ* entry no. | Date | Location | Recipient |
|---|---|---|---|
| 5.34.9 | 1.30.294 | Sirmium | Maximianus |
| 3.36.20 | 1.30.294 or 2.3.294 or 10.3.294 | *Sirmium* | Pactumeia |
| 4.10.9 | 2.1.294 | **Sirmium** | Glyco |
| 4.35.13 | 2.1.294 | Sirmium | Zosimus |
| 4.2.10 | 2.4.294 | Sirmium | Crispinus |
| 4.49.12 | " | " | Egus Crispinus |
| 4.50.8 | 2.4.294 | Sirmium | Maxima Valentina |
| 3.15.2 | 2.4.294 | Sirmium | Nica |
| 2.50.7 | 2.5.294 | *Sirmium* | Marina |
| 9.22.16 | 2.6.294 | Sirmium | Fortunatus |
| 3.37.4 | 2.6.294 | **Sirmium** | Herodae |
| 3.28.21 | 2.8.294 | **Sirmium** | Alexander |
| 6.20.13 | 2.8.294 | Sirmium | Antistia |
| 4.9.3 | 2.8.294 | **Sirmium** | Galatia |
| 6.30.11 | 2.8.294 | Sirmium | Philumena |
| 6.55.6 | 2.8.294 | **Sirmium** | Posidonius |
| 8.44.25 | 2.8.294 | **Sirmium** | Saturnina |
| 2.32.1 | 2.8.294 | **Sirmium** | Soter |
| 2.45.2 | " | " | " |
| 5.3.12 | 2.8.294 | Sirmium | Timoclea & Cleotima |
| 8.47.8 | 2.9.294 | *Sirmium* | Isio |
| 7.16.25 | 2.9.294 | *Sirmium* | Licentianus |
| 4.19.17 | 2.9.294 | *Sirmium* | Paulina |
| 7.26.7 | 2.9.294 | *Sirmium* | Pecus |
| 5.56.4 | 2.11.294 | Sirmium | Aurelius |
| 4.6.9 | 2.11.294 | Sirmium | Bibulus |
| 4.51.4 | 2.11.294 | **Sirmium** | Domitius Aphobius |
| 8.42.18M | " | " | " |
| 4.6.8 | 2.11.294 | **Sirmium** | Flavianus |
| 9.22.17 | 2.11.294 | Sirmium | Menelaus |
| 5.37.19 | 2.11.294 | Sirmium | Vindicianus |
| 4.2.11 | 2.12.294 | Sirmium | Maximianus |
| 7.52.5 | 2.12.294 | Sirmium | Valentinus |
| 2.36.3 | 2.13.294 | Sirmium | Laurentius |
| 3.28.22 | 2.13.294 | Sirmium | Statilla |
| 7.32.8 | 2.14.294 | *Sirmium* | Cyrillus |
| 9.1.14 | 2.14.294 | *Sirmium* | Aelia |
| 6.59.3 | 2.15.294 | Sirmium | Ulpiana |
| 4.13.4 | 2.18.294 | Sirmium | Achaeus |
| 6.15.5 | 2.18.294 | Sirmium | Plato |

| *CJ* entry no. | Date | Location | Recipient |
|---|---|---|---|
| 8.37.8 | 2.18.294 | **Sirmium** | Posidonius |
| 6.29.2 | 2.18.294 | Sirmium | Soterichus |
| *Coll.* 3.244–5 | 2.20.294 | Sirmium | Aurelius Ennius Lucellus & Marcus Severinus |
| 6.20.14 | 2.23.294 | Tricornium | Stratonica |
| 3.32.20 | 2.24.294 | | Quartilla |
| 9.1.15 | 2.27.294 | | Lupio |
| 6.42.25 | 2.28.294 | | Iuliana |
| 8.35.7 | 2.28.294 | | Menandra |
| 8.27.15 | 3.1.294 | Sirmium | Aviana |
| 2.34.2 | 3.3.294 | *Sirmium* | Procula |
| 4.50.9 | 3.3.294 or 5.3.294 or 7.3.294 | Sirmium | Eminius Rufinianus |
| 6.37.17 | 3.5.294 | *Sirmium* | Eutychianus |
| 9.22.18 | 3.5.294 | *Sirmium* | Maximus |
| 4.16.5 | 3.6.294 | Sirmium | Iulius |
| 3.22.4M | 3.6.294 | **Sirmium** | Sisinnia |
| 4.38.7 | 3.7.294 | Sirmium | Aurelius Isio |
| 7.14.11 | 3.7.294 | **Sirmium** | Maxima |
| 7.10.6 | 3.7.294 | **Sirmium** | Midus |
| 9.22.19 | 3.8.294 | *Sirmium* | Cosmia |
| 2.4.23 | 3.8.294 | *Sirmium* | Tatianus |
| 7.16.26 | 3.9.294 | *Sirmium* | Molentus |
| 8.53.21 | 3.11.294 | *Sirmium* | Antonia |
| 8.50.13 | 3.11.294 | *Sirmium* | |
| 4.29.17 | 3.13.294 | *Sirmium* | Alexander |
| 2.4.26 | 3.13.294 | *Sirmium* | Dionysia |
| 2.12.19 | 3.14.294 | *Sirmium* | Firmus |
| 4.38.8 | 3.16.294 | *Sirmium* | Herodes & Diogenes |
| 7.2.11 | 3.17.294 | Sirmium | Laurina |
| 2.32.2 | " | " | " |
| 8.50.14 | 3.17.294 | **Sirmium** | Severa |
| 5.18.8 | 3.20.294 | Sirmium | Sallustia |
| 4.10.13 | 3.22.294 | *Sirmium* | Barsimius |
| *Cons.* 9.18 | 3.25.294 | **Sirmium** | Sergia & Anagius |
| 7.26.8 | 3.25.294 | **Sirmium** | Severus |
| 4.38.9 | " | Sirmium | " |
| 8.53.22 | 3.26.294 | Sirmium | Diomedes |
| 6.57.2M | 3.26.294 | Sirmium | Metrodora |
| 4.35.14 | 3.27.294 | Sirmium | Hermianus |
| 8.2.2 | 3.27.294 | **Sirmium** | Marcus |

| *CJ* entry no. | Date | Location | Recipient |
|---|---|---|---|
| 8.19.3 | 3.27.294 | **Sirmium** | Theophilus |
| 3.41.5 | 3.28.294 | **Sirmium** | Menophilus |
| 3.38.6 | 3.28.294 | Sirmium | Thesidiana |
| 7.34.3 | 3.30.294 | Sirmium | Apollinarius |
| 3.31.8 | 3.30.294 | **Sirmium** | Asterius |
| *Cons.* 6.18 | " | " | Aurelius Asterius |
| 6.59.4 | " | " | " |
| 7.16.27 | " | " | " |
| 5.34.10 | 3.30.294 | **Sirmium** | Florentinus |
| 5.36.5 | 3.30.294 | **Sirmium** | Zeno |
| 8.44.26 | 3.31.294 | Sirmium | Neo |
| 4.22.3 | 4.1.294 | Sirmium | Marina |
| 6.22.3 | 4.2.294 | Sirmium | Licinius |
| 7.49.1 | 4.3.294 | **Sirmium** | Acte |
| 7.45.9 | 4.3.294 | **Sirmium** | Domnus |
| 4.10.10 | 4.3.294 | **Sirmium** | Rufinus |
| 7.32.9 | 4.3.294 | Sirmium | Sergius |
| 8.27.16 | 4.3.294 | **Sirmium** | Silvanus |
| 2.4.24M | 4.4.294 | Sirmium | Victorinus |
| 8.27.17 | 4.4.294 | **Sirmium** | Agape |
| 8.46.7 | 4.4.294 | **Sirmium** | Dupliana |
| 5.28.6 | 4.5.294 | Sirmium | Domna |
| 5.62.18 | 4.5.294 | **Sirmium** | Sabinus |
| 4.38.10 | 4.6.294 | *Sirmium* | Aurelia Gordiana |
| 9.41.14 | 4.6.294 | *Sirmium* | Constantius |
| 8.4.3 | 4.6.294 | *Sirmium* | Ulpia & Proclina |
| *CHV* 1.1 | 4.7.294 | Sirmium | Aurelius Alexius |
| 5.71.16 | 4.8.294 | **Sirmium** | Eutychia |
| 6.16.2 | 4.8.294 | Sirmium | Firmus |
| 9.41.15 | 4.9.294 | *Sirmium* | Maximus |
| 7.16.28M | 4.10.294 | Sirmium | Eurymedon |
| 8.4.4 | 4.10.294 | Sirmium | Hyginus |
| 4.13.5 | 4.11.294 | **Sirmium** | Lampetius |
| 4.23.3 | 4.11.294 | Sirmium | Sotera |
| 6.42.26 | 4.12.294 | Sirmium | Gaianus |
| 2.4.25 | 4.12.294 | **Sirmium** | Marcella & Cyrilla |
| 8.41.5 | 4.12.294 | Sirmium | Septimia |
| 4.35.15 | 4.15.294 | **Sirmium** | Aurelius Precarius Athenaeus |
| 7.4.12 | 4.15.294 | Sirmium | Irenaeus |
| 5.59.2 | 4.15.294 | **Sirmium** | Serena |

| *CJ* entry no. | Date | Location | Recipient |
|---|---|---|---|
| 5.28.7 | 4.15.294 | Sirmium | Tryphaena |
| 6.55.7 | 4.16.294 | Sirmium | Aemiliana |
| 8.46.8 | " | " | " |
| 2.53.5 | 4.16.294 | **Sirmium** | Licinianus |
| 2.20.7 | 4.16.294 | **Sirmium** | Sebastianus |
| 3.1.7 | 4.18.294 | Sirmium | Irena |
| 6.59.5 | 4.18.294 | **Sirmium** | Iustina |
| 4.1.8 | 4.20.294 | **Sirmium** | Alexander |
| 8.40.22 | 4.20.294 | **Sirmium** | Hermianus |
| 6.35.10 | 4.20.294 | Sirmium | Silvana |
| 4.22.2 | 4.22.294 | **Sirmium** | Soter |
| 4.13.3 | 4.22.294 | Sirmium | Theogenes |
| 5.43.9 | 4.23.294 | *Sirmium* | Ammianus |
| 6.32.3 | 4.26.294 | **Sirmium** | Aristotle |
| 4.20.7 | 4.26.294 | *Sirmium* | Diogenes & Ingenuus |
| 8.27.18 | 4.26.294 | *Sirmium* | Gaianus |
| 4.8.1 | 4.26.294 | *Sirmium* | Hermogenes |
| *FV* 270 | 4.27.294 | Sirmium | Caecilia Anagriana |
| 4.17.1 | 4.27.294 | Sirmium | Macedona |
| 4.1.9 | 4.27.294 | Sirmium | Marcianus |
| 8.46.9 | 4.27.294 | Sirmium | Nicagoras |
| 2.21.6 | 4.27.294 | Sirmium | Sententia |
| 1.18.6 | 4.27.294 | **Sirmium** | Taurus & Pollio |
| 5.12.20 | 4.27.294 | Sirmium | Tiberius |
| 6.49.5 | 4.27.294 | Sirmium | Verissimus |
| 2.3.25 | 4.28.294 | Sirmium | Euhemerus |
| 6.9.6 | 4.28.294 | Sirmium | Frontina |
| 5.44.5 | 4.28.294 | **Sirmium** | Tigranus |
| 4.65.26 | 4.29.294 | *Sirmium* | Aurelius Opilio & Hermius |
| 6.1.2 | 4.29.294 | *Sirmium* | Pompeianus |
| 5.31.10 | 4.30.294 | Sirmium | Priscus |
| 4.8.2 | 5.1.294 | **Sirmium** | Aristaenetus |
| 2.35.1 | 5.1.294 | Sirmium | Isidora |
| 6.21.14 | 5.3.294 | Aureus Mons | heredes Maximi |
| 4.51.5 | 5.8.294 | Sirmium | Aurelius Aeger |
| 2.4.27 | 5.9.294 | *Sirmium* | Cato |
| 4.7.6 | 5.18.294 | **Sirmium** | Eutychia |
| 6.59.1 | 5.18.294 | Sirmium | Varianae |
| 4.29.15 | 6.1.294 | Sirmium | Agrippinus |
| 6.58.7 | 6.16.294 | Sirmium | Ammianus |
| 4.18.1 | 6.25.294 | Sirmium | Felix |

| *CJ* entry no. | Date | Location | Recipient |
|---|---|---|---|
| 1.18.7 | 7.2.294 | *Sirmium* | Zoe |
| 2.4.28 | 7.5.294 | *Sirmium* | Sapparta |
| 6.58.8M | 7.7.294 | Sirmium | Silanus |
| 4.9.1 | 7.20.294 | Sirmium | Ulpius |
| 4.10.11 | 7.25.294 | *Sirmium* | Paula |
| 5.12.15 | 7.25.294 | Sirmium | Ulpiana |
| 5.16.22 | 8.1.294 | Sirmium | Arsinoe |
| 2.25.1 | 8.11.294 | *Sirmium* | Aphobius |
| 6.24.10 | 8.17.294 | Sirmium | Asclepiada |
| 4.2.12 | 8.18.294 | *Sirmium* | Theophanius |
| 9.18.2 | 8.20.294 | Sirmium | Tiberius |
| 3.42.9 | 8.25.294 | | Faustinus |
| 3.37.5 | 8.25.294 | | Secundinus |
| 1.18.8 | 8.28.294 | | Dionysia |
| 4.19.21M | 9.8.294 | Singidunum | Crispus |
| 3.28.23 | 9.9.294 | *Singidunum* | Philippa |
| 3.29.8 | 9.11.294 | *Singidunum* | Auxanon |
| 9.20.12 | 9.12.294 | Singidunum | Mucianus |
| 8.44.27 | 9.15.294 | | Theophilus |
| 4.65.28 | 9.17.294 | | Tuscianus Neo |
| 2.21.7 | 9.22.294 | | Severa |
| 2.54.1M | 9.26.294 | Viminacium | Catulus |
| 6.50.14 | 9.26.294 | Viminacium | Faustina |
| 5.12.23 | 9.27.294 | Viminacium | Diogenes |
| 8.55.6 | 9.27.294 | Viminacium | Herennia |
| 6.42.27 | 9.27.294 | Viminacium | Olympias |
| 8.53.23 | " | " | " |
| 5.12.22 | 9.27.294 | **Viminacium** | Polybiana |
| 8.38.6 | 9.27.294 | **Viminacium** | Septimius & Eustolius |
| 2.4.29 | 9.28.294 | **Viminacium** | Marcia |
| 3.33.11 | 9.28.294 | Viminacium | Theodotus |
| 5.52.3 | 9.28.294 | **Viminacium** | Zoticus |
| 4.32.23 | 9.29.294 | Viminacium | Iason |
| 4.35.16 | 9.29.294 | **Viminacium** | Uzandus |
| 7.62.10 | 9.30.294 | Viminacium | Titianus |
| 6.2.16 | 10.1.294 | Viminacium | Artemidorus et alii |
| 6.59.6 | 10.1.294 | **Viminacium** | Publicianus |
| 7.23.1 | 10.3.294 | | Rufinus |
| 8.44.28 | 10.5.294 | Cuppae | Maximianus |
| 6.59.7 | 10.6.294 | | Nicolaus |
| 4.33.5 | 10.8.294 | Ratiaria | Pullius Iulianus Eucharistus |

| *CJ* entry no. | Date | Location | Recipient |
|---|---|---|---|
| 7.60.3 | 10.10.294 | Ratiaria | Fortunata |
| 8.13.21 | 10.10.294 | Ratiaria | Vitus |
| 3.32.21 | 10.10.294 | **Ratiaria** | Herodes |
| 6.59.8M | 10.10.294 | Ratiaria | Iusta |
| 2.4.30 | 10.11.294 | Cebrum | Antoninus |
| 7.16.31 | 10.11.294 | | Corsiana |
| 8.42.19 | 10.11.294 | | Diogenes |
| 8.37.9 | 10.13.294 | Varianae | Capito |
| 2.3.26 | 10.13.294 | Varianae | Cornelia |
| 8.35.8 | 10.18.294 | **Transmarisca** | Aurelius |
| 6.42.28 | 10.18.294 | Transmarisca | Gaius |
| 3.35.6 | 10.18.294 | **Transmarisca** | Plinius |
| *Cons.* 9.19 | 10.19.294 | | Aurelius Hermogenes |
| 4.10.12 | 10.20.294 | | Iovinus |
| 4.64.7 | 10.20.294 | | Timotheus |
| 4.5.8 | 10.21.294 | **Durostorum** | Ziparus |
| 8.41.6 | " | Durostorum | " |
| 9.22.20 | 10.22.294 | Durostorum | Rufinus |
| 2.56.1 | 10.24.294 | | |
| 2.4.32 | 10.25.294 | **Reginassi** | Cyrillus |
| 4.20.8 | 10.25.294 | Reginassi | Derulo |
| 5.18.9 | 10.25.294 | **Reginassi** | Marcia |
| 4.21.10 | 10.25.294 | Reginassi | Victorinus |
| *Cons.* 6.17 | 10.26.294 | Marcianopolis | Aurelius Secundinus, optio |
| 5.12.24 | 10.27.294 | Anchialos | Aurelius & Lysimachus |
| 5.51.11M | 10.28.294 | Anchialos | Chrysiana |
| 8.31.2 | 10.28.294 | **Anchialos** | Claudia |
| 6.50.17 | 10.28.294 | Anchialos | Gaius |
| 4.25.5 | 10.28.294 | **Anchialos** | Gaius |
| 8.47.9 | 10.28.294 | Anchialos | Marcianus |
| 8.42.20 | 10.28.294 | **Anchialos** | Eucratides |
| 3.32.22 | 10.30.294 | **Develtus** | Diodotus |
| 8.50.17 | 10.30.294 | Develtus | Diogenia |
| 6.36.5M | 10.30.294 | Develtus | Flavia |
| 5.16.23M | 11.1.294 | Burtudizum | Caeciliana |
| 2.3.28M | 11.3.294 | Burtudizum | Leontius |
| 8.35.9 | 11.3.294 | Burtudizum | Mucianus |
| 7.16.32 | 11.5.294 | **Heraclea** | Athenais |
| 7.53.9 | 11.5.294 | **Heraclea** | Glyco |
| 7.48.3 | 11.5.294 | Heraclea | Phileta(s) |
| 5.18.10 | 11.7.294 | Heraclea | Epigonus |

| *CJ* entry no. | Date | Location | Recipient |
|---|---|---|---|
| 2.3.27 | 11.8.294 | Heraclea | Aurelius Chresimus |
| 7.35.6 | 11.8.294 | Heraclea | Doleus |
| 8.27.19 | 11.8.294 | Heraclea | Livia |
| FV 325 | 11.8.294 | Heraclea | Aurelia Panthera |
| 2.4.34 | 11.8.294 | **Heraclea** | Ptolemais |
| FV 314 | 11.9.294 | Melantias | Aurelius Apollonidas |
| 2.4.33 | 11.9.294 | Melantias | Euchrysius |
| 7.16.33 | 11.10.294 | **Byzantium** | Melitiana |
| 2.4.31M | 11.10.294 | Byzantium | Proculus |
| 8.27.20 | 11.10.294 | Byzantium | Sabinus |
| 5.12.25 | 11.11.294 | Pantichium | Eutychianus |
| 6.22.4 | 11.11.294 | Pantichium | Rhodon |
| 4.21.11 | 11.11.294 | **Pantichium** | Theagenes |
| 4.29.18 | 11.11.294 | Pantichium | Zoticus |
| 7.16.34 | 11.13.294 | *Nicomedia* | Hermiona |
| 4.2.13M | 11.14.294 | Nicomedia | Fronto |
| 3.32.25 | 11.16.294 | Nicomedia | Eugnomius |
| 3.32.24 | 11.16.294 | **Nicomedia** | Iulianus |
| 3.32.23 | 11.16.294 | **Nicomedia** | Magniferus |
| 4.19.19 | 11.16.294 | Nicomedia | Menander |
| 4.32.24 | 11.18.294 | *Nicomedia* | Culcia |
| 4.25.6 | 11.18.294 | *Nicomedia* | Onesima |
| 6.44.5 | 11.18.294 | *Nicomedia* | Severa |
| 9.1.16 | 11.20.294 | Nicomedia | Callitychus |
| 6.55.8 | 11.20.294 | Nicomedia | Catonia |
| 8.8.3M | 11.20.294 | Nicomedia | Euodia |
| 4.23.4 | 11.20.294 | **Nicomedia** | Faustina |
| 4.24.12 | 11.20.294 | Nicomedia | Heraiscus |
| 8.50.18 | 11.20.294 | **Nicomedia** | Tryphonianus |
| 5.62.20 | 11.22.294 | Nicomedia | Charitinus |
| 3.32.26M | 11.22.294 | **Nicomedia** | Heliodorus |
| 2.4.35 | 11.24.294 | Nicomedia | Ammonius |
| 4.22.4 | 11.24.294 | **Nicomedia** | Decius |
| 6.54.8 | 11.25.294 | *Nicomedia* | Iulius & Zenodorus |
| 6.23.13 | 11.26.294 | **Nicomedia** | Euripides |
| 3.36.21 | 11.26.294 | **Nicomedia** | Fortunatus |
| 3.36.22 | 11.26.294–12.27.294 | *Nicomedia* | Dionysius |
| 3.36.23 | 11.26.294–12.27.294 | *Nicomedia* | Hermogenes |
| 9.35.9 | 11.26.294 | Nicomedia | Nonna |
| 6.19.2 | 11.26.294 | Nicomedia | Theodorus |
| 4.49.14 | 11.27.294 | **Nicomedia** | Aurelius Ruso |

| *CJ* entry no. | Date | Location | Recipient |
|---|---|---|---|
| 4.2.15 | 11.27.294 | Nicomedia | Charidemus |
| 8.43.3 | 11.27.294 | **Nicomedia** | Demetria |
| 5.38.6 | 11.27.294 | **Nicomedia** | Epictetus |
| 4.10.14 | 11.27.294 | Nicomedia | Hermodotus & Nicomachus |
| 4.1.10 | 11.27.294 | **Nicomedia** | Protogenes |
| 9.20.13 | 11.27.294 | **Nicomedia** | Severinus |
| 4.7.7 | 11.27.294 | Nicomedia | Zenonida |
| 10.32.12M | 11.27.294 | **Nicomedia** | Zoticus |
| 6.30.12 | 11.29.294 | **Nicomedia** | Antonius |
| 3.31.9 | 11.29.294 | Nicomedia | Demophilia |
| 7.14.12 | 11.29.294 | **Nicomedia** | Quieta |
| 7.56.4 | 11.29.294 | **Nicomedia** | Soterianus |
| 8.35.10 | 12.1.294 | Nicomedia | Aquilina |
| 4.51.6 | 12.1.294 | **Nicomedia** | Aurelius Rufus |
| 4.21.12 | 12.1.294 | Nicomedia | Dionysia |
| 4.16.6 | 12.1.294 | **Nicomedia** | Domnus |
| = 7.72.7 | " | " | " |
| 2.31.2 | 12.1.294 | **Nicomedia** | Hymnoda |
| 8.17.9 | 12.2.294 | **Nicomedia** | Asclepiodotus |
| 4.49.13 | 12.2.294 | **Nicomedia** | Flavius Alexander |
| 4.5.9 | 12.2.294 | Nicomedia | Gratiana |
| 4.19.20 | 12.2.294 | Nicomedia | Phronima |
| 4.20.6 | 12.2.294 | Nicomedia | Tertullus |
| 4.38.11 | 12.3.294 | **Nicomedia** | Aurelius Paternus |
| 4.6.10 | 12.3.294 | Nicomedia | Cononiana |
| 8.42.21 | 12.3.294 | **Nicomedia** | Rufus |
| 3.28.24 | 12.3.294 | Nicomedia | Successus |
| 9.20.14 | 12.4.294 | Nicomedia | Callisthenes |
| 5.34.8M | 12.4.294 | **Nicomedia** | Euelpistus |
| 3.38.7 | 12.4.294 | Nicomedia | Severianus & Flavianus |
| 8.40.23 | 12.5.294 | Nicomedia | Antipater |
| 7.16.35M | 12.5.294 | **Nicomedia** | Atellius |
| 5.45.2 | 12.5.294 | **Nicomedia** | Marcus |
| 3.38.8 | 12.5.294 | **Nicomedia** | Nicomachus |
| 4.64.8 | 12.5.294 | Nicomedia | Paulina |
| 8.17.10 | 12.5.294 | **Nicomedia** | Polydeuca |
| 7.16.36 | 12.5.294–12.16.294 | *Nicomedia* | Theodora |
| 7.16.37 | 12.5.294–12.16.294 | *Nicomedia* | Olympius |
| 2.4.36 | 12.6.294 | *Nicomedia* | Achilleus |
| 6.23.14 | " | " | " |
| 6.42.29 | " | " | " |

| CJ entry no. | Date | Location | Recipient |
|---|---|---|---|
| 5.59.3 | 12.6.294 | *Nicomedia* | Gaius |
| = 7.26.9 | " | " | " |
| 5.75.5 | 12.7.294 | **Nicomedia** | Eugenia |
| 7.14.13 | 12.7.294 | **Nicomedia** | Menander |
| 5.71.17 | 12.7.294 | **Nicomedia** | Philippus |
| 6.20.15 | " | " | " |
| 7.4.13 | 12.7.294 | **Nicomedia** | Pythagorida |
| 6.56.2M | 12.7.294 | **Nicomedia** | Rhesa |
| 8.44.29 | " | Nicomedia | " |
| 4.16.7 | 12.8.294 | Nicomedia | Apolaustus |
| 3.38.9 | 12.8.294 | Nicomedia | Demetrianus |
| 2.11.22 | 12.8.294 | Nicomedia | Domitianus |
| 1.18.9 | 12.8.294 | **Nicomedia** | Gaius & Anthemius |
| 6.37.18 | 12.8.294 | **Nicomedia** | Iustinus |
| 9.12.5 | 12.8.294 | Nicomedia | Oplo |
| 2.24.5 | 12.8.294 | **Nicomedia** | Valentinus |
| 8.42.22 | 12.9.294 | **Nicomedia** | Gratus |
| 6.37.19 | 12.9.294 | Nicomedia | Nico |
| 7.33.10 | 12.9.294 | **Nicomedia** | Reginus |
| *Cons.* 5.6 | 12.10.294 | Nicomedia | Aurelius Dexter |
| 8.13.22 | 12.11.294 | Nicomedia | Antiochianus |
| 6.30.13 | 12.11.294 | Nicomedia | Archepolis |
| 8.6.1M | 12.11.294 | Nicomedia | Cyrillus |
| 6.36.6 | 12.11.294 | Nicomedia | Demosthenes |
| 4.34.10 | 12.12.294 | Nicomedia | Septimia Quadratilla |
| 5.73.3M | 12.13.294 | Nicomedia | Agatha |
| 6.2.17 | 12.13.294 | **Nicomedia** | Conon |
| 8.54.5 | 12.13.294 | Nicomedia | Dexippus |
| 8.44.30 | 12.13.294 | **Nicomedia** | Hastius |
| 2.26.5M | 12.13.294 | Nicomedia | Marcianus |
| 3.39.1 | 12.13.294 | Nicomedia | Nicephorus |
| 5.39.5 | 12.13.294 | **Nicomedia** | Onesima |
| 5.42.4 | 12.13.294 | Nicomedia | Tertullus |
| 6.30.14 | 12.14.294 | Nicomedia | Flavia |
| 8.44.31 | 12.15.294 | Nicomedia | Agathus |
| 4.29.19 | 12.15.294 | Nicomedia | Faustina |
| 5.62.21 | 12.15.294 | Nicomedia | Paramonus |
| 3.32.27 | 12.15.294 | Nicomedia | Philadelphus |
| 5.17.6 | 12.15.294 | Nicomedia | Phoebus |
| 9.9.26 | " | " | " |
| 6.59.9 | 12.15.294 | Nicomedia | Sopatros |

| *CJ* entry no. | Date | Location | Recipient |
|---|---|---|---|
| 3.32.28 | " | " | " |
| 2.40.4 | 12.15.294 | Nicomedia | Stratonica |
| 4.6.11 | " | " | " |
| 5.49.2M | 12.15.294 | Nicomedia | Grata |
| 5.58.3 | 12.15.294 | **Nicomedia** | Thesis |
| 4.9.10 | 12.16.294 | **Nicomedia** | Alexander |
| 4.43.1 | 12.16.294 | Nicomedia | Aurelia Papiniana |
| 7.62.11 | 12.16.294 | **Nicomedia** | Aurelius |
| 10.40.7 | " | " | " |
| 4.48.6 | 12.18.294–12.25.294 | Nicomedia | Aurelius Cyrillus |
| 4.49.16 | " | " | " |
| 4.31.12 | 12.16.294 | Nicomedia | Lucius Cornelianus |
| 8.13.23 | 12.16.294 | Nicomedia | Macedonius |
| 10.32.8M | 12.16.294 | Nicomedia | Platonianus |
| 8.41.7 | 12.16.294 | **Nicomedia** | Zoilus |
| 4.21.13 | 12.17.294 | Nicomedia | Leontius |
| 8.29.5 | 12.17.294 | Nicomedia | Nonna |
| 7.16.38 | 12.17.294 | Nicomedia | Philoserapis |
| 4.49.15 | 12.18.294 | Nicomedia | Aurelius Antoninus Aelianus |
| 4.44.14 | 12.18.294 | Nicomedia | Aurelius Basilida |
| 8.13.24 | 12.18.294 | Nicomedia | Marcus |
| 8.35.11 | 12.18.294 | **Nicomedia** | Neo |
| 9.25.10 | 12.18.294 | Nicomedia | Paulus |
| 8.42.23 | 12.18.294 | Nicomedia | Vatius |
| 5.62.22 | 12.19.294 | Nicomedia | Hermodorus |
| 5.14.7 | 12.19.294 | Nicomedia | Philetus |
| 9.20.15 | 12.20.294 | Nicomedia | Pomponius |
| 4.22.5 | 12.20.294 | **Nicomedia** | Victor |
| 4.37.5 | 12.21.294 | Nicomedia | Aurelius Theodorus |
| 2.4.37 | 12.21.294 | Nicomedia | Basilissa |
| 8.40.24 | 12.22.294 | *Nicomedia* | Pergamius |
| 4.19.22 | 12.24.294 | **Nicomedia** | Agathoclea |
| *FV* 326 | 12.24.294 | **Nicomedia** | Aurelia Agemacha |
| 3.39.2 | 12.24.294 | Nicomedia | Tatianus |
| 2.4.38 | 12.24.294 | Nicomedia | Theodotianus |
| = 6.31.3 | " | " | " |
| 2.6.4 | " | " | " |
| = 6.19.1 | " | " | " |
| 3.31.10 | " | " | " |
| 4.29.20 | " | " | " |

| *CJ* entry no. | Date | Location | Recipient |
|---|---|---|---|
| *Cons.* 6.12 | 12.25.294 | Nicomedia | Aurelius Altinus |
| 5.53.5 | 12.25.294 | Nicomedia | Artemidorus |
| *Cons.* 6.11 | 12.25.294 | **Nicomedia** | Cretianus Maximus |
| 4.19.23 | 12.25.294 | **Nicomedia** | Menelaus |
| 7.14.14 | 12.26.294 | **Nicomedia** | Aristotle |
| 8.13.25 | 12.26.294 | Nicomedia | Dracontius |
| 6.37.20 | 12.26.294 | **Nicomedia** | Eutychianus |
| 7.16.39 | 12.26.294 | **Nicomedia** | Eutychius |
| 9.16.6 | 12.26.294 | Nicomedia | Philiscus |
| 8.42.24 | 12.26.294 | Nicomedia | Rufinus |
| 7.29.4 | 12.26.294 | **Nicomedia** | Serapio |
| 7.72.8 | 12.27.294 | Nicomedia | Aelis |
| 6.58.9 | 12.27.294 | Nicomedia | Damagoras |
| 6.59.10 | 12.27.294 | **Nicomedia** | Danuvius |
| 5.12.26 | 12.27.294 | **Nicomedia** | Demosthenes |
| 7.20.2 | 12.27.294 | **Nicomedia** | Milesius |
| 8.40.25 | 12.27.294 | **Nicomedia** | Philippus |
| 5.17.5M | 12.27.294 | Nicomedia | Scyrio |
| 1.18.10 | 12.28.294 | **Nicomedia** | Amphia |
| 6.34.3 | 12.28.294 | **Nicomedia** | Eutychis |
| 3.36.24 | 12.28.294 | **Nicomedia** | Socrates |
| 6.20.16 | " | " | " |
| 8.42.25 | 12.30.294 | Nicomedia | Antellianus |
| 6.2.18 | 12.30.294 | Nicomedia | Dionysodorus |
| 3.34.12 | 12.30.294 | Nicomedia | Valeria |
| 3.36.15 | 293 | | Theophila |
| 4.35.10 | 293 | | Aurelius Papius |
| 4.38.3 | 293 | | Valeria Viacra |
| 6.23.10 | 293 | | Menophilianus |
| 7.2.10 | 293 | | Germanus |
| 7.16.9 | 293 | | Proculus |
| 7.16.10 | 293 | | Stratius |
| 7.16.11 | 293 | | Faustinus |
| 7.16.15 | 293 | | Palladius |
| 7.16.19 | 293 | | Paulus |
| 7.33.3 | 293 | | Antonius |
| 7.72.4 | 293 | | Clearchiana |
| 8.4.2 | 293 | | Alexander |
| 8.27.13 | 293 | | Theodota |
| 8.40.20 | 293 | | Aurelius |
| 8.44.18 | 293 | | Eutychius |

| *CJ* entry no. | Date | Location | Recipient |
|---|---|---|---|
| *Cons.* 4.10 | 293 | | Flavius Rumitalus |
| *Cons.* 6.16 | 293 | | Iulius Pancratius |
| 4.65.27 | 294 | | Maximianus Agopous |
| 5.62.19 | 294 | | Dionysius |
| 6.8.2 | 294 | | Eumenes |
| 6.9.5 | 294 | | Maximus |
| 7.16.29 | 294 | | Troila |
| 7.16.30 | 294 | | Eutychius |
| 7.33.8 | 294 | | Celsus |
| 7.33.9 | 294 | | Demosthenes |
| 8.50.15 | 294 | | Mucatraulus |
| 10.32.9 | 294 | | Aurelius |
| 10.32.10 | 294 | | Aurelius |
| 10.32.11 | 294 | | Maximus |
| 4.2.14 | undateable | | Hadrianus |
| 4.30.10 | undateable | | Mucazanus |
| 4.30.11 | 4.10.??? | | Eutychianus |
| 4.30.12 | undateable | | Severianus |
| 4.31.10 | undateable | | Iulius Nicander |
| 4.31.11 | undateable | | Claudius Iulius & Paulus |
| 4.31.13 | after 12.16.294 | | Aurelius Bassus |
| 4.32.18 | undateable | | Aurelius Castor |
| 4.32.19 | undateable | | Aurelia Irenea |
| 4.32.20 | undateable | | Aelius Nicopolitanus |
| 4.32.21 | undateable | | Chresimon |
| 4.32.22 | 7.15.??? | | Cominius Carinus |
| 4.35.17 | undateable | | Aurelius Gorgonius |
| 4.35.20 | undateable | | Aurelius Epagathus |
| 4.38.12 | after 3.3.294 | | Aurelius Pacianus |
| 4.38.13 | after 3.3.294 | | Aurelius Decius Lollianus |
| 4.37.2 | undateable | | Pannonius |
| 4.37.3 | 8.27.??? | | Aurelius Victorinus |
| 4.37.4 | undateable | | Aurelius Celer |
| 4.39.8 | undateable | | Vigilianus |
| 4.49.17 | undateable | | Hermianus & Hermippus |
| 4.52.4 | undateable | | Ulpianus |
| 4.52.5 | undateable | | Olympianus |
| 4.53.7 | undateable | | Fabianus Muscus |
| 4.53.8 | undateable | | Auxanoni |
| 4.64.3 | undateable | | Barcus Leontius |
| 4.64.4 | undateable | | Leontius |

| CJ entry no. | Date | Location | Recipient |
|---|---|---|---|
| 4.64.5 | undateable | | Theodolana |
| 4.64.6 | undateable | | Protogenes |
| 4.65.29 | undateable | | Aurelius Iulianus |
| 5.3.13 | undateable | | Alexander |
| 5.3.14 | undateable | | Aurelia |
| 5.4.13 | undateable | | Onesimus |
| 5.4.14 | undateable | | Titius |
| 5.4.15 | undateable | | Titianus |
| 5.4.16 | undateable | | Rhodon |
| 5.59.1 | undateable | | Antonianus |
| 6.2.19 | after 12.30.294 | | Mnestheus |
| 6.36.4 | undateable | | Stratonicus |
| 7.1.3 | undateable | | Attia |
| 7.2.13 | undateable | | Martial |
| 7.4.11 | undateable | | Flavianus |
| 7.11.6 | undateable | | Olympius |
| 7.11.7 | undateable | | Zoticus |
| 7.18.2 | undateable | | Melana |
| 7.27.3 | undateable | | Rhodanus |
| 7.29.3 | undateable | | Diocletianus |
| 7.34.2 | undateable | | Dionysius |
| 7.34.4 | undateable | | Livia |
| 7.34.5 | undateable | | Zosimus |
| 7.35.7 | undateable | | Cassander |
| 7.36.2 | undateable | | Marcella |
| 7.43.11 | undateable | | Valerius |
| 7.45.7 | undateable | | Isidora |
| 7.45.8 | undateable | | Licinius |
| 7.45.10 | undateable | | Menodorus |
| 7.45.11 | undateable | | Titianus |
| 7.62.7 | undateable | | Neo |
| 7.62.8 | undateable | | Oppianus |
| 7.64.9 | undateable | | Rufinus |
| 7.71.4 | undateable | | Chilo |
| 7.71.5 | undateable | | Myro |
| 7.72.6 | undateable | | Agathemerus |
| 7.75.6 | undateable | | Menandra |
| 8.48.4 | 10.15.??? | | Colonia |
| 9.47.14 | undateable | | Vitalis |
| 9.47.15 | undateable | | Agathemerus |
| 9.49.6 | undateable | | Gaudentius |

| CJ entry no. | Date | Location | Recipient |
|---|---|---|---|
| 9.51.11 | undateable | | Philippus |
| 9.51.12 | undateable | | Trypho |
| 10.32.13 | undateable | | Protus |
| 10.40.6 | undateable | | Marcellus |
| 10.41.3 | undateable | | Nicia |
| 10.42.8 | undateable | | Longinus |
| 10.42.9 | undateable | | Marcia |
| 10.43.4 | undateable | | Reginus |
| 10.47.2 | undateable | | Cassius |
| 10.51.3 | undateable | | Celer |
| 10.51.4 | undateable | | Reginus |
| 10.52.5 | undateable | | Marcia |
| 10.53.5 | undateable | | Concedemon |
| 10.54.1 | undateable | | Hermogenes |
| 10.58.1 | undateable | | Lucillus |
| 10.62.4 | undateable | | Alexander |
| 12.36.5 | undateable | | Philostratus |
| *P.Amh.* 2.27 | undateable | | Severus, Aurelius |

*Notes*

The following entries have been changed from Krüger's 1877 edition on the basis of their incorrect dates or locations. I have not included in this list entries that I emended following the suggestions of Mommsen in that same edition, but following Barnes' practice (*New Empire*) I have marked them on the table above according to the following scheme: *CJ* 1.22.2M.

*CJ* 2.4.39. Was dated to 12.28.294 at Sirmium. Year changed to 293 to suit the location.

*CJ* 3.31.7. Was dated to 7.22.294. Year changed to 293 to preserve the temporal sequence of the title.

*CJ* 4.2.14. Was dated to 293, but appears between two entries dating to 294. Neither date nor year can be determined.

*CJ* 4.30.11. Was dated to 4.10. Year is probably, but not certainly 294, as 4.30.9 is dated to December, most likely 293.

*CJ* 4.35.11. Date was . . . *k. Iun.* in 293. Month changed from *Iun.* to *Ian.* to suit the location. Given the subsequent entry, was dated to sometime between 12.14.293 and 12.16.293.

*CJ* 4.35.16. Was dated to 9.29, but lacked a year. Given previous entries in title, most likely 294.

*CJ* 4.35.18. Was dated to 9.25.294 at Sirmium. Year changed to 293 to suit the location, though does break sequence.

*CJ* 4.35.19. Was dated to 10.19.294 at Sirmium. Year changed to 293 to suit the location.

*CJ* 4.49.9. Was dated to 5.18.293 at Philippopolis. The distance from Adrianople to Philippopolis was 119 miles, which could be covered in about six days. The last entry before leaving Adrianople was dated to 5.13.293. It is possible that *CJ* 4.49.9 has the correct date, though an entry placed at Verona on the 18th could actually be from Beroea, a large place at which Diocletian may well have stopped. It is probable, therefore, that (following Mommsen) that the date should be changed from *xv k. Iun.* to *xv k. Iul* (6.17).

*CJ* 4.51.5. Was dated to *viii id. M.* in 294 at Sirmium. 5.8.294 (taking *M.* to stand for *Mai*) has been favored following Honoré, though 3.8.294 (with *M.* standing for *Mart.*) is equally likely.

*CJ* 5.12.14. Was dated to 11.2.293 at Philippopolis. Date changed from *iv n. Iun.* to *iv n. Nov.* to suit location.

*CJ* 5.12.15. Was dated to 7.25.293 (*viii k. Aug.*) at Sirmium. Year changed to 294 to suit location.

*CJ* 5.12.24. Was dated to 10.27.294 at Antioch. Location should be changed to Anchialos. (The entry at Marcianopolis on 10.26.294, Cons. 6.17, is problematic, as the journey from there to Anchialos was just over 80 miles. Perhaps it should be moved, and perhaps Reginassi is another name for or is very close to Marcianopolis.)

*CJ* 5.12.25. Was dated to 11.11.294 at Antioch. Location changed to Pantichium to suit date; place name incorrectly copied at some point, possibly on the model of the previous entry.

*CJ* 5.12.27. Was dated to 12.27.294 at Sirmium. Year changed to 293 to suit the location.

*CJ* 5.16.18. Was dated to 6.29.293 at Serdica. Change date from *iiii k. Iul.* to *iiii k. Aug.* (7.29.293) to aid route of itinerary. See below at *CJ* 8.44.21.

*CJ* 5.24.1. Was dated to 6.16.294 at Beroea. Year changed to 293. Journey from Beroea to Philippopolis should take approximately three days, which is not possible given this entry and the two at Philippopolis dated to the following day. I propose that the date be changed from *xvi k. Iul.* to *xviii k. Iul.* (14.6.293), allowing a little more time to make the journey.

*CJ* 5.49.2. Was dated to *xviii k. Nov.* 294. Date does not exist and should be changed to *xvii k. Nov.*

*CJ* 5.51.12. Was dated to 11.22.294 at Sirmium. Year changed to 293.

*CJ* 5.71.13. Was dated to 8.25.293 at Sirmium. Date changed from *viii k. Sept.* to *viii id. Sept.* (9.6.293) to maintain the sequence of entries in the title. *k.* may have been copied erroneously from the previous entry.

*CJ* 5.71.16. Was dated to 4.8.294 at Anchialos. Location should be deleted, following mss. *VPL.*

*CJ* 6.2.19 *sine die*. Follows an entry on 12.30.294. Most likely dates to 294 and therefore to 12.30 or 12.31.

*CJ* 6.19.1. Lacking date and year. Shares a recipient and much text with *CJ* 2.6.4 (*iiii k. Ian.*). Should both be changed to *viiii k. Ian.* (12.24) to suit *CJ* 2.4.38 (=6.31.3), 3.31.10 and 4.29.20, possibly all to the same recipient.

*CJ* 6.21.14. Was dated to 5.3.294 at Aurris. Location could be Aureus Mons, near Sirmium. Date supports the identification. Compare with the conjecture of Barnes, *New Empire*, 53.

*CJ* 6.50.14. Was dated to 9.26.293 at Viminacium. Year changed to 294 to suit the location.

*CJ* 6.58.9. Was dated to 6.26.294 at Nicomedia. Date changed from *vi k. Iul.* to *vi k. Ian.* (12.27.294) to suit the location.

*CJ* 6.59.2. Was dated to 5.19.293 at Verona. Either this could be a Western entry or it should be placed at Beroea and its date changed from *xiiii k. Iun.* to *xvii k. Iul.* (6.15.293) to almost coincide with *CJ* 5.24.1, another entry from Beroea.

*CJ* 7.2.11. Was dated to 3.17.293 at Sirmium. Year changed to 294 to allow time for journey from Sirmium to Heraclea.

*CJ* 7.16.39. Was dated to 12.26.294 at Sirmium. Abbreviated notation *s* was incorrectly expanded to Sirmium. Location deleted. (Alternatively, the year should be changed to 293.)

*CJ* 7.62.11. Dated to *xvii k. Ian.* (12.16), though the exact year of Diocletian's reign is unknown. The previous entry dates to 294 and the subsequent entry to 314. The year is more likely to be 294 than any subsequent year.

*CJ* 8.13.15. Was dated to 5.3.293 at Heraclea. Heraclea was copied mistakenly from the previous entry; Adrianople is probably the correct location.

*CJ* 8.13.21. Was dated to 10.30.294 at Ratiaria. Date needs to be changed from *iii k. Nov.* to *viii* or *vi id. Oct.* (10.8 or 10.10, following Mommsen), though it is hard to justify the necessary changes to every element of the date.

*CJ* 8.13.26. Was dated to 12.27.294 (*vi k. Ian.*) at Sirmium. Year changed to 293 and date changed to *viiii k. Ian.* to suit the location and to match the date of *CJ* 4.10.6, probably to the same recipient. (Alternatively, the location should be removed.)

*CJ* 8.42.20. Was dated to 10.28.294 at Adrianople. This is a very problematic entry. While the Peutinger Map does not show clearly the route between Anchialos and Heraclea, the Antonine Itinerary demonstrates clearly that Adrianople was not a stopping point between these two points. Even if Adrianople were a stopping point, the court could not have traveled between Develtus and Adrianople in less than one day. Perhaps Adrianople is a miswriting for a location between Sirmium and Luciona visited by the court exactly one year earlier. Alternatively, the date needs somehow to be changed from *iv k. Oct.* to *iv id. Mai* to bring it into line with other entries from that location in 294. Another alternative is to keep the date and conjecture that Adrianople was inserted by a scribe unsure of the correct location but aware that Adrianople was in the vicinity. Finally, Adrianople may have been misread for Anchialos (probably in abbreviated form.) This last option has been followed. (The fact that the recipient's name, Eucratis, is Greek may support keeping the entry in the East, rather than moving it west of Sirmium.)

*CJ* 8.44.21. Was dated to 6.21.293 at Serdica. Date changed from *xi k. Iul.* to *xi k. Aug* (7.22.293). Month may have been incorrectly copied from previous entry. Because of this change Diocletian now goes from Philippopolis to Serdica to Viminacium without doubling back once to Philippopolis.

*CJ* 8.53.13. Was dated to 5.18.293 at Sirmium. Date changed from *xv k. Iun.* to *xv k. Ian.* (12.18.293) to suit the location.

*CJ* 9.12.4. Was dated to 6.15.293 at Sirmium. Date changed from *xvii k. Iul.* to *xvii k. Ian.* (12.16.293) to suit the location.

*FV* 325. Was dated to 11.9.294 at Heraclea. Date changed from *v id. Nov.* to *vi. id. Nov.* (11.8.294) to suit the location and time required for the journey from Heraclea to Melantias.

The following entries have been changed on the basis that they should be joined with another entry to the same recipient. They are listed here either because I have not followed Mommsen/Krüger or because I have accepted one of their two or more alternative suggestions.

*CJ* 2.32.1. Was dated to 2.8.294 (*vi id. Feb.*) at Sirmium to Soter. Should be joined with *CJ* 2.45.2 on 2.13.294 (*id. Feb.*). Should both be dated to *vi id. Feb.*

*CJ* 2.40.4. Was dated to 12.15.294 (*xviii k. Ian.*) at Nicomedia to Stratonica. Should be joined with *CJ* 4.6.11 at 12.16.294 (*xvii k. Ian.*). Should both be dated to *xviii k. Ian.*

*CJ* 3.31.8. Was dated to 3.30.294 (*iii k. Apr.*) at Sirmium to Asterius. Should be joined with *CJ* 7.16.27 and *Cons.* 6.18 on the same day and with *CJ* 6.59.4 on 4.5.294 (*non. Apr.*). *CJ* 6.59.4 should be changed to *iii k. Apr.* (though the change is tricky).

*CJ* 3.31.10. Was dated to 12.20.294 (*xiii k. Ian.*) at Nicomedia to Theodotianus. Should be joined with *CJ* 4.29.20 on 12.24.294 (*viiii k. Ian.*), *CJ* 2.4.38 on 12.25.294 (*viii k. Ian.*) and *CJ* 2.6.4 on 12.29.294 (*iiii k. Ian.*). All should probably be dated to *viiii k. Ian.*

*CJ* 3.32.18. Was dated to 12.24.293 (*viiii k. Ian.*) at Sirmium to Clarus. Should be joined with *CJ* 8.43.2 on 12.27.293 (*vi k. Ian.*). Should both be dated to *viiii k. Ian.*

*CJ* 3.36.18. Was dated to 12.15.293 (*xviii k. Jan.*) at Sirmium to Domna. Should be joined with *CJ* 2.3.24 on 12.16.293 (*xvii k. Jan.*). Both entries should be dated to *xviii k. Ian.*

*CJ* 4.5.8. Was dated to 10.18.294 (xv k. *Nov.*) to Ziparus. Should be joined with *CJ* 8.41.6 on 10.21.294 (*xii k. Nov.*) at Durostorum. Both should be dated to *xii k. Nov.* as this date suits the location Durostorum.

*CJ* 4.48.6. Was dated to 12.18.293 (*xv k. Ian.*) at Nicomedia to Aurelius Cyrillus. Should be joined with *CJ* 4.49.16 on 12.24.294 (*viii k. Ian.*). Both entries could be dated to *xviii k. Ian.* (12.15.294) to suit the location and as a reasonable compromise for scribal errors in both dates.

*CJ* 5.1.1. Was dated to 4.14.293 (*xviii k. Mai*) to Bianor. Should be joined with *CJ* 9.12.3 dated to 4.24.293 (*viii k. Mai*). Both entries should be dated to *xviii k. Mai.*

*CJ* 5.16.17. Was dated to 4.24.293 (*viii k. Mai*) at Heraclea to Capitolina. Should be joined with *CJ* 8.42.11 (*v k. Mai*) on 4.27.293. Should both be dated to *viii k. Mai.*

*CJ* 5.71.17. Was dated to 12.7.294 (*vii id. Dec.*) at Nicomedia to Philippus. Should be joined with *CJ* 6.20.15 on 12.13.294 (*id. Dec.*). Should both be dated to *vii id. Dec.*

*CJ* 6.42.29. Was dated to 12.6.294 (*viii id. Dec.*) at Nicomedia to Achilleus. Should be joined with *CJ* 2.4.36 on 12.8.294 (*vi id. Dec.*) and *CJ* 6.23.14 on 12.13.294 (*id. Dec.*). All three entries should be dated to *viii id. Dec.*

*CJ* 6.50.17. Was dated to 10.28.294 (*v k. Nov.*) at Anchialos to Gaius. Should be joined with *CJ* 4.25.5 on 10.29.294 (*iv k. Nov.*). Should both be dated to *v k. Nov.* to allow time for travel.

*CJ* 6.55.7. Was dated to 2.14.294 (*xvi k. Mart.*) at Sirmium to Aemiliana. Should be joined with *CJ* 8.46.8 from 4.16.294 (*xvi k. Mai*) and be moved to same day by changing *Mart.* to *Mai.*

*CJ* 6.59.9. Was dated to 12.18.294 (*xv k. Ian.*) at Nicomedia to Sopatros. Should be joined with *CJ* 3.32.28 on 12.25.294 (*viii k. Ian.*) Krüger suggests changing *viii k. Ian.* to *xv k. Ian.* But *CJ* 3.32.28 could also date to *xviii k. Ian.* (12.15.294); it is then possible that both entries should have that same date, which combines *xv* and *viii.*

*CJ* 7.2.11. Was dated to 3.17.293 (*xvi k. Apr.*) at Sirmium to Laurina and should be joined with *CJ* 2.32.2 on 3.18.294 (*xv k. Apr.*). Both should be dated to *xvi k. Apr.* (3.17.294) to suit the location.

*CJ* 7.26.8 *sine die* to Severus. Should be joined with *CJ* 4.38.9 on 3.25.294 and should therefore take its date.

*CJ* 7.72.9 to Aurelius Gerontius. Was dated to 8.19 (*xiiii k. Sept.*) in 293 or 299. Should be joined with *CJ* 3.21.1 (*xiiii k. Sept.* 293) and *CJ* 4.50.7 (*xiiii k. Sept.* 293). Should therefore be dated to 293.

*CJ* 8.13.26. Was dated to 12.27.293 (*vi k. Ian.*) at Sirmium to Mauricius. Should be joined with *CJ* 4.10.6 on 12.24.293 (*viiii k. Ian.*). Should both be dated to *viiii k. Ian.*

*CJ* 9.33.3. Was dated to 1.7.293 (*vii id. Ian.*) at Sirmium to Euelpistus. Should be joined with *CJ* 4.10.7 on 12.30.293 (*iii k. Ian.*) and *CJ* 5.34.8 on 1.4.294 (*ii non. Ian.*). While it seems that the entries do share a recipient, nevertheless there seem to be no simple solutions for aligning their dates and so the entries have not been grouped together.

*CJ* 10.40.7 *sine die* to Aurelius. Should be joined with *CJ* 7.62.11 (*xvii k. Ian.*) and should therefore also be dated to 12.16.294.

The following entries are either copies of each other or one is an edited copy of the other:

*CJ* 2.4.38 and 6.31.3.
*CJ* 2.6.4 and 6.19.1.
*CJ* 4.16.6 and 7.72.7.
*CJ* 5.59.3 and 7.26.9.

The following entries are located at places otherwise unknown:

*CJ* 4.20.8 and *CJ* 4.21.10 at Reginassi. The location remains unidentified; perhaps it is Marcianopolis.

*CJ* 6.20.14 at Trimontium. This is the alternative name for Philippopolis, though the location does not suit the date of the entry (2.23.294). Trimontium has probably been written instead of the less familiar, but more plausible Tricornium, which is located near Sirmium.

*CJ* 6.21.14 at Aurrii. Probably written for Aureus Mons (see above).

*CJ* 7.19.5 at Beraca. Amended to Heraclea (see above).

*CJ* 9.20.10 at Lucione and *CJ* 9.20.11 at Lucionae. These names have been identified as Luciona, modern Lugio, located to the north-west of Sirmium on the Danube.

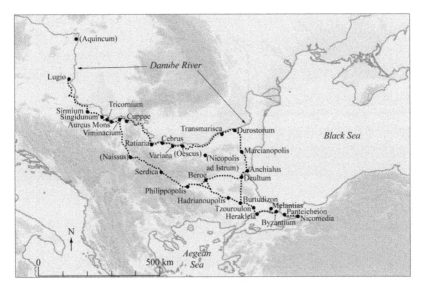

*Map Copyright 2008, Ancient World Mapping Center*

Places marked on this map follow the spelling used by the AWMC (and therefore the *Barrington Atlas*) and differ from the spellings used elsewhere in this book as follows:

Anchialus = Anchialos
Beroe = Beroea
Burtudizon = Burtidizum
Cebrus = Cebrum
Deultum = Develtus
Hadrianoupolis = Adrianople
Herakleia = Heraclea
Lugio = Lucione
Panteichion = Pantichium
Tzouroulon = Tzirallum
Variana = Varianae

The location of Reginassi cannot be identified and therefore does not appear on this map.

# NOTES

## Preface & Acknowledgments

1. Honoré, *Severan Lawyers*, 164.
2. Brown, *Augustine of Hippo,* 9. Augustine's description of his father is found in *Conf.* II, iii, 5.
3. Crook, "Review of E. Champlin," 233.
4. Ibid., 233–34. Millar, *Crowd in Rome*, 203, states that the "middle class" at Rome could be defined as having a minimum of 10 percent of the wealth required of *equites* and 5 percent of that required of senators.
5. Purcell, "Way We Used to Eat," 339.
6. Education for most children was until about the age of eleven: Marrou, *History of Education,* 359 nn. 3–4, referring to Suet. *Ner.* 7.

## Introduction

1. The declaration was made to Krt, a Canaanite god, by his son. The lines are cited by Brown, *Poverty and Leadership,* 69, who quotes from Gray, "Social Aspects," 173–74.
2. Speech of Mr. Cushing, of Massachusetts, on the Right of Petition, as connected with petitions for the abolition of slavery and the slave trade in the District of Columbia in the House of Representatives, January 25, 1836 (Washington: Gales & Beaton, 1836).
3. On the claims of early Near Eastern rulers to protect the vulnerable, see Fensham, "Widow, Orphan, and the Poor," passim, and on Hammurabi, p. 129. There are also further examples in the laws of Ur-Namma (ca. 2100 BC) and Lipit-Ishtar (ca. 1930 BC), for which see Roth, *Law Collections,* 16–17 and 25, respectively.
4. Weinfeld, *Social Justice,* 225, gives an example of praise of a charitable Hittite ruler.
5. For a text, see Cavigneaux and Böhmer, *Uruk,* 60–61, no. 115. A translation is conveniently accessible at the Electronic Text Corpus of Sumerian Literature based at the University of Oxford (http://etcsl.orinst.ox.ac.uk/cgi-bin/etcsl.cgi?text=c.3*#),

text 3.3.01. The translated text above, of lines 6–8 from ETCSL, follows the readings of the majority of manuscripts.

6. Hallo, "Individual Prayer," 76–80.

7. Another example of early petitioners' vulnerability is found in the petition of a widow to an official written in Hebrew and dating in the ninth to seventh centuries BC. In humility, she refers to herself as the official's servant and asks for his support. On this text, see Shanks, "Three Shekels."

8. On pleas for fairness rather than legal remedy, see Dobbs-Allsopp, "Genre," 50.

9. On written petitions generally, see Alexander, "Aramaic Epistolography," 158. On the evidence found of letters deposited at statue bases, see Hallo, "Individual Prayer," 79. On the structure of petitions, Alexander, "Aramaic Epistolography," 164.

10. Dobbs-Allsopp, "Genre," 52, on the basis of 2 Sam. 14:4.

11. See Fensham, "Widow, Orphan, and the Poor," 138, on the Israelite David receiving petitions.

12. The translation comes from VerSteeg, *Law in Ancient Egypt*, 23.

13. The Egyptian court allowed petitioners to present their cases orally or, if they lived far from the court, in writing. On procedure, see VerSteeg, ibid., 68–70.

14. Ibid., 52 n. 94.

15. See, for example, Ewick and Silbey, *Common Place*, 101.

16. On manumission, see Weinfeld, *Social Justice*, 193 n. 33.

17. The original publication is in *PSI* 402. See White, *Form and Structure*, appendix 2, for further examples of Greek petitions and letters. *PSI* 402 is the second document in the appendix.

18. The translation comes from White, ibid.

19. On this text and others of the period, see White, ibid.

20. See the critical edition of Parkinson, *Eloquent Peasant*.

21. From the *Bellum Alexandrinum* 52.2, we learn that a petitioner purportedly asked (*postularet*) for something from Cassius in his capacity as *praetor peregrinus* and requested (*peteret*) a response (*responsum*). The technical vocabulary suggests that this was petition and response, not a casual enquiry and informal reply. On early Roman petitioning, see also the first edition of Fergus Millar's *Emperor in the Roman World* (hereafter referred to as *ERW*[1]), p. 466. That the receipt of petitions was widespread is suggested by the fact that Sertorius received petitions orally in Spain in the 80s BC (Plut. *Sert.* 20.3).

22. On this petition to an official sent by a Jewish woman in Arabia, see Bowersock, "Babatha Papyri," 338–40, and Cotton, "Guardianship of Jesus," 106–107.

23. On the variety of texts called *libelli*, see *RE*, s.v. "*libellus.*" They were sent as well as received by Roman rulers. Suetonius names Caesar's recommendations of individuals to the various voting tribes *libelli: et edebat per libellos circum tribum missos scriptura breui: 'Caesar dictator illi tribui. commendo uobis illum et illum, ut uestro suffragio suam dignitatem teneant.' (Div. Iul. 41.2)*

24. Suet. *Div. Iul.* 81: *tandem Decimo Bruto adhortante, ne frequentis ac iam dudum opperientis destitueret, quinta fere hora progressus est libellumque insidiarum indicem ab obuio quodam porrectum libellis ceteris, quos sinistra manu tenebat, quasi mox lecturus commiscuit.*

25. On Caesar working at the games, see Suet. *Div. Aug.* 45; Caesar gave his ring

to the father of Pompeius Trogus, who also dealt with his letters and assemblies, according to Just. *Epit.* XLIII 5.12. The references come from Millar, *ERW*[1], 213.

26. *CIL* 6.5181 = *ILS* 1676. Augustus may also have had help. Cassius Dio has Maecenas advise him, "Moreover, for your judicial work and your correspondence, to help you attend to the decrees of the states and the petitions of private individuals, and for all other business which belongs to the administration of the empire, you must have men chosen from the knights to be your helpers and assistants" (Cassius Dio 52.33.5, trans. E. Carey) though this is probably a retrojection of current practice.

27. On the experience of *a libellis* in the first and second centuries, see Millar, *ERW*[1], 102–105.

28. *D* 20.5.12: *rescriptum est ab imperatore libellos agente Papiniano.*

29. *Not. Dig. Occ.* XVII: *Magister libellorum cognitiones et preces tractat.*

30. On this, see Millar, *ERW*[1], 242 and Nörr, "Interloqui de plano" 542–43.

31. Cassius Dio 77.18.2 and 78.4.2–3.

32. For a good, brief overview of the development of the system, incorporating recent bibliography, see Hauken, *Petition and Response*, 303–13.

33. *RE*, s.v. "libellus."

34. For example, P.Amh. II 63, P.Col. VI 123, P.Oxy. IV 705, P.Oxy. VII 1020 (though this could date to AD 198) and P.Oxy. LX 4068. Some of their responses to petitions are preserved in the *Apokrimata* (P.Col. VI 123); yet other responses are found in the *Codex Gregorianus,* on which see below.

35. On the controversy, see Hauken, *Petition and Response*, 303–304, who is confident that Aphrodisias 14 is a private petition and is in agreement with Reynolds, *Aphrodisias and Rome*, 113, who calls it a subscript.

36. The constitution of Trajan that is referenced could, however, come from either a petition or a letter. Other constitutions dating to Hadrian's reign are quoted in *D* 40.12.43, 48.8.4.2, 48.8.14 and 48.15.6pr. Many more constitutions are quoted from the reigns of Marcus Aurelius, Antoninus Pius, and Lucius Verus, including *D* 1.7.39 and 2.15.3pr.

37. Simon, *Konstantinisches Kaiserrecht*, 6–7. They are most likely letters, although Simon is unsure. It is possible that entries looking like rescripts, with a salutation in the dative, are actually letters because the words *suo salutem* have been omitted after the recipients' names. On the various forms of address used in the Theodosian Code, see Matthews, *Laying Down the Law*, 217.

38. Scholars have pointed to imperial pronouncements limiting the use of rescripts; for example, Constantine ruled that *subscriptiones contra ius* had no force of precedent (*CTh* 1.2.2). But this ruling may simply reveal that petitioners were approaching multiple potential respondents, a situation which could give rise to rescripts that contradicted earlier legislation and each other. On the view that later Roman emperors were increasingly distant from their subjects and restricted their opportunities to present petitions, see especially MacMullen, *Corruption*, 110. Against this view, see Harries, *Law and Empire*, especially chap. 4. The former's view is undermined by a ruling (*CTh* 9.21.4.1) in which Constantine offers dispensations to his subjects on the basis of their gender and legal knowledge and capacity.

39. *Not. Dig. Occ.* XVII.

40. Simon, *Konstantinisches Kaiserrecht*, 7–8. FV 32, 33, 273, 274, and 291. FV 34,

287 and 290 may also be attributable to Constantine. Though its salutation may suggest that it is a rescript, *FV* 36 is probably a letter.

41. On the development of litigation *per rescriptum,* see Maggio, "Note critiche."

42. *CJ* 1.23.7. An inscription to the *gens* of Orcistus illustrates the law, which includes a text directed to the *gens* and a response to an official about them. The first text, which is brief and resembles earlier rescripts, seems to have been signed originally by the emperor. The second, described as a *pragmatica sanctio,* is longer and resembles one of the constitutions preserved in the *CTh* or post-dating Diocletian's reign in the *CJ* that look like letters or edicts. The text is presented and discussed by Feissel, "Adnotatio de Constantin," 256–57 and also discussed in his "Pétitions aux empereurs," 36.

43. On *adnotationes,* see Feissel, "Adnotatio de Constantin," 259–60 and 266 and "Pétitions aux empereurs," 36–38. On earlier *adnotationes,* see Corcoran, *Empire of the Tetrarchs,* 57–58.

44. *CTh.* 1.2.1: *adnotationes nostras sine rescriptione admitti non placet.*

45. The late Roman position of *quaestor* was probably introduced under Constantine. For the evidence, see Harries, "Roman Imperial Quaestor," 153. Peachin, *Iudex vice Caesaris,* 197, proposes the reorganization of the three *scrinia* under a *quaestor* as early as AD 314 on the basis that other legal reforms, especially in the area of appeals, were being introduced in that decade.

46. On these changes, see Zuckerman, "Deux Dioscore d'Aphroditè," 82–83.

47. Feissel, "Pétitions aux empereurs," Annexe 1 (pp. 45–49). He does admit (p. 42) that what look like rescripts to petitions are sometimes responses to requests made in person or to legislative requests from officials. Kramer, "P.Strasb.Inv. 1265," 155–61.

48. Feissel, "Pétitions aux empereurs,"34.

49. Feissel, ibid., 36.

50. On estate owners as respondents and the Church answering petitions, see Gascou, "Pétitions privées," 96–97 and 94, respectively.

51. See the list of petitions, including identification of petitioners, of Fournet and Gascou, "Liste des pétitions."

52. On bishops as arbiters, see Brown, *Poverty and Leadership,* 67; Rapp, *Holy Bishops,* 242–52. On Symeon Sylites, see ibid., 251.

53. Ibid., 240–41.

54. Finn, *Almsgiving,* 265–68.

55. Brown, *Poverty and Leadership,* 68 n. 110 cites Augustine, *de opera monachorum* 29.37; and Possidius, *Vita Augustini* 19.

56. Brown, *Poverty and Leadership,* 67–68.

57. Brundage, *Medieval Canon Law,* 10.

58. On this collection, see Winroth, *Gratian's Decretum.*

59. Morris, "Citizen Attitudes," 748–49. From his sixth-century examples, P.Oxy. I 130 and P.Oxy. XXVII 2479, we find petitioners calling themselves Πιηοῦτ[ο]ς ὑμετέρ(ου) δούλου ("Pieous, your slave") and Ἀνοὺπ ἐλεεινοῦ ὑμετέρου δούλου ("Anoup, your pitiable slave"), respectively.

60. Zuckerman, "Deux Dioscore d'Aphroditè," 90, though he is not entirely convinced at this interpretation of the absence of evidence.

61. Khan, "Medieval Arabic Petitions," 24–26, on the careful use of formulas to express the status relationship between petitioner and addressee.

62. Hauken, *Petition and Response*, no. 1, III.1–3 (p. 8); no. 3, lines 48–54 (pp. 39–40); no. 5, lines 73–76 (p. 89); no. 6, lines 31–32 (p. 148).

63. Khan, *Legal and Administrative Documents*, no. 86 (pp. 359–60), no. 87 (pp. 361–64), and no. 89 (pp. 369–71), for example. On the Christian, Jewish, and Muslim traditions of petitioning about poverty, see Cohen, "Feeding the Poor," 417–18.

64. On Muslim influences on Jewish petitioners, see Cohen, "Four Judaeo-Arabic Petitions," 448. On the Genizah texts in general, see Khan, *Legal and Administrative Documents*. Khan's collection contains petitions (documents 70–92, pp. 321–73) and responses (nos. 103–107, pp. 413–19). On procedure, see Cohen, "Four Judaeo-Arabic Petitions," 448.

65. Examples of petitions are found in Khan, "Medieval Arabic Petitions," 12–18. Further examples are found in Khan, *Legal and Administrative Documents;* asking for money: documents 80 (pp. 344–45), 82 (pp. 348–49); for employment: 84 (pp. 352–53); for a murder investigation: 74 (pp. 330–31).

66. On the petitions of men and women in poverty trying to feed their families, see Cohen, "Four Judaeo-Arabic Petitions," 449–65. See also Cohen, "Feeding the Poor," on poverty in the Genizah texts.

67. Cohen, "Voice of the Poor."

68. Baha' al-Din, *Sirat Salah al-Din* (*Life of Saladin*), 13. Also in the east but somewhat later, we find an unpublished Yemeni liturgical text of the fifteenth century containing a collection of all the documents one might need in life, such as divorce documents and contracts of sale. It includes as the final document a pro forma petition, which would otherwise have been available to a potential petitioner at the court who collected the unfilled petition, entered his or her own details, and then presented it. The petition was answered and signed at the bottom.

69. On petitioning in the Byzantine Empire, see generally Nystazopoulou-Pélékidou, "*Déiseis* et les *lyseis.*"

70. Macrides, "Ritual of Petition," 364–65.

71. Ibid., 368–69.

72. See Sidonius Apollinaris, *Ep.* 1.2

73. On ancient petitions, see Dodd, "Hidden Presence."

74. TNA SC 9/1 and 9/2 are two parliamentary rolls that record the activities of a local scribe (I owe the reference to Musson, "Ancient Petitions"). On scriveners, the medieval successors to Roman *tabelliones,* see Ramsay, "Scriveners and notaries," 118–21 and 123–27, especially 127 on their importance to non-elites.

75. On letters of remission, see Davis, *Fiction in the Archives;* she analyzes the status of suppliants on p. 18. I am grateful to Deborah Lyons for recommending her work.

76. Al-Haifi, "Streamlining the Bureaucracy." His complaints were "any dealings with the government by the public at large involve a myriad of red tape and bureaucratic procedures. In many cases all this red tape is enough to scare any petitioner and may actually lead to the deprivation of countless citizens from government services." "There are so many different steps involved in getting a certain petition through any of the majority of the Government ministries and authorities that one is inclined to believe that logic and common sense have no place in Government administration of its various functions." "There are no set procedures that are clearly laid out and outlined to the public to be able to determine ahead of time the

requirements of certain transactions and the flow chart for the various processing tasks ahead." "It is not clear what led to the development of almost an impossible bureaucratic framework that costs the concerned petitioners a great length of time, and requires substantial expense (both direct and opportunity cost) and of course a lot of patience." "Some people manage to speedily complete the procedures in the minimum of time, as they enjoy the ample influence their social and political positions may generate, all under the noses of the 'normal' people that must go through all the tedious steps, many of which are practically and logically unnecessary."

77. The First Amendment states: "Congress shall make no law . . . abridging . . . the right of the people . . . to petition the government for redress of grievances." "Government" is usually interpreted as the three branches: legislative, executive, and judicial. Europeans may petition their Parliament on the basis of Article 194 of the EC Treaty: "Any citizen of the Union, and any natural or legal person residing or having its registered office in a Member State, shall have the right to address, individually or in association with other citizens or persons, a petition to the European Parliament on a matter which comes within the Community's fields of activity and which affects him, her or it directly."

78. The Charter of the United Nations, Chapter 13, Article 87 provides that "the General Assembly and, under its authority, the Trusteeship Council, in carrying out their functions, may . . . accept petitions and examine them in consultation with the administering authority."

79. An Internet site that hosts petitions is www.petitiononline.com. It allows a subscriber to post the text of a petition, wait for interested individuals to add their names, and then deliver the petition when he or she is satisfied with the number of signatures received. The Internet's importance to communication between people and with their governments about political issues is discussed by Gore, *Assault on Reason*, 262–65.

80. Marriage: *CJ* 5.27.1pr; liturgies: P.Mich. XIV 675.

## 1. Seeking Justice in the Roman World

1. The *leges regiae* are collected in *FIRA*² i 3–18. It was said that Romulus had instituted the system of patronage in part to ensure legal protection for the weaker in society. The Roman system of patronage may, according to Sirks, "Making a Request," 135, have been the origin of petitioning: "The rescript system is a development of the existing habit at Rome to present requests to patrons by way of a *libellus*." Just as Near Eastern rulers were expected to care for their vulnerable subjects, so Roman patrons provided protection for their clients.

2. Saller, *Personal Patronage*, 193–94, notes that evidence for patronage among the non-elites is all but non-existent, though it was widespread. In his account of Libanius as the client of the provincial governor, Saller describes how he became the focus of potential petitioners, who swarmed to him with requests for help, such as speeding up or rescheduling a trial (p. 151).

3. Ignorance of law among lawyers was not restricted to the Roman Empire. According to Lemmings, *Professors of the Law*, 113, "The only substantive 'qualifications' for entry to the Georgian inns of court were financial; the ability to pay the admission fees of the house and its termly duties. There were certainly no strict educational

requirements of the kind which are obligatory at the modern inns and universities, and so the early schooling of barristers was a matter of parental choice and cultural prejudice." Even at university, would-be barristers learned languages, philosophy, and the other liberal sciences, but not law (ibid., 118).

4. Quint. *Inst.* 2.3. This attitude may have changed with the rising importance of the law schools, especially that at Beirut, in the later Roman period.

5. Harries, *Law and Empire,* 13.

6. *Edictum de maximis pretiis* (hereafter *EMP*) 7.72–73.

7. *EMP* 7.1.

8. Ulpian: *D* 48.19.9.4, cited in *RE* s.v. *tabellio.* My assessment here differs from that presented in *EDRL* s.v. *tabellio,* which claims that lawyers advised their clients about legal problems and *tabelliones* assisted with drawing up relevant documents. I believe that such was the *tabelliones'* experience that many people went to them directly, rather than making a prior visit to a lawyer. Cuias, with reference to *Nov.* 44 *de tabellionibus,* calls them *publici contractuum scriptores vel testamentorum.* The reference is from Pfaff, *Tabellio und Tabularius,* 8. For introductions to these ubiquitous, yet shadowy figures of the Roman legal world see Pfaff, as well as *RE* s.v. *tabellio* and *EDRL* s.v. *tabellio.* The longest contemporary description of their activities is found at *D* 48.19.9.4–9.

9. Some documents contain a symbol resembling a letter N scored through vertically, which has been taken to stand either for *narratio* or *nomikos,* an alternative name for *tabellio* in Hellenistic Egypt and the Byzantine east. See Crook, *Legal Advocacy,* 116–18, and Harries, *Law and Empire,* 107, for discussions of possible interpretations.

10. That they knew law is indicated by the fact that they are sometimes mentioned with jurists. See, for example, *D* 48.19.9.4.

11. See, for example, P.Stras. I 15 (l. 5), P.Oxy. VIII 1121, P.Oxy. IX 1206, P.Mich. VIII 508, P.Ryl. II 117 and P.Dura 29 and 30, in which individuals are named, who have written on behalf of one party. P.Hamb. I 4, refers to a νομογράφος ("notary," LSJ), who may be a *tabellio.* For a list of *tabelliones* in the later Roman period, see *RE* s.v. *tabellio,* which uses inclusion of the phrase ὑπ' ἐμοῦ ("by me") as evidence of the work of a *tabellio.* P.Lips. I 28, an adoption of ad 381, contains the signature of a *tabellio:* δι' ἐμοῦ Φιλοσαράπδος ἐγρά(φη) (Philosarapdos wrote on my behalf). This phrase, which is in a different hand from the body of the petition, may be interpreted, I believe, as the imprimatur of a *tabellio,* under whose direction a scribe wrote the preceding document.

12. Operating from *stationes: CJ* 8.11.12; *D* 42.4.7.13, *D* 47.10.15.7. Charges: *EMP* 7.41.

13. On the guidelines: *CJ* 4.21.17. *CTh* 9.19.1.1 threatened that *tabelliones* might be called on to confirm their authorship of transactions subsequently found to be illegal. Justinian, who may have been restating earlier principles, required that every *tabellio* seek permission to operate and follow certain guidelines, such as ensuring that all relevant parties signed an agreement. His *Nov.* 44.1.4 authorizes only *tabelliones,* and on certain occasions their representatives, to draw up legally valid documents for money in the *fora.*

14. This document and several others pertaining to the case are translated and discussed in Evans Grubbs, *Women and the Law,* 257–60.

15. P.Sakaon 36.

16. *D* 50.13.1.10–11.

17. Constantine's legislation is preserved as *CTh* 1.16.7. Not long after, Valentinian and Valens again had to order that *defensores civitatis* control charges levied by advocates, staff-chiefs, *exceptores*, and enforcement officers so as to look after the "harmless rustics" (*CTh* 1.29.5).

18. On the costs of going to court, Harries, *Law and Empire*, 100–101. For the levying of charges by the writers (*scholastici*) and issuers (*officiales*), see *FIRA*² i 64.

19. Some jurists were aware of the banal but time-consuming calls on a litigant's time: *D* 4.6.15.3. (The reference is from Crook, *Law and Life,* 96 n. 145.)

20. *D* 48.2.8. Those who were barred could, however, hire an advocate to appeal to a *iudex*.

21. Even if that attitude has disappeared from modern Western law, the disadvantages of low social status are still keenly felt, as the second quotation at the start of this chapter demonstrates. Ewick and Silbey's sociological study examines attitudes to and experiences of law among a cross-section of people in New Jersey.

22. A modern analogy comes from rural Wales, where farmers make up the majority of magistrates on one particular bench. The preponderance of farmers in a stable rural community can be advantageous in complex cases involving farming matters, but can also raise issues of bias for or against various parties—farmers and non-farmers; locals and newcomers. See Harding and Williams, *Legal Provision,* 68–70.

23. Harries, *Law and Empire,* 99.

24. On the linguistic issue in Egypt, where Demotic was the local language, see Fewster, *Bilingualism.* She notes that some legal documents in Egypt were written in Greek or Demotic or both (229), but that any communication with the Roman administration had to be conducted in Greek (225). Roman law was aware of the issue; *fideicommissa* could be made in any language (*D* 32.11.pr), as could stipulations, although jurists are cautious on this point (*D* 45.1.1.6).

25. Harries, *Law and Empire,* 108. The experience for Romans became far worse after AD 337, when it seems that advocates no longer spoke for their client; rather, they simply offered advice, leaving the client to speak for himself, according to Tellegen-Couperus, *Short History,* 132.

26. Much of my discussion of out-of-court methods of dispute resolution is informed by Harries, *Law and Empire,* 172–90. For examples of arbitration documents, see P.Princ. II 79, P.Berl. Möller 1 (an agreement between two women), and P.Oxy. XXXVI 2768.

27. On the process, see *D* 4.8.

28. Certain groups were probably excluded, such as wards under guardianship, women, the mad, the deaf and the dumb, by analogy with restrictions against such people acting as judges or public officials. Ulpian at *D* 8.3.7 says simply that an *arbiter* could be freeborn or a freedman, but he could not be a slave.

29. For discussion of two arbitration documents, see Gagos and Sijpesteijn, "Settling a Dispute," and also P.Oxy. XII 1562.

30. *CTh* 2.55.4.

31. For discussion of oaths, see Matthews, "Roman Law," 37–38, who points

out that resolution by the exchange of oaths used to be thought fitting for a legally unsophisticated people. But Roman jurists thought exchange of oaths an effective method of resolution with greater authority than a judgment (Paul, *D* 12.2.2). This method may seem naive, probably because it relied on the compunction of parties to tell the truth in court. But it also required the first oath to go unchallenged; if there was a challenge by the other party, evaluation of the oaths was left to the judge. Cases in American and European courts today also assume that parties and their counsels tell the truth and also make the judge (and jury) responsible for deciding between the parties' stories.

32. Coriat, *Prince législateur,* 317. It is certainly not the case that all petitioners belonged to the middling sort. Some were of elite status, as the early fourth-century petition of Aurelius Adelphios, preserved as *CPR* XVIIA, demonstrates.

33. *CIL* 3.12336 = *IGRR* 1.674 = *Syll3* 888 = *IGBulg* IV, 2236. On this inscription, see most recently Hauken, *Petition and Response,* 74–139, and "Structures and Themes," 13–22. The best text is that of Hallof, "Inschrift von Skaptopara," which, together with the translation of Hauken presented in *Petition and Response,* can be found in appendix I.

34. Though very rare in the *CJ,* a few rescripts dealt with issues that had already been decided in court, but which the petitioner was considering bringing to appeal. On these petitioners and the rescripts to them, see Coriat, *Prince législateur,* 339.

35. Examples of this third type of petition include notices of intention to act as a guardian, notices of sale, and declarations of adherence to a law; for example, during Decius's persecution of Christians in AD 250, individuals petitioned asking for a certificate to confirm that they had sacrificed to the old gods (e.g. P.Oxy. XXIV 3929). Further examples are provided in *EDRL,* s.v. "*libellus.*"

36. See Oliver, *Greek Constititions,* 1–18, for a succinct and accurate description of an epistle, its features and uses. Nörr, "Zur Reskriptenpraxis," §II, points out that sometimes, with inadequate evidence, it is impossible to tell the difference between an epistle and a rescript.

37. *CJ* 2.13.1, 2.56.1, 3.22.5, 5.12.21, 7.33.6, 7.62.9, 9.1.13, and 9.9.25.

38. On petitions to provincial officials, see Haensch, "Bearbeitungsweisen," and *Capita Provinciarum;* also Thomas, "Subscriptiones," and Burton, "Proconsuls."

39. Petition to an *epistrategos:* P.Yale inv. 1086. Petitions to centurions: P.Euphrates 5 and P.Mich. inv. 6127 (AD 193). *Scrinia libellorum* under *duces* are listed in *Not. Dig. Or.* XL, XLI, XLII; the *duces* of Pannonia and Thracia apparently did not have *scrinia libellorum,* perhaps because of scribal omission. A fuller list of the provincial officials who were eligible to receive petitions is given by Tibiletti, "Frammento di petizione," 48–51.

40. Haensch, "Bearbeitungsweisen" 488–89.

41. Bad business deals: P.Mich. inv. 264, 265 and 6354. Property disputes: P.Col. X 276 and P.Oslo II 23. Inheritance: P.Mich. inv. 1946. Family disappearance: P.Tebt. II 333. Ephebe list: P.Oxy. IX 1202. Tax complaint: P.Wisc. inv. 56. Freedom from liturgy: P.Mich. inv. 5473 and 6351. Applications for guardians: P.Mich. inv. 3805 and P.Tebt. II 326.

42. "First and foremost, petitions appear to be a cry for help from someone who is unable to assert his or her own rights," according to Hobson, "Impact of Law," 209. The texts discussed by Herrmann, *Hilferufe,* are expressions of this lack of power.

43. On the costs of trials and alternative methods of resolution, see Harries, *Law and Empire,* especially chap. 9.

44. *CIL* 8.10570 = 8.14464.

45. On the dangers of petitioning, see Williams, "Epigraphic Texts," 189.

46. On P.Sakaon 31 and several others pertaining to the case, see Evans Grubbs, *Women and the Law,* 257–60. Although a rescript could not reopen a case that had already been judged unfavorably (*CJ* 2.4.16), Aurelia Artemis was able to petition to begin a second trial because no judgment had been made in the first.

47. On validating petitions: *CJ* 6.32.2.

48. See P.Oxy. XLII 3017, ll. 10–13.

49. On counter petitions: *CJ* 2.14.1.3 and 8.39.2.

50. Ewick and Silbey, *Common Place,* 103.

51. Petitions cannot adjourn a trial: *CJ* 3.11.2. On *quaestiones,* see *CJ* 1.21.2; on adultery, see *CJ* 9.9.17pr. On using a petition to bring an appeal, see *CJ* 1.21.1 and 3.11.5. On the guarantees bestowed by a petition, see *CJ* 7.62.12.

52. On the harsh penalties for faking responses or obtaining them fraudulently, see *CJ* 9.22.3 and 5.47.1.

53. *CJ* 1.23.2: *ea, quae ad ius rescribuntur, perennia esse debent.*

54. Petitioning as a group allowed: *CJ* 1.23.1; the restrictions: *CJ* 7.68.2.

55. On the history and current state of the text, see Hauken, *Petition and Response,* 76–84, who includes a sketch of the stone. The most recent and best text is that of Hallof, "Inschrift von Skaptopara," according to whom the stone cannot be found (p. 405).

56. On the rhetorical nature of petitions, see Hauken, *Petition and Response,* 261–88.

57. For evidence of people being employed to search for suitable supporting material, see P.Oxy. XIV 1654. On petitioners drafting petitions: T.Vindol. II 344 is a draft petition from a civilian associated with a garrison to the provincial governor. It is a good example of someone drafting a petition unaided because, as the editors describe, "the text is repetitive and the word order is awkward" (Bowman, Thomas, and Adams, *Vindolanda Writing-Tablets,* 329).

58. On the *formula Baetica,* preserved as FIRA iii, n. 92, see Crook, *Law and Life,* 245. *EMP* 7.41.

59. On scribes writing for the illiterate in Egypt, see, for example, Hanson, "Ancient Illiteracy," 166–68. The *formula Baetica* was most likely used by *tabelliones* as a template; dossiers such as that of the sixth-century notary Dioscuros, preserved in P.Cairo Masp. III 67019, 67283 and 67352 (this last is a draft of a petition), were probably kept by many *tabelliones.* On this dossier, see Fournet, "Entre document et literature," 74, who notes that a philosopher Horapollon copied his petition from a model over a century old. Abbreviations: P.Euphrates 1 and 5 respectively.

60. Hauken, *Petition and Response,* 258–95 and "Structures and Themes," 13–18.

61. For example, *CIG* 2.2018 dates to the reign of Diocletian and includes his names, albeit in truncated form. Other inscriptions would have provided notaries with emperors' full names and titles, for example, *CIG* 2.2022 dating to the reign of Septimius Severus. These sorts of inscriptions could be found even at small locations such as Tzirallum, on Diocletian's route in AD 292–4 (*CIG* 2.2023). On abbreviated

titles in petitions and responses, see Peachin, *Roman Imperial Titulature,* 15–17 and Williams, "Epigraphic Texts," 201.

62. For example, in P.Ryl. II 617 the slightly expanded phrase δέησις καὶ ἱκεσία is set off from the rest of the text and centered on its own line as a heading.

63. On petitioners' titles and place of origin, see for example P.Oxy. XLVII 3366, ll. 5–6: δημοσίου [γρ]αμματικοῦ (grammarian of the deme). P.Ryl. II 618 provides the petitioners full title and place of origin: ἀρχιπρο[φήτου τῆς λαμπροτά] της ᾿Αλεξα[νδρέων] πόλεως τῆ[ς με]γάλη[ς . c. 27] [ c. 10 ἀλλ]ων πόλε[ων ? ] ("chief priest of the great and most illustrious city of the Alexandrians . . . thank other cities"); P.Ryl. II 617, l. 5 gives just the place: ἀπὸ κώμη[ς c. 6]εχώνσιος Λε[οντο]πολίτου νομοῦ (from the village . . . of the district of Leontopolis). On variations in name, see Verhoogt, "Family Papers," 145: Sarapammon, who features in multiple documents, appears variously as Marcus Aurelius Sarapammon, Aurelius Sarapammon, and Sarapammon.

64. A particularly elaborate petition, P.Oxy. VI 899, includes a main petition, probably to the *epistrategos* (according to the original editors), as well as two trial accounts, an official letter, two other petitions, more trial proceedings, another official letter, and an imperial rescript. Crook, *Legal Advocacy,* 68–69: "They [the petitions in Egypt of the Ptolemaic and Roman periods] often read just like an advocate's *narratio* of his client's case in court, to the extent that [in] some of the texts it is uncertain whether they are the one or the other." He discusses using petitions as *narrationes* at p. 113.

65. From Alexandria, for example, P.Oxy. XII 1405, XLIII 3105, and LXIV 4437, and P.Amh. II 63, all of which date to Severus and Caracalla's visit.

66. Pliny, *Ep.* 10.106.

67. The idea was proposed by Wilcken, "Zu den Kaiserreskripten," 23, and refuted by Williams, "Libellus Procedure," 96, who points out that sending petitions through governors would be pointless, for if governors could deliberately omit to send petitions concerning matters they would probably eventually have to judge anyway, petitioners would try to circumvent them. The only evidence we have for rescripts being sent elsewhere is that officials' answers to Arsinoites's petitions were posted first at Alexandria and then Arsinoe (P.Yale I 61). But this was a special dispensation for individuals petitioning not the emperor, but the governor at Alexandria.

68. For the difficulties of presenting a petition at the assizes, see P.Oxy. XXII 2343. Septimius Heracleides's representative Nemesianus tried several times to approach the prefect, but found him dealing with embassies and other business. The account of Lewis, *Life in Egypt,* 189, is updated by Coles, "P.Oxy. XXII 2343 Revisited," 110–11.

69. Kelly, *Ruling,* 114–29 describes the time and money constraints that faced people approaching the imperial court in the later Roman period, as well as the frustrations of hopeful petitioners, ambassadors, and litigants.

70. ἔντυχέ μοι πρὸ βήματος ("petition me at the tribunal") in P.Oxy. XLII 3017.

71. D 1.16.9.4: *Observare itaque eum oportet, ut sit ordo aliquis postulationum, scilicet ut omnium desideria audiantur, ne forte dum honori postulantium datur vel improbitati ceditur, mediocres desideria sua non proferant, qui aut omnino non adhibuerunt, aut minus frequentes neque in aliqua dignitate positos advocatos sibi prospexerunt.*

72. An argument against my proposition is that in one inscription we find *alia*

*manu* preceding *scripsi* in CIL 8.10570, but not *recognovi*. Williams, "Epigraphic Texts," 189, argues that the emperor added both. But Williams acknowledges that in SB I 4639 the Greek equivalents of the two terms are in different hands, with ἀνέγνων ("I acknowledged") probably belonging to an official checking the script before it was signed by the prefect. Other scholars believe that *recripsi* and *recognovi* were written by the emperor and *magister* respectively, including Nörr, "Zur Reskriptenpraxis," 12 n. 36, but he does allow for *rescripsi* being written by a member of *scrinium* and *recognovi* by the emperor (though *IGSK* 24.1 [Smyrna II 1] 597 seems to argue against this). Their justifications are summarized by Hauken, *Petition and Response,* 124–25. A significant point in my favor is that, as Williams, "Epigraphic Texts," 193–94, points out, both *scripsi* and *recognovi* are in the first person singular and this remains the case even when there are joint emperors ruling. According to Wilcken, "Zu den Kaiserreskripten," 6, the emperor wrote *scripsi,* the *magister* wrote *recognovi.*

73. Hermann, *Hilferufe,* and Hauken, *Petition and Response,* discuss other petitions of this sort. Hauken's interpretation of the response to the Skaptopareni (122–24) is followed in this discussion.

74. Nörr, "Zur Reskriptenpraxis," 23, 33. Originals were posted, despite the risks of weather damage and theft; petitioners took copies, not the originals, back home with them.

75. Hauken, *Petition and Response,* 82. The omission is noted by Hallof, "Inschrift von Skaptopara," 423, who follows Mommsen's opinion that the petitioners may not have understood the meaning of the rescript when it was put up.

76. Williams, "Libellus Procedure," 101–3. *D* 8.3.16 and *D* 16.1.2.3 may contain rescripts in Greek, but perhaps Callistratus and Ulpian, the jurists who quoted them, found them translated in a Greek archive. Alternatively, the texts could be letters produced by the *scrinium epistolarum Graecarum.*

77. For example, *CIL* 3, Suppl. 2, 14203 = *IG* 12.5.132 = *Syll*³ 2.881, the so-called *Sacrae Litterae* of AD 204. For further discussion, see Drew-Bear, Eck, and Herrmann, "Sacrae Litterae." Further examples are found in the so-called *Apokrimata,* P.Col. VI 123, if these are in fact rescripts, on which see Schiller and Westermann, *Apokrimata,* Schiller and Youtie, "Second Thoughts," Lewis, "Imperial Apokrimata," and Turpin, "Apokrimata."

78. Temple of Apollo: Hauken, "Structures and Themes," 12; at the *stoa* of a gymnasium: P.Oxy. XLII 3018.

79. The posting of petitions and their responses was posited by Wilcken and has been accepted by all subsequent scholars, with the exception of d'Ors and Martín, "Propositio Libellorum," 117–18, who believe the documents were made available in reading rooms. Williams, "Publication of Imperial Subscripts," 292–94, criticizes this theory for being anachronistic. Nörr, "Zur Reskriptenpraxis," believes only the rescripts, not the petitions, were posted up, though his view has been soundly contradicted by Williams, "Epigraphic Texts," 202–3, who points out that the response to the Skaptopareni was copied from the *liber libellorum rescriptorum . . .* surely proving that responses were posted along with their petitions or *libelli.*

80. Not all copies have as many authenticating details as the Skaptoparean text, however: P.Mich. inv. 6554 (AD 290), for example, lacks a specific location.

81. See, for example, P.Mich. inv. 6554.

82. The phrase on Greek copies [ἐκ τ]εύχου[ς συγκ]ολλησίμω[ν βιβ]λειδίων (from the rolls of the petitions glued together) proves that the originals of petitions and responses were archived in rolls. For roll and sheet numbers, see for example P.Ryl. II 220, l. 78: α′ τεύχους, α′ τόμου, κολλήματος ρδ′ (from the first group of rolls, first roll, sheet 104) and also D'Ors and Martín, "Propositio Libellorum." On the length of the sheets, see Clarysse, "Tomoi Synkollesimoi," 349 52. Meyer, *Legitimacy and Law,* 196–201, suggests that petitions and responses may also have been written on wooden *tabulae,* which were presumably posted alongside the papyrus sheets.

83. Diocletian and Maximian's declaration: *Sancimus, ut authentica ipsa atque [et?] originalia rescripta et [ex?] nostra manu subscripta, non exempla eorum, insinuentur* (*CJ* 1.23.3).

84. P.Flor. III 382, another example and dating to 222/3 AD, was most likely the work of a lawyer or *tabellio* who had access to a store of rescripts and other legal documents. It contains one rescript dating to AD 200, another to 216, and two to 199; it also contains the texts of a couple of imperial letters and an edict. Katzoff, "P.Col. 123," surveys scholars' conjectures for the use of the Apokrimata. He, along with Schiller and Williams, gives most credence to the idea that the texts were preserved for a lawyer, who would use them as precedent in court.

85. In the first category belongs, for example, P.Oxy. VII 1020; P.Amh. II 63 belongs to the second.

86. Another possibility is that it was copied from a more official but hitherto unknown collection preceding those of Gregorian and Hermogenian that brought together legally useful rescripts. We know of the collection of Papirius Justus (see Volterra, "Ouvrage de Papirius Justus"), but there may have been others. Collections could also be made of documents for personal records. For example, the people of Antinoopolis kept a dossier of three letters (not rescripts) sent to them on various matters by Gordian III, which has been preserved as P.Vindob. G 25945. On this dossier, see Hoogendijk and van Minnen, "Drei Kaiserbriefe."

## 2. The Rescript System

1. For the most recent brief summary of the nature, purpose and textual history of the *CG* and *CH,* see Corcoran, "Publication of Law," 56–65. Some entries preserved in an epitome of the *CG* date to as late to AD 295, but were probably added later. The rescript collection of Papirius Justus may have been the first of its kind, but it was not official and its author seems not to have preserved the rescripts in their entirety with their accompanying rubric. On the *CG* generally, see Rotondi, "Fonti del Codice Giustinianeo," and most recently Sperandio, *Codex Gregorianus.*

2. It is likely that Maximian and the Caesars also answered petitions sent to their courts, since there are a few rescripts from the west, presumably from the court of Maximian. On rescripts being given from all four courts, see Barnes, *New Empire,* 48–49.

3. On there being three editions of the *CH,* see *CSEL* 10.172. On the career of Hermogenian, see most recently Salway, "Equestrian Prefects," 129–30, who suggests that he was *magister a libellis,* praetorian prefect, suffect consul, proconsul of Asia, and finally urban prefect. On Hermogenian and his legal *Epitome,* see Liebs, *Hermogenians Iuris Epitomae,* and Dovere, *De Iure.*

4. On the differences between ancient archives and libraries, see Brosius, *Ancient Archives,* 10–11, and Culham, *Archives and Alternatives,* though her focus is on the Republican period.

5. On the *CG* and *CH* as successors to the Praetor's rescripts, see Harries, *Law and Empire,* 15.

6. The first extant instance of the word *codex* being applied to the *CH* is at *CTh* 1.1.5. On the use of the codex form in judicial circles at this time, see Wenger, *Quellen des römischen Rechts,* 90, 93.

7. According to Collinet, *Histoire de École,* 77–78, 264–65, the *CG* and *CH* were studied in law schools (cited by Turpin, "Roman Law Codes," 626). The *Codex Justinianus* was certainly was the focus of the final year's study at Beirut under Justinian (Collinet, ibid., 241).

8. The *CH* as a private undertaking: Cenderelli, *Ricerche sul Codex Hermogenianus,* 15–16, sets out the argument but rejects it. Harries, *Law and Empire,* 64, claims, "Even the widespread perception that the efforts of Gregorius and Hermogenian were, in some sense, 'official' may derive from the privileged position granted retrospectively to their Codes by Theodosius." The *CG* and *CH* were derived from imperial archives: Gregorian's entries reflect the *damnatio memoriae* of Geta: Honoré, "Severan Lawyers," 171; the *CH*'s entries come from the years when Hermogenian was producing them for the imperial archives. There seems to be no other source for the entries.

9. The numbers of books in the *CG* and titles in the *CH* are based on the reconstructions of Krüger, Mommsen and Studemund, *Collectio,* 236–45.

10. This conjecture is made more plausible by the fact that the patriotic (or obedient) printers of a 1475 edition of the *CJ* held at Yale University's Beinecke Library inserted several laws of the reigning German monarch, Frederick III, into their text (*Codex Justinianus: with the Glossa ordinaria of Accursius* (June) [Nuremberg: J. Sensenschmidt & A. Frisner, 1475]).

11. Stereotype: Krüger, *Codex Iustinianus,* of 1877. Editions of the *CJ* do not always follow this model, placing the various elements in a different order.

12. Krüger, *Codex Iustinianus,* 29. One variant *SP* occurs seven times: *CJ* 6.50.15, 6.50.17, 6.53.6, 6.54.8 = 11.31.2, 6.55.6, 6.58.5, 6.59.6.

13. On the first theory, Honoré, *Emperors and Lawyers,* 1st ed. (hereafter *E&L*[1]), 27–28; on the second, Honoré, *Emperors and Lawyers,* 2nd ed. (hereafter *E&L*[2]), 53, which he now follows.

14. On *CJ* 1.23.3, see Corcoran, *Empire of the Tetrarchs,* 58.

15. Rescripts were preserved for the *CJ,* in my opinion, primarily because they contained clear statements of legal principles. This is not to suggest, however, that there were not other considerations. For example, Turpin, "Roman Law Codes," suggests that entries in the *CJ* were chosen to simplify and quicken trials (p. 623); they could not be *contra ius* (627) and had to provide an authoritative statement of general law (629). Corcoran, *Empire of the Tetrarchs,* claims that the intention for the *CH* was to provide a comprehensive (or even complete) range of material from AD 293–294 (pp. 27–28), but sensibly points out that those rescripts were chosen in a very uneven way that left much to chance or individual choice (p. 11).

16. In a body of evidence in ancient history, this is a large number; in the social sciences, it is rather small.

17. Comparing the absence, presence, and forms of recipients' names in the earliest manuscripts of the *CJ*, Krüger, *Kritik des justinianischen Codex*, 32–40, suggests that the *Codex* was edited as early as the seventh century; some place-names may have been removed around this time.

18. Halfmann, *Itinera Principum*, 10 and 51.

19. Ibid., 113.

20. Ibid., 51.

21. *HA, Alex. Sev.* 45.2. On which see Halfmann, *Itinera Principum*, 75. On the experience of road travel through the empire, see also Salway, "Travel, itineraria, and tabellaria," 32–34.

22. On the problems faced by officials sourcing suitable supplies and aides for the imperial party, see P. Panop.Beatty I 53–59.

23. *RE* XVII 1 s.v. "Nikomedia," 491, and according to M. Mirkovic, "Sirmium—Its History," 37, 59, there may also have been imperial accommodation at Sirmium.

24. *Palatia* mentioned in contemporary sources have sometimes been identified as imperial residential palaces, though Coriat, *Prince législateur*, claims that some of these were probably administrative buildings (192–96).

25. Given that Antoninus Pius as proconsul of Asia stayed at Smyrna in the house of a local prominent man, Campanile, "Infanzia della provincia," 287–88, thinks that governors during the *conventus* stayed at the houses of eminent citizens.

26. Halfmann, *Itinera Principum*, 89.

27. Emperors at lodging places: Casson, *Travel*, 184–85. Diocletian's early years: *RE* VII A 2, s.v. "Diokletianus."

28. Halfmann, *Itinera Principum*, 108.

29. The numbers are unclear in part because we cannot be certain that permanent court officials customarily traveled with the emperor. Winterling, *Aula Caesaris*, 89 n. 36, sounds the note of caution.

30. Halfmann, *Itinera Principum*, 75–81; evidence for the procurator's responsibilities: P.Panop. Beatty I 30 ff.

31. See the collected inscriptions in Herrmann, *Hilferufe*. Sometimes the burden may have been lifted by a grant to fund centrally local *mansiones*. *CIL* V 8987, in which the emperor Julian ordered that state-funded *mansiones* be constructed in the provinces of Venetia and Histria to lessen the burden of requisitioning on locals and of excessive distances on beasts of burden, is the latest example we have of local beneficences that are first attested in the reign of Nerva. On this text, see Kolb, "Cursus fiscalis."

32. This itinerary is based on my catalog of the extant rescripts from 293–294 listed in appendix 2.

33. *Itinerarium Antonini* used at end of third century: Salway, "Travel, itineraria, and tabellaria," 39–40. *CJ* 8.42.20 was dated to October 28 or 31 and placed at Adrianople; now it is dated to October 31 and no longer placed at Adrianople (see appendix 2).

34. *D* 2.11.1.

35. This calculation roughly agrees with Casson's suggestion that on a normal terrain without any difficult slopes a carriage could travel between twenty and thirty miles in a six-hour day; forty to forty-five miles would be possible, but would require "an exhaustingly long and hard day's travel" (Casson, *Travel*, 189). Halfmann, *Itinera*

*Principum,* 86, estimates that the imperial train covered twenty to thirty kilometers (roughly 12.5–18 miles) per day.

36. This figure is confirmed by modern maps' measurements of the distance between Golubac and Arcar (approximating to ancient Cuppae and Ratiaria), in particular those of ViaMichelin's digital mapping service (www.viamichelin.com/viamichelin/gbr/tpl/hme/MaHomePage.htm).

37. If *CJ* 6.59.7 was answered en route, only a little more time would have been freed up for the journey.

38. These locations have been supplied on the basis of *FV* 325 from Heraclea on the 8th and *FV* 314 from Melantias on the 9th.

39. On Valerian's capture with his praetorian prefect, see Potter, *Empire at Bay,* 255–56. On Valens's officials at Adrianople, see Ammianus Marcellinus 31.12.10 and 31.15.2.

40. The response to her comprises *CJ* 2.19.9, 2.20.6, 2.31.2, and 4.48.8.

41. On Fergus Millar's conception of the role of emperors and their authorship of responses, see most recently *ERW*², 640, 644–52. Millar, A. N. Sherwin-White, and W. Williams believe that the emperor wrote (or at least formulated) the responses (see respective entries in the bibliography). Indeed, according to Millar, *ERW*², 640, there was no government apparatus that functioned on behalf of the emperor while he was absent; all constitutions issued in the name of the emperor were issued where the emperor was. Their opponents, D. Nörr and T. Honoré, claim that emperors delegated the task to officials. Honoré has faced fierce criticism for using stylistic analysis to reveal the work of individual *magistri a libellis* (Gustafson, review of Tony Honoré, and Millar, "New Approach"); he argues for the primary authorship of *magistri* but concedes some input from assistants or members of a team (*E&L*², 31).

42. On Honoré's methodologies and conclusions, see especially *E&L*², 56–70, and also his preface.

43. *CJ* 6.49.4 and 7.2.12 refer to constitutions of Antoninus Pius, *CJ* 5.17.5 to a pronouncement by Marcus Aurelius.

44. The text of *CJ* 3.33.3 reads: *Si patri tuo usus fructus legatus est, defuncto eo nihil ad te pertinet, cum morte eius, cui fuerat legatus usus fructus vel alio modo adquisitus, ad proprietatem regredi solet. **Usufructuario** autem **superstite licet dominus proprietatis rebus humanis eximatur, ius utendi fruendi non tollitur;*** the text excerpted for *FV* 42 is in bold.

45. On camaraderie in the *scrinia,* see Kelly, *Ruling,* 36–37, 111.

46. On *supernumerarii* in other departments, ibid., 69.

47. On officials' brief tenure: Jones, *Later Roman Empire,* 380–83, and Kelly, *Ruling,* 39. On the possibility that Arcadius Charisius was Hermogenian's predecessor, see Honoré, "Arcadius, also Charisius." On the number of officials in the *scrinium, CJ* 12.19.10 of AD 470 limits the number of *libellenses* to 34.

48. Alternative suggestions are that the *scrinium* may have written and posted up these entries the day the petitions were handed in; *CJ* 2.4.33 would also have been processed in one day. Or it may have refused to receive petitions more than one day before it left a location, so that it could post responses at the same place. The date and location of *CJ* 2.4.33, however, would seem to contradict this suggestion.

49. Nörr, "Zur Reskriptenpraxis," 13, adduces evidence (albeit for responses from the Egyptian prefect) that responses were posted for three days.

50. Perhaps some rescripts were put up at a location, copied by the *scrinium* for its records and by Hermogenian for his codex, and then left there. But this scheme was burdensome for the *scrinium*. Three texts would be required of some responses—one for posting, one for archiving, and one for Hermogenian's Code. Another alternative is that responses may have been posted for some time at one location and then brought to the next by officials who followed on after the main convoy. Employing these officials, however, seems wasteful.

51. Wilcken, "Zur Propositio libellorum," 22–23, makes this claim on the basis of P.Oxy. IV 705, ll. 36–39: ἐτιμήσατε μὲν οὖν καὶ ὑμεῖς αὐτοὺς [i.e., the Oxyrhynchites] ἐπιδη/μήσ[αν]τες τῷ ἔθνει [i.e. Egypt] πρώτοις μετὰ Πηλου/σιώτας μεταδόντες τῆς εἰς τὸ δ[ικ]αστήριο[ν ὑμῶ]ν / εἰσόδου. ("And so you honored them, visiting their province and granting them, along with the Pelusians, first entry to your court.") There may be an allusion in the *Historia Augusta* (*HA, Hadrian* 12.4) to rules limiting the availability of the governor to the population local to each stopping point on the *conventus: omnibus Hispanis Tarraconem in conventum vocatis*. The reference comes from Halfmann, *Itinera Principum*, 122.

52. Nörr, "Zur Reskriptenpraxis," 33–37, followed by Halfmann, *Itinera Principum*, 152, claims that responses sent on from Rome were posted at Rome while Caracalla was variously in Germany, the east, and Egypt. But unlike his sojourn in Egypt, these other journeys were military campaigns, during which the system of petition and response may not have functioned in the normal way.

53. Only entries that can be dated to a particular month with certainty are included.

54. The higher number could also reflect Hermogenian's decision to begin amassing entries for his code, according to Corcoran, *Empire of the Tetrarchs*, 27–28.

55. Another dip occurred in Sirmium. The first few months of 293 were quiet, with January, February, and early March showing only twenty-nine entries. With Hermogenian's tenure probably beginning in March, perhaps Hermogenian had limited access to or insufficient time to look through the entries produced in the months before he took office.

### 3. The Rescript System in Context

1. Hoddinott, *Bulgaria in Antiquity* and *Thracians*, provides the most useful introductions to the area. More detailed analyses are provided by Mócsy, *Gesellschaft und Romanisation* and *Pannonia and Upper Moesia*. For a recent bibliography, along with very a brief history of archaeological research in Bulgaria, see Vagalinski, "Archaeology in Bulgaria."

2. On Balkan geography, Katicic, "Balkanprovinzen," 103: "Zum größten Teil ist es rauhes Gebirgsland, klimatischen und kulturellen Einflüssen der Küstenstreifen nur schwer zugänglich, unwegsam und unwirtlich, wo Fremdlinge nur schwer ihren Weg von Tal zu Tal finden können." Also Talbert and Bagnall, *Barrington Atlas*, 310–11.

3. Katicic, "Balkanprovinzen," 112–13.

4. On the survival of the Thracian language, see ibid., 113. Various inscriptions that mention Thracian gods testify to the persistence of the religion, for example, *CIL* 3.6120. On native naming practices, Kolendo, "Relation village/campagne," 93–94.

5. On the language split, see especially Gerov, "Lateinisch-griechische

Sprachgrenze," 149, fig. 1, according to which people at Appiaria, Cebrus, Cuppae, Durostorum, Lucionum, Ratiaria, Singidunum, Sirmium, Transmarisca, Varianae, and Viminacium (all places on Diocletian's route in 293–294) wrote in Latin; those at Anchialos, Beroea, Burtudizum, Byzantium, Develtus, Adrianople, Heraclea, Marcianopolis, Melantias, Nicomedia, Pantichium, Philippopolis, Serdica, and Tzirallum wrote in Greek. On retaining Thracian as a spoken language, see Gerov, ibid., 158; on the course and nature of the split, see ibid., 149–65.

6. Soldiers and the Romanized likely to commission inscriptions: MacMullen, "Epigraphic Habit," 238–41. Salomies, "Names and Identities," 80, points out that of the 62,360 individuals in Osbourne and Byrne, *Foreign Residents*, only 5,691 are women.

7. On locations where the epigraphic habit was strong, see Bodel, *Epigraphic Evidence*, 7–9. Fewer inscriptions in the third century: MacMullen, "Epigraphic Evidence," especially 233–37. Difficulty of dating private inscriptions: Bodel, ibid., 50.

8. Poulter, "Roman Towns," 109.

9. Dintchev, "Classification," 40, who also assesses the original sizes of settlements on the basis of "other objective criteria: the number and the type of the architectural complexes and buildings with public and private destination, and the nature and the amount of movable stock found in excavations" (p. 42).

10. On the size of Augustan Rome, Favro, *Urban Image*, 218–19, gives a minimum of 500 hectares, producing a maximum population density of 2,000 people per hectare (assuming Beloch's estimate of the population at 1 million, though Beloch, *Bevölkerung*, 412, suggests 800,000 for the first three centuries of the Principate). The later Aurelianic Wall enclosed an area of about 1,300 hectares, producing a density of over 700 per hectare. Storey, "Population of Ancient Rome," however, proposes that Rome was home to 450,000 people living in approximately 1,400 hectares, giving a population density of 324 people per hectare and making his Rome spacious by comparison. Following Storey's lower estimate but taking a population figure of 750,000 (arrived at on the basis of Hopkins, *Conquerors and Slaves*, 98, who thinks that a number between 800,000 and 1,000,000 is reasonable, and Lo Cascio, "Popolazione," 58, who proposes between 650,000 and 700,000), I am working from the calculation that the population density inside the Aurelianic Wall would have been 576 people per hectare. I am grateful for Carlos Noreña's help on this matter.

11. Jones, *Later Roman Empire*, 479.

12. The reading of an imperial edict at a *conventus*: Crook, *Legal Advocacy*, 187. On the *acta consistorii*, see Harries, *Law and Empire*, 39.

13. *OLD*, s.v. *forum* [6, 7].

14. On the form and function of a basilica, see Vitruvius, *De arch.* 5.1.4–10, and MacDonald, *Architecture*, 114–15.

15. The *formula Baetica* was found *ad ostia Baetis fluminis* (*FIRA*[2] iii 92), and therefore not in an urban setting.

16. Overworked governors: Jones, *Later Roman Empire*, 479.

17. Huchthausen in a number of articles ("Soldaten des 3. Jahrhunderts," "Herkunft und ökonomische Stellung," "Kaiserliche Rechtsauskünfte," "Zu kaiserlichen Reskripten" and *Frauen fragen*) has tabulated numbers of petitioners in different status groups. These are the first articles that have tried to identify recipients' status.

On the numbers of women petitioning under Alexander Severus, see Sternberg, "Reskripte des Kaisers," especially p. 510. On petitioners under the Tetrarchy, see Corcoran, *Empire of the Tetrarchs,* chap. 5.

18. On guardianship of women, see Gardner, *Women in Roman Law,* 5–29; on guardianship in Egypt, see also Sheridan, "Women without Guardians." For a good recent discussion about selective use of guardians, see Vandorpe, "Apollonia," especially 329–31.

19. Womanly weakness: Gaius *Inst.* 1.144 (although compare 1.190); Ulpian at *D* 16.1.2.2.

20. On the size of the army: Jones, *Later Roman Empire,* 679; Nicasie, *Twilight of Empire,* 75, cites John Lydus's statement that Diocletian's army numbered 390,000. Adult population: two-thirds of 54 million population estimated by Beloch, *Bevölkerung,* 507; in agreement, Parkin, *Demography and Roman Society,* 5.

21. On the difficulties of estimating slave numbers: Parkin, ibid., 121; slaves numbered 10 percent of the Egyptian population: MacMullen, "Late Roman Slavery," 364.

22. The only entries containing references to senatorial status are *CJ* 3.22.3 and 2.19.6, which are both to women whose opponents are senators. Entries certainly to decurions: *CJ* 6.55.6; 10.32.06; 10.32.07; 10.32.08; 10.32.09; 10.32.12; 10.32.13; 10.40.06; 10.53.03; 10.59.01; possibly to decurions: 4.13.3; 10.32.11 (probably); 10.47.2.

23. Hobson, "Impact of Law," 209.

24. Especially true if one accepts a literacy rate of 5–10 percent (Harris, *Ancient Literacy,* 272), as most do. On using *tabelliones:* Hauken, "Structures and Themes," 14.

25. Nörr, "Zur Reskriptenpraxis," 18, has claimed that if an entry in the *CJ* is addressed to a freedman or a soldier, it is probably a letter. But given the form of these nine entries, it is unlikely.

26. Campbell, *Roman Army,* 269–71. Soldiers' advantages in the legal system: their cases were heard quickly and at a time convenient to them (Juvenal, *Sat.* 16), and a military judge would presumably be biased toward them (soldiers' cases could be heard before a military or civilian court). They also enjoyed partial immunity from taxation, and veterans had the same status as decurions (*D* 49.18.3). See also Garnsey, *Social Status,* 247–49.

27. Huchthausen, "Soldaten des 3. Jahrhunderts," 24, calculates that about 4 percent of petitioners over the third century were soldiers.

28. For example, P.Euphrates 5. Centurions could also receive petitions from civilians; for example, P.Mich. inv. 6127, a petition from a civilian complaining about violence and intimidation by another civilian. *Scrinia libellorum* under *duces: Not. Dig. Or.* XL, XLI, XLII.

29. MacMullen, *Soldier and Civilian,* 12.

30. Huchthausen, "Soldaten des 3. Jahrhunderts," 36.

31. Military issues include military privilege and responsibility, terms of service and retirement, the *peculium castrense* and wills, the effects of absence, private disagreements stemming from one's status as a soldier, familial and marital problems stemming from absence, theft from garrisons and depots, and inheritance, as well as other private disagreements unconnected to military status. These topics, which appear in entries to soldiers from the time of Hadrian until the reign of Diocletian, are listed by Huchthausen, "Soldaten des 3. Jahrhunderts," 26.

32. Huchthausen, "Soldaten des 3. Jahrhunderts," 37 claims that contrary to previous opinion, soldiers were not deprived of cash when they were on duty; they did have a disposable income which they used for property and other acquisitions, over which they sometimes encountered legal problems.

33. Women recipients in the *CG*: Huchthausen, "Herkunft und ökonomische Stellung," 200–204. Female petitioners in Egypt: Hobson, "Impact of Law," 209. More generally, see also Volterra, "Femmes." It appears that the proportion of women petitioners increased into the third century. Huchthausen, ibid., 213, calculates that women of free birth and with citizenship numbered 15 percent of all recipients in the second century AD, but 28 percent in the third. There was, however, a decline in the numbers of private petitioners in the post-Classical period that was especially marked among women, which was accompanied by an apparent restriction of access to petitioners of a higher social standing. On the decline, see Bagnall, "Women's Petitions."

34. *CJ* 3.38.6 and 8.38.4. Though see also below, n. 48.

35. Huchthausen, "Zu kaiserlichen Reskripten," provides the categories and examples. Women petitioning about their property: *CJ* 3.33.9; 4.19.16; 5.3.12; 5.39.4; 5.73.3; 8.55.6. A female slave owner: *CJ* 4.57.6. Women in business: *CJ* 2.4.28; 4.23.1; 4.25.4; 7.45.7; 8.37.5.

36. See especially Vandorpe, "Apollonia."

37. A convenient collection of documents illustrating women's involvement in non-familial legal activities problem is found in Rowlandson and Bagnall, *Women and Society,* chap. 5.

38. Hobson, "Impact of Law," 209.

39. Freedwomen threatened with slavery: *CJ* 6.3.12; 7.16.23. Free women contesting their perceived servile status: for example, *CJ* 4.19.17; 7.14.7; 7.14.11; 7.16.16; 7.16.22.

40. *CJ* 1.19.1.

41. On this concept, see Ankum, "Favor libertatis."

42. The proportion of male to female slaves (2:1) is roughly comparable with that of free men to free women. It is likely, however, that some free women had guardians or representatives petition for them; women claimed as slaves, however, were probably of such low status that they are unlikely to have had such protection.

43. MacMullen, "Late Roman Slavery," 359–60.

44. Rural slaves: ibid., 375 and 380 n. 97, on entries in law codes relating to private property and tax liability that attest to slaves in farming.

45. *D* 48.10.7pr. See also Gaius, *Inst.* 4.14. The statement from the *Digest* is, however, contradicted by *D* 40.12.7.5, which states that *quaestio status* is to be initiated by a slave.

46. *CJ* 4.34.9, 6.2.16, 6.21.14 and 8.44.20. Katzoff, "P.Col. 123," 568–69, suggests that the address to a named individual *et aliis* or *et ceteris* may signify that the rescript in question was sent to that individual and also, with the same wording, to other unrelated individuals. There may be many more rescripts to groups if we understand *vos* as addressing multiple individuals, even if only one recipient is named, though those recipients may have petitioned about a legal problem independently of others also affected by it. Alternatively *vos* might be used formally.

47. The true number could be higher, because in some cases scribes may have

wrongly inserted *et* and made one person into two people. Equally, they may have omitted *et* and made two people into one person.

48. The two (inexplicable) exceptions are *CJ* 2.3.27 and 3.32.15.

49. On recipients with multiple names in the *CTh*, see Matthews, *Laying Down the Law*, 219–21.

50. Curiously, the two 1475 editions of the *CJ* held in the Beinecke Library at Yale University contain no multiple names. Perhaps at some point an over-zealous medieval editor brought the end of book four into line with the rest of the Code (interestingly, he knew which name to keep). Alternatively, both editions were copied from a manuscript containing only single names that is no longer extant.

51. The following reference works have been helpful in this task: Solin, *Griechischen Personennamen*, Salomies and Solin, *Repertorium*, and Minkova, *Personal Names*.

52. Identifiable names: for example, the *cognomen* of Aurelius Nica Decaria (*CJ* 4.44.13). Another petitioner is identified as *Aurelius Loreus qui et Enucentrius* (*FV* 42); his is the only alias from AD 293–294 in the *CJ*. His latter two names defy analysis; the closest name to Enucentrius is Encratius, listed in Kajanto, *Supernomina*, 67 and 68.

53. For example, one scribe turned Glusie, attested in one manuscript (M), into Culcia, a more Latin name (*CJ* 4.32.24), and we find Epigathus (C) and Epazaptus (M) instead of Epagathus in *CJ* 4.65.25.

54. Huchthausen, "Herkunft und ökonomische Stellung," 206, citing Solin, *Beiträge*.

55. Solin, "Ancient Onomastics," 8.

56. One example of an alias is given above in n. 52.

57. *CJ* 4.07.05 Bithus—Thracian; 2.12.17 Mardonius—eastern; 8.42.14 Cuta—eastern; 4.44.07 Mucatraulus—Thracian; 4.23.02 Auluzanus—Thracian; 3.13.03 Iuda—Semitic; 4.10.13 Barsimius—perhaps Thracian; 5.44.05 Tigranus—eastern; 2.04.28 Sapparta—probably eastern; 4.35.16 Uzandus—perhaps African; 4.20.08 Derulo—foreign; 6.56.02 Rhesa—Thracian; 4.30.10 Mucazanus—Thracian; 4.53.08 Auxanoni—Thracian; 8.50.15 Mucatraulus—Thracian.

58. The Thracian names could be explained as evidence for a sort of reversed Romanization, appearing as people went back to their roots; see Salway, "What's in a Name?" 135.

59. Barbarians had entered the Roman Empire and had (been) settled in their thousands from the first century AD. For a convenient list of figures and sources for barbarian settlement, see Frier, "Demography," 810–11. De Ste Croix's list of barbarian immigrations into the Roman Empire remains a useful summary (*Class Struggle*, 509–13). On the Dacian migrations south, see Diaconescu, "Towns of Roman Dacia," 125–28. On prisoners of war settled in Thrace under Diocletian, see Lieu, "Captives, Refugees, and Exiles," 487, from the evidence of *Pan. Lat.* IV/8.21.1. On barbarian settlements, MacMullen, "Barbarian Enclaves."

60. Solin, "Ancient Onomastics," 8, has complained that "the use of Latin and Roman names in the Greek East has yet to receive the attention it deserves, being treated so far in a rather slapdash way, in spite of its clear significance for the study of Romanization and of the Latin element in the Greek half of the Mediterranean."

61. The fact that Diocletian's court stopped at smaller locations near Heraclea

suggests that petitioners at the city were locals. On the connection between locations at which petitions were received and the makeup of petitions, see Huchthausen,
"Thrakerreskripte," 8.

62. See chapter 2 n.51.

63. On the date of Galerius's investiture, see Barnes, *New Empire*, 4 n. 8. On the
mint at Heraclea, which seems to have opened in AD 292 or 293, see Sayar, *Perinthos-
Herakleia*, 77.

64. *CJ* 3.34.8 to Anicetus on January 1, 293.

65. Duval, "Ville impériale," 59–61, warns that while Sirmium can be labeled an
imperial residence, it was not necessarily a capital. There is no firm evidence for a
permanent space for the court. For a general history of Sirmium, see Mirkovic, "Sirmium—Its History." Other surveys of work at the site are Boskovic, Duval et Gros,
*Recherches archeologiques*, and Milosevic, *Arheologija i istorija Sirmijuma*.

66. On the problems of following the *conventus*, see Burton, "Proconsuls," 99–102.

67. The city had an enceinte of approximately one square kilometer or one hundred hectares, according to Poulter, "Use and Abuse," 106. On my method of calculating the population, see above n. 10. Duval, "Résidences impériales," 67, estimates a
population of 60,000–70,000.

68. V. Popovic, "Survey of the Topography," 122–25. Also Duval, "Ville impériale,"
71. On precious metal workshops supplying the court and, presumably, wealthy
locals, see I. Popovic, "Production of Gold."

69. See Popovic, "Survey of the Topography," 127–29, on the area around the
forum. The possible site of the basilica is not to be confused with the *horrea*. Duval,
"Ville impériale," 65, fig. 2, and 70–71.

70. Location of imperial palace: Popovic, "Survey of the Topography," 128, although there is disagreement from Duval, "Résidences impériales," 130, as to whether
this complex can be properly labeled an imperial palace; it contained private and
public spaces but may not have been used as a permanent space for emperors and
the court until the fourth century (Duval, "Ville impériale," 77–78). Bath complexes:
Poulter, "Use and Abuse," 107–108.

71. *Horrea*: Poulter, "Use and Abuse," 106.

72. *CHV* 2. The petitioner, Ennius Saturninus, was instructed to approach the proconsul of Africa with his case. Ennius was a visitor to Sirmium, perhaps a trader. It is
unlikely that he brought or sent the petition from Africa (contra Barnes, *New Empire*,
197): no other rescript at Sirmium mentions officials in other places, suggesting that
petitions were seldom delivered over great distances.

73. Poulter, "Use and Abuse," 108–109. Also *Not. Dig. Oc.* 32.49, 50, 54.

74. The inscriptions, mostly from *CIL*, are collected by Mirkovic, "Sirmium—Its
History," 60–90. Latin names are found in *CIL* 3.3237 and 3240, Syrian in *ILS* 3.7528.

75. Mirkovic, "Sirmium et l'armée romaine," 639.

76. Inscriptions mentioning women are *CIL* 3.3242, 3244, 3245, 6441, 6442.

77. The Greek inscriptions are nos. 105–12 in Mirkovic, "Sirmium—Its History"
pp. 89–90. Two inscriptions date to the Tetrarchy: *CIL* 3.3231 contains a wish for the
health of Diocletian and Maximian; in *ILS* 2.3458 a Latin-named soldier refers to the
columns of the new baths of Licinius.

78. Manufacturing: for example, Ivanov, "Roman Cities," 148: "Within the Roman

towns of the Moesias and Thrace and in their territories, there flourished centres of craftsmanship and art, catering for the needs of all social classes . . . The manufacturers of luxury and household goods were Thracians and immigrants from the western and especially the eastern provinces of the Roman empire." Immigration: Mócsy, *Pannonia and Upper Moesia*, 227–30.

79. One civilian foreigner, perhaps with a Syrian name, is found in *CIL* 3.6443.

80. *CJ* 4.2.9.

81. *CJ* 7.14.4. On Aurelian and Palmyra, see Kuhoff, *Diokletian*, 433–34.

82. Located on *TIR* L34. *Barrington*, however, includes only three large settlements (Cuccium, Malata, and Bassiana), four smaller settlements, of which two are *castella*, and three *mansiones* (map 21). *TIR* seems overly optimistic about the number of local ancient sites.

83. Stambaugh, *Ancient Roman City*, 253.

84. *CJ* 2.12.19; 2.36.3; 3.32.11; 3.32.17; 3.34.10; 4.51.4; 4.51.5; 4.65.26; 5.12.18; 6.38.2; 7.32.7; 8.14.5; 8.34.2; 9.22.18.

85. See, for example, *CJ* 5.71.15 and 5.71.16, which mentions a *praedium rusticum vel suburbanum*.

86. Hire of an *ager*: *CJ* 4.65.25. Contract with *coloni*: *CJ* 4.10.11. The rescript suggests that the *coloni* were still tenant farmers, not yet quasi-slaves. On the development of the colonate in the Balkans during this period, see Johne, "Entwicklung."

87. *CJ* 3.35.5; 4.2.8; 4.44.9; 4.49.10; 5.3.10. Animal husbandry was probably of cattle: Henning, *Südosteuropa*, 104, fig. 49.

88. *CJ* 4.2.10; *CJ* 4.49.12.

89. *CJ* 4.38.8.

90. *CJ* 3.32.16; 3.34.9.

91. *CJ* 1.18.6. *CJ* 4.65.21 also mentions olive oil.

92. *CJ* 4.25.4.

93. *CJ* 9.25.1. The *tria nomina* clung on despite the developments described by Salway, "What's in a Name," 133–36.

94. *CJ* 9.18.2. *Ars mathematica* should be understood as astrology.

95. *CJ* 4.7.5: "You say that you considered your wife for sale on the open market: wherefore you understand that your petition contains a confession of pimping and there is no (room for) action on the secured amount on account of the shameful reason for taking the payment. For although the shame was practiced by both sides and with payment of the amount the second claim would cease, nevertheless arising from a stipulation made against good morals, by the authority of the law, it is shown that the actions are to be denied." On jurists' moral indignation in the time of Diocletian, see Honoré, *E&L*², 159.

96. *Senatus consulta*: for example, *CJ* 7.9.3; 4.29.15. *Carbonianum edictum*: *CJ* 6.17.1. *Lex Falcidia*: for example, *CJ* 8.3.1; 6.39.3. *Lex Cornelia*: *CJ* 2.53.5. Opinion of Papinian: *CJ* 5.71.14. Constitution of Antoninus Pius: *CJ* 7.2.12.

97. For example, *CJ* 8.37.6; *CJ* 6.9.6.

98. For example, *CJ* 5.74.2; *Cons.* 6.15; *CJ* 7.14.4.

99. *Procuratores*: for example, *CJ* 4.35.11; *CJ* 5.61.2; *FV* 326. A *procurator ducenarius* is attested at Sirmium in *CIL* 3.6439.

100. If Dessau is right in dating *ILS* 1.2255 and *ILS* 3.9107 to the early Principate,

then the city was called Heraclea before the reign of Diocletian. The earliest firm evidence is the rescript *FV* 284 from AD 286.

101. Calculating on the basis of Sayar, *Perinthos-Herakleia,* map 1, the enceinte (including the area by the sea and the theater) measures 0.46 square kilometers or 46 hectares (using the population density I proposed above in n. 10). Theater and stadium: Sayar, ibid., 60–61. For an overview of recent work on Heraclea (drawing mostly on Sayar), see Crow, "Recent Research," 342–43.

102. The basilica: Sayar, *Perinthos-Herakleia,* 61. A structure also identified as a basilica has been found in the lower city, but its location near the city walls, its probable dating to the fifth century, and the presence of mosaics at the site mean it is most likely a Christian church. On palaces at Heraclea, see *Expositio totius mundi,* L: *Heraclea vero excellens opus habet et theatrum et regale palatium.* The latter probably refers to a building sometimes used by the emperors. The provincial palace may have been close by.

103. *CJ* 5.16.17.

104. See above at n. 24.

105. Local businesses: Sayar, *Perinthos-Herakleia,* 68–69.

106. Ibid., 183–398, inscriptions 179, 32, 31, 49A,B.

107. *RE* XIX 1, s.v. "Perinthos[1]," 808.

108. Harbor: Sayar, *Perinthos-Herakleia,* 59.

109. The other names include one German and one eastern, as well as possibly Egyptian, Thracian, Slavic, and Celtic.

110. *CIL* 3.731. *Tropaiophoros* is otherwise attested in Latin only in Apuleius, *Mun.* 37, but naturally occurs more often in Greek, in writers of the imperial period including Plutarch (Plut. *Rom.* 16), Dionysios of Halicarnassus (3.31) and Dio Chrysostom (49.15). On linguistic borrowings and code-switchings, see Adams, *Bilingualism,* 18–28.

111. Gothic population: *RE* XIX 1, s.v. "Perinthos[1]," 809. Craftsmen: Poulter, "Use and Abuse," 100 n. 1. Locals of the middling sort: Hoddinott, *Thracians,* 158. Upwardly mobile Thracians: ibid., 163.

112. Straßenknotenpunkt: *RE* XIX 1, s.v. "Perinthos[1]," 808. Surrounding settlements: Sayar, *Perinthos-Herakleia,* map V; although the lack of a scale and a key render this map somewhat unhelpful.

113. *CJ* 5.71.12.

114. Some of the rescripts from Tzirallum (e.g., *CJ* 2.3.21) refer to court cases, which must have been heard at Heraclea.

115. Governors may have answered petitions addressed to the emperor but delivered to the provincial court. Petitioners at Heraclea, who already had such petitions ready to take to the governor, could therefore have handed them to the emperor's officials without any need for rewriting. Otherwise, petitioners would perhaps have hired notaries to re-address their petitions to the emperor. I think it less plausible that the emperor's officials would have answered petitions addressed to local officials.

116. *Lex Fabia: CJ* 9.20.9. *Lex Julia de vi: CJ* 9.12.3. *Consuetudo regionis: CJ* 4.65.19.

117. Halfmann, *Itinera Principis,* 124, who also mentions soldiers, speakers, judges, servants, slaves, animal trainers, craftsmen, and prostitutes.

118. Ibid., 125. He uses Antioch, Diocletian's winter quarters, as an example of a city that benefited from the emperor's visits.

### 4. Using the System

1. The format of the *CJ* entries discussed in this chapter follows that of Honoré's palingenesia (accompanying *E&L²*), in which the *CJ* entry number is followed by the recipient's name in the dative, the date in modern style, and the location. I have chosen this format for its simplicity, brevity, and ease of understanding.

2. The symbolic importance of rescripts to petitioners will be discussed in following chapter.

3. For a general introduction to the role of law in people's lives, see Crook, *Law and Life*. This chapter contains anecdotes (a source of evidence Crook disparages: 34–35). Though I follow the skepticism of Saller, "Anecdotes as Historical Evidence," toward anecdotes and share his view that "anecdotes reveal the striking" rather than reflect the typical (81), I hope they will form the basis for some important comments on the importance of rescripts and on the light they shed on people's lives and the role of the state in their lives. (Saller introduces his arguments against anecdotes in "Anecdotes as Historical Evidence," and elaborates them in "Domitian and His Successors.") The general approach of Huchthausen, *Frauen fragen*, is also to tell stories; the way in which she structures her discussion has helped me to put together this chapter.

4. Merry, *Getting Justice*, 103.

5. Ewick and Silbey, *Common Place*. Their investigation, carried out in the 1990s in New Jersey, interviewed 430 people.

6. Playing "with the law": ibid., 48; law as an arena of contest: 131.

7. An example of popular mistrust of the law is the formula *Dolus malus abesto et ius civile* (sometimes replaced with *iuris consultus*), which is found most often in funerary inscriptions and is discussed by Nörr, *Rechtskritik*, 52–54.

8. Ewick and Silbey, *Common Place*, 47–48. The term is taken from the final chapter of Kafka's *The Trial*, "Before the Law," which Ewick and Silbey discuss briefly at pp. 74–77.

9. Ibid., 48–49.

10. On repeated court experience leading to increased confidence in navigating the legal system, see Merry, *Getting Justice*, 145. On the importance of humble self-presentation in petitions, see Harries, *Law and Empire*, 185–86.

11. *CJ* 4.23.1.

12. According to Borkowski, *Textbook on Roman Law*, 257, "*vis maior* included disasters such as floods, storms, earthquakes; also violent theft, i.e., robbery . . . *Vis maior* is often described as 'act of God' but, in view of the inclusion of robbery, 'overwhelming force' would be a more accurate and theologically less objectionable translation." For explanations of the legal terms that appear in the rescripts I am discussing in this chapter, see especially *EDRL* and also Borkowski, *Textbook on Roman Law*.

13. Ewick and Silbey, *Common Place*, 132: "In addition to costs, however, our respondents also acknowledged the significant consequences of players' different levels of skill and experience. In other words, legality comes with costs that are differentially burdensome, and thus legality is differentially available." On legal knowledge among Romans, see Peachin, *Iudex vice Caesaris*, 34–53 *passim* (though his discussion is focused on the knowledge of judges and lawyers).

14. The description by Cotton, "Guardianship of Jesus," 103–107, of Babatha's legal dealings suggests that she too had some legal knowledge or had received good advice. Like Sisola, we cannot know for certain how much input Babatha, as opposed to a scribe, lawyer, or friends, had in composing her legal documents and in deciding strategy; we can simply point out that those assumed to be formally uneducated in law nevertheless put their name to legal documents and took part in legal procedures.

15. Julianus returned from captivity to find someone exercising the first maxim on his property (see below); the second would seem to be a fundamental concept in the law of persons and is the basis for the defenses in many *quaestiones status*. On individuals ignorant of the law but nevertheless having a keen sense of injustice, see Ewick and Silbey, *Common Place*, 40.

16. I am following the definition of equity provided by Watson, "Equity," 24, as "a response of the legal system to modify the effect of the law in particular circumstances." The increase in the number of equitable rescripts in the third century from the reign of Alexander Severus is noted by Talamanca, "Aequitas," who surveys the scale and scope of equity during the Principate. The role of the emperor in producing equitable pronouncements of various types is discussed by Buckland, *Equity in Roman Law*, 8–14, who credits them to emperors' whims and legal ignorance.

17. For an extended discussion of Roman law and custom in the third century focusing on examples of individuals from Dura Europos using local procedures, see Connolly, "Women at the Edge."

18. The legal expertise and juristic activities of individuals brought into the imperial court to serve as *magistri* are discussed by Millar, *ERW*[1], 94–97. I am aware, however, that Millar is able to find inscriptions that mention only *magistri* and cite juristic works written only by them; the identities or juristic activities of the junior officials of the *scrinium* are nowhere attested, and we should therefore view them simply as employees.

19. On the uses of the *Apokrimata*, see chapter 1 n. 84.

20. Honoré, "Severan Lawyers," 164.

21. The numbering of books, titles, and constitutions is ancient, as can be seen from the Verona fragments of the *CJ* (Krüger, *Fragmenta Veronensia*), which probably date to the sixth or seventh century given their script, and those constitutions that were copied onto papyrus in the sixth century (see Amelotti and Migliardi Zingale, *Costituzioni giustinianee*, for example, pp. 21–22).

22. Such discomfort could be the motivation for the judgment expressed in *CJ* 3.31.8, which is continued by *CJ* 6.59.4 and 7.16.27, and Cons. 6.18. Arrianus was named a slave by Leonidas, who persuaded Aurelius Asterius's co-heir to join the claim, thus depriving him of his inheritance. Arrianus's status was investigated and he was found to be free. The discomfort of the rescript's authors with slavery can be inferred from their insistence that individuals such as Arrianus not be investigated multiple times, but be left to live in undisturbed freedom.

23. *D* 40.12.1.pr. See on this Connolly, "Quasi ancilla," 17.

24. On decurions and their sons, see *D* 50.2.

25. It seems that Egus Crispinus's debtors had decided to pay him in wine, believing this to be a simple way to defraud him. But he realized their trickery. Perhaps he was tipped off; alternatively he may have had a good nose (and palate).

26. Michael Peachin is the main proponent of this theory, from whose work and guidance I have benefited. On possible identifications of the official recipients of rescripts, see especially Peachin, "Epigraphy."

27. The rescripts dating to AD 293–294 are listed in appendix 2. Nearly all the entries up to and including AD 304 are rescripts. Letters to magistrates comprise many of the post-304 entries in the *CJ* and contain the name and title of the official recipient. Imperial audiences and judgments are found mostly after 304, but a few are of an earlier date, such as the *sententia* of 304 preserved as *CJ* 9.1.17. Other types of entries include decrees, such as 1.17.2 addressed to the Senate and the Roman people, and judgments, such as that rendered by Constantine to a group of veterans in *CJ* 12.46.1.

28. There is some confusion, for example, about the nature of *CJ* 8.50.1, whose recipient was *Ovinio.* The use of the dative case should suggest Ovinius was a private petitioner, but *D* 49.15.9 records a letter to *Ovinius Tertullus,* the governor of Moesia Inferior, on the same issue. On the basis of the contents and its recipient's name, Krüger, correctly in my view, believes that the text was originally a letter, which was later incorrectly edited into a rescript.

29. While the problem of substitution is surely very old, Egus's rescript may have been the one preserved because earlier statements had been imprecisely expressed, lost, or deemed unimportant by an earlier compiler. Accident plays a large part in the preservation of rescripts.

30. *CJ*.2.19: De his quae vi metusve causa gesta sunt; *CJ*.2.20: De dolo malo; *CJ*.2.31.0. Si adversus transactionem vel divisionem minor restitui velit; *CJ*.4.44: De rescindenda venditione.

31. Huchthausen, "Herkunft und ökonomische Stellung," 200.

32. On female guardians in Egypt, see Cotton, "Guardianship of Jesus," 96 n. 27; in Arabia, ibid. p. 97.

33. *CJ* 8.50.7 also expresses condemnation, not of the recipient but of the woman who had ransomed from barbarians and then attempted to prostitute the recipient's daughter. On this text, see Connolly, "Roman Ransomers," 122–23.

34. On mixed-income housing at Pompeii, see Wallace-Hadrill, *Houses and Society,* 75–82.

35. On this text and a number of similar cases, see Herrmann-Otto, *Ex ancilla natus,* 405–406.

36. See Gardner, *Women in Roman Law,* 213.

37. See Connolly, "Quasi ancilla," on slaves petitioning and confusions between slaves and free persons.

38. Judges might also benefit from the direction of a rescript. Crook, *Legal Advocacy,* 174–75, points out that even provincial governors were untrained in the law; they were therefore reliant on the legally educated members of their *consilium;* see Weaver, "Consilium praesidis."

39. Krüger chooses Dionysiadae as the dative form from among a number of manuscript variants; I have chosen a related female nominative form that is well attested according to the *Lexicon of Greek Personal Names,* though there is no syntactical relationship between them. It seems impossible to recover the recipient's name given the manuscript evidence available; later scribes may have incorrectly Latinized a Greek name.

40. See, for the example, Dixon, "Sentimental Ideal," 109–11 and *Roman Family,*

107. Emotional detachment from children is manifested usually in the ancient sources with the death of a very young child; thereafter detachment was, as the rescript suggests, the result of extreme poverty.

41. For a longer discussion of *postliminium* and ransoming and a discussion of some of the rescripts on these topics, see Connolly, "Roman Ransomers."

42. Kuhoff, *Diokletian,* 429.

43. Borkowski, *Textbook on Roman Law,* 264, states that a contract for *locatio conductio* "was made when the parties agreed on the subject-matter of the hire and on the amount of the payment." The contract could end with the expiration of the agreed term or, if there was no agreed term, at any time. The term in Antonia's case was one year, so she had broken the contract by accepting a higher payment of oil from another party and now faced stiff financial penalties. As Buckland, *Manual,* 291, explains, "renunciation by the lessor at an unreasonable time, even if there was no term, would entitle the tenant to claim compensation for expenses of which he had not yet obtained the benefit."

44. *EDRL,* s.v. *recedere,* referring to *D* 2.14.58.

45. On the dangers of petitioning, particularly of reprisals upon publication, see Williams, "Epigraphic Texts," 189.

46. The phrase *idcirco minus* introduced by either *ne* or *non* has been found by Honoré in this entry, as well as *CJ* 1.22.1, 6.23.11, 6.36.4, 7.16.35, 1.18.9 (to Gaius and Anthemius), 4.21.12 and 4.44.12 (Honoré, *E&L²,* 173 n. 426). But he has also found examples of the phrase from AD 241 and 243 (p. 122 n. 669). Clustering of this phrase in the reign of Diocletian supports Honoré's notion of individual *magistri* leaving their stylistic mark on their work.

47. In this notion he would be unsuccessful, as *CJ* 7.16.35 indicates: (Atellio s. 5 Dec 294 Sirmium) *Non idcirco minus, quod pupilli res velut tutor administrasse dicitur, ex eius persona servitutis pati quaestionem potest.* "Just because someone is said to have managed the affairs of a guardian as tutor, having held that position, he can no less be subject to an investigation into his servile status."

48. *CJ* 7.16.14 (Quintianae d. 28 Apr 293 Heraclea) *Imperatores Diocletianus, Maximianus. Lite ordinata in possessione libertatis is, de cuius libertate quaeritur, constituitur et interim pro libero habetur.* "When an investigation is under way, the person whose liberty is subject to investigation is considered to be in possession of liberty and is considered meanwhile a free person."

49. The importance of law in the everyday lives of Romans outside Egypt is pointed out by Crook, *Law and Life,* 7–8, 33–35, and Peachin, *Iudex vice Caesaris,* 3–6. The work of Kehoe, *Investment, Profit, and Tenancy,* on patterns of tenancy in Egypt has revealed the frequency with which tenants entered into new contracts. His findings might be applied more widely and borne in mind when considering other legal transactions.

50. On the normative and validating power of writing, see Ewick and Silbey, *Common Place,* 101. Also de Certeau, *Practice of Everyday Life,* 140: "The act of suffering oneself to be written by the group's law is oddly accompanied by a pleasure, that of being recognized (but one does not know by whom), of becoming an identifiable and legible word in a social language, of being changed into a fragment within an anonymous text, of being inscribed in a symbolic order that has neither owner nor author."

51. The form of a legal case was important in a legal system in which the formulary procedure had not long before given way to *cognitiones extra ordinem.*

52. Merry, *Getting Justice,* 97.

53. Ibid., 44: "The use of law instead of violence is an important aspect of the distinction that the more respectable segments of the working class draw between themselves and those they consider more disreputable." On law as daunting, Ewick and Silbey, *Common Place,* 106: "Aspiring toward grandeur and permanence law houses itself in monumental buildings of marble and granite and arranged its agents behind desks, counters, and benches. It expresses itself in a language that is arcane and indecipherable to most citizens."

54. Non-Western communities: Friedman, *Legal System,* 134–35.

55. Nörr, "Zur Reskriptenpraxis," 5–6.

56. In some sense, then, the members of the *scrinium* could be regarded as gate-keepers of the law, reinterpreting petitioners' stories before applying the law to them. I do not wish to press the analogy any further, however, because I do not think these officials tried to reduce the number of petitioners with the intention of depriving them of access to law.

57. On rules in legal systems, see Friedman, *Legal System,* 27–28.

58. Ibid., 26–27.

59. This is, admittedly, a very broad statement and is meant simply to suggest that the laws satisfied many people much of the time. There may have been opposition in the minds of women, slaves, peasants, and others to some laws, but there is little evidence of widespread resistance to particular laws. Ando, *Imperial Ideology,* 374, points out the lack of resistance, but is unwilling to attribute it entirely to social satisfaction. He points out that many Romans obeyed laws probably through self-interest or fear.

60. On the need to maintain a balance between law and justice, see Ewick and Silbey, *Common Place,* 39. The term "society" needs qualification: laws are usually made with the wealthy in mind, with the result that some legislation is the product of attempts to balance their interests and those of the wider community. On this issue, see Frier, *Landlords and Tenants,* 185–90 and especially 205–209.

### 5. The Emperor and His Petitioners

1. For an example of a wealthy person using petition and response, see chapter 1 n. 32.

2. Some petitions might not pose a question to be answered or might not pose a legal question. This is, of course, an argument from silence, as these petitions were not kept and never answered.

3. Brown, *Poverty and Leadership,* and Cohen, "Feeding the Poor." On definitions of Roman poverty, see especially Humfress, "Poverty and Roman Law," whose view that poverty was not necessarily defined economically I share.

4. Brown, *Poverty and Leadership,* 69.

5. Ibid., 70.

6. More exaggerated claims of poverty are to be found in the medieval ancient petitions. For example, Alice de Prestwich claimed that having been robbed of £200 of property (an enormous sum for the period), she had no means to run her estate.

Even University College, Oxford tried to plead poverty in its petition complaining of a wealthy grocer alleged to have stolen some of its land (and the king in his response acknowledged its straitened circumstances). The examples, from the National Archives, Special Collections, Ancient Petitions SC 8/6/295 and 8/19/915A–C respectively, were made known to me by Anthony Musson.

7. The translation comes from Parsons, "Petitions and a Letter," 437.

8. There are rescripts dating to AD 286 at Nicomedia, Byzantium, and Heraclea; 290 at Sirmium, Adrianople, and Byzantium; 291 at Sirmium and Tzirallum.

9. Licinius and Galerius may also have answered petitions. Galerius may have been in Egypt in 293 (Barnes, *New Empire,* 62), where Severus and Caracalla had created a precedent for emperors answering petitions as they toured.

10. On communications from the emperors during the Tetrarchy, see Corcoran, *Empire of the Tetrarchs,* and more briefly "Publication of Law" and "Tetrarchy: Policy and Image."

11. Praetor's Edict: Lenel, *Palingenesia Iuris Civilis,* has attempted a partial reconstruction. *Sententiae et epistulae Hadriani:* Böcking, *Corpus Iuris Romani Anteiustiniani,* 193–214. Entry 9 is most certainly in response to a written petition (*per libellum*). There were also collections of jurists' work, such as the *responsa* and *quaestiones* of Papinian, which may have been the product of official roles at the imperial court. These are also collected by Lenel, ibid.

12. Coriat, *Prince législateur,* 420–22.

13. Hauken, *Petition and Response,* 298: "The emperors implemented their objectives by directly responding to the approaches of their subjects."

14. Sirks, "Making a Request," 129–30.

15. Ando, *Imperial Ideology,* 111–15, 368, describes the circulation of texts in the provinces emanating from the imperial court, which could have extended from provincial governors to their junior officials.

16. According to Sirks, "Making a Request," 129–30, changes in law were implemented gradually and other methods of promulgation (such as making speeches before the Senate) could be used. True, though I think the argument above is more compelling.

17. Mitchell, "Requisitioned Transport," 107, ll. 23–25: "Mansionem omnibus qui erunt ex / comitatu nostro et, militantibus ex omnibus provincis et principis optimi libertis et servis et iumentis / eorum gratuitam praestari oportet, ita ut reliqua ab invitis gratuita non e(x)sigant." There is also a Greek rendering on the same inscription.

18. Ibid., 127–28; other texts: 111–12, especially also 114 nn. 21–22.

19. For example, P.Oxy. VII 1020, XLII 3018 and LXIV 4437.

20. With this point, Honoré, *E&L*[2], 39, references Coriat, "Technique du rescrit," 333–42. Millar, *ERW*[1], 547, makes a similar point.

21. Corcoran, *Empire of the Tetrarchs,* 42, also proposes that rescripts of interest were circulated in the Roman administration.

22. Coriat, *Prince législateur,* 341, 357.

23. On this entry, *CJ* 7.14.4, see chapter 4.

24. The new rule is clearly expressed in *CJ* 8.50.2 (Publiciano pp. June 12, 241) *Ab hostibus redempti, quoad exsolvatur pretium, in causam pignoris constituti quam in*

*servilem condicionem videntur esse detrusi*; also in *CJ* 8.50.6 (Iusto pp. 1 Feb 291) . . . *si qui captos ab hostibus redemerint, accepto pretio redemptos suae ingenuitati restituant.*

25. See Connolly, "Roman Ransomers."

26. I am identifying here a process that was later formalized as the *suggestio*, which consisted of provincial officials passing up information to the imperial court to inform legislation. On *suggestio*, see Harries, *Law and Empire*, 47–53.

27. While there is no direct evidence, it does not seem far-fetched to suggest that *magistri* on the *consilia* would have sometimes passed on information about socially or politically significant legal problems identified by petitions, especially given the influence that some *consilium* members wielded over imperial policy, as Crook has identified (*Consilium Principis*, chap. IX).

28. Numbers of provinces: Jones, *Later Roman Empire*, 42–43. The timing of the provincial reform is much debated, since there is little evidence suggesting possible dates. The *termini post* and *ante quem* seem to be 293 and 305, with 297 favored by many scholars (probably following Mommsen) on the basis of the Verona List. See Kuhoff, *Diokletian*, 369–70. Barnes, *New Empire*, 209–25, whose dates I am following, suggests, "It is more probable that Diocletian ordained the division of provinces and the creation of dioceses in 293 at a single stroke, that his reforms were put into effect immediately, or at least with all deliberate speed, and that only minor changes were made thereafter" (p. 225). Diocletian may then have traveled through the lower Danube provinces in 293–294 in order to visit his new provincial capitals (previously the provincial capitals were Aquincum in Pannonia Inferior, Viminacium in Moesia Superior, Marcianopolis in Moesia Inferior, Heraclea in Thracia, and Nicomedia in Bithynia). The new provinces and their capitals were Adrianople in Haemimontus, Heraclea in Europa, Viminacium in Moesia Superior Margensis, Ratiaria in Dacia Ripensis, Serdica in Dacia Mediterranea, and Philippopolis in Thracia. For Diocletian, the journey consisted of stopping at every old and new provincial capital except Aquincum (though he may have visited here in the summer of 294), inducting Galerius, escorting him to Byzantium, and then inspecting the Danube frontier.

29. Lactantius, *de Mortibus Persecutorum* 7.4.

30. Coriat, *Prince législateur*, 341–42. Meyer-Zwiffelhoffer, *Politikos archein*, 277, also sees rescripts as a means of controlling governors. The inclusion of rescripts, along with *mandata* and edicts, in archives or on inscriptions also placed pressure on governors to adhere to the decisions of their predecessors. The rescripts thus reduced governors' *Handlungsspielraum* (288) but perhaps also strengthened them for giving judgments in court, since they knew they had the support of the emperor. Nevertheless, as Meyer-Zwiffelhoffer notes, provincials could also call on the authority of the emperor to defend themselves against the provincial governor (288–289).

31. Coriat, *Prince législateur*, 366–67.

32. Ibid., 379–80.

33. Meyer-Zwiffelhoffer, *Politikos archein*, 281.

34. Coriat, *Prince législateur*, 411.

35. Ibid., 451.

36. On the simplification of law under Diocletian, see especially Taubenschlag, "Römisches Recht," 266–81. A sentimental and somewhat fanciful interpretation of

Diocletian's rescript is that it stems from his origins as the son of a freed slave (*RE* s.v. "Diocletianus," 2419–20).

37. Friedland et al., *Access to the Law*, 1: "Why should citizens have access to the law? The simple answer is that good citizenship requires it. Citizens should be able easily to ascertain their rights and obligations. An increasing number of statutory and other provisions place positive obligations on members of the public, but a citizen cannot be expected to fulfil these obligations unless he knows of them. A basic assumption of our legal system is that the citizen knows the law; for example, section 19 of the Criminal Code provides that 'ignorance of the law by a person who commits an offence is not an excuse for committing that offence.'"

38. The story concerning Hadrian is told by Dio LXXI, 6, 1 (the reference comes from Millar, *ERW*[1], 3). The story bears striking similarity to those told about Philip II (Plut. *Mor.* 179 C-D), Demetrius Poliorcetes (Plut. *Demetr.* 42.7), and Antipater (Stobaeus, *Flor.* III, 13, 48). There is also a selection of anecdotes about emperors' legal diligence (or lack of it) in Peachin, *Iudex vice Caesaris*, 80–82.

39. The quotation in full: *Verum quotiens adesset, nihil praeterea agebat, seu vitandi rumoris causa, quo patrem Caesarem vulgo reprehensum commemorabat, quod inter spectandum epistulis libellisque legendis aut rescribendis vacaret* (Suet. *Div. Aug.* 45). The gerundive construction may be used here simply to replace a phrase containing gerunds and direct objects, but it could also retain the notion of obligation or necessity, thus revealing the burden that the system of petition and response placed on the shoulders of Roman rulers. The anecdote attests to Augustus's workload and his assiduity, but it may also reveal that the emperor was not a fan of the games.

40. Suet. *Div. Aug.* 50: *In diplomatibus libellisque et epistulis signandis initio sphinge usus est, mox imagine Magni Alexandri, novissime sua, Dioscuridis manu scalpta, qua signare insecuti quoque principes perseverarunt. ad epistulas omnis horarum quoque momenta nec diei modo sed et noctis, quibus datae significarentur, addebat.*

41. Hauken, *Petition and Response*, 124–25, emends SIGNAVI to SIGNA VI[I] and persuasively argues that it refers to the seven witnesses to the authenticity of petition of the Skaptopareni and its response.

42. Dio LXXI, 6, 1.

43. For example, a *dupondius* of Tiberius dating to AD 22–23 includes the inscription IUSTITIA below the head of Livia on the obverse. A *sesertius* and a *denarius* of Hadrian both show the female *Iustitia* holding a scepter, presumably as she dispenses justice. The legend on the *sestertius* is IVSTITIA AVG COS III PPP. There are also various depictions of magistrates on stone, which may have been modeled on those of emperors. The depictions are not always easy to interpret. They may show magistrates sitting in judgment, though they could also be receiving petitioners. Schäfer, *Imperii Insignia*, 50–56, who interprets them as trial scenes, provides a thorough discussion of the genre, accompanied by a useful series of illustrations on plate 31.

44. Rossano Gospels folio 8R, reproduced in Weitzmann, *Book Illumination*, 90, with a discussion on p. 92.

45. Halfmann, *Itinera Principum*, 123. Also Millar, *ERW*[1], 370.

46. Halfmann, *Itinera Principum*, 124.

47. For example, Millar, *ERW*[1], 31–32 quotes from *Pan. Lat.* III (II) 10.5, on Diocletian and Maximian's meeting at Milan in the winter of AD 290–291: "All the fields were filled with crowds not only of men rushing to see, but with herds of beasts

leaving their remote pastures and woods; the peasants vied with each other in reporting what they had seen to all the villages. Altars were lit, incense thrown on, libations poured, sacrificial victims slain." The presence of emperors has a magical effect and urges men to worship the gods in thanks.

48. Halfmann, *Itinera Principum*, 112–17.

49. Coriat, *Prince législateur*, 180.

50. Suet. *Div. Aug.* 53.

51. For example, in the exchange between Constantine and a group of veterans in *CJ* 12.46.1 the artificiality of the veterans' questions and statements and the emperor's responses suggests that our record is not of an impromptu exchange, but rather a series of carefully crafted statements summarizing unwritten negotiations between the veterans and Constantine's officials. In some texts, however, the emperors seem to have voiced their opinions stridently, perhaps extemporaneously. For example, *CGL* III p. 32, 13ff. (§4) records Hadrian giving the following response: *Petente quodam de suo filio quoniam eum neglegeret valetudinarium et pauperem et pascere nollet, in quo omnes facultates suas expenderat, Adrianus dixit iuveni: custode patrem tuum; ideo enim te genuit. cura ergo, ne iterum de te apud me queratur.* But responses such as this, which seem to have been given *de plano*, may not have resulted from the same process that I described in chapter 1. On responses given *de plano*, see Nörr, "Interloqui de plano," from whom I have taken the Hadrianic text.

52. Greenberg, *Studies in the Bible*, 104.

53. Ibid., 103–104.

54. Naiden, *Ancient Supplication*, 386–87, demonstrates how the language of the petition sent by the Skaptopareni contains language in its archaism has parallels with that used in Greek supplications. Not all petitioners, however, were so humble. For example, an Egyptian petitioner of the New Kingdom wrote the following to a local official: "One of my subordinates came and reported to me that you have reckoned for me an excessive amount of barley as (tax-)assessment on my field in the district of Village-of-Re. What's the meaning of wronging me thus? I am the one you've picked on to penalise, out of the whole body of taxpayers! That's just fine! I am an attendant of Pharaoh, close to his presence. I shall not be approaching you, to make my complaint to you. I shall approach one . . . (in far higher authority!)" *Papyrus Anastasi* V 27:3ff, trans. Kitchen, *Pharaoh Triumphant*, 133. I owe the reference to David Boardman.

55. Brown, *Poverty and Leadership*, 69.

56. Fest. 185 M. = 200 L, on which see *RE* s.v. "pontifex," 1206. On the importance of the emperor as *pontifex maximus*, see Sirks, "Making a Request," 131.

57. The image in Hellenistic thought of the ruler as νόμος ἔμψυχος could also be applied to rulers in many other periods, including the Roman. On the image, see Adam, *Clementia Principis*, 45. On ancient evidence for statues of Roman emperors as offering asylum, see Pékary, *Das römische Kaiserbildnis*, 130–31.

58. Emperors were guardians of the law: Coriat, *Prince législateur*, 176–78. There were harsh penalties for passing off false rescripts as genuine, according to *CJ* 9.22.3, which threatens *maiorem severitatem*.

59. On the need for emperors to be accessible, Peachin, *Iudex vice Caesaris*, 90. On the maintenance of legal instability, ibid., 10–13.

60. On these qualities, Adam, *Clementia Principis*, 36–37.

61. Millar, *ERW*[1], 516, cites the following example of imperial indulgence from Ammianus Marcellinus 16.5.12: "When [Julian] was approached by the parents of a girl who had been carried off, and when the man who had violated her had been found guilty, he gave as his verdict that he should be relegated. When they complained that they were being unfairly treated because the man had not been punished by death, he replied, 'Let the laws find fault with my *clementia*, but it is right that an emperor of indulgent disposition should be superior to all laws.'"

62. On statements of the emperor's adherence to the law: Honoré, *E&L*[2], xii. On the *apologiae*, Corcoran, *Empire of the Tetrarchs*, 296–97.

63. On the importance of emperors' adherence to the law, see Harries, *Law and Empire*, 213.

64. This is especially true of the son of Constantine, whose hand, an orator in AD 321, claimed, "already rejoiced in 'bountiful subscription'" (*Pan. Lat.* X (4) 37.5, referenced by Millar, *ERW*[1], 207).

65. I am grateful to Ann Hanson for this suggestion.

66. On the importance of status to imperial charity, see Humfress, "Poverty and Roman Law." On private charity among pagan Romans, who seem to have differentiated between the deserving and undeserving poor, see Parkin, "Pagan Almsgiving."

67. A similar point is made by Adam, *Clementia Principis*, 29–30, who notes that an emperor's *securitas* is supported by his giving of justice. With imperial *securitas* guaranteed, the emperor can in turn help his subjects—and keep their support. Ma, *Antiochos III*, 171, has the following to say about the system of petition and response used by Antiochus III: "By allowing itself to be constrained or petitioned into giving privileges (i.e., lessening demands), the empire of domination channelled the energies of the ruled into petition rather than resistance or defection, into improving the immediate situation rather than challenging the framework of imperial authority." Though the governmental situations are not identical, this conceptualization of the Hellenistic system could be applied also to the Roman.

68. On the power of *exempla*, see Peachin, "Exemplary Government." While his concern is with the prerogatives that emperors enjoyed thanks to *exempla*, I think that *exempla* also created expectations for emperors in the eyes of their subjects.

69. This is probably the best explanation for the numbers of petitions answered. It is hard to know what evidence could show that Diocletian was actively encouraging or discouraging the answering of petitions, especially given the smaller numbers of rescripts preserved from previous and subsequent years.

70. I agree with the general point made by Millar, *ERW*[2], 646: "The fact that it was generally known that in principle the emperor, wherever he might happen currently to be, was open to the receipt of petitions, and could be imagined as attending to individual worries or problems and as giving effective rulings on legal issues which were of concern to private persons, is of great significance in itself, a significance wholly unaffected by the statistical exiguousness of the number of petitions actually answered." Of course, I contest his assumption that emperors alone answered all petitions since it is based on literary evidence. I also contest his use of the phrase "statistical exiguousness," compared to what evidence is the total number of rescripts exiguous? Reports of the burden of the rescript system may indicate that considerable numbers of rescripts were produced, as do the *CG* and *CH*, even in their extant edited forms.

71. *CJ*.1.19.2. Constantine's concern about the burden on his officials is expressed in *CTh* 1.15.1. Julian also complains of the burden of letters and βίβλοι following him (Julian *Ep.* 98 Bidez, 402b; the reference comes from Millar, *ERW*¹, 211), though βίβλοι may not necessarily refer to petitions.

72. On this idea see Ewick and Silbey, *Common Place*, 93–94.

73. Kelly, *Ruling*, 114, describes an exchange between former British prime minister Margaret Thatcher and a member of Parliament, who was indignant at her failure to respond personally to a letter. Thatcher's response was that her job simply did not allow her the time to reply in this way to all the correspondence she received.

74. Bowersock, "Emperor's Burden," 347, in his review of Millar, comments that if, as an official, a man concentrated solely on everyday bureaucracy, he would not rise through the ranks and certainly not to be emperor.

75. Millar, "Emperor, Senate, Provinces," 166: "The Republic, it may be, can be seen from Rome outwards. To take this standpoint for the Empire is to lose contact with reality. Not only the pattern of the literary evidence, or the existence of an immense mass of local documents, but the very nature of the Empire itself, means that it can only be understood by starting from the provinces and looking inward."

76. Corcoran, *Empire of the Tetrarchs*, 169.

77. On this notion, see Ando, *Imperial Ideology*, 78, who cites Habermas's theory that consensus presupposes communication accepted by both sides.

78. Peachin, *Iudex vice Caesaris*, 203.

79. Corcoran, "Tetrarchy: Policy and Image," 39–40.

80. Jones, *Later Roman Empire*, 578. Christol, "Ascension de l'ordre," 622–23, however, sees that equestrians often took the top positions in the *scrinia*, a situation that was maintained under Diocletian (Lepelley, "Triomphe à la disparation," 633), and therefore Jones's claim may be overstated. It is striking that the ἐπὶ τῶν δεησέων of the Byzantine period came from grand families (Morris, Epi tôn deêseôn, 131–34); during this period the rescript system became less accessible to the non-elites. The two phenomena may be connected, but it is unclear whether the former caused the latter, or vice versa.

81. This is certainly not the only nexus of relationships in the Roman imperial administration—there was an important interdependence between the emperor, the *magister memoriae*, or *magister epistulae* and the provincial governors, which was important for the access it gave the emperor to his subjects and their concerns. Meyer-Zwiffelhoffer, *Politikos archein*, 284–89, examines the relationship between provincial governors and the emperor: as emperors from the second century increasingly consulted governors, so governors also more and more involved the emperor in legal questions. Those questions were probably most frequently raised by rescripts. Another important person frequently in the nexus was the *tabellio*, who helped his client receive help from the emperor via his officials.

82. I owe the expression to Michael Peachin. Williams, *Diocletian*, 131–32, for example, is clear in his condemnation of the edict; Rees, *Diocletian and the Tetrarchy*, 44, however, offers a more nuanced critique that recognizes the influence of Lactantius's condemnation (II 6 7.6–7), as does Kuhoff, *Diokletian und die Epoche*, 543. In his detailed discussion of the text and the inscriptions' history, Kuhoff criticizes the edict as unworkable (550) but allows that it may have increased public confidence in the government (564).

83. There is a wealth of bibliography on this topic, since emperors could use many media to present themselves, such as monumental architecture, statuary, inscriptions, and coinage. Some important works are Zanker, *Power of Images*, Noreña, "Communication of the Emperor's Virtues" (and the extensive bibliography he cites in the first two notes of this article), and Wallace-Hadrill, "Civilis princeps."

84. Yavetz's *Plebs and Princeps* is a notable exception to the omission of the middling sort from analyses of imperial self-representation, along with Ando, *Imperial Ideology.* Millar, *ERW*[1,2] (especially chaps. 5 and 8), has led the way in incorporating the middling sort into discussion of imperial communication. See also Peachin, "Rome the Superpower," 145. Millar, *Crowd in Rome*, Mouritsen, *Plebs and Politics*, and Sünskes Thompson, *Demonstrative Legitimation*, are concerned with the influence of non-elites living in Rome on political events at Rome. A potential set of clues for emperors' feelings of obligation toward answering the middling sort is a couple of rescripts to disgruntled petitioners who claimed to be dissatisfied with previous responses (*CJ* 2.19.1 of AD 223 and *CJ* 8.43.1 of AD 212). These texts are discussed in Nörr, *Rechtskritik*, 51. Peachin, "Rome the Superpower," 149 and 152, while looking at, among other things, emperors' responsibilities to the Senate, military, and plebs, points out that acting as a judge is one responsibility.

### Conclusion

1. This work will be helped greatly by the forthcoming collaborative edition of Frederick Blume's unpublished translation of the *CJ*, which is directed by Bruce Frier.

2. Suet. *Div. Aug.* 50 and 45 respectively.

3. *HA, Alex. Sev.* 31.1, trans. Millar, *ERW*[1], 221.

4. Quoted by Hopkins, "Rules of Evidence," 181. The account comes from Hirth, *China*, 71.

5. Macrides, "Ritual of Petition," 358–59.

6. Sidonius Apollinaris, *Ep.* II 9: *circa nonam recrudescit molis illa regnandi. redeunt pulsantes, redeunt summoventes; ubique litigiosus fremit ambitus, qui tractus in vesperam cena regia interpellante rarescit.*

7. Agapetos Diakonos, *Ekthesis Kephalaion Parainetikon* sections 8, 23 and 52, cited by Zuckerman, "Deux Dioscore d'Aphroditè," 81 n. 17.

8. Zuckerman, ibid., 80, who cites Procopius, *Anecdota* XIII, 1.

9. Morris, "Epi tôn deêseôn," 127–28, who gives further examples of medieval and modern rulers receiving petitions in public. Also Macrides, "Ritual of Petition," 358–64.

10. Toynbee, *Experiences*, 361–62.

11. Khan, *Legal and Administrative Documents*, 305, quoting Sirat Salah al-Din, ed. Sayyal, 13.

12. According to Joinville's *Histoire de Saint Louis*, reproduced in Michaud and Poujoulat, *Nouvelle Collection*, 184.

13. Toynbee, *Experiences*, 362.

14. Ibid., who mentions yet another nice anecdote showing how these stories gain credence from being in print and from their almost credible circumstances: "At [Turkish] Yozgad in 1948 it was still practicable for the provincial governor to hold open court, but already before that date, in Washington, D.C., President Franklin

D. Roosevelt's children's only means of getting access to their father was, so I have been told, to make an appointment with him through the White House secretariat" (p. 363). (This probably happened only once. Roosevelt's aggrieved children—who would all have been in their late teens or twenties—probably wished simply to make a point.)

15. McGrory, "Ruling Class," 25. I came across this story independently of Morris, "Epi tôn deêseôn," 128 n. 13; I am delighted that the story has made an impact on those working on petitioning, but disappointed not to have found further modern evidence of this practice.

16. Xenophon, *Cyropaedia* 7.5.37 f. This example and the following come from Wallace-Hadrill, "Civilis Princeps," 33–34.

17. Plut., *Demetr.*, 18.41–42.

18. Suet., *Tib.* 40, referenced by Millar, *ERW*[1], 36–37. Millar follows with this anecdote about Vespasian: "Vespasian once had occasion to interrogate one of his muleteers as to whether he had been bribed to get down and shoe the mules, in order to give time for a litigant to approach" (Suet., *Vesp.* 23.2).

19. On anecdotes as often unreliable evidence for ancient history, see Saller, "Anecdotes as Historical Evidence" and "Domitian and His Successors." I believe that the anecdotes Millar uses illustrate imperial virtues and vices, not typical behavior.

20. The pressures on emperors' time and their need to delegate responsibilities are the subject of Peachin, *Iudex vice Caesaris*.

21. The exception under Diocletian is that he granted slaves access to the administration. My theory complements Millar, *ERW*[2], 651–52: "'Petition-and-response' . . . remains essentially a model; setting-up and deploying that model is one way of asking questions about the role of the emperor, the nature of imperial government and the character of Graeco-Roman antiquity as a civilisation. If viewed as expressions of a culture, with the aid of as many as possible of the varied and curious viewpoints on its workings which this particular civilisation happens to have left for us to encounter, the operations of government may seem no less interesting, and no less baffling, than does that culture itself."

22. Brown, *Poverty and Leadership*, 71. It is notable that the poor have shared concerns through the ages: too little food, insecure employment, and threats of violence and intimidation from those more powerful. The repetition of these problems seems to undermine attempts to see pleas for pity in certain periods as reflecting concerns particular to that period. As long as there is economic or physical suffering, there will be petitions and they will necessarily share themes.

23. I am grateful to Simon Corcoran and Benet Salway for stimulating conversation on this subject.

### Appendix 2

1. A facsimile of this edition of the *CJ* was reprinted by Keip Verlag in 1998.

2. Barnes, *New Empire*, 52–54, and Honoré, *E&L*[2], 163–65 and also 181 nn. 556–58, where he supplies years for otherwise undated entries on the basis of their style. See also his palingenesia, though he does not supply explanations for changes he makes to dates and places. The dates and locations of the entries are also considered by Mommsen, "Über die Zeitfolge."

3. For example, *CJ* 4.44.6 and 4.44.7 were both dated by Honoré to before December 1, 293, but can also be dated to after October 18. Therefore they can be placed at Sirmium.

4. *Codex Justinianus*, published at Nuremberg by Johann Sensenschmidt and Andreas Frisner, June 24, 1475. Held at Beinecke Library, Yale University, New Haven, Connecticut. Other errors include *CJ* 2.12.16 Patronia for Paconia, 2.21.3 Acianus to Attianus, 2.21.4 Isidus for Isidorus, 2.20.4 Emandara for Menandra, 2.12.17 Martenius for Mardonius, 2.20.5 Ampirosa for Aphrodisia, 2.54.1 Attalus for Catulus, and 2.4.32 Cerilus for Cyrillus. Other divergences may add information to the names we already have: for 2.3.27 Krüger has Aurelius Chresimus, whereas the Yale edition has Cornelius Chresimus. Perhaps the recipient's name was Aurelius Cornelius Chresimus. For 2.4.34 Krüger has Ptolemais, while the Yale edition has Ptolemais and Cerillus, perhaps an additional recipient whose name disappeared from other editions. For 1.18.10 Krüger has Amphia; the Yale edition has Philippus, perhaps also an additional recipient.

5. For a list of the Western entries, see Barnes, *New Empire*, 56–61, and the comments of Corcoran, *Empire of the Tetrarchs*, 34. See also Wieling, "Gesetze der Herculier." I disagree, however, with many of Wieling's allocations of rescripts to the West. His thesis (p. 629) that few Western rescripts from the Caesars are extant because they were juristically inferior to those from the East is unlikely; archival issues explain their low number (and that of the Western Augusti too).

# BIBLIOGRAPHY

Adam, Traute. *Clementia Principis: Der Einfluss hellenistischer Fürstenspiegel auf den Versuch einer rechtlichen Fundierung des Principats durch Seneca.* Kieler historische Studien, vol. 2. Stuttgart: E. Klett, 1970.

Adams, J. N. *Bilingualism and the Latin Language.* New York: Cambridge University Press, 2003.

Alexander, Philip S. "Aramaic Epistolography." *Journal of Semitic Studies* 23 (1978): 155–70.

Al-Haifi, Hassan. "Streamlining the Bureaucracy." *Yemen Times,* March 11–14, 2004. http://yementimes.com/article.shtml?i=719&p=opinion&a=1 (accessed September 8, 2007).

Amelotti, Mario, and Livia Migliardi Zingale. *Le costituzioni giustinianee nei papiri e nelle epigrafi.* 2nd ed. Legum Iustiniani imperatoris vocabularium. Subsidia; 1. Milano: Giuffráe, 1985.

Ando, Clifford. *Imperial Ideology and Provincial Loyalty in the Roman Empire.* Berkeley: University of California Press, 2000.

Ankum, Hans. "Der Ausdruck *favor libertatis* und das klassische römische Freilassungsrecht." In *Unfreie Arbeits- und Lebensverhältnisse von der Antike bis in die Gegenwart: Eine Einführung,* ed. Elisabeth Herrmann-Otto, 82–100. Hildesheim: Olms, 2005.

Bagnall, Roger S. "Women's Petitions in Late Antique Egypt." In *La pétition à Byzance: Table ronde, XXe congrès international des études byzantines, 19–25 août 2001,* ed. Denis Feissel and Jean Gascou, 53–60. Paris: Association des amis du centre d'histoire et civilisation de Byzance, 2004.

Barnes, Timothy. *The New Empire of Diocletian and Constantine.* Cambridge, Mass.: Harvard University Press, 1982.

Beloch, Julius. *Die Bevölkerung der griechisch-römischen Welt.* Leipzig: Duncker & Humblot, 1886.

Böcking, Eduard. *Corpus iuris Romani anteiustiniani.* Vol. 1. Bonn: A. Marcus, 1835.

Bodel, John. "Epigraphy and the Ancient Historian." In *Epigraphic Evidence: Ancient History from Inscriptions*, ed. John Bodel, 1–56. London: Routledge, 2001.

Borkowski, J. A. *Textbook on Roman Law*. International student ed. London: Blackstone, 1994.

Boskovic, Djurdje, Noel Duval, Pierre Gros et al. "Recherches archeologiques a Sirmium: Campagne Franco-Yougoslavie de 1973." *MEFR (A)* 86, no. 1 (1974): 597–620.

Bowersock, Glenn. "The Emperor's Burden." Review of *The Emperor in the Roman World (31BC–AD 337)*, by Fergus Millar. *CPh* 73, no. 4 (1978): 346–51.

———. "The Babatha Papyri, Masada, and Rome." Review of *Masada II: The Yigael Yadin Excavations 1963–1965. Final Reports: The Latin and Greek Documents*, by Naphthali Lewis, Hannah Cotton, and Joseph Geiger. *JRA* 4 (1991): 336–44.

Bowman, Alan K., J. David Thomas, and J. N. Adams. *The Vindolanda Writing-Tablets (Tabulae Vindolandenses II)*. London: British Museum, 1994.

Brosius, Maria. *Ancient Archives and Archival Traditions: Concepts of Record-Keeping in the Ancient World*. Oxford: Oxford University Press, 2003.

Brown, Peter Robert Lamont. *Augustine of Hippo: A Biography*. New ed. London: Faber, 2000.

———. *Poverty and Leadership in the Later Roman Empire*. Menahem Stern Jerusalem Lectures. Hanover, N.H.: University Press of New England, 2002.

Brundage, James A. *Medieval Canon Law*. London: Longman, 1995.

Buckland, W. W. *A Manual of Roman Private Law*. Cambridge: Cambridge University Press, 1925.

———. *Equity in Roman Law: Lectures Delivered in the University of London, At the Request of the Faculty of Laws*. Buffalo, N.Y.: W.S. Hein, 2002.

Burton, Graham P. "Proconsuls, Assizes, and the Administration of Justice under the Empire." *JRS* 65 (1975): 92–106.

Campanile, Domitilla. "L'infanzia della provincia d'Asia: l'origine dei 'conventus iuridici' nella provincia." In *Gli stati territoriali nel mondo antico*, ed. Cinzia Bearzot, Franca Landucci Gattinoni, and Giuseppe Zecchini, 271–88. Milano: V&P università, 2003.

Campbell, J. B. *The Emperor and the Roman Army, 31 BC–AD 235*. Oxford: Clarendon, 1984.

Casson, Lionel. *Travel in the Ancient World*. London: Allen & Unwin, 1974.

Cavigneaux, Antoine, and R. M. Boehmer. *Uruk: Altbabylonische Texte aus dem Planquadrat Pe XVI-4/5 nach Kopien von Adam Falkenstein, Ausgrabungen in Uruk-Warka*. Endberichte, vol. 23. Mainz am Rhein: von Zabern, 1996.

Cenderelli, Aldo. *Ricerche sul Codex Hermogenianus*. Università di Milano. Facoltà di Giurisprudenza. Studi di Diritto Romano; ser. 2, no. 4. Milano: A. Giuffrè, 1965.

Christol, Michel. "L'ascension de l'ordre équestre. Un thème historiographique et sa réalité." In *L'ordre équestre: histoire d'une aristocratie: IIe siècle av. J.-C.—IIIe siècle ap. J.-C.: Actes du colloque international (Bruxelles-Leuven, 5–7 octobre 1995)*, ed. Ségolène Demougin, Hubert Devijver, and Marie-Thérèse Raepsaet-Charlier, 613–28. Rome: Écolefrançaise de Rome, 1999.

Clarysse, Willy. "Tomoi Synkollesimoi." In *Ancient Archives and Archival Traditions: Concepts of Record-Keeping in the Ancient World*, ed. Maria Brosius, 344–59. Oxford: Oxford University Press, 2003.

Cohen, Mark R. "Four Judaeo-Arabic Petitions of the Poor from the Cairo Geniza." *Jerusalem Studies in Arabic and Islam* 24 (2000): 446–65.

———. "Feeding the Poor and Clothing the Naked: The Cairo Geniza." *Journal of Interdisciplinary History* 35, no. 3 (2005): 407–21.

———. "The Voice of the Poor in the Middle Ages from the Cairo Geniza." Lecture, Yale University, New Haven, January 26, 2006.

Coles, Revel. "P.Oxy. XXII 2343 Revisited." *ZPE* 61 (1985): 110–14.

Collinet, Paul. *Études historiques sur le droit de Justinien*. Vol. 2, *Histoire de École de droit de Beyrouth*. Paris: L. Larose & L. Tenin, 1912.

Connolly, Serena. "Women at the Edge: Gender and Ethnicity in Law at Dura-Europos." *Diotima: Gender and Diversity in Place: Proceedings of the Fourth Conference on Feminism and Classics*, 2004. www.stoa.org/diotima/essays/fc04.

———. "*Quasi ancilla, quasi libera*: Diogenia and the Everyday Experience of Slaves." *AJAH* 3–4 (2004–2005 [2007]): 171–88.

———. "Roman Ransomers." *AHB* 20, no. 1–4 (2006): 115–31.

Corcoran, Simon. *The Empire of the Tetrarchs: Imperial Pronouncements and Government, AD284–324*. Oxford: Clarendon, 1996.

———. "The Publication of Law in the Era of the Tetrarchs—Diocletian, Galerius, Gregorius, Hermogenian." In *Diokletian und die Tetrarchie: Aspekte einer Zeitenwende*, ed. Alexander Demandt, Andreas Goltz, and Heinrich Schlange-Schöningen, 56–73. Berlin: Walter de Gruyter, 2004.

———. "The Tetrarchy: Policy and Image as Reflected in Imperial Pronouncements." In *Die Tetrarchie: Ein neues Regierungssystem und seine mediale Präsentation*, ed. Dietrich Boschung and Werner Eck, 31–61. Wiesbaden: Reichert, 2006.

Coriat, Jean-Pierre. "La technique du rescrit à la fin du principat." *SDHI* 51 (1985): 319–48.

———. *Le prince législateur: La technique législative des Sévères et les méthodes de creation du droit impérial à la fin du Principat*. Bibliothèque des Écoles françaises d'Athènes et de Rome; fasc. 294. Palais Farnèse: École française de Rome, 1997.

Cotton, Hannah. "The Guardianship of Jesus Son of Babatha: Roman and Local Law in the Province of Arabia." *JRS* 83 (1993): 94–108.

Crook, John. *Consilium Principis: Imperial Councils and Counsellors from Augustus to Diocletian*. Cambridge: Cambridge University Press, 1955.

———. *Law and Life of Rome*. London: Thames & Hudson, 1967.

———. Review of *Final Judgments: Duty and Emotion in Roman Wills 250 BC–AD 250*, by Edward Champlin. *JRS* 82 (1992): 232–34.

———. *Legal Advocacy in the Roman World*. London: Duckworth, 1995.

Crow, James. "Recent Research on the Late Antique Cities of Eastern Thrace (*provincia-europa*)." In *The Roman and Late Roman City: The International Conference, Veliko Turnovo, 26–30 July 2000*, ed. Liudmila Ruseva-Slokoska, Rumen Teofilov Ivanov, Ventisislav Dinchev et al., 342–51. Sofia: Prof. Marin Drinov Academic Publ. House, 2002.

Culham, Phyllis. "Archives and Alternatives in Republican Rome." *CPh* 84, no. 2 (1989): 100–15.

Davis, Natalie Zemon. *Fiction in the Archives: Pardon Tales and Their Tellers in Sixteenth-Century France*. Stanford, Calif.: Stanford University Press, 1987.

de Certeau, Michel de. *The Practice of Everyday Life*. Berkeley: University of California Press, 1984.

de Ste Croix, Geoffrey E. M. *The Class Struggle in the Ancient Greek World from the Archaic Age to the Arab Conquests*. Ithaca, N.Y.: Cornell University Press, 1981.

Diaconescu, Alexandru. "The Towns of Roman Dacia: An Overview of Recent Research." In *Roman Dacia: The Making of a Provincial Society*. JRA Supplementary Series, no. 56, edited by William S. Hanson and Ian Haynes, 87–142. Portsmouth, R.I.: Journal of Roman Archaeology, 2004.

Dintchev, Ventzislav. "Classification of the Late Antique Cities in the Dioceses of Thracia and Dacia." *Archaeologia Bulgarica* 3, no. 3 (1999): 39–73.

Dixon, Suzanne. "The Sentimental Ideal of the Roman Family." In *Marriage, Divorce, and Children in Ancient Rome,* ed. Beryl Rawson, 99–113. New York: Oxford University Press, 1991.

———. *The Roman Family*. Baltimore: Johns Hopkins University Press, 1992.

Dobbs-Allsopp, Fred W. "The Genre of the Mesad Hashavyahu Ostracon." *Bulletin of the American Schools of Oriental Research* 295, no. 3 (1994): 49–55.

Dodd, Gwilym. "The Hidden Presence: Parliament and the Private Petition in the Fourteenth Century." In *Expectations of Law in the Middle Ages,* ed. Anthony Musson, 135–49. Woodbridge, UK: Boydell, 2001.

D'Ors, Alvaro, and Fernando Martín. "Propositio libellorum." *AJPh* 100 (1979): 111–24.

Dovere, Elio. *De iure: Studi sul titolo 1. delle Epitomi di Ermogeniano*. Pubblicazioni della Facoltà di giurisprudenza. Ser. 1: Giuridica/Università di Cagliari; 56. Torino: G. Giappichelli, 2001.

Drew-Bear, Thomas, Werner Eck, and Peter Herrmann. "Sacrae Litterae." *Chiron* 7 (1977): 355–83.

Duval, Noël. "Sirmium 'ville impériale' ou 'capitale'?" *Corso di cultura sull'arte ravennate e bizantina* 26 (1979): 53–90.

———. "Les résidences impériales: Leur rapport avec les problèmes de légitimité, les partages de l'empire et la chronologie des combinaisons dynastiques." In *Usurpationen in der Spätantike: Akten des Kolloquiums "Staatsstreich und Staatlichkeit," 6.–10. März 1996, Solothurn/Bern: Elf Beiträge,* ed. Timothy Barnes, François Paschoud, and Joachim Szidat, 127–53. Stuttgart: F. Steiner, 1997.

Evans Grubbs, Judith. *Women and the Law in the Roman Empire: A Sourcebook on Marriage, Divorce, and Widowhood*. London: Routledge, 2002.

Ewick, Patricia, and Susan S. Silbey. *The Common Place of Law: Stories from Everyday Life*. Chicago: University of Chicago Press, 1998.

Favro, Diane G. *The Urban Image of Augustan Rome*. New York: Cambridge University Press, 1996.

Feissel, Denis. "L'adnotatio de Constantin sur le droit de cité d'Orcistus en Phrygie." *AnTard* 7 (1999): 255–67.

———. "Pétitions aux empereurs et formes du rescrit dans les sources documentaires du IVe au VIe siècle." In *La pétition à Byzance: Table ronde, XXe congrès international des etudes byzantines, 19–25 août 2001,* ed. Denis Feissel and Jean Gascou, 33–52. Paris: Association des amis du centre d'histoire et civilisation de Byzance, 2004.

Fensham, F. Charles. "Widow, Orphan, and the Poor in Ancient Near Eastern Legal and Wisdom Literature." *Journal of Near Eastern Studies* 21, no. 2 (1962): 129–39.

Fewster, Penelope. "Bilingualism in Roman Egypt." In *Bilingualism in Ancient Society: Language Contact and the Written Word*, ed. J. N. Adams, Mark Janse, and Simon Swain, 220–45. Oxford: Oxford University Press, 2002.

Finn, Richard. *Almsgiving in the Later Roman Empire: Christian Promotion and Practice*. Oxford Classical Monographs. Oxford: Oxford University Press, 2006.

Fournet, Jean-Luc. "Entre document et littérature: La pétition dans l'antiquité tardive." In *La pétition à Byzance: Table ronde, XXe congrès international des études byzantines, 19–25 août 2001*, ed. Denis Feissel and Jean Gascou, 61–74. Paris: Association des amis du centre d'histoire et civilisation de Byzance, 2004.

Fournet, Jean-Luc, and Jean Gascou. "Liste des pétitions sur papyrus des Ve–VIIe siècles." In *La pétition à Byzance: Table ronde, XXe congrès international des études byzantines, 19–25 août 2001*, ed. Denis Feissel and Jean Gascou, 141–96. Paris: Association des amis du centre d'histoire et civilisation de Byzance, 2004.

Friedland, Martin L., Peter E. S. Jewett, Linda J. Jewett et al. *Access to the Law: A Study Conducted for the Law Reform Commission of Canada*. Toronto: Carswell-Methuen, 1975.

Friedman, Lawrence Meir. *The Legal System: A Social Science Perspective*. New York: Russell Sage Foundation, 1975.

Frier, Bruce. *Landlords and Tenants in Imperial Rome*. Princeton, N.J.: Princeton University Press, 1980.

———. "Demography." In *The Cambridge Ancient History*. Vol. 11, *The High Empire, A.D. 70–192*, ed. Alan K. Bowman, Peter Garnsey, and Dominic Rathbone, 787–816. Cambridge: Cambridge University Press, 2000.

Gagos, Traianos, and P. J. Sijpesteijn. "Settling a Dispute in Fourth Century Small Oasis (P.Mich.Inv. No. 4008)." *ZPE* 105 (1995): 245–52.

Gardner, Jane. *Women in Roman Law and Society*. London: Croon Helm, 1986.

Garnsey, Peter. *Social Status and Legal Privilege in the Roman Empire*. Oxford: Clarendon, 1970.

Gascou, Jean. "Les pétitions privées." In *La pétition à Byzance: Table ronde, XXe congrès international des études byzantines, 19–25 août 2001*, ed. Denis Feissel and Jean Gascou, 93–103. Paris: Association des amis du centre d'histoire et civilisation de Byzance, 2004.

Gerov, Boris. "Die lateinisch-griechische Sprachgrenze." In *Die Sprachen im römischen Reich der Kaiserzeit: Kolloquium vom 8. bis 10. April 1974*, ed. Günter Neumann and Jürgen Untermann, 147–65. Köln; Bonn: Rheinland-Verlag; Habelt [in Komm.], 1980.

Gore, Albert. *The Assault on Reason*. New York: Penguin, 2007.

Gray, John. "Social Aspects of Canaanite Religion." *Vetus Testamentum* Suppl. 15 (1966): 170–92.

Greenberg, Moshe. *Studies in the Bible and Jewish Thought*. JPS Scholar of Distinction Series. Philadelphia: Jewish Publication Society, 1995.

Gustafson, Mark. Review of *Emperors and Lawyers*, 2nd ed. *BMCR* 95, no. 10.17 (1995).

Haensch, Rudolf. "Die Bearbeitungsweisen von Petitionen in der Provinz Aegyptus." *ZPE* 100 (1994): 487–546.

———. *Capita provinciarum: Statthaltersitze und Provinzialverwaltung in der römischen Kaiserzeit*. Kölner Forschungen, vol. 7. Mainz am Rhein: von Zabern, 1997.

Halfmann, Helmut. *Itinera Principum: Geschichte und Typologie der Kaiserreisen im Römischen Reich.* Heidelberger althistorische Beiträge und epigraphische Studien, Vol. 2. Stuttgart: F. Steiner Verlag Wiesbaden, 1986.

Hallo, William. "Individual Prayer in Sumerian: The Continuity of a Tradition." *Journal of the American Oriental Society* 88, no. 1 (1968): 71–89.

Hallof, Klaus. "Die Inschrift von Skaptopara: Neue Dokumente und neue Lesungen." *Chiron* 24 (1994): 405–41.

Hanson, Ann. "Ancient Illiteracy." In *Literacy in the Roman World*, ed. Mary Beard, Alan Bowman, Mireille Corbier et al., 159–98. Ann Arbor: Dept. of Classical Studies, University of Michigan, 1991.

Harding, Christopher, and John Williams. *Legal Provision in the Rural Environment: Legal Services, Criminal Justice, and Welfare Provision in Rural Areas.* Cardiff: University of Wales Press, 1994.

Harries, Jill. "The Roman Imperial Quaestor from Constantine to Theodosius II." *JRS* 78 (1988): 148–72.

———. *Law and Empire in Late Antiquity.* Cambridge: Cambridge University Press, 1999.

Harris, William. *Ancient Literacy.* Cambridge, Mass.: Harvard University Press, 1989.

Hauken, Tor. *Petition and Response: An Epigraphic Study of Petitions to Roman Emperors, 181–249.* Monographs from the Norwegian Institute at Athens, vol. 2. Bergen; Jonsered, Sweden: Norwegian Institute at Athens; Distributor, P. Åstrøms förlag, 1998.

———. "Structures and Themes in Petitions to Roman Emperors." In *La pétition à Byzance: Table ronde, XXe congrès international des études byzantines, 19–25 août 2001*, ed. Denis Feissel and Jean Gascou, 11–22. Paris: Association des amis du centre d'histoire et civilisation de Byzance, 2004.

Henning, Joachim. *Südosteuropa zwischen Antike und Mittelalter: Archäologische Beiträge zur Landwirtschaft des 1. Jahrtausends u.Z.* Schriften zur Ur- und Frühgeschichte, 42. Berlin: Akademie Verlag, 1987.

Herrmann, Peter. *Hilferufe aus römischen Provinzen: Ein Aspekt der Krise des römischen Reiches im 3. Jhdt. n. Chr.* Joachim Jungius-Gesellschaft der Wissenschaften; Jahrg. 8, 1990 Heft 4. Hamburg: Verlag Vandenhoeck & Ruprecht, 1990.

Herrmann-Otto, Elisabeth. *Ex ancilla natus: Untersuchungen zu den "hausgeborenen" Sklaven und Sklavinnen im Westen des Römischen Kaiserreiches.* Forschungen zur antiken Sklaverei, vol. 24. Stuttgart: F. Steiner, 1994.

Hirth, Friedrich. *China and the Roman Orient.* Leipzig: G. Hirth, 1885.

Hobson, Deborah W. "The Impact of Law on Village Life in Roman Egypt." In *Law, Politics, and Society in the Ancient Mediterranean World*, ed. Baruch Halpern and Deborah W. Hobson, 193–219. Sheffield: Sheffield Academic Press, 1993.

Hoddinott, Ralph F. *Bulgaria in Antiquity: An Archaeological Introduction.* New York: St. Martin's Press, 1975.

———. *The Thracians.* London: Thames & Hudson, 1981.

Honoré, Tony. "The Severan Lawyers: A Preliminary Survey." *SDHI* 28 (1962): 162–232.

———. *Emperors and Lawyers.* London: Duckworth, 1981.

———. "Arcadius, also Charisius." *Index (Quaderni camerti di studi romanistici; International Survey of Roman Law)* 22 (1994): 163–79.

———. *Emperors and Lawyers*. 2nd ed. Oxford: Clarendon, 1994.

Hoogendijk, Francisca A. J., and Peter van Minnen. "Drei Kaiserbriefe Gordians III. an die Bürger von Antinoopolis." *Tyche* 2 (1987): 41–74.

Hopkins, Keith. *Conquerors and Slaves*. Sociological Studies in Roman History, vol. 1. Cambridge: Cambridge University Press, 1978.

———. "Rules of Evidence." Review of *The Emperor in the Roman World (31 B.C.–A.D. 337)*, by Fergus Millar. *JRS* 68 (1978): 178–86.

Huchthausen, Liselot. "Soldaten des 3. Jahrhunderts u. Z. als Korrespondenten der kaiserlichen Kanzlei." In *Altertumswissenschaft mit Zukunft: Dem Wirken Werner Hartkes gewidmet*, 17–51. Berlin: Akademie-Verlag, 1973.

———. "Herkunft und ökonomische Stellung weiblicher Adressaten von Reskripten des Codex Iustinianus (2. und 3. Jh. u. Z.)." *Klio* 56 (1974): 199–228.

———. "Kaiserliche Rechtsauskünfte an Sklaven und in ihrer Freiheit angefochtene Personen aus dem Codex Iustinianus." *Wissenschaftliche Zeitschrift der Universität Rostock, Gesellschafts- und Sprachwissenschaftliche Reihe* 23, no. 3 (1974): 251–57.

———. "Zu kaiserlichen Reskripten an weibliche Adressaten aus der Zeit Diokletians (284–305 u.Z.)." *Klio* 58 (1976): 55–85.

———. "'Thrakerreskripte' aus dem Codex Iustinianus." *Historia: Acta Universitatis Nicolae Copernici* 13 (1979): 7–20.

———. *Frauen fragen den Kaiser: Eine soziologische Studie über das 3. Jh. n. Chr.* Konstanz: Universitätsverlag, 1992.

Humfress, Caroline. "Poverty and Roman Law." In *Poverty in the Roman World*, ed. E. M. Atkins and Robin Osborne, 183–203. Cambridge: Cambridge University Press, 2006.

Ivanov, Teofil. "The Roman Cities of Moesia and Thrace (Modern Bulgaria)." In *Ancient Bulgaria: Papers Presented to the International Symposium on the Ancient History and Archaeology of Bulgaria, University of Nottingham, 1981*, ed. A. G. Poulter, 129–54. Nottingham: University of Nottingham, Dept. of Classical and Archaeological Studies, Archaeology Section (Part 2), 1983.

Johne, Klaus-Peter. "Die Entwicklung von Kolonenwirtschaft und Kolonat." In *Ländliche Besiedlung und Landwirtschaft in den Rhein-Donau-Provinzen des Römischen Reiches: Vorträge eines Internationalen Kolloquiums vom 16.–21. April 1991 in Passau*, ed. Helmut Bender and Hartmut Wolff, 73–86. Espelkamp: Leidorf, 1994.

Jones, A. H. M. *The Later Roman Empire, 284–602: A Social, Economic, and Administrative Survey*. Oxford: B. Blackwell, 1964.

Kajanto, Iiro. *Supernomina: A Study in Latin Epigraphy*. Commentationes humanarum litterarum, vol. 40, no. 1. Helsinki, 1967.

Katicic, Radoslav. "Die Balkanprovinzen." In *Die Sprachen im römischen Reich der Kaiserzeit: Kolloquium vom 8. bis 10. April 1974*, ed. Günter Neumann and Jürgen Untermann, 103–20. Köln: Rheinland-Verlag; Habelt [in Komm.], 1980.

Katzoff, Ranon. "On the Intended Use of P.Col. 123." In *Proceedings of the Sixteenth International Congress of Papyrology: New York, 24–31 July 1980*, ed. Roger S. Bagnall, 559–73. Chico, Calif.: Scholars Press, 1981.

Kehoe, Dennis P. *Investment, Profit, and Tenancy: The Jurists and the Roman Agrarian Economy*. Ann Arbor: University of Michigan Press, 1997.

Kelly, Christopher. *Ruling the Later Roman Empire*. Revealing Antiquity, 15. Cambridge, Mass.: Belknap Press of Harvard University Press, 2004.

Khan, Geoffrey. "The Historical Development of the Structure of Medieval Arabic Petitions." *Bulletin of the School of Oriental and African Studies* 53, no. 1 (1990): 8–30.

———. *Arabic Legal and Administrative Documents in the Cambridge Genizah Collections*. Cambridge: Cambridge University Press, 1993.

Kitchen, Kenneth A. *Pharaoh Triumphant: The Life and Times of Ramesses II, King of Egypt*. Monumenta Hannah Sheen dedicata, 2. Warminster, UK: Aris & Phillips, 1982.

Kolb, Anne. "Cursus Fiscalis: Eine Inschrift aus Concordia in der Tradition Kaiserlicher Politik." In *Römische Inschriften: Neufunde, Neulesungen, und Neuinterpretationen. Festschrift für Hans Lieb Zum 65. Geburtstag dargebracht von seinen Freunden und Kollegen. Arbeiten zur romischen Epigraphik und Altertumskunde*, vol. 2, ed. Hans Wolfgang Lieb, Regula Frei-Stolba, and M. Alexander Speidel, 191–204. Basel: Friedrich Reinhardt, 1995.

Kolendo, Jerzy. "La relation ville/campagne dans les provinces Danubiennes." In *Ländliche Besiedlung und Landwirtschaft in den Rhein-Donau-Provinzen des Römischen Reiches: Vorträge eines Internationalen Kolloquiums vom 16.–21. April 1991 in Passau*, ed. Helmut Bender and Hartmut Wolff, 87–99. Espelkamp: Leidorf, 1994.

Kramer, Bärbel. "P.Strasb.Inv. 1265 + P.Strasb. 296 recto: Eingabe wegen ANDRAPO-DISMOS (= *plagium*) und SULHSIS (= *furtum*)." *ZPE* 69 (1987): 143–61.

Krüger, Paul. *Kritik des justinianischen Codex*. Berlin: Weidmann, 1867.

Krüger, Paul, ed. *Codicis Justiniani fragmenta Veronensia*. Berlin: Weidmann, 1874.

———. *Codex Iustinianus*. Berlin: Weidmann, 1877.

Krüger, Paul, Theodor Mommsen, and Wilhelm Studemund. *Collectio librorum iurisanteiustiniani in usum scholarum*. Berolini: apud Weidmannos, 1878.

Kuhoff, Wolfgang. *Diokletian und die Epoche der Tetrarchie: Das römische Reich zwischen Krisenbewältigung und Neuaufbau (284–313 n. Chr.)*. Frankfurt am Main: P. Lang, 2001.

Lemmings, David. *Professors of the Law: Barristers and English Legal Culture in the Eighteenth Century*. Oxford: Oxford University Press, 2000.

Lenel, Otto, and Luigi Capogrossi Colognesi. *Palingenesia iuris civilis*. 2 vols. Roma: Cigno Galileo Galilei, 2000.

Lepelley, Claude. "Du triomphe à la disparation: Le destin de l'ordre équestre de Dioclétien à Théodose." In *L'ordre équestre: Histoire d'une aristocratie: IIe siècle av. J.-C.—IIIe siècle ap. J.-C.: Actes du colloque international (Bruxelles-Leuven, 5–7 octobre 1995)*, ed. Ségolène Demougin, H. Devijver, and M. Th Raepsaet-Charlier, 629–57. Rome: Ecole française de Rome, 1999.

Lewis, Naphtali. "The Imperial Apokrimata." *RIDA*, 3rd ser., 25 (1978): 261–78.

———. *Life in Egypt under Roman Rule*. Oxford: Clarendon, 1983.

Liebs, Detlef. *Hermogenians Iuris Epitomae. Zum Stand der Römischen Jurisprudenz im Zeitalter Diokletians*. Göttingen: Vandenhoeck & Ruprecht, 1964.

Lieu, Samuel. "Captives, Refugees, and Exiles: A Study of Cross-Frontier Civilian Movements and Contacts between Roman and Persian from Valerian to Jovian." In *The Defence of the Roman and Byzantine East: Proceedings of a Colloquium Held at* the University of Sheffield in April 1986. BAR International series 297, ed. Philip Freeman and D. L. Kennedy, 2:475–505. Oxford, UK: B.A.R., 1986.

Lo Cascio, Elio. "Il popolazione." In Roma imperiale: Una metropoli antica, ed. Elio LoCascio, 3–76. Roma: Carocci, 2000.

Ma, John. Antiochos III and the Cities of Western Asia Minor. Oxford: Oxford University Press, 2002.

MacDonald, William Lloyd. The Architecture of the Roman Empire. Rev. ed. Vol. 2, Yale Publications in the History of Art, 17, 35. New Haven, Conn.: Yale University Press, 1982.

MacMullen, Ramsay. "Barbarian Enclaves in the Northern Roman Empire." Antiquité classique 32 (1963): 552–61.

———. Soldier and Civilian in the Later Roman Empire. Harvard Historical Monographs, 52. Cambridge: Harvard University Press, 1963.

———. "The Epigraphic Habit in the Roman Empire." AJPh 103 (1982): 233–46.

———. "Late Roman Slavery." Historia 36, no. 3 (1987): 359–82.

———. Corruption and the Decline of Rome. New Haven, Conn.: Yale University Press, 1988.

Macrides, Ruth. "The Ritual of Petition." In Greek Ritual Poetics, ed. Dimitrios Yatromanolakis and Panagiotis Roilos, 356–70. Washington, D.C.: Center for Hellenic Studies, 2004.

Maggio, Lucio. "Note critiche sui rescritti postclassici. 1. Il c.d processo per rescriptum." SDHI 61 (1995): 285–312.

Marrou, Henri. A History of Education in Antiquity. Translated by George Lamb. New York: New American Library, 1964.

Matthews, John. Laying Down the Law: A Study of the Theodosian Code. New Haven, Conn.: Yale University Press, 2000.

———. "Roman Law and Barbarian Identity in the Late Roman West." In Ethnicity and Culture in Late Antiquity, ed. Stephen Mitchell and Geoffrey Greatrex. London: Duckworth/Classical Press of Wales, 2000.

McGrory, Daniel. "Ruling Class." The Times Magazine, July 20, 2002.

Merry, Sally Engle. Getting Justice and Getting Even: Legal Consciousness among Working-Class Americans. Chicago: University of Chicago Press, 1990.

Meyer, Elizabeth A. Legitimacy and Law in the Roman World: Tabulae in Roman Belief and Practice. Cambridge: Cambridge University Press, 2004.

Meyer-Zwiffelhoffer, Eckhard. Politikos archein: Zum Regierungsstil der senatorischen Statthalter in den kaiserzeitlichen griechischen Provinzen. Stuttgart: Steiner, 2002.

Michaud, Jean-François, and Jean-Joseph-François Poujoulet. Nouvelle collection des memoires pour servir à l'histoire de France, depuis le XIIIe siècle jusqu'à la fin du XVIIIe; précédés de notices pour caractériser chaque auteur des mémoires et son époque; suivis de l'analyse des documents historiques qui s'y rapportent. Vol. 1. Paris: Chez l'éditeur du Commentaire analytique du code civil, 1836.

Millar, Fergus. "The Emperor, the Senate, and the Provinces." JRS 56 (1966): 156–66.

———. The Emperor in the Roman World: 31 BC–AD 337. London: Duckworth, 1977.

———. "A New Approach to the Roman Jurists." Review of Emperors and Lawyers and Ulpian, by Tony Honoré. JRS 76 (1986): 272–80.

———. *The Emperor in the Roman World: 31 BC–AD 337.* 2nd ed. Ithaca, N.Y.: Cornell University Press, 1992.

———. *The Crowd in Rome in the Late Republic.* Ann Arbor: University of Michigan Press, 1998.

Miloševic, Petar. *Arheologija i istorija Sirmijuma.* Novi Sad: Matica srpska, 2001.

Minkova, Milena. *The Personal Names of the Latin Inscriptions in Bulgaria.* Studien zurklassischen Philologie, vol. 118. New York: Peter Lang, 2000.

Mirkovic, Miroslava. "Sirmium—Its History from the 1 Century A.D. to 582 A.D." In *Sirmium I,* ed. Vladislav Popovic, 5–90. Beograd: Archaeological Institute, 1971.

———. "Sirmium et l'armée romaine." *Arheoloéski vestnik. Acta archaeologica* 41 (1990): 631–41.

Mitchell, Stephen. "Requisitioned Transport in the Roman Empire: A New Inscription from Pisidia." *JRS* 66 (1976): 106–34.

Mócsy, András. *Gesellschaft und Romanisation in der römischen Provinz Moesia Superior.* Amsterdam: Adolf M. Hakkert, 1970.

———. *Pannonia and Upper Moesia: A History of the Middle Danube Provinces of the Roman Empire.* London: Routledge & K. Paul, 1974.

Mommsen, Theodor. "Über die Zeitfolge der Verordnung Diocletians und seiner Miteregenten." *Abhandlungen der Königliche Akademie der Wissenschaften zu Berlin* (1860): 349–447.

Morris, Rosemary. "What Did the epi tôn deêseôn Actually Do?" In *La pétition à Byzance: Table ronde, XXe congrès international des études byzantines, 19–25 août 2001,* ed. Denis Feissel and Jean Gascou, 125–40. Paris: Association des amis du centre d'histoire et civilisation de Byzance, 2004.

Morris, Royce L. B. "Reflections of Citizen Attitudes in Petitions from Late Roman and Byzantine Oxyrhynchus." In *Akten des 21. Internationalen Papyrologenkongresses, Berlin, 13.–19.8.1995,* ed. Bärbel Kramer, Herwig Maehler, Wolfgang Luppe et al., 744–49. Stuttgart: B. G. Teubner, 1997.

Mouritsen, Henrik. *Plebs and Politics in the Late Roman Republic.* Cambridge: Cambridge University Press, 2001.

Naiden, Fred S. *Ancient Supplication.* New York: Oxford University Press, 2006.

Nicasie, Martinus Johannes. *Twilight of Empire: The Roman Army from the Reign of Diocletian until the Battle of Adrianople.* Dutch Monographs on Ancient History and Archaeology, vol. 19. Amsterdam: J. C. Gieben, 1998.

Nörr, Dieter. *Rechtskritik in der Römischen Antike.* München: Verlag der Bayerischen Akademie der Wissenschaften: in Kommission bei C. H. Beck, 1974.

———. "Zur Reskriptenpraxis in der hohen Prinzipatszeit." *ZRG Röm. Abt.* 98 (1981): 1–46.

———. "Zu einem fast vergessenen Konstitutionstyp: Interloqui de plano." In *Studi in onore di Cesare Sanfilippo,* 3:521–43. Milano: Dott A Giuffrè Editore, 1983.

Nystazopoulou-Pélékidou, Marie. "Les *déiseis* et les *lyseis,* une forme de pétition à Byzance du Xe siècle au début du XIVe." In *La pétition à Byzance: Table ronde, XXe congrès international des études byzantines, 19–25 août 2001,* ed. Denis Feissel and Jean Gascou, 105–24. Paris: Association des amis du Centre d'histoire et civilisation de Byzance, 2004.

Oliver, James Henry, and Kevin Clinton. *Greek Constitutions of Early Roman Emperors from Inscriptions and Papyri*. Memoirs of the American Philosophical Society, vol. 178. Philadelphia: American Philosophical Society, 1989.

Osborne, Michael J., and Sean G. Byrne. *The Foreign Residents of Athens: An Annex to the Lexicon of Greek Personal Names: Attica*. Leuven: Peeters, 1996.

Parkin, Anneliese. "'You Do Him No Service': An Exploration of Pagan Almsgiving." In *Poverty in the Roman World*, ed. E. M. Atkins and Robin Osborne, 60–82. Cambridge: Cambridge University Press, 2006.

Parkin, Tim G. *Demography and Roman Society*. Ancient Society and History. Baltimore: Johns Hopkins University Press, 1992.

Parkinson, Richard B. *The Tale of the Eloquent Peasant*. Oxford: Griffith Institute, 1991.

Parsons, Peter. "Petitions and a Letter: The Grammarian's Complaint (P.Coll.Youtie 66)." In *Collectanea Papyrologica: Texts Published in Honor of H. C. Youtie (= P.Coll. Youtie II)*, ed. Ann Hanson, 409–46. Bonn: Rudolf Habelt, 1976.

Peachin, Michael. *Roman Imperial Titulature and Chronology, A.D. 235–284*. Studia Amstelodamensia ad epigraphicam, ius antiquum et papyrologicam pertinentia, 29. Amsterdam: Gieben, 1990.

———. *Iudex vice Caesaris: Deputy Emperors and the Administration of Justice during the Principate*. Heidelberger althistorische Beiträge und epigraphische Studien, vol. 21. Stuttgart: F. Steiner, 1996.

———. "Epigraphy, Prosopography and the Evidence of the Codex Justinianus." In *International Congress of Greek and Latin Epigraphy XI (Congresso internazionale di epigrafia greca e latina), 1997*, 545–51. München: Beck, 1999.

———. "Rome the Superpower: 96–235 CE." In *A Companion to the Roman Empire*. Blackwell Companions to the Ancient World. Ancient History, ed. D. S. Potter, 126–52. Malden, Mass.: Blackwell, 2006.

———. "Exemplary Government in the Early Roman Empire." In *Crises and the Roman Empire: Proceedings of the Seventh Workshop of the International Network Impact of Empire, Nijmegen, June 20–24, 2006*, ed. Olivier Hekster, Gerda de Kleijn, and Danièlle Slootjes, 75–95. Leiden: Brill, 2007.

Pekáry, Thomas. *Das römische Kaiserbildnis in Staat, Kult, und Gesellschaft: Dargestellt Anhand der Schriftquellen*. Berlin: Gebr. Mann Verlag, 1985.

Pfaff, Ivo. *Tabellio und Tabularius: Ein Beitrag zur Lehre von den römischen Urkundspersonen*. Wien: Manz, 1905.

Popovic, Ivana. "The Production of Gold and Silver Workshops in late Roman Sirmium." In *The Roman and Late Roman City: The International Conference, Veliko Turnovo, 26–30 July 2000*, ed. Liudmila Ruseva-Slokoska, Rumen Teofilov Ivanov, Ventìsislav Dinchev et al., 383–85. Sofia: Prof. Marin Drinov Academic Publ. House, 2002.

Popovic, Vladislav. "A Survey of the Topography and Urban Organization of Sirmium in the Late Empire." In *Sirmium*, ed. Vladislav Popovic, 119–33. Beograd: Archaeological Institute, 1971.

Potter, David S. *The Roman Empire at Bay: AD 180–395*. London: Routledge, 2004.

Poulter, Andrew. "Roman Towns and the Problem of Late Roman Urbanism: the Case of the Lower Danube." *Hephaistos* 5–6 (1983–1984): 109–32.

———. "The Use and Abuse of Urbanism in the Danubian Provinces during the Later

Roman Empire." In *The City in Late Antiquity,* ed. John Rich, 99–135. London: Routledge, 1992.

Purcell, Nicholas. "The Way We Used to Eat: Diet, Community, and History at Rome." *AJPh* 124 (2003): 329–58.

Ramsay, Nigel. "Scriveners and Notaries as Legal Intermediaries in Later Medieval England." In *Enterprise and Individuals in Fifteenth-Century England,* ed. Jennifer Kermode, 118–31. Stroud, UK: Alan Sutton, 1991.

Rapp, Claudia. *Holy Bishops in Late Antiquity: The Nature of Christian Leadership in an Age of Transition.* Berkeley: University of California Press, 2005.

Rees, Roger. *Diocletian and the Tetrarchy: Debates and Documents in Ancient History.* Edinburgh: Edinburgh University Press, 2004.

Reynolds, Joyce Maire, and Kenan T. Erim. *Aphrodisias and Rome: Documents from the Excavation of the Theatre at Aphrodisias.* Journal of Roman Studies Monographs, no. 1. London: Society for the Promotion of Roman Studies, 1982.

Roth, Martha Tobi. *Law Collections from Mesopotamia and Asia Minor.* Atlanta, Ga.: Scholars Press, 1995.

Rotondi, Giovanni. "Studi sulle Fonti del Codice Giustinianeo." In *Studi sulla Storia delle Fontie sul Diritto Pubblico Romano,* 110–265. Pavia: Tipografia e Legatoria Cooperativa, 1922.

Rowlandson, Jane, and Roger S. Bagnall. *Women and Society in Greek and Roman Egypt: A Sourcebook.* Cambridge: Cambridge University Press, 1998.

Saller, Richard P. "Anecdotes as Historical Evidence for the Principate." *G&R* n.s., 27, no. 1 (1980): 69–83.

———. *Personal Patronage under the Early Empire.* Cambridge: Cambridge University Press, 1982.

———. "Domitian and His Successors." *AJAH* 15, no. 1 (1990): 4–18.

Salomies, Olli, and Heikki Solin. *Repertorium nominum gentilium et cognominum Latinorum. Editio nova addendis corrigendisque augmentata, Alpha-Omega. Reihe A, Lexika, Indizes.* Konkordanzen zur klassischen Philologie, 80. Hildesheim: Olms-Weidmann, 1994.

———. "Names and Identities: Onomastics and Prosopography." In *Epigraphic Evidence: Ancient History from Inscriptions,* ed. John Bodel, 73–94. London: Routledge, 2001.

Salway, Benet. "What's in a Name? A Survey of Onomastic Practice from c. 700 B.C. to A.D. 700." *JRS* 84 (1994): 124–45.

———. "Travel, Itineraria, and Tabellaria." In *Travel and Geography in the Roman Empire,* ed. Colin Adams and Ray Laurence, 22–66. London: Routledge, 2001.

———. "Equestrian Prefects and the Award of Senatorial Honours from Severus to Constantine." In *Herrschaftsstrukturen und Herrschaftspraxis: Konzepte, Prinzipien, und Strategien der Administration im römischen Kaiserreich: Akten der Tagung an der Universität Zürich, 18.–20.10.2004,* ed. Anne Kolb, 111–32. Berlin: Akademie Verlag, 2006.

Sayar, Mustafa. *Perinthos-Herakleia (Marmara Ereglisi) und Umgebung: Geschichte, Testimonien, griechische und lateinische Inschriften.* Wien: Verlag der Österreichischen Akademie der Wissenschaften, 1998.

Schäfer, Thomas. *Imperii insignia, sella curulis und fasces: Zur Repräsentation römischer Magistrate.* Mainz: Verlag P. von Zaben, 1989.

Schiller, Arthur, and William Linn Westermann. *Apokrimata: Decisions of Septimius Severus on Legal Matters. Text, Translation, and Historical Analysis.* New York: Columbia University Press, 1954.

Schiller, Arthur, and Herbert C. Youtie. "Second Thoughts on the Columbia Apokrimata (P.Col.123)." *Chronique d'Égypte* 30 (1955): 327–45.

Shanks, Hershel. "Three Shekels for the Lord." *Biblical Archaeology Review* 23, no. 6 (1997): 28–32.

Sheridan, Jennifer. "Women without Guardians: An Updated List." *BASP* 33 (1996): 117–31.

Sherwin-White, A. N. "Trajan's Replies to Pliny: Authorship and Necessity." *JRS* 52 (1962): 114–20.

Simon, Dietrich V. *Konstantinisches Kaiserrecht: Studien anhand der Reskriptenpraxis und des Schenkungsrechts.* Forschungen zur byzantinischen Rechtsgeschichte, vol. 2. Frankfurt am Main: Klostermann, 1977.

Sirks, Boudewijn. "Making a Request to the Emperor: Rescripts in the Roman Empire." In *Administration, Prosopography, and Appointment Policies in the Roman Empire: Proceedings of the First Workshop of the International Network Impact of Empire (Roman Empire, 27 B.C.–A.D. 406), Leiden, June 28–July 1, 2000,* ed. Lukas de Blois, 121–35. Amsterdam: Gieben, 2001.

Solin, Heikki. *Beiträge zur Kenntnis der griechischen Personennamen in Rom.* Commentationes humanarum litterarum, 48. Helsinki: Societas Scientiarum Fennica, 1971.

———. "Ancient Onomastics: Perspectives and Problems." In *Roman Onomastics in the Greek East: Social and Political Aspects,* ed. Athanasios D. Rizakis, 1–10. Athens: Kentron Hellenikes kai Romaikes Archaiotetos; Diffusion de Boccard, 1996.

———. *Die griechischen Personennamen in Rom: Ein Namenbuch.* 2nd ed. Berlin: W. de Gruyter, 2003.

Sperandio, Marco Urbano. *Codex Gregorianus: Origini e vicende.* Pubblicazioni dell'Istituto di diritto romano e dei diritti dell'Oriente mediterraneo, 80. Napoli: Jovene, 2005.

Stambaugh, John E. *The Ancient Roman City.* Ancient Society and History. Baltimore: Johns Hopkins University Press, 1988.

Sternberg, Thomas. "Reskripte des Kaisers Alexander Severus an weibliche Adressaten." *Klio* 67 (1985): 507–27.

Storey, Glenn. "The Population of Ancient Rome." *Antiquity* 71 (1997): 966–78.

Sünskes Thompson, Julia. *Demonstrative Legitimation der Kaiserherrschaft im Epochenvergleich: Zur politischen Macht des stadtrömischen Volkes.* Stuttgart: Steiner, 1993.

Talamanca, Mario. "L'aequitas nelle costituzioni imperiale del periodo epiclassico." In *Aequitas: giornate in memoria di Paolo Silli: atti del convegno, Trento, 11 e 12 aprile 2002,* ed. Gianni Santucci, 53–273. Padova: CEDAM, 2006.

Talbert, Richard J. A., and Roger S. Bagnall. *Barrington Atlas of the Greek and Roman World. Map by Map Directory, vol. 1.* Princeton, N.J.: Princeton University Press, 2000.

Taubenschlag, Rafael. "Das römische Recht zur Zeit Diokletians." *Bulletin international* de l'Académie polonaise des sciences et des lettres, classe d'histoire et de philosophie (1919): 141–281.

Tellegen-Couperus, Olga E. *A Short History of Roman Law.* London: Routledge, 1993.

Thomas, J. David. "Subscriptiones to Petitions to Officials in Roman Egypt." In *Egypt and the Hellenistic World: Proceedings of the International Colloquium, Leuven, 24–26 May 1982,* ed. E. Van't Dack, P. Van Dessel, and W. van Gucht, 369–82. Lovanii: Studia Hellenistica, 1983.

Tibiletti, Giuseppe. "Frammento di Petizione." *Aegyptus* 54 (1974): 44–51.

Toynbee, Arnold Joseph. *Experiences.* New York: Oxford University Press, 1969.

Turpin, William. "Apokrimata, Decreta, and the Roman Legal Procedure." *BASP* 18 (1981): 145–60.

———. "The Purpose of the Roman Law Codes." *ZRG* 104 (1987): 620–30.

Vagalinski, Lyudmil. *Roman and Late Antique Archaeology in Bulgaria.* 2000. www .nipissingu.ca/department/history/muhlberger/orb/bulgbib.htm.

Vandorpe, Katelijn. "Apollonia, a Businesswoman in a Multicultural Society (Pathyris, 2nd–1st Centuries B.C)." In *Le rôle et le statut de la femme en Egypte hellénistique, romaine et byzantine: Actes du colloque international, Bruxelles-Leuven, 27–29 novembre 1997,* ed. Henri Melaerts and Leon Mooren, 326–36. Paris: Peeters, 2002.

Verhoogt, Arthur M. F. W. "Family Papers from Tebtunis: Unfolding a Bundle of Papyri." In *The Two Faces of Graeco-Roman Egypt,* ed. A. M. F. W. Verhoogt and S. P. Vleeming, 141–53. Boston: Brill, 1998.

VerSteeg, Russ. *Law in Ancient Egypt.* Durham, N.C.: Carolina Academic Press, 2002.

Volterra, Edoardo. "L'ouvrage de Papirius Justus constitutionum libri XX." In *Symbol aeiuridicae et historicae Martino David dedicatae,* ed. Johan A. Ankum, Robert Feenstra, and Wilhelmus F. Leemans, 215–23. Leiden: Brill, 1968.

———. "Les femmes dans le 'inscriptiones' des rescrits impériaux." In *Xenion: Festschrift für Pan. J. Zepos anlässlich seines 65. Geburtstages am 1. Dezember 1973,* ed. Ernst von Cämmerer, 717–24. Athens: Ch. Katsikalis, 1973.

Wallace-Hadrill, Andrew. "Civilis princeps: Between Citizen and King." *JRS* 72 (1982): 32–48.

———. *Houses and Society in Pompeii and Herculaneum.* Princeton, N.J.: Princeton University Press, 1994.

Watson, Alan. "Equity in the Time of Cicero." In *Aequitas and Equity: Equity in Civil Law and Mixed Jurisdictions,* ed. Alfredo Mordechai Rabello, 23–28. Jerusalem: Hebrew University, 1997.

Weaver, Paul. "Consilium praesidis: Advising Governors." In *Thinking Like a Lawyer: Essays on Legal History and General History for John Crook on his Eightieth Birthday,* ed. Paul McKechnie, 43–62. Leiden: Brill, 2002.

Weinfeld, Moshe. *Social Justice in Ancient Israel and in the Ancient Near East.* Jerusalem: Magnes; Minneapolis: Fortress, 1995.

Weitzmann, Kurt. *Late Antique and Early Christian Book Illumination.* London: Chatto & Windus, 1977.

Wenger, Leopold. *Die Quellen des römischen Rechts.* Wien: A. Holzhausen, 1953.

White, John Lee. *The Form and Structure of the Official Petition; A Study in Greek Epistolography.* Missoula, Mont.: Society of Biblical Literature, 1972.

Wieling, Hans. "Die Gesetze der Herculier." In *Collatio iuris romani: Études dédiées à*

*Hans Ankum à l'occasion de son 65e anniversaire*, ed. Robert Feenstra et al., 619–32. Amsterdam: J. C. Gieben, 1995.

Wilcken, Ulrich. „Zu den Kaiserreskripten." *Hermes* 55 (1920): 1–42.

———. "Zur propositio libellorum." *Archiv für Papyrusforschung* 9 (1930): 15–23.

Williams, Stephen. *Diocletian and the Roman Recovery*. London: B.T. Batsford, 1985.

Williams, Wynne. "The Libellus Procedure and the Severan Papyri." *JRS* 64 (1974): 86–103.

———. "The Publication of Imperial Subscripts." *ZPE* 40 (1980): 283–94.

———. "Epigraphic Texts of Imperial Subscripts: A Survey." *ZPE* 66 (1986): 181–207.

Winroth, Anders. *The Making of Gratian's Decretum*. Cambridge Studies in Medieval Life and Thought; 4th ser., 49. Cambridge: Cambridge University Press, 2000.

Yavetz, Zvi. *Plebs and Princeps*. London: Oxford University Press, 1969.

Zuckerman, Constantin. "Les deux Dioscore d'Aphroditè ou les limites de la pétition." In *La pétition à Byzance: Table ronde, XXe congrès international des études byzantines, 19–25 août 2001*, ed. Denis Feissel and Jean Gascou, 75–92. Paris: Association des amis du centre d'histoire et civilisation de Byzance, 2004.

# INDEX

**Serena Connolly** is Assistant Professor of Classics at Rutgers University, New Brunswick, New Jersey.